# Madness
## in the making

# MADNESS
# IN THE MAKING

The Triumphant

Rise and Untimely

Fall of America's

Show Inventors

# DAVID LINDSAY

KODANSHA INTERNATIONAL
*New York • Tokyo • London*

Kodansha America, Inc.
114 Fifth Avenue, New York, New York 10011, U.S.A.

Kodansha International Ltd.
17-14 Otowa 1-chome, Bunkyo-ku, Tokyo 112, Japan

Published in 1997 by Kodansha America, Inc.

Library of Congress Cataloging-in-Publication Data
Lindsay, David, 1957–
    Madness in the making : the triumphant rise and untimely fall of
America's show inventors / David Lindsay.
        p.      cm.
    Includes bibliographical references and index.
    1. Inventions — United States — History.    2. Inventors — United
States — History.    I. Title.
    T21.L46    1997
    609'.73 — dc21                                              97-39617
    ISBN 1-56836-203-X

Book design by Debbie Glasserman

Manufactured in the United States of America on acid-free paper

97 98 99 00 RRD 10 9 8 7 6 5 4 3 2 1

*To the memory of*
*John Robert Lindsay, Jr.*

Joseph Faber's fabulous talking machine. *Courtesy Meserve-Kunhardt Collection*

# Contents

## Introduction

# INVENTING THE PAST

When I first felt the impulse to write a book about the inventors of the nineteenth century, I imagined it as an exercise in chaos. I had done some initial research, and a nonlinear approach seemed suitable to the subject. So I set off on my task, gravitating toward the outrageous and the unlikely, a thrill seeker in the archives.

There was only one problem. As I began to follow promising leads (laughing gas, coffin alarms, baby incubators), I came to see a pattern. At first, it was simply a recurring image: a crowd gathered before a figure, his features not quite clear, a machine beside him. Then I noticed that, again and again, nineteenth-century inventors had connections to conventional theater. So much for my anarchic approach. At this point, I felt an obligation to find out what these connections meant.

The subject of invention being a large one, I was also forced at this point to make certain choices. One of these was to limit my inquiry, loosely, to the United States. Doing so helped me simplify a subject that, under the best of circumstances, threatens to become tangled in analysis. At the same time, I moved beyond the confines of the nineteenth century in both directions until the connection between inventors and the stage disappeared. I ran these two values—invention and theater—side by side, like a proof, trying my best not to hedge the facts to fit the supposition. What I discovered was a phenomenon with its own internal coherence and its own implications about the culture at large.

As a result of this unsolicited discovery, this book is *not* many things. It is not, for example, a bid to rewrite the inventor's canon. My aim, after all, was not to right wrongs but to trace a cultural pattern. In doing so, I have left out individuals whom some readers might consider important. Worthy a subject as he is, Charles Goodyear does not make an appearance. Rufus Porter, founder of *Scientific American*, fails to figure as prominently as perhaps he should. Certainly, I omitted a discussion of *pluviculture*—the rainmaking industry of the early twentieth century—only with a gathering sense of remorse.

There was little I could do to bridge these gaps. To my knowledge, this is the first time such a thing as a show inventor has been explored in depth, and it was enough to make the phenomenon evident without striving for encyclopedic proportions. The binding of a book can only be so thick before it begins to sag, and along with it, the reader's interest.

By the same token, I have tried not to spend an inordinate amount of time debating who really invented what. Peruse the extant material for an hour or two and you will begin to doubt the very idea of originality, as the qualifiers pile up and the terminology grows thick with caveats. "The first light bulb to burn continuously for more than forty hours in a contained vessel that did not break" is not the kind of phrase that can be served up with great elan, not more than once anyway.

To make matters more difficult, inventors tend to treat facts as something plastic, suitable more for their own hagiography than anything else. This kind of self-exaltation is interesting in itself, but it also begs a certain amount of caution. History is full of hazy documentation, and in the case of inventors, the haziness will often be accompanied by willful untruths. Henry Ford, for example, backdated the invention of his automobile by several years in order to finesse a struggle with another patent holder. As a result of such widespread practices, there is less consensus among historians of technology than might be expected.

At times, this lack of consensus will even assume international proportions, as individual nations rush to claim credit for changing the world. Though America is the primary focus of the discussion here, I make no special plea for my native land on this account. Every industrialized country seems to have its own technological creation myth, with its own pantheon of inventors, and this is simply the one I have chosen to tell.

That said, I had no urge to write a book that remained oblivious to the particularities of time and place altogether. Inventions represent an addition to society, a moment from which there is no turning back. They are "firsts" by definition, and carry with them a sense of the irreversible that is best conveyed by days, months, years. Then, too, where I synthesized material from arcane sources, I felt a need to include more data rather than less. As I say, the story of the show inventor is by no means exhausted with this book, and it seems only fair to give the next historian who comes along a place to start.

Closing out my list of negations, I have to admit that this book is not about science, either. Rather than donning the gloves of the specialist, I tried to imagine myself as a curious witness in the house. Others could parse the intricacies of electromagnetic theory or aerodynamics; mostly I was interested in the show. As it turns out, this bias has forced me into very little revisionism when it comes to individual inventors. Only in the piecing together of their many stories does a different moral emerge.

Of course, after viewing so many gala events in my mind's eye, it was probably inevitable that I would start to imitate the performers themselves. I saw a little of myself in every character that runs through these pages, but to the extent that I identified an ideal, I tried to model my approach after that of Alexander Graham Bell, who balanced sense and sensationalism better than most. I also found myself treating my material as if it were its own kind of invention, attaching this phenomenon to that, setting up the chains of events that brought a point most clearly to light. An analogous machine for this labor might be the later version of the panorama, which slowly scrolls an epic scene from American history, its motion suggesting a voyage. At any rate, having now adjusted the screws and dusted off the exterior, I hope, like any inventor, to have created something that has the twin values of being both novel and useful.

And like any inventor, I cannot honestly claim to have operated alone. My prior art—the inventions upon which my own is based—can be found in the bibliography. As for my muckers, to borrow Edison's term for his assistants, I can only say that without them, I would still be sitting in a cafe making feeble excuses as this book destroyed me from the inside out. For this act of rescue, I wholeheartedly thank everyone who supported me in ways both great and small.

More pointedly, I want to thank Dolores Briante and Dean George Daly for instructing me on the ins and outs of New York University's Bobst Library; Cyntia Karnes for economizing my search at the National

Archives; Kathleen McDonough for doing the same at the Library of Congress; Miroslava Malesevic for making the trip to the Tesla Museum in Belgrade; the staff at the New York Public Library's Brooke Russell Astor Reading Room for Rare Books and Manuscripts for their willingness to help with even the smallest detail; Bipin Parmar for showing me around the Royal Institution in London; Paul Roth and my brother John Lindsay-Poland for searching expeditions that exceeded the call of duty; Mary Dallmann, who, along with Harry Miller, valiantly braved the 300-odd linear feet of the McCormick Collection at the State Historical Society of Wisconsin; Joseph Lanza for his astute advice; Allen Koenigsberg, who mined gems from mountains of data; Joe Lauinger for directing me to important theatrical sources; Dominique Janeo, artistic director of the Big Apple Circus, and Menzi Behrnd-Klodt of the Circus World Museum; Cheryl Malone and William H. Richter at the University of Texas at Austin; John Rudlin; Bob Fairbrother; Beth Fredrick; and Robert Shapiro.

Special gratitude is due to Goran Djordjevic, who not only supplied me with a wealth of information but helped me articulate myself through many confusing months; to Lazar Stojanovic and Michael Benson, whose vigorous readings kept me to the straight and narrow; to Frederic Schwarz, who was gracious enough to look over the manuscript for factual errors; and to Mike Shatzkin, who has been as much a friend as an agent. Finally, there are those who cannot be thanked enough: my editor, Philip Turner; my mother; and of course, Leslie, custodian of my soul and tireless tough-love critic. You're right, you're right.

# A TIME MACHINE
# IN A BRIEFCASE

If you spend enough time in New York's Grand Central Station, you are likely to come across an unusual figure. Elderly and bespectacled, Jack Marchand wears a jacket, a tie, and a hat that has survived several generations of fashion. But it's the briefcase that tells the story. If you say so much as hello, he will open it up and produce a mimeographed newsletter, written in his own spidery hand, called the *Street Rag*.

This newsletter, which comes out whenever it comes out, contains Marchand's life work—diagrams for electric-car batteries, explanations of world-trade practices, words of advice and support. There is other information to be gleaned, but so intricate is the scrawl that most of it could slip by you unnoticed. You squint to make out the bold print in the upper left-hand corner: "Back copies are available. See distributor or vendor. Also ask friends and others for them."

You look around. No other distributors seem to be in sight.

Having seen this much, you may feel you have filled your quota of interesting encounters for the day. But if you are willing to go further, Marchand is likely to suggest that you join him someplace where he can show you more of what he's got in his briefcase.

The two of you walk a few blocks through midtown Manhattan. Dusk is blowing the heat from the city air; the traffic careens down the avenues. You pass the New York Public Library, its lions frozen in their fury, and arrive at the corner of Forty-second and Sixth. To your right stands the National Debt Clock, a billboard that broadcasts the running tab of the federal government—an ongoing tale of disaster. To your left Bryant Park offers a merciful half-block of green against the urban steel. . . . You walk in and sit at a bench. Marchand settles himself carefully and opens his briefcase. He unfolds a diagram, then unfolds it again, extending it past the edge of the bench until it brushes the ground. Then he begins to tell you about his plans for a worldwide transportation system.

A tube some thirty feet off the ground, he explains, will whisk his electric cars from New York to Tokyo through a vacuum, at a speed of 2,000 miles an hour. "Like an electron gun," he says dryly. The system will be powered by huge solar banks in the deserts of the world, poised high above the sands. Recharging booths at regular points, a standard size battery—it will work. He knows it will work. But try telling that to the Department of Transportation. They toyed with him half a lifetime ago, then left him twisting in the wind.

He adjusts his glasses and moves on to some of his other ideas—a stadium roof designed like a folding fan, a radio battery that needs no recharging. You listen as the twilight gathers. When you question him, he reluctantly admits that he has been an inventor all his life, moving from one job to the next in the tristate area, contriving machines that improve on other machines—jig borers, plastic-lid production machinery. But this he finds uninteresting. He touches the point of his pencil to a diagram, returning to the subject at hand.

Marchand talks on and on, drawing his information from a seemingly inexhaustible well. Several times, in the midst of it all, you experience a kind of shock that he is present, that you are present—that this is happening at all.

By the time he is done, the sun is beginning to set. You say good-bye, and as he walks off down the city streets, his hat slowly sinking in the throng, you feel almost as if you have traveled back in time, to an era when inventors were part of a hurdy-gurdy world of curiosities and marvels. Looking up at the National Debt Clock and turning the numbers backward in your mind, you can almost feel the texture of that age, a glimpse of Bryant Park as it was long ago. The night air plays tricks on your eyes, conjuring the dim outline of an inventor who once stood on this very same ground, beneath the vaulted roofs of New York's Crystal Palace . . .

It was hailed as the *Iliad* of the nineteenth century. Here, anatomical and surgical inventions gleamed. Faces captured in daguerrotype peered

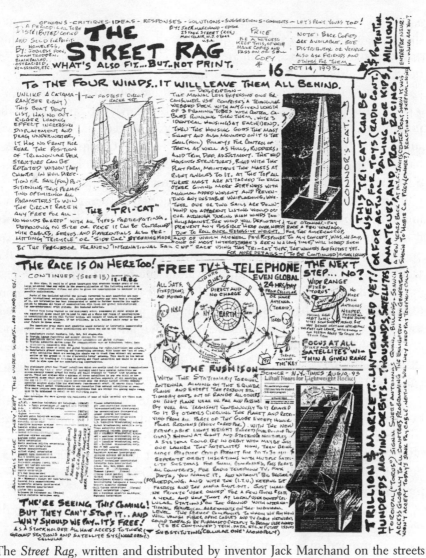

The *Street Rag*, written and distributed by inventor Jack Marchand on the streets of New York in the 1990s. *Author's Collection*

out at curious passersby. Locomotives glistened under the gaslights. Engines roared. Brakes hissed. To ensure robust attendance, the master of ceremonies—none other than Phineas T. Barnum—brought in other kinds of attractions as well. An orchestra played, boisterous and overstocked with musicians. Pyrotechnics were promised. A chunk of the "great CALIFORNIA CEDAR TREE" stood on solemn display.

In this sea of wonders, a burly, forty-three-year-old man attracted little notice as he stepped up to a contraption that rose almost 300 feet into the air. Elisha Graves Otis was not, after all, a well-known personality; nor had his appearance been heavily advertised. A few minutes later, however, everyone would know his name.

The most practical of circumstances had led Otis to this moment. As a young man, he had worked throughout the New York area, repairing machinery, sometimes improving it. Then one day in 1852, he was supervising the relocation of the Yonkers Bedstead Company to the east bank of the Hudson River, when it occurred to him that he could build a special platform hoist for moving the plant's heavy machinery.

The device was relatively simple. He attached a wagon spring to both the top of a platform and a cable. When weight was put on the platform, it kept the spring in place. But if the cable broke, the spring would snap open, engaging a set of saw-tooth, ratchet-bar beams and breaking the platform's fall. This feature made elevators safe for the first time.

Otis didn't give his accomplishment much thought. Rather than announcing it to the heavens, he made plans to join the gold rush, which was raging in California at the time. Then Benjamin Newhouse, owner of a Manhattan furniture business and sponsor of a Turkish armchair exhibit at the Crystal Palace, contacted him with bad news: an elevator cable had snapped at Newhouse's plant at 275 Hudson Street.

Hoping to avoid future disasters, Newhouse implored Otis to build two safety elevators for him. Otis agreed, and before he was finished with the job, a nearby picture-framing business put in an order for another one. That was enough for the inventor to unpack his bags. On September 20, 1853, he formed the E. G. Otis Company and began manufacturing his invention.

Six months later, however, people still doubted that an elevator could be safe for passengers, and sales were anything but brisk. Landlords, it seemed, needed more than abstract assurances.

Perhaps it was Newhouse, the exhibitor of Turkish armchairs, who came up with the solution. Or perhaps Barnum himself caught wind of what was going on at the Otis factory. In any event, Otis decided to secure exhibit space at the Crystal Palace. There, people could see for themselves how safe his elevator was.

And so the inventor, turned out in top hat and tails, stepped onto the platform. Fairgoers paused in their tracks as they caught sight of a figure rising—and rising and rising—up toward the sky itself. What was he doing? Was he mad? Surely it seemed so when he ordered his assistant to cut the rope that held him aloft! But Otis did not fall. Rather than crashing, the elevator quickly came to a halt, caught by the ratchet-bar beams that sprang into place.

"All safe, gentlemen," the daredevil called out, doffing his hat with a bow as the crowd breathed a sigh of relief. "All safe."

The Crystal Palace demonstration paid off handsomely. The following year, Otis sold fifteen safety elevators. The year after that, his orders nearly doubled, and soon Otis elevators ran in the Eiffel Tower and the Washington Monument. In the end, they made possible the skyscrapers whose shadows now close around Bryant Park.

A different world, a different time. As you look down at the copy of the *Street Rag* that Marchand has hastily thrust in your hand, it all seems so unlikely, as if it were a dream . . .


But it was not a dream. One hundred years ago and more, America was a land of show inventors—a thousand Elisha Otises, a thousand Jack Marchands, each of them vying for the greater part of the public's attention.

These people are the subject of this book. They have all appeared in other books and they have been called many things, but never *show inventors*. The term is a product of hindsight, a construct imposed on the past.

Strictly speaking, a show inventor can be identified by his predilection for presenting inventions to live audiences. The show inventor, quite simply, shows his invention. But historically he was something more. The nineteenth-century show inventor had a well-defined place in society, and his character bore a signature stamp. Because the job of promoting unlikely goods required a persuasive authority figure, he was often a man of European descent. Yet he was not likely to hail from a wealthy family because, for all his authority, he was usually forced to operate on the margins of society. With his disorienting object in hand, he was an outsider who brought chaos, and often comedy, to the status quo. He promoted excess over thrift, passion over moderation, risk over safety. He was an improviser, a jokester, a rhetorician. It was not at all unusual for him to perform feats of physical prowess, or to appeal to man's lower nature.

Perhaps most important, the show inventor encouraged his audience to suspend its disbelief: in addition to showing his invention, he *put on* a show. Those with the means and the moxie did so in the truest sense, using patter, stage effects, brightly colored props, eye-popping showbills and trained animals. Indeed, the leap from acting to innovation was not so very great. It is no coincidence that Otis performed his death-defying feat on Barnum's watch. Many other nineteenth-century inventors had direct experience in the theater, as if it were a sister occupation to the mechanical arts.

In drawing on this connection, the show inventors created a truly spectacular form of theater. After all, an invention, then as much as now, had the power to change the way people conducted their daily affairs. Fashion, theories, customs, governments, empires—all these could come and go. But an invention like dynamite was proof positive that things would never be the same, and the show inventor who succeeded in dramatizing such a thing created a rite of passage that had implications far beyond the confines of the stage: the technological spectacle.

Besides inspiring audiences, the inventor's show heaped outrageous popularity on the inventors themselves. Thomas Edison was bigger by far than Edwin Booth, the most famous American actor of the nineteenth century. Alexander Graham Bell remains a household name long after Edwin Forrest, a contemporaneous actor, has been forgotten. In fact, the show inventors were the nation's first superstars. Long before the advent of professional sports and stadium concerts, the purveyors of mechanical wonders dazzled the public with their achievements and provided the stuff of myth. The most successful of them attained a celebrity on par with the Beatles or Elvis Presley.

The world has changed a great deal since the days of the Crystal Palace. Inventors rarely command front-page headlines. Crowds no longer gather to hear them orate. The show inventor has fallen into decline. And yet this figure, for all his excess and absurdity, has had a far-reaching impact on American culture—an impact that continues to be felt today. Fortunately, in a case of reason meeting the raconteur, his tale also makes for an engaging one, even from the very beginning.

*Part One*

# CARNIVAL ApPROACHES

POET:    What glitters, lives but for a moment;
         What has real worth survives for all posterity.

PLAYER: Don't talk about posterity to me!
         Suppose I chose to preach posterity,
         who'd entertain the present generation?
         Amusement's what they want, and what they'll get.

                                            —*Goethe*, Faust

## Chapter One

# RUMORS OF LIGHTNING

The sky is cobalt blue, the earth barren and lifeless. To all outward appearances, it's an ordinary winter afternoon. Then, faintly, a noise comes floating on the breeze. The cacophony grows louder and louder until a procession appears. Women dressed as soldiers, mutes carrying birdcages, mock warriors preparing for battle, masked figures everywhere—suddenly the street is thronged with improbable characters.

"Sir!" a masked figure from among them shouts. "Your great-great-grandfather owes my family an enormous debt!" Displaying an odd book, this man holds forth on the many injustices his forebears have incurred. He insists that you see the bill of exchange for yourself. When you look to see what is written there, however, he slams the book shut in a blast of flour. Momentarily blinded, you grope for solid ground, only to be met by a team of specialists. A masked groom dusts you off. A masked sweeper sweeps you along. A fool whispers high-flown nonsense in your ear. You try to break free, but now the doctor and the apothecaries take their turn. "He is pale!" cries one. "He is ill!" cries another. Together, they implore you to accept their services. Their remedies, they assure you, are more effective than any others.

Carnival season is on.

. . .

The age of the American show inventors followed a long arc, from the early days of the new Republic to the dark years of the Great Depression. During that time, they changed the shape of the world and, in the process, established the technological spectacle as an enduring feature of popular culture. Many of them got rich for their efforts. A few became superstars beyond their wildest dreams.

The one thing almost none of them enjoyed, however, was security. By nature of their trade, show inventors were constantly battling to maintain their position. Their experiments generally required that they squander vast amounts of money, and with each new invention, they ran the risk of being censured as swindlers or, worse, ridiculed as misguided fools. In this, they bore little resemblance to the celebrated Yankee craftsmen, or to the high-minded scientists of the Enlightenment. For all their ingenuity and insight, the show inventors claimed a closer kinship with a chorus of masked revelers, and their struggle most closely resembled the procession of Carnival as it came face to face with the procession of Lent.

Taking place in southern Europe in the heart of winter, Carnival was a Catholic tradition developed as a response to the dilemma of dwindling food supplies. In the days leading up to Shrove Tuesday, the poor pretended to be rich, the men dressed as women, pranks were played. Elaborate masks gave ordinary citizens the appearance of exotic animals. Outlandishness and excess were encouraged. Inevitably, the festivities ceased on the first day of Lent, Ash Wednesday, when the penitents, donning sacks, delivered themselves over to the church—and to the iconography of archangels and saints—for a somber, forty-day period of abstinence.

Disorder meeting order, excess meeting economy—this theme was sounded throughout the Industrial Revolution. Many a show inventor would face his crowds with an implausible item that threatened the existing order even as it promised an end to scarcity. His was a mad day in the sun, when all bets were off and anything could happen. But it could be an exceedingly short day if the forces of order saw fit to squelch his efforts.

The conflict between Carnival and Lent was sometimes illustrated in a traditional dramatic performance called the *Contrasto between Master Carnival and Lady Lent*. Contrast is the key word. These two characters greet each other with increasingly foul insults until they fall to blows. Finally, Lady Lent strikes Master Carnival down:

> [Master] Carnival must die of course, but not until he has called
> in Doctors and magicians, heard and even attempted their bur-
> lesque prescriptions, and made a ridiculous will, leaving to his sis-
> ters his "credits never acquired," to his wife "property not bought,"
> and to others still less desirable gifts; then amidst howls of grief
> from members of the family, Lent summons her enemy's soul.

Like the fate of Master Carnival, an invention moved in one direction
only: into the hands of the lenten forces. At first, it precipitated a crisis,
a change in the existing patterns of life. Who could tell? Perhaps it was
simply a form of madness. The show inventor was able to minimize this
crisis for a time by staging dramas, which placed his device within an
understandable, if imaginary, framework. By enacting a ritual that contained both disorder and order, threat and rescue, suspense and reso-
lution, he was able to gain a powerful hold on the public imagination.

Sooner or later, however, an invention's survival depended on its economic value—its ability to generate either profits or savings. It had to
meet the test of an organizing, or economizing, force. If it failed to
increase the bounties of society, the show inventor was left to replay the
absurd bequeathing of "credits never acquired"—inventions never given
a chance. If it succeeded, it became part of the new order—it became
a product. Then another invention came along, and the process began
all over again.

Clearly, in such a situation, it behooved the show inventors to enlarge
the audience's tolerance for chaos and to suspend its disbelief for as
long as possible. Whenever the carnivalesque mood waxed stronger, the
party was extended, the inventors gained in stature, and the improbable
offerings multiplied. In this sense, the clash between disorder and order
resulted in a vector, the outcome of which would determine the course
of history.

At the heart of this effort was the inventor's show, which not only
exposed the public to specific inventions but allowed inventors to flex
their creative muscles. Inventors as a class, it seems, are propelled by
some mysterious urge to think across categories, linking steering wheels
to weapons, flames to musical scales, navigational courses to the shape
of the universe. Naturally, then, when they had greater access to the
public through the show, the scope and variety of inventions increased.

In the glory days of the show inventor—the period between the Civil
War and the Crash of '29—an astonishing variety of inventions passed

into fact. Dynamite, gas-fueled cars, electric cars, radio, computers, fax machines, airplanes, rocketry (including the multistage rocket), telephones, television, machine guns, refrigerators, robotics, radar, x-rays, fluorescent lighting, incandescent lighting, movies, solar power, video recording, the phonograph (including stereo)—all these existed as working prototypes, even if some of them did not appear in commercial form until later.

The years following the show inventor's decline, if just as active, have been less diverse. The atom bomb, the transistor, genetic engineering, the geostationary satellite, and the photocopier make up one possible list of significant developments since the beginning of the depression. Other candidates may be rounded up and the facts argued from various standpoints—impact, performance, cost, widespread use, and permanence. It can even be debated whether an ever-widening array of earth-shattering inventions is desirable after a certain point. Nevertheless, the basic principle remains: when they had an authentic public, show inventors were able to loose their freewheeling imaginations upon the world.

The backyard mechanic as a Carnival figure, enmeshed in a cosmic struggle between chaos and order—on the face of it, the comparison might seem forced. Yet historically it is not. In fact, the show inventor himself rose out of a character closely associated with Carnival. In demeanor, approach, and motive, the show inventor was very much like the mountebank.

The figure of the mountebank first appeared in the sixteenth century, not long after the death of Leonardo da Vinci, in the city piazzas and village squares of what is now Italy. Known as the *montimbanchi*—literally the "bench mounter"—this man made quite a name for himself as the peddler of bogus notions. His bench might be a simple plank thrown across two barrels, or it might be a grander affair with an upstage curtain, behind which he would mix his elixirs and tend to patients with more unseemly maladies. Invariably, the mountebank would wax eloquent on the virtues of his potions; often, these would turn out to be little more than a puff of flour blown in an innocent's face.

As witnessed by Sir Thomas Coryat, an Englishman on a Continental tour in the sixteenth century, the mountebank was, among other things, a close relative of the dramatist:

These Mountebankes at one end of the stage place their trunke, which is replenished with a world of *new-fangled trumperies* . . . While the musicke plays, the principall Mountebanke which is the Captaine and ring-leader of all the rest, opens the trunk and sets abroach his wares; after the musicke hath ceased, he maketh an oration to the audience of halfe an hour long, or almost an hour. . . . After the chiefest Mountebankes first speech is ended, he de-liuereth out his commodities little by little, the iester still playing his part and the musicians singing and playing on their instruments. (Italics mine.)

Indeed, the mountebank and the jester crossed paths often. An early French illustration depicts a masked mountebank at Notre Dame flanked by two performers, one of whom supports a monkey on his shoulders. Some accounts mention the presence of *saltimbanchi*, who tumbled on and off the stage to collect the mountebank's fees. Others have noted the development of shows in which the player caricatured a sick patient as a foil for the doctor's oratory. But regardless of these variations, the actors belonged to a theatrical tradition known as *commedia dell'arte*.

From the mid-1500s to the mid-1700s, commedia dell'arte flourished in outdoor markets and village squares, first in Italy, and ultimately throughout the Continent. Technically, the term *arte* designated actors who performed on a professional basis, but the form was more distinct than that. Relying on stock characters, improvised dialogue, clowning, and acrobatics, it was loud, low, and comic — the vaudeville of its time.

In what were usually three-act plays, the commedia dell'arte actors improvised from a *canovaccio*, or general plotline, posted at the back of the stage. It was the commedia dell'arte actors who performed the *Contrasto between Master Carnival and Lady Lent* during Carnival season. Generally, though, they relied on a more diverse set of characters to entertain their audiences. The lower-class clowns were known as the *zanni*, from the diminutive for "Giovanni," or "John." The zanni could be a generic servant with his own distinct mask, or he could inhabit more developed roles, all of which required an expertise in acrobatics. The character Arlecchino was a zanni, as were Brighella and Colombina. Counterbalancing the zanni were the so-called Old Men: the miserly Pantalone, the humpbacked Pulcinella, the cowardly Capitano, and the verbose Dottore, whose fellow actors sometimes had to carry him from the stage before his speech was over.

To break up the action, commedia dell'arte players used a device known as a *lazzo*. Today, we would call this a gag. There were innumerable *lazzi*, which every actor was required to know—the Lazzo of the Stupid Discovery, the Lazzo of Nightfall, the Lazzo of the Ladder, and so on. One exceptionally popular lazzo was the administering of an enema to an unwitting victim. Another was the pratfall in all its various forms. A more refined lazzo involved a character who reproached the Dottore with the criticism, "You are not a doctor." To which the Dottore, taking offense, replied: "I am not a Doctor." And back and forth they would go. Many lazzi live on today in the realm of popular comedy: the Lazzo of Arlecchino's Portrait, in which a spy looked through a hole cut into a painting, was performed as early as 1685.

Curiously, commedia dell'arte also bore more than a passing resemblance to supernatural ceremony. With few exceptions, the players wore masks that determined their character. These masks echoed an earlier tradition, prevalent in cultures throughout the world, in which the tribe paid fealty to a particular animal as its guiding spirit. Thus Arlecchino was a monkey or a cat, Brighella half dog and half chicken, Pantalone a chicken or a turkey. Each character had an identifying posture and gait that mimicked their mother-animal. Some scholars believe that the masks themselves were made of animal skins.

This mixture of the sacred and profane gave rise to seemingly contradictory characterizations. Arlecchino, who in France developed into the *harlequin*, was simultaneously a rascal-servant and a master of dark, infernal powers. Pantalone, though nominally a tight-fisted patron, used his purse as a codpiece, suggesting an exaggerated phallus. If there was comedy in the commedia, there was also a hint of magic, and of fertility cults.

The mountebanks borrowed freely from the commedia dell'arte tradition, and the boundary between the groups was indistinct at best. While mountebanks employed commedia dell'arte troupes to support them, comedians gave the zanni Brighella many of the mountebank's qualities. Ever fleet of foot and quick of tongue, Brighella could be counted on to hoodwink his friends. And it was Brighella who, much like his real-life counterpart, prepared love potions and hawked the philosopher's stone.

Both the mountebank and the player felt free to cross over to the other's terrain. Maurice Sand, a chronicler of commedia dell'arte, records a Giovanni Bissoni, who began his career as a clown in Bologna, then became a mountebank in Milan before reverting to acting again and touring France and Italy as Scapino. The most famous mountebank in Paris during the early 1700s, the inimitable Tabarin, took his name from the Tabarinos, a family of commedia dell'arte actors. Mountebanks developed a stock dramatic form for selling their wares, in which the mountebank played an officious doctor and the zanni a comic patient. On the trestle stage, drama and commerce were never far apart.

The alliance between mountebanks and players was informal at best (hardly anything they did was committed to posterity), but it proved remarkably resilient. Though the commedia dell'arte troupes mutated as they traveled, they were slow to lose their flavor. By the 1600s, the zanni had reached England, where he became the "zany," or sometimes the "Merry Andrew," and left his trace in other traditions—mumming, the Punch and Judy shows, even some of Shakespeare's plays. (The influence of commedia dell'arte on *The Tempest* formed the basis of most early critiques.) In France and Italy, commedia dell'arte became more formal as it was incorporated into commedia erudita, the plays of Molière, and operas such as *I Pagliacci*. The zany was even popular enough in northern climes to make a cameo in the prelude to Goethe's *Faust*.

The mountebank, meanwhile, lived on in his own various guises: the patent medicine man, the huckster, the street peddler, and—as his "newfangled trumperies" became more elaborate—the show inventor. Yet he never lost his dramatic pedigree. Comedy, improvisation, and acrobatics remained staples of his repertoire. He could behave like clever Arlecchino when faced with a Pantalone-like businessman, or like the cantankerous Pulcinella when threatened with competition. Certainly, he could become a doctor with frightening speed. And, inadvertently or not, he would find himself replaying the gags from his earlier incarnation for many decades hence.

Among the most telling lazzi in the commedia dell'arte tradition was the Lazzo of the New World. In this gag, recorded in Paris as late as 1740, Arlecchino entices Pantalone (or sometimes the Dottore) to look into a peep-show machine, inside which awaits a view of the continent across the sea. While his customer complies, Arlecchino passes a love letter to the stock character Celia, perhaps with his zig-zag device (a hinged contraption that prefigured the extended boxing glove in twentieth-century cartoons). Typically, this lazzo ends with Arlecchino smashing the peephole machine over his victim's head.

The zanni Arlecchino lures Pantalone to look into his peep-show machine in the Lazzo of the New World. Drawing by G. Zocchi, Paris, circa 1740. *Author's Collection*

Whether such a New World machine was ever sold is unknown, but its appearance was certainly prescient. At the time this gag was performed, commedia dell'arte was losing its potency. The playwright Carlo Goldoni delivered a fatal blow to the form when he introduced written scripts and removed the actors' masks. By 1750, the form was all but gone.

The show inventor, however, was just beginning his ascent. No longer bound by the mask, he began to transfer its animalistic power into simple mechanical devices, and gradually into more complex forms. Soon he was making marionettes and their relatives the automata, which had their successes in Jacques de Vaucanson's mechanical duck and Baron von Kempelen's chess player. Another variation, and one more crucial to the story of eighteenth-century America, was the electrical novelty.

In 1747, Gianfrancesco Pivati of Venice announced a kind of miracle: he had used electricity to draw "Peruvian balsam vapors" out of a hermetically sealed glass globe. In Bologna and Turin, two other men immediately reported similar results. No sooner had they made their claims, however, when a Frenchman named Abbé Nollet undertook a tour of Italy, disproving these and other mountebanks along the way. Nollet was a dedicated debunker. When he returned to Paris, he would dispatch three of his fellow countrymen—the showman Delor, the botanist T. H. Dalibard, and a naturalist named Buffon (which, ironically, was also a stage name used by zanies)—for trying to pass off the quack theories of an American printer named Benjamin Franklin.

These names represent a turning point—the moment when the twin rituals of Carnival and Lent began to break from their seasonal origins. By the mid-eighteenth century, the mountebanks were becoming show inventors proper. With their lazzolike machine by their sides, they would impose their will on the planet and make it their stage. They would actually make a New World.

In America, however, they almost did not survive at all.


By the middle of the eighteenth century, Philadelphia was beginning to shed its reputation for solemnity. Drinking in public was common by 1750, though the Quakers still routinely deplored it. Lotteries were drawn widely and received an ambivalent reaction from the town elders—they disapproved of them, but they held them, too. In 1740, "gentlemen with families" held dances at Christ Church until William Seward padlocked the door, bemoaning the insurgency of "devilish diversions." Dancers broke the lock, and, by 1749, their society balls were thriving.

But for all the signs of growing leniency in Philadelphia, it would be hard to imagine a more inhospitable ground for colorful street shows. In 1723, a commedia dell'arte troupe took care to play on the outskirts of town, where it was less likely to be harassed. In late 1749, Thomas Kean and Walter Murray attempted the first theatrical performance inside city limits, on Pine Street near the wharfs on the Delaware River. The common council saw the engagement as an invitation to waste money on sinful pleasures and, on January 5, 1750, asked the troupe to leave town.

Four years later, when producer Lewis Hallam tried to introduce Philadelphians to a play called *Love Makes a Man, or the Fop's Fortune*, the Quakers brought pressure to bear. Miraculously, by opening night, the fare had been transformed into a palliative called *The Fair Penitent*. Even so, protests continued throughout the run. So virulent was their opposition to theater that, in 1759, Philadelphians attempted to outlaw stage plays permanently—and would have succeeded had the king not struck the law down.

The mountebanks were not received any better than their actor cousins. In 1757, the Philadelphia clergyman William Smith complained that "Quacks abound like locusts in *Egypt* . . . the Profession is under no Kind of Regulation . . . Any Man at his Pleasure sets up for Physician, Apothecary, and Chirurgeon." Nor was this a fleeting sentiment among the colonists. In 1772, New Jersey passed an act to regulate the practice of medicine, with an eye toward thinning the ranks of the mountebanks. The following year, Connecticut passed the more comprehensive "Act for the suppressing of Mountebanks." The wording is revealing:

> Be it therefore enacted by the Governor, Council and Representatives, in General Court assembled, and by the authority of the same, That no mountebank, or person whatsoever under him, shall exhibit or cause to be exhibited on any publick stage or place whatsoever in this Colony, any games, tricks, plays, jugling or feats of uncommon decsterity and agility of body, tending to no good and useful purposes, but tending to collect together numbers of spectators and gratify vain and useless curiosity.

America was not a Catholic country. Its churches had no public traditions comparable to the procession of Lent. On the contrary, the

Protestant faith answered the problems of scarcity through private acts. The good man kept to himself and worked hard, praying in solitude for his rewards, lest he fall prey to the "vain and useless curiosities" offered to idle crowds. And so the American equivalent to Lent—its economizing force—developed along its own peculiar lines. Rather than distinguishing between mountebanks and honest performers, the colonial authorities defined public exhibition itself as the problem. The battle would not be waged between spectacles of order and disorder, but over the right to put on a show at all.

This was the mood in 1747 when Benjamin Franklin sat in a crowd in Boston. A bawdy man who was not averse to running the occasional dirty joke in his *Poor Richard's Almanack*, Franklin had come to see a Scotsman named Dr. A. Spencer conduct an electrical demonstration. The performance, as it turned out, was very much in keeping with his sensibilities. As a boy was suspended from the ceiling by silk cords, the Philadelphia printer became alert. When the doctor drew "sparks of fire" from the boy's face and hands, his curiosity turned to amazement.

At forty, Franklin had found an avocation. He immediately availed himself of Spencer's equipment, then ordered more from Peter Collinson, an English friend. First, he tried his own variation on Spencer's experiment and drew sparks from a boy on a glass stool. Before long, he and Ebenezer Kinnersley, a fellow Philadelphian, were electrifying "upon Wax, in the Dark, a Book that has a double line of Gold round upon the Covers." In a daring move, Franklin even assumed the role of the quack and tried to treat a paralytic patient with electricity.

In April 1749, a few months before Kean and Murray began their ill-fated run on Pine Street, Franklin despaired of finding any use for this potent force of nature and expressed his wish for an inventor's show. "Chagrin'd a little," he wrote to his friend Collinson, "that We have hitherto been able to discover Nothing in the Way of Use to Mankind . . . 'tis proposed to put an End to them this Season somewhat humorously in a Party of Pleasure on the Banks of the Schuylkill." Expanding on this imaginary scene, he proposed to kill turkeys with electricity, then roast them on an "electrical Jack, before a Fire kindled by an Electrical Bottle." After toasting the famous electricians of Europe, he and his guests would drink from "Electrified Bumpers under the Discharge of Guns from the Electrical Battery."

But Franklin had to watch his step. Not only were quacks frowned upon in Philadelphia, he had been personally singled out for his activities as a journalist and sometime militia organizer. In 1748, Thomas

Penn, the leader of colonial Pennsylvania, declared him "a Dangerous Man . . . of a very uneasy Spirit." If Franklin wanted to make his experiments known, he would have to conduct his electric Carnival by circuitous means. He would have to become a cipher.

Franklin never did stage his riverside electrical spectacle. He did, however, sponsor his colleague Kinnersley's efforts along similar lines. In 1751, Kinnersley began a series of "experiments for money" (as Franklin called them in his autobiography) with the title "For the Entertainment of the Curious." Colonists who attended this show were feted to a two-part debut of marvels, including "a Shower of Sand which rises as it falls," "A Piece of Money drawn out of a Person's Mouth in spite of his Teeth, yet without touching the Money of the Person," and, more dubiously, a flash of lightning made to avoid a woman sitting in its path and to strike instead "the Image of a Negro standing by, and seeming to be further out of Danger."

Kinnersley's show was not entirely given over to tricks. Tucked in among the "astonishing wonders" was "An Experiment, shewing how to preserve Houses, Ships &c. from being ever struck by lightning." In other words, Kinnersley demonstrated Franklin's lightning rod (although in this case the lightning was probably simulated with sparks) at least a year before the famous kite experiment took place. If he is not remembered for this today, it was not for lack of celebrity in his time, since the lectures were said to be popular. More likely, Kinnersley's lectures were received as entertainments, to be enjoyed or admonished, but not to be judged on their scientific merits.

Franklin himself maintained a certain distance from these performances. Though he was supplying the theoretical underpinnings of the show and even wrote Kinnersley's text, his name was nowhere attached to the lectures. In fact, he seemed determined to keep as low a profile as possible. This strategy may have kept him in the good graces of the town elders, but it also posed a paradox: In the absence of a proof, he could never hope to make his ideas known. Yet if he did try to demonstrate his ideas, he could never hope to be taken seriously.

Franklin's interest in science, not to mention his willingness to flirt with "quackery," isolated him from his fellow colonists. But if, unlike the French and English scientists of his day, he had few compatriots with whom he could confer, he could always confer from afar. Ever the good press man, he mailed his ideas to Collinson, who in turn "got them read" at the Royal Society. One such letter, written by Franklin in 1751, contained a proposal called the sentry-box experiment:

Newport, March 16. 1752.

*Notice is hereby given to the Curious,*

That at the COURT-HOUSE, in the Council-Chamber, is now to be exhibited, and continued from Day to Day, for a Week or two;

A COURSE of EXPERIMENTS, on the newly-discovered

# Electrical FIRE:

Containing, not only the most curious of those that have been made and published in *Europe*, but a considerable Number of new Ones lately made in *Philadelphia*; to be accompanied with methodical LECTURES on the Nature and Properties of that wonderful Element.

By *Ebenezer Kinnersley.*

## LECTURE I.

I. OF Electricity in General, giving some Account of the Discovery of it.

II. That the Electric Fire is a real Element, and different from those heretofore known and named, and *collected* out of other Matter (not created) by the Friction of Glass, &c.

III. That it is an extremely subtile Fluid.

IV. That it doth not take up any perceptible Time in passing thro' large Portions of Space.

V. That it is intimately mixed with the Substance of all the other Fluids and Solids of our Globe.

VI. That our Bodies at all Times contain enough of it to set a House on Fire.

VII. That tho' it will fire inflammable Matters, itself has no sensible Heat.

VIII. That it differs from common Matter, in this; its Parts do not mutually attract, but mutually repel each other.

IX. That it is strongly attracted by all other Matter.

X. An artificial Spider, animated by the Electric Fire, so as to act like a live One.

XI. A Shower of Sand, which rises again as fast as it falls.

XII. That common Matter in the Form of Points attracts this Fire more strongly than in any other Form.

XIII. A Leaf of the most weighty of Metals suspended in the Air, as is said of *Mahomet's* Tomb.

XIV. An Appearance like Fishes swimming in the Air.

XV. That this Fire will live in Water, a River not being sufficient to quench the smallest Spark of it.

XVI. A Representation of the Sensitive Plant.

XVII. A Representation of the seven Planets, shewing a probable Cause of their keeping their due Distances from each other, and from the Sun in the Center.

XVIII. The Salute repulsed by the Ladies Fire; or Fire darting from a Ladies Lips, so that she may defy any Person to salute her.

XIX. Eight musical Bells rung by an electrified Phial of Water.

XX. A Battery of eleven Guns discharged by Fire issuing out of a Person's Finger.

## LECTURE II.

I. A Description and Explanation of Mr. *Muschenbroek's* wonderful Bottle.

II. The amazing Force of the Electric Fire in passing thro' a Number of Bodies at the same Instant.

III. An Electric Mine sprung.

IV. Electrified Money, which scarce any Body will take when offer'd to them.

V. A Piece of Money drawn out of a Person's Mouth in spite of his Teeth; yet without touching it, or offering him the least Violence.

VI. Spirits kindled by Fire darting from a Lady's Eyes (without a Metaphor).

VII. Various Representations of Lightning, the Cause and Effects of which will be explained by a more probable Hypothesis than has hitherto appeared, and some useful Instructions given, how to avoid the Danger of it: How to secure Houses, Ships, &c. from being hurt by its destructive Violence.

VIII. The Force of the Electric Spark, making a fair Hole thro' a Quire of Paper.

IX. Metal melted by it (tho' without any Heat) in less than a thousandth Part of a Minute.

X. Animals killed by it instantaneously.

XI. Air issuing out of a Bladder set on Fire by a Spark from a Person's Finger, and burning like a Volcano.

XII. A few Drops of electrified cold Water let fall on a Person's Hand, supplying him with Fire sufficient to kindle a burning Flame with one of the Fingers of his other Hand.

XIII. A Sulphurous Vapour kindled into Flame by Fire issuing out of a cold Apple.

XIV. A curious Machine acting by means of the Electric Fire, and playing Variety of Tunes on eight musical Bells.

XV. A Battery of eleven Guns discharged by a Spark, after it has passed through ten Foot of Water.

As the Knowledge of Nature tends to enlarge the human Mind, and give us more noble, more grand, and exalted Ideas of the AUTHOR of Nature, and if well pursu'd, seldom fails producing something useful to Man, 'tis hoped these Lectures may be tho't worthy of Regard & Encouragement.

☞ Tickets to be had at the House of the Widow Allen, in Thames Street, next Door to Mr. John Tweedy's, Price Thirty Shillings each Lecture. The Lectures to begin each Day precisely at Three o'Clock in the Afternoon.

One of America's first inventor's shows was *For the Entertainment of the Curious*, put on in the 1750s by Ebenezer Kinnersley, a colleague of Benjamin Franklin. Among the attractions was the simulated use of a lightning rod. *Brown University Libraries*

To determine the question Whether the Clouds that contain Lightning are electrified or not, I would propose an Experiment to be try'd where it may be done conveniently.

On the Top of some high Tower or Steeple, place a Kind of Sentry Box big enough to contain a Man and an electrical Stand.

From the Middle of the Stand let an Iron Rod rise, and pass bending out of the Door, and then upright 20 or 30 feet, pointed very
sharp at the End. If the Electrical Stand be kept clean and dry, a
Man standing on it—when such clouds are passing low, might be
electrified and afford Sparks, the Rod drawing Fire to Him from a
Cloud.

The Royal Society gave little credence to Franklin's ideas, and even
laughed outright at a paper on the "Sameness of Lightning with Electricity," which he had originally written for Kinnersley. Undaunted, Collinson turned to a publisher and had the papers printed in pamphlet
form.

Collinson's tenacity soon paid off. With publication, word of the
sentry-box proposal spread to France and ultimately to the court of King
Louis XV, who gave his imprimatur for French scientists to try it out.
A location was chosen for the experiment, and on May 10, 1752, in a
garden in Marly, eighteen miles outside of Paris, the botanist Dalibard—
Abbé Nollet's nemesis—erected a rod forty feet into the air. When a
storm cloud passed over the site, a guard or dragoon named Coiffier
came forward with a jar in hand and the nerve to draw a spark. At 2:20
in the afternoon, a man forgotten by history became the first to trap
lightning in a bottle.

Immediately, the race was on in Europe to repeat the experiment.
The French electrical showman Delor did so on May 18. (Calling his
performance the "Philadelphia Experiments," Delor also drew large
sparks from a battery, created a momentary electrical portrait, and otherwise fascinated the French king with Franklin's repertoire of tricks.)
Englishman John Canton, a schoolmaster and electrical experimenter,
met with success across the channel not long thereafter.

With this the encomiums flowed, from the likes of Immanuel Kant,
who called Franklin a "modern Prometheus," and John Adams, who
gushed that Franklin's status was "more universal than that of Liebniz
or Newton, Frederick or Voltaire; and his character more esteemed and
beloved than all of them." Caught unawares, Abbé Nollet, who had
done so well in exposing the electrical mountebanks of Italy, had failed
to debunk Franklin at all.

Meanwhile, back in Philadelphia, Franklin proceeded apace, apparently unaware that he had become the man of the hour in the Western
world. He was edging his way toward his own sentry-box experiment
but, as he later explained, was delayed while a new tower was being

constructed atop Christ Church. Tired of waiting, he hit upon the make-shift idea of using a kite instead. And so, one day in the summer of 1752, Benjamin Franklin set out into a field and performed his renowned kite experiment.

*Maybe.*

As fixed as this experiment has become in the textbooks of the world, the best researchers on the subject have never been able to prove that Franklin really flew that kite. He took along only one witness—his son William—and afterward failed to write down any of the particulars of the experiment, even though he had been taking detailed notes on electrical phenomena for at least five years. His only bid at documentation was a letter to his friend Peter Collinson in England in October 1752, in which he described the experiment as a recommendation rather than a matter of record. In the *Pennsylvania Gazette*, he simply repeated this letter. In fact, the only detailed account of the incident came from Joseph Priestley, a British scientist and Franklin's friend. Yet even Priestley did not record his own hearsay account until 1767—some fifteen years after the fact.

The lengths to which Franklin went to avoid being seen as a performer are extraordinary. Indeed, had he chosen to emulate his contemporaries in France or Italy, he would have behaved differently on almost every count. The European experimenter of his day would have organized a riverside "electric picnic" without compunction, perhaps even throwing in a mention of "Peruvian balsam vapors" for good measure. Certainly, he would have made himself, not Kinnersely, the star of his traveling show. And when the time came to prove his theories, he would have advertised his sentry-box proposal throughout his immediate environs, carried it out before a crowd, and then, if he had the means, quickly published a narrative account of the episode.

Yet Franklin did none of these things. He did not even leave behind the simplest artifacts that might have served as historical souvenirs. The kite he is supposed to have used is not on exhibit anywhere in the world today. The key he is supposed to have held does not sit beneath polished glass for tourists to admire. There may never have been a key.

Scholars still debate the confusing nature of Franklin's activities during this period. Impatience, fear, and modesty have all been put forward as motives (with reservations on each count) to explain why a man such as Franklin—not one to shun recognition in other areas—stole away to conduct his landmark experiment. The possibility that he may never have conducted it only clouds the issue further. Unless, of course, the confusion itself is a telltale clue—the sign of a man improvising under adverse conditions.

Was Franklin anxious to avoid appearing before a crowd? Did he bluff, delay, and delegate his way to recognition in order to escape the tar brush of the lowly mountebank? The prevailing attitudes of the times suggest as much, even if he was reacting to them only on an unconscious level. Among other things, they explain why he was so keen on having Europeans perform his sentry-box experiment.

In Europe, theater was an accepted fact of life. One theatrical tradition had its roots in religious mystery plays and morality plays. First overseen by the church and then by kings, this branch of drama eventually developed into a form of high theater. Through the spectacle of Lent overtaking Carnival, low theater had also been integrated into European society and even into the courts themselves; in a society where court jesters sat beside the throne, for Delor to perform before the king was perfectly normal. There were still aspects of European drama that ruffled the dander of the authorities in Franklin's day, but a guard capturing lightning before a French crowd was hardly cause for moral outrage.

American theater, on the other hand, had no roots in either state or religious matters at all. From the very beginning, theatrical producers like Thomas Kean and Lewis Hallam put on plays with an eye toward profit alone, and any questions about the deeper significance of their shows would have met with a puzzled look. In 1752, American performances were presumed to be entirely commercial, a fact that only added to their impropriety in the eyes of the Protestant clergy.

Given the abyss between the American and European attitudes, Franklin's belated account (as delivered by Priestley) makes sense whether it is fiction or fact. After all, a man climbing on top of a church in the center of town and summoning the Lord's power into his hand was bound to be viewed as a gaudy, money-grubbing scheme at best, and more likely as sheer blasphemy. Much better to get a European to do the job with the blessings of a European government, and then to conduct his own experiment in the manner of strolling player—on the outskirts of town, or not at all.

If this was Franklin's plan, it worked quite well. The demonstrations in Europe took on the trappings of high theater, which in turn allowed Franklin's American contemporaries to compare him to Prometheus without fear of reprisal. Only years later did he permit his own demonstration to be described in any detail, by which time he had long since been lionized. In this way, Franklin was spared any association with the chirurgeons, who set up without any regulation, and the players, who were generally asked to leave town. Pulling his invisible levers, he remained instead a private figure. And by failing to appear before his fellow citizens, he had offered himself up not as a conniving, hardscrabble conjurer, but as a dignified man with brilliant thoughts on his mind.

There was one shortcoming to this plan, though. Franklin's ability to avoid an appearance before an American crowd may have kept his electrical discoveries from looking like some kind of crass scheme. But in fact, there *was* some kind of scheme. Though Franklin had no interest in patenting his lighting rod, he had thought a demonstration might popularize its use. In this case, a no-show show did not bring in the orders. The colonists, who had never actually seen fire brought safely to the ground, were reluctant to install the invention in their homes, and the local churchmen seized the opportunity to denounce it as heresy. By the time lightning rods began to appear on American rooftops, they were already a common sight on the Continent.

Franklin's approach could never be a permanent solution to the problem of introducing an invention. Few colonists could call upon European friends to further their aims, and even if they could, obfuscation was hardly the most effective method of popularizing a physical object. For an invention to pass into general use, it had to be put before American audiences. The voice of unreason needed its say.

As it turned out, however, the voice of unreason suffered all the more as the colonies graduated into nationhood. Indeed, when Thomas Jefferson became the official overseer of American inventions, his style seemed to indicate that, if anything, Franklin had done his job altogether too well.

When the U.S. Patent Office began operations on April 10, 1790, a three-man board was assigned to process the applications, with Jefferson at the helm. For the red-headed Virginian to bear the brunt of the workload was only natural. He was, after all, secretary of state, a Founding Father, and heir to Franklin's legacy by popular acclaim. He was no stranger to inventions, either. Over the course of his life, he invented a dumbwaiter, a plow, a fireproof ceiling, a weather vane, a swivel chair, an adjustable music stand, a turnstile, a double-door opening mechanism, and possibly a wind-powered saw mill. It is revealing, though, that he designed every one of his inventions for his own private use at his

Monticello home. However ingenious he showed himself to be, he disapproved of any inventor who tried to exploit the public for commercial gain.

To be fair, Jefferson had reasons to be wary of commercialism that the earlier church authorities did not. In the 1790s, British industrialists were darkening the English countryside with their "Satanic mills" and using their newfound wealth to lord over the masses—an example of the disruptive power of invention at its worst. Closer to home, Alexander Hamilton, then secretary of the treasury, had begun arguing that Yankee capitalists needed a wider berth for their ambitions. One of the more immediate effects of Hamilton's campaign was a sharp increase in financial speculation.

Jefferson looked upon these trends with a heavy heart. In his mind, the exemplar of democratic ideals was the agrarian life—self-sufficient, essentially private, far from the venalities of the marketplace. During his tenure as secretary of state, he engaged in an increasingly bitter fight with Hamilton, and found himself complaining of the "Immense sums . . . filched from the poor & ignorant, and fortunes accumulated by those who had been poor enough before," even as he wrote longingly of the day when he could return to his rural Virginia home. Of course, the mountebank who gratified the "vain and useless curiosity" of crowds with his half-cocked contraptions was not so different from the speculator who "filched from the poor and innocent" with his investment schemes. Thus, for Jefferson, the old church biases remained in effect. Public appeals, commercialism, and danger were all of a piece.

Ironically, Jefferson later drew support for his cautious sensibility from his illustrious forebear. In 1812, as an aging statesman, he wrote to Dr. Thomas Cooper: "You know the just esteem which attached itself to Dr. Franklin's science, because he always endeavored to direct it to something useful in private life." By something useful in private life, he could hardly have meant the attractions that Ebenezer Kinnersley offered for the price of admission—sand made to hang in midair, a coin drawn from a man's closed mouth. But that, apparently, was the price of obfuscation: such a subtle operator was Franklin that his actions came to support the very attitude he had once finessed.

Then again, Jefferson had to justify himself somehow, because the new patent laws supported *both* sides of the debate. It was true, of course, that the American system solved many of the inequities that had marred the colonial laws. Where British patents had cost as much as seventy pounds, the U.S. Patent Office asked the equivalent of a mere six. Surely this was a triumph of Jeffersonian ideals, as it made legal protection affordable to the common man for the first time. But the new laws also awarded a seventeen-year monopoly to patent holders, a fact that boded well for Hamilton's dreams of robust capitalization. Worse, the low cost of applying—equitable as it was—threatened to give even the poorest mountebank a legitimacy he had never enjoyed before.

Rather than ushering in a golden age of invention, then, Jefferson braced himself for the storm and began methodically rejecting any application that smacked of disingenuous intent. In the end, he outdid himself. So strict were his standards that during his first year he awarded only three patents. By the time he left the position four years later, only thirty-seven inventions had made it into the record books.

As secretary of state, Jefferson enjoyed tremendous authority over inventors; he was essentially the nation's economizing force concentrated in a single man. He was not alone in his prejudices, however. In 1787, David Rittenhouse, an early American astronomer, wrote Jefferson a letter, warning of an "abundance of projectors and pretenders to new Discoveries, some of them ridiculous enough." That Rittenhouse put something called a "self-moving boat" at the top of his list was little cause for wonder. This invention had sprung from the mind of an unruly traveler—uneducated, solicitous, America's first major show inventor. And in a gesture charged with symbolism, John Fitch had chosen to debut his boat at the very site where the new nation was being formed.

## Chapter Two

# A PASSION FOR PRIVACY

On August 22, 1787, the delegates of the Constitutional Convention in Philadelphia had occasion to see a very obvious performance put on in the center of town. Strolling down to the Front Street wharves from Independence Hall or their lodgings at the Indian Queen, they came upon a man who began telling them excitedly about a vessel he had built. It moved against the tide without the aid of wind or hand, he said, but was powered instead by steam.

To the delegates in their elegant wigs, satin breeches, brightly colored coats, and laced stockings—an assembly that Jefferson described from his distant perch in France as "demigods"—John Fitch must have looked every bit as dubious as the craft he was advertising. By the time he was twenty-one and married, he had already been a farmer, a store clerk, a sea merchant, a clockmaker, a silversmith, and a brass worker. Deserting his wife only a few months after their wedding, he joined the loose-knit network of merchants known as Yankee peddlers who wandered from town to town selling candles, tinware, or clocks, and offering their services for repairs.

These peddlers, known at the time as chapmen, resembled the mountebanks to a degree. Like the dubious Dottores of Italy, they became famous as the merchants of notions, and they were just as amenable to any tall tale that might help them sell their wares. Their audiences, however, were far less sophisticated than those in European or even American cities. Traveling the backroads of the colonies and beyond, the peddlers traded with Indians and uneducated whites, who generally required very little prompting to suspend their disbelief. On the eighteenth-century frontier, any theater at all was a lot.

The chapmen also had to endure less welcoming traveling conditions than those of their European counterparts. Some pushed handcarts. Those who were better off rode horseback or in horse-drawn wagons. Often, the road was nothing more than a dirt path or "corduroy"—a series of logs laid side by side. Crossing bodies of water was especially difficult.

Presented with such challenges on an almost constant basis, the Yankee peddlers developed a distinctive brand of inventiveness: the mechanics on the road became mechanics *of* the road. They devised many methods of spanning rivers—wooden bridges, rope bridges, makeshift dams. Sometimes they would rig up a wire ferry, which was a scow with a wire network set up overhead, and a long pole for working the craft along the wires.

Such was the life for Fitch then. After plodding through Pittsfield, Massachusetts, Albany, and New York City, he surfaced in 1769 as a button maker and clock cleaner in Trenton, New Jersey, then during the war as a gunsmith and a trader in Bucks County, Pennsylvania. A land purchase debacle in the early 1780s led to his capture by Indians on the Ohio River and his eventual imprisonment by the British in Canada. After his release in 1783, he continued his efforts to buy land in Kentucky and Ohio.

By April 1785, Fitch had grown tired of the transient life and, while traveling this terrain for the umpteenth time, he saw his way out. No more corduroys. No more wire ferries. He would turn in his hardships for steamships.

For two years, he labored to complete a workable model of this invention; by 1787, he was finished. All the signs seemed to point to success. The new American patent system, being hammered out even as Fitch's boat idled at the dock, promised to favor ordinary citizens— and what better symbol of the new republic could there be but this remarkable invention, unveiled in the capital city?

Good chapman that he was, Fitch beseeched the delegates to try it out for themselves. A few did, among them Dr. Samuel Johnson, who hailed from Fitch's hometown of Windsor, Connecticut. Most, however, simply pronounced it interesting and went back to the more serious business of debating the articles and clauses of the Constitution. General Washington kept his distance. So did Benjamin Franklin.

Franklin's indifference was especially perplexing. Fitch simply couldn't understand why such a far-seeing inventor would fail to get excited about a boat that moved of its own accord. Had he been studying style instead of steam, however, Fitch might have seen the silent treatment coming. Only nine years earlier, the Continental Congress had delivered its most severe injunction yet regarding live performances:

> Whereas, frequenting play-houses and theatrical entertainments has a fatal tendency to divest the minds of people from a due attention to the defence of their Country and preservation of their liberties;
>
> Resolved, That any person holding an office under the United States who shall act, promote, encourage or attend such play, shall be deemed unworthy to hold such office and shall be accordingly dismissed.

Such sentiments were not designed to stem the tide of invention; the same gathering had openly voiced the need to improve the state of American manufactures. But if invention and theatrical entertainments were to come together, that was another thing again.

So there stood Fitch, a man with the mud of the Ohio River on his boots, soliciting the nation's future officeholders—many of whom had attended that earlier congress—to take part in a mechanical spectacle. At the moment, his closest counterpart in the New World was John Brenon, who was currently treating New Yorkers to a show involving balloon ascensions, tricks on the slack wire, a stunt in which a fowl was beheaded and then restored to life, and, for a finale, a cure for toothaches "without drawing. No cure, no pay. For the poor Gratis."

Fitch's rival in the invention of the steamboat, James Rumsey, had spared himself such comparisons. A few years earlier, Rumsey had shown George Washington a small model of his invention when the general showed up at his tavern. This approach required a great deal less from its esteemed audience than a public performance did. There was none of the disorder inherent in any crowd, none of the vulgar appeals of the showman. Nor was there any real risk. Washington did not have worry that, after expressing his approval, the steamboat might be seen to fail. Fascinated, he had offered Rumsey his glowing endorsement.

Fitch's boat, on the other hand, was the very picture of risk. When it failed to move as quickly as advertised and no eminent figure came forward in its defense, the crowd let loose its scorn. "I could not suppress my indignation," remembered Jacques Pierre Brissot de Warville, "upon seeing Americans frustrate and discourage with sarcastic jeers the noble efforts of one of their fellow citizens."

To his credit, Fitch did not give up right away. After building a more powerful version, he put on another show, this one at the Front Street wharves. A mile was measured out along the riverside, a flag placed at each end, and the progress timed with a stopwatch. The stockholders were impressed, and on April 16, 1790, Fitch pulled away from shore on the first commercial steamboat operation in the world—a good twelve years before Robert Fulton floated one of his own.

Ironically, Franklin managed to foil Fitch in death as in life: on April 17, the day after Fitch's maiden voyage, a special, black-bordered edition of Franklin's *Pennsylvania Gazette* announced that the great statesman was dead. An estimated twenty thousand people attended the funeral—the largest gathering in Philadelphia up to that time—and the mourning continued well into June, when the French observed a national day of remembrance. No doubt a bold commercial undertaking in the midst of this collective grief left a bad aftertaste for many Philadelphians. The *Gazette*, newly headed by the eminent man's grandson, Benjamin Franklin Bache, refused to run the advertisements for it.

Undaunted, Fitch ran excursions between Philadelphia and Trenton throughout the summer, traveling a total of two to three thousand miles and carrying an estimated hundreds of passengers, who had been plied with beer and sausages. But that was the best things got for him. His Virginia patent, a colonial monopoly patterned after the old British laws, required that he build a boat capable of bearing a load of twenty tons before the end of the year. Try as he might, he could not satisfy the demand.

The situation reached the height of absurdity when the Patent Office granted the same patent to both Fitch and Rumsey. This made no sense, Fitch complained to Jefferson, especially since the patent described Rumsey's boat, which was clearly inferior. (It never traveled a distance greater than 150 yards.) When Fitch offered to show his papers, however, Jefferson pursed his lips and succinctly revealed his bias against show inventors and their marketplace mentality.

"It would be too much," said the secretary of state, "like tampering with judges out of doors."

From then on, Fitch descended ever deeper into anonymity, a man without a context. He went to Europe hoping for better luck but returned empty-handed. A wanderer to the last, he ended up in Bardstown, Kentucky, living in a tavern and carefully avoiding any mention of himself in connection with steamboats. On July 7, 1798, his mind addled by alcohol, he gave up. "Nobody will believe that poor John Fitch can do anything worthy of attention," he wrote, and ended his travels once and for all with a draught of poison.

John Fitch was not a bad mechanic or a misguided dreamer. He was simply a pioneer on too many levels at once. Not only did he bring forth the first practical steamboat from the backroads (where he was a pioneer in the original sense of the word), he was also the first major American inventor to appeal directly to the public.

Ultimately, it was this last accomplishment that damaged him most. Crawling out of the frontier, he had tried to deal with the nation's elite in broad daylight, just as he might have sold nutmegs to a Menongahelan log splitter. That was too steep an offer for the Founding Fathers, so it was left to Fitch to provide the first example of a classic American figure: the inventor as unreconstructed wild man.

If Oliver Evans, whose mechanical miller came second on David Rittenhouse's list of "ridiculous projects," fared any better than John Fitch, it was because he persisted long enough to see the glimmer of a different nation.

As the Republic emerged from the hardships of war, the harsh attitudes toward performers showed signs of softening. The playwright Royall Tyler still tapped a popular sentiment in 1787, when he described the typical playhouse as "the devil's drawing-room." Yet several years later, audiences were flocking to see his comedy The Contrast, in which the character of Jonathan clowned it up onstage as America's first home-grown zany. In New York, moralists still deplored the custom of reserving one section of the house for prostitutes. Yet when the first Park Theater—designed by the French inventor Marc Isambard Brunel—opened in 1797, it signaled a more durable dramatic tradition for the country. The stage was attaining the status of a necessary evil, and the fortunes of Oliver Evans improved accordingly.

Evans was not a typical man for his time, or for any time. Benighted with a game leg and two eyes that didn't seem to belong to each other, he spent his life constucting devices that, practical as they were, invariably looked slightly demented. No doubt his inability to draw did not help matters. Beginning with rough pencil sketches, he would proceed to a chalkboard, where he worked out his diagrams in full scale, with nothing but a two-foot rule, a straight-edge square, and a compass to guide him. Thanks to this crude procedure, any attempts at a graceful design were soon lost to ad hoc—and unwittingly comical—solutions.

Certainly, Evans was accustomed to ridicule from an early age. As a child in Maryland, he tested the patience of his family with a card-punching machine that continually failed to perform as intended. The young inventor was not easily discouraged, however, and by 1782, he had built his first "Mechanical Miller."

Nothing could have prepared his fellow colonists for the sight. A descender, a conveyor belt, a rotating rake, a grain elevator, and pulleys all conspired to generate flour, making the contraption the ancestor of all assembly lines and a precursor to Rube Goldberg's sensibility by more than a century. More importantly, it turned a job that formerly required two or three men into a solo affair.

True to character, Jefferson had his reservations about this invention, insisting that it be tolerated only within "the compass of the private family." When Evans applied for a patent in 1790, Jefferson complained that the device simply combined a number of inventions already in existence. "I can conceive how a machine may improve the manufacturing of flour," he wrote, "but not how a *principle* abstracted from any machine can do it." But in the end, he could not argue with originality, and he was compelled to award Evans a patent—the third in U.S. history.

With the turn of the century, Evans grew braver, but no more acclaimed for his efforts. In 1800 or 1801, in his shop on Philadelphia's Market and Ninth streets, he applied a steam engine of his own design to the task of milling and began exhibiting it to the public. The reaction of the crowd provided its own brand of comedy. After breaking and grinding twelve tons of plaster of Paris in a period of twenty-four hours, Evans thought to highlight the powers of his machine by having it saw marble. Yet this elicited more brow-furrowing than understanding.

"I thought this was sufficient to convince thousands of spectators of the utility of my discoveries," Evans recounted, "but I frequently heard them inquire if the power could be applied to saw timber, as well as stone . . . and though I answered in the affirmative, I found they still doubted."

Philadelphians, unfamiliar with the principles of steam power, had

Oliver Evans paraded his Orukter Amphibolos ("amphibious digger"), the first self-propelled vehicle in America, through Philadelphia's Center Square in 1805. Model by Greville Bathe. *Smithsonian Institution*

yet to grasp that the miracle lay not in the saw but in the engine. To address this ignorance, Evans screwed up his courage and decided to apply his engine "to many new uses and to introduce it and them to the public notice."

There is no doubt that Evans knew how to rouse the public's attention. Built in 1805, his steam dredge was the first self-propelled vehicle in America and many years ahead of its time. A model reconstructed by Evans's biographer, Greville Bathe, gives some indication of just how spectacular it was. A long wooden wagon supported a mad assemblage of parts: a conveyor belt, buckets for removing the mud from the belt, a paddlewheel, oars, and the various machinery that connected these components into a single unwieldy unit. Dwarfed beneath it all, on a strut extending from the front, sat the driver *cum* helmsman.

In language befitting its style, Evans dubbed his behemoth the Orukter Amphibolos, or "amphibious digger." For several days, he set it loose in Philadelphia's Center Square, allowing its heaving glory to be fully absorbed and, all but announcing that he intended this event to be received as a show, requested a twenty-five-cent donation from spectators. Then he took the wheel and chugged off into the Schuylkill River, where, after puttering around for a while, he anchored his machine and commenced dredging mud from the riverbed.

All this commotion generated no notice whatsover. Even though Evans had advertised in *Relf's Philadelphia Gazette,* and even though, aside from a few initial difficulties with the wheels, the machine functioned well enough, not a single newspaper reviewed his spectacular performance. Of course, it could not have helped that the *Philadelphia Gazette* itself regarded steam power as the tool of mountebanks. On July 13, 1800, a reporter for the paper had called steam engines a "ridiculous project" and hoped that "the good people of my native city will no longer be duped by chimeras."

After the Orukter Amphibolos failed to win any admirers, Evans became increasingly hangdog about his prospects. That same year, he composed a tract with the pessimistic title, *The Abortion of the Young Steam Engineer's Guide*. But if nothing else, he was tenacious. In 1806, when Jefferson rigged up a mechanical miller of his own, the aborted young steam engineer slapped him with a bill. Jefferson, who by this time was the president of the United States, grumbled that "If the bringing together under the same roof various useful things before known . . . enables him to an exclusive use of all these, either separately or combined, every utensil of life might be taken from us by a patent." Then he quietly paid up.


Minor victories aside, show inventors profited little from their efforts in the Jeffersonian era. To be effective, one had to bend to dictates of the day; in other words, privacy was the best policy. Of course, those who demanded privacy could never be completely satisfied, because the revelation of an invention was an unavoidably social act, with all the potential disorder that attended such things. Still, there were ways of playing down the clamor of the moment when the machine was exposed.

Ironically, one of these methods was developed by Jefferson himself. Because he believed that inventions should be useful and not simply spun from fanciful theories, the secretary of state felt obliged to verify that they worked, which meant that he had to see them for himself. For starters, inventors were required to send a scale model of their invention to the U.S. Patent Office. Even then Jefferson was usually not satisfied until the inventor made a personal appearance to explain the device.

If this was not a performance per se, it was not very far from being an audition. Unable to keep invention from being a completely asocial endeavor, Jefferson, like the Quakers a generation earlier, required that his inventors appear before him in the role of the Fair Penitent. Those who did so invariably got better results. As it turned out, however, this strategy did not always serve Jefferson himself very well. In fact, Eli Whitney—the dashing Romantic who invented the cotton gin—managed to use one such meeting to subvert Jefferson's aims altogether.

In 1797, Whitney was laid up in his native Connecticut, his life in wild disarray. He had impressed Jefferson with his gin four years earlier, but things had gone horribly sour since then. When he tried to extract a fee of one pound of cotton for every three that farmers produced with his invention, they had responded by making their own gins and paying nothing. Then, unable to control himself any longer, he had declared his love for the fiancée of his business partner, Phineas Miller. Inevitably, a schism began to grow between them. "I have labored hard against the current of Disappointment which has been threatening to carry us down the Cataract of destruction," wrote Whitney to Miller in a desperate eleventh-hour plea, "but I have labored with a shattered oar." Miller ignored him.

Deep in the winter of his discontent, Whitney brooded. His New Haven friends worried that he never left the house. Even so, he was not yet ready for the poison that John Fitch, a few hundred miles to the southwest, was beginning to contemplate as the only solution. Instead, Whitney decided that the problem lay with business backers in general. As he remembered his success in showing Jefferson his cotton gin, an idea came to him. Would the government itself, he wondered, back him on some sort of project?

Whitney studied the government and decided that it needed a screw press. Forthwith, he proposed the manufacture of "presses and dies for the execution of the Stamp Act" to Oliver Wolcott, who had succeeded Jefferson as secretary of state. After that failed to make an impression, Whitney hit upon a favorite of states the world over: guns. At the time, Congress was particularly worried about Napoleon, who seemed ready to attack most any nation he could locate on the map. Playing on this fear, Whitney was able to initiate the practice of government contracts for arms manufacturers—a custom that continues to this day.

The contract was astoundingly generous. Effective June 21, 1798, it called for Whitney to produce ten thousand muskets, the first four thousand of which would be delivered in a year and a half. For each musket delivered, he would receive $13.40, for a grand total of $134,000. He would also receive advances along the way should that become necessary. What made this handsome sum all the more astonishing was the fact that Whitney had almost no knowledge of gun making whatsoever and that, at the time, the best armories were unable to produce more than five thousand guns a year.

Whitney felt confident he would work all that out. He set up a factory in East Haven, Connecticut, and proceeded to divide labor to an extent never before attempted. He assigned his workers menial tasks on a need-to-know basis. Instead of making an entire lock, the worker would engage himself only in planing or some other monotonous activity.

As bored as his workers became, Whitney drove them hard. Sounding very much like a contemporary manager, he wrote to Wolcott that "there is no branch of the work that can proceed well, scarcely for a single hour, unless I am present." Perhaps he meant this as an advance apology, because come his first deadline on September 30, 1799, he had no muskets to show for himself. He hadn't even equipped his armory.

Hoping to extend his contract, Whitney did the most expedient thing: he improvised. In another letter to Wolcott, he announced a "new principle" in manufacturing. This principle, he claimed, would revolutionize the arms industry even as it improved the quality of the goods. "One of my primary objects," he said, "is to form tools so the tools themselves shall fashion the work and give to every part its just proportion—which when once accomplished, will give expedition, uniformity, and exactness to the whole." Wolcott and his staff were intrigued, and an extension was granted. After all, Whitney was proposing to make real a dream that had been aired as far back as 1775—the manufacture of interchangeable parts.

Public demonstrations may have been anathema to the Founding Fathers, but Whitney soon discovered that private demonstrations were not. On January 8, 1801, before an audience that included President John Adams and Whitney's old friend, President-elect Thomas Jefferson, the inventor demonstrated that he could fit ten different locks into the same musket using nothing but an ordinary screwdriver. He then did one better and took one hundred different locks apart, scrambled their pieces, and put them back together "by taking the first pieces which come to hand." His audience, not least Jefferson, was amazed.

Whitney had no trouble getting extensions after that. Public leaders exalted him, and in 1812, the government awarded him another contract, this time for fifteen thousand guns. Sightseers began to make stops at his armory, hoping to catch a glimpse of this titan of a man. From the depths of his depression he had risen to the heights of heroism and received a sobriquet that formally admitted him into the ranks of the elite: after his 1801 demonstration, Elizur Goodrich, a congressman from Connecticut, wrote to his lawyer to say that the government now considered him the "Artist of his Country."

More astute observers might have deemed him an artist of a different sort. As the historian (and Whitney apologist) Merritt Roe Smith has pointed out, when twentieth-century industrial archeologists started mulling through the artifacts, they discovered that the gun parts were not even remotely interchangeable. Even more damaging was the presence of identifying numbers on Whitney's individual lock components, which would not have been necessary with interchangeable parts. Smith himself is categorical on the matter: "Whitney must have staged his 1801 demonstration with specimens specially prepared for the occasion."

For a shell game of this order, one is tempted to award Whitney the title of America's first court jester, except that court jesters generally received more meager rewards. Certainly, the exhibition evinced the mountebank's expert touch. By offering frothy predictions of "new principles," Whitney primed his audience in advance. Then, like Rumsey before him, he put on a private show, free of moral stigma or social disorder. The luminaries who beheld Whitney's gun locks ran no risk of being embarrassed in front of the common folk. And so they were drawn in by a time-honored showman's trick: the confidence game.

Of course, anyone can be fooled once. But why, when Whitney failed to achieve interchangeability in his subsequent deliveries, did the government continue to reward him with contracts? Didn't Jefferson and company care about that?

Perhaps, but Whitney's demonstration also realized a dream that the Founders themselves had set into motion. The need for interchangeable parts had first been voiced in the presence of Jefferson and Adams at the Continental Congress in 1775. With Whitney, that call had been made real—or rather, it had been dramatized.

In fact, the entire musket-lock episode exudes a slightly illicit air, as if the American heads of state secretly enjoyed mechanical performances (within reasonable limits) but could only indulge such forbidden pleasures behind closed doors. One might even say that a gathering such as the one Whitney convened was a kind of private family, within the compass of which a certain amount of excess was permissible—especially if the audience could interpret the proceedings as something other than a theatrical event.

As it turned out, the nomenclature of the times made a second interpretation readily available. The word *technology*, ubiquitous as it is today, did not come into popular usage until after Jefferson's death. Instead, the preferred term to describe both new inventions and established devices was *the mechanical arts*—and to the extent that an invention could be thought of as "art," it had redemptive qualities that low theater did not. This notion may seem odd at first glance, but Jefferson's aesthetic cravings bear it out.

For as much as he disdained "tampering with judges out of doors," Jefferson maintained a lifelong appetite for architecture, music, and, most of all, painting and sculpture. Being a man of morals, he was hard put to reconcile his passions with his station. As best as he could justify it, art could "give a pleasing and innocent direction to accumulations of wealth which could otherwise be employed in the nourishing of coarse and vicious habits." The painted image, in his view, was the nobleman's answer to vice—a respectable substitute for the pleasures of Carnival.

The vogue in the European art world supported this view. Throughout much of the eighteenth century, artists and rulers alike promulgated a style known as history painting. Born of aristocratic desires, history paintings were meant to be exhibited and sold with discretion, in marked contrast to the commercial fare hawked in the open markets. By the same token, common scenes meant very little to the history painter, whose job it was to glorify the moments that made his nation great. And glorify them he did. Around his kings and generals, he was likely to conjure clouds where there had been dust; angels where there had been devils. In fact, many of these paintings depicted the very figures that appeared in the procession of Lent—archangels, seraphim, the orderly forces of good.

Given the imprimatur of royalty, Jefferson followed this pleasing and innocent direction with vigor. During his tenure as U.S. plenipotentiary in France between 1784 and 1789, he collected as many paintings and sculptures as he could and brought them back to his crowded art gallery in Monticello. He joined the Société de 1789 and spoke admiringly of his fellow member, the artist David. To James Madison he wrote, somewhat sheepishly, "You see that I am an enthusiast on the subject of the arts."

As a statesman, Jefferson also had his own stake in the course that history painting might take, and he exercised it on occasion. It goes without saying that he posed for his own portraits. But he also saw fit to collaborate with the painter John Trumbull on *The Signing of the Declaration of Independence*—a representation of his own crowning moment.

Jefferson was also called upon to render his artistic judgment when the time came for the French artist Jean-Antoine Houdon to make a statue of George Washington. The American painter Benjamin West had created a stir some years earlier when his *Death of General Wolfe* depicted its hero surrounded by the usual grandeur but, shockingly, dressed in modern clothes. Was Washington to take his place in the pageant of history in contemporary attire as well? Jefferson ventured that he should, and that Houdon was the only sculptor worthy of the job.

Such matters were not to be taken lightly. With the image of the fledgling Republic at stake, art mattered. By extension, then, any inventor who qualified as an "artist" could be condoned, even as his commercial, open-air counterparts were shunned.

Whitney, for his part, encouraged such an interpretation by convening with the Founding Fathers far from the marketplace and, incidentally, showing them what they already wanted to see. There were, however, more literal ways of bringing out the artistic dimension of a mechanical device. For example, the inventor might actually be an artist.

A dark, imperious figure, Robert Fulton started out his career in the very circles that so fascinated Jefferson. As a young painter in 1787, he went to England and studied with Benjamin West, whose landmark painting had inspired a modern wardrobe for Washington's statue. Fulton soon began to have ideas of a more mechanical nature, though, and in 1794 he bolted from his teacher's studio and found his way to France. In 1797, he started publicizing a number of inventions in Paris. Only one of these was his own: a torpedo that worked intermittently. The others, which functioned much better, included a submarine stolen outright from the American inventor David Bushnell, a rope-making machine stolen from a Reverend Edmund Cartwright, and a panorama more graciously borrowed from the Scottish inventor Robert Barker.

This last invention was an early example of the show inventors' love of heights, which would surface again and again in the decades to come. Described in Fulton's 1799 French patent as "a circular picture without boundaries and the method of painting all the countryside, all the towns and villages . . . and other objects which can be seen from the summit of a mountain or tower or other eminence," it was almost arrogant in its scale. Leaving the boulevard Montmartre, spectators walked through a tunnel and up a spiral staircase to enter a forty-six-foot-wide circular building. At the apex, the view opened onto an immense painting of their beloved city, lighted by a central clerestory window.

The panaroma was just the kind of spectacle that would have met with a press blackout in Philadelphia. Parisians, however, were enthusiastic. One tourist noted that "[p]atrons . . . become so absorbed in the nuances of the view that they forget it is a mere illusion." The locals, for whom spectacles were more *de rigueur* than *gauche*, did this praise one better and made the panorama the subject of a music hall song: "Everybody goes or is going / To the pano, pano, panorama." Before long, Fulton was able to put up a second building, this one celebrating the "Evacuation of Toulouse by the British in 1793"—a surefire crowd pleaser.

Fulton next demonstrated a steamboat, which, as he himself admitted, was taken almost wholesale from John Fitch's diagrams. The French loved this show as much as they had his panorama and declared it a complete success. But almost immediately, Fulton began to feel the curse of the original inventor upon him. His backer, Robert R. Livingston, a New York patroon and the U.S. minister plenipotentiary to France (the same title formerly held by Jefferson), had agreed to appear at the demonstration on the Seine. True to patrician form, come showtime, Livingston disappeared to the Alps, pleading hot weather.

Fulton had promised to return to the United States after his steamboat demonstration, but it was clear from Livingston's actions that a public performance would give pause to the American elite, so he began instead to insert himself into the iconography of his nation. Before leaving France, he had a bust of himself made by Jefferson's favorite sculptor, Jean-Antoine Houdon. Then, rather than returning home, he went to England, where he renewed his friendship with Benjamin West and proposed to buy a painting or two from him.

By this time, West counted among his accomplishments the *American Commissioners of the Preliminary Peace Negotiations with Great Britain*, for which the British contingent had declined to sit, leaving the canvas blank on one side. More in keeping with Fulton's line of work, he had recently completed *Benjamin Franklin Drawing Electricity from the Sky*, as part of his Peace Commissioners series.

The painting is testimony to art's remarkable powers of revision. If Franklin indeed performed this experiment, he had done so in a field under a makeshift roof, alone but for the company of his son. In West's portrayal, however, he is surrounded by cupidlike figures. One prepares the kite on the ground, even as another holds taut the bolt from which the twine has been unreeled. Two more cupids inspect an elaborate array of laboratory equipment, unaccountably transported into the middle of a thunderstorm. In the center, Franklin sits on a rock, his legs splayed, his knuckles drawing a large spark from the key. His clothes are windswept, his bold face jutting upward, his beneficent eyes set in a stern face. The sum effect is to make Franklin into a solemn and unapproachable hero—a noble inventor, rather than the humane and earthy man he was in real life.

Fulton bought two paintings—*Ophelia before the King and Queen* and *King Lear in the Storm at the Hovel on the Heath*—with a third thrown in by West to show his affection. Sometime during this period, Fulton also suffered West to paint his own likeness. *Portrait of Robert Fulton*, completed in 1806, is considered a precursor to the Romantic movement. Fulton sits indoors, a young man with large enchanting eyes. Behind in the distance, a ship is being successfully blown up at sea with his torpedo—the same torpedo that had yet to function properly.

And so with his three West paintings and a Boulton-Watt steam engine in tow, Fulton returned to the States on December 13, 1806, fully equipped to demonstrate the power of the grand historical style and to be received as a noble inventor himself. Upon his arrival, he donated the West paintings to the Pennsylvania Academy of Fine Arts, just then being established, with an appeal to the institution to buy as much of the artist's work as possible. His country was grateful for the gesture: he was quickly elected a director of the American Academy of Fine Arts and a fellow of both the New-York Historical Society and the American Philosophical Society.

Then, in January 1807, Fulton gave a demonstration of his torpedo at a friend's estate outside Washington for a private audience that included Secretary of State James Madison and Secretary to the Navy Robert Smith. That much was in keeping with the Whitney protocol, and the statesmen expressed their satisfaction. But Fulton was not yet in the clear, and in July of that year, he attempted another demonstration on the southern tip of Manhattan to much less salubrious effect.

Though only a few local politicians were invited to witness the demonstration at the Battery, pedestrians inevitably grew curious and gathered round, craning their necks to see what the fuss was about. Ignoring them, Fulton fired a torpedo out toward a brig that was anchored near

Ellis Island. No explosion ruffled the waves. A second attempt resulted in the charge going off only one hundred yards offshore. By this time, most of the crowd had dispersed and gone home for dinner. Fulton, unfazed, persisted until he hit his target.

This was the event that came to be known as "Fulton's Folly." The *Commercial Advertiser*, a popular newspaper of the time, dutifully panned it as a bungled demonstration. Washington Irving, writing under a pen name, went further and satirized it. "The young ladies were delighted with the novelty of the show," he wrote, "and declared that if war could be conducted in this manner it would become a fashionable amusement; and the destruction of a fleet as pleasant as a ball or a tea party."

Fulton had suffered the fate of show inventors before him, and at this point, he could easily have gone the way of John Fitch. But as he now knew, the messy truth could always be arranged into more attractive form. Explaining that the shortcomings of his torpedo were easily corrected, he informed President Jefferson by mail that the people of New York seemed *pleased* with his demonstration.

Of course, in being depicted by West and Houdon, Fulton had also joined the procession of the historically significant, which in addition to Benjamin Franklin, included John Adams, John Jay, a host of characters from the Bible, and Jefferson himself. Thus, Jefferson did not see Fulton as a dangerous profiteer as much as a fellow "enthusiast of the arts"—perhaps even a potential addition to his Monticello gallery. Enthralled, he gave vent to his passions. Not only did he give Fulton the benefit of the doubt, he offered him the title of colonel.

Fulton turned the offer down but accepted the general show of encouragement. By August 9, 1807, his *North River Steamboat*, often mistakenly referred to as the *Clermont*, was painted and ready to go. Wise to the ways of his patrician backer now, he gave a test demonstration the first time out. A private demonstration followed a week later with Robert Livingston—vaguely encouraged by Jefferson's approval—in attendance.

This time, Fulton did his best to control the conditions. The affair was by invitation only, with each man "elegant in spotless ruffles and professionally arranged hair; each lady dimpled charmingly from under a correct bonnet, from over a stylish dress." With everything so carefully managed, it was as pleasant, one might say, as a ball or a tea party. But where Whitney actually performed in private, Fulton only made it *seem* as if his launch was a private event. The one thing he could not control was the uninvited crowd along Manhattan's West Side, which had gathered to watch him bomb once again.

No doubt Fulton would have preferred a wholly private performance at this point (he did not advertise the event and submitted to advance coverage in only one newspaper: the *National Intelligencer*), but a steamboat equipped with immense paddlewheels was not easily hidden. Unable to will away the rabble, he fell back on his strategy from the Battery demonstration and disregarded it. Later, he spoke of the hecklers as a distant force to be suffered as one suffers beggars: "I number a few sarcastic remarks," he wrote. "This is the way ignorant men compliment what they call philosophers and projectors." The Livingston clan behaved similarly, bravely boarding the boat as if no one was looking.

And so a curious situation developed. By the time the *North River* was a speck on the North River, everyone involved was a reluctant witness to Fulton's success—the public because it wanted to see him fail, and the patricians because they would have preferred to stay at home. On August 17, 1807, fifty-five years after Franklin's apocryphal act, America had unwittingly backed into its first successful public performance of an invention.

Empowered at last, Fulton went on to develop more steamboats, including a terrifying cannon-proof warship called, aristocratically enough, *Fulton the First*. Meanwhile, a certain contradiction may have dawned on Jefferson as he sat in the President's House. He had harangued Evans about the derivative nature of his mechanical miller, yet he let Fulton's steamboat pass, even though it was essentially the same invention introduced by Fitch twenty years earlier. (What's more, Fulton's boat was slower than Fitch's.) Then again, Evans was a publicist who could not draw and Fulton a renowned painter who disdained the vulgarities of advertising (or so it seemed from Jefferson's vantage point), so what, really, could be done?

Given the yawning chasm between the fates of Evans and Fitch on the one hand and Whitney and Fulton on the other, the lessons of the early Republic are clear. There was no gain in strenuously demonstrating the worth of an invention through commercial appeals to the public when the authorities could be cultivated to much greater effect with assurances of high-minded purposes. Yet even when the fears of the existing powers were assuaged, the overall pattern remained flawed. Only a few inventors stood any chance of satisfying Jefferson's stringent demands, and when those inventors offered bogus or borrowed ideas, the system became weaker again.

Indeed, in looking back at the Jeffersonian era, it appears like a bubble, separated from the rest of history. This perception is reinforced by the lack of inventions that have survived that time. The cotton gin, the musket, the many varieties of making potash—these devices seem vexingly remote. Then again, what about . . . the car?

Some historians have defended Whitney's 1801 demonstration, on the grounds that he recognized the importance of interchangeable parts at such an early date. He was, it is said, ahead of his time. Applying this argument strictly, though, Oliver Evans deserved equal, perhaps even greater, accolades. He did invent a self-propelling vehicle, after all, and unlike Whitney's interchangeable system, his invention had the advantage of actually working. Evans's decision to introduce his inventions to "the public notice" was also prescient—by the end of the Civil War, it would be the norm. In fact, all Evans really lacked in becoming the "Artist of his Country" was the blessing of Thomas Jefferson.

This was no small thing. Because the government rewarded inventors who mitigated the troubling aspects of the public demonstration and punished those who did not, the diversity of invention was limited so severely as to change the course of history. In a country that championed the kind of inventor who felt free to pass his hat among the crowd, Americans could well have been tooling around in Evansmobiles by the 1820s.

The constrictive trend established by Jefferson reached its endgame in 1802, when he appointed Dr. William Thornton to the newly established position of patent commissioner. If Jefferson had been overwrought about the perils of profiteering, at least he cared. Thornton, on the other hand, behaved like the consummate patrician, privately amusing himself with his own projects, oblivious to the needs of the nation altogether. Thornton's private family was a family of one.

Circumstances, it must be said, gave Thornton all the berth he wanted. The Patent Act of 1793 dispensed with the need for an invention to be "sufficiently useful or important," making the job of patenting essentially a clerical one. The need for an examination—the private audition that Whitney used to cultivate Jefferson even as he demonstrated his cotton gin—was also struck from the requirements. In 1802, Congress went whole hog, eliminating the three-man board and retaining only a single patent chief, or commissioner.

Arriving a few months later, Thornton interpreted his territory as a fiefdom and ruled it as such until his death in 1828. He was a doctor by title but preferred to follow the professions of author, painter, architect, political economist, and inventor—any profession, in fact, except medicine. He kept records or not as he saw fit, made arbitrary decisions about fees, and casually granted himself patents, managing a tally of eight, most for improvements in winemaking and stills.

Thornton was generally in high spirits, but given the opportunity, he could be downright destructive. No sooner were the wheels of Fulton's *North River* wet than Thornton wrote to the inventor looking for a percentage, suggesting that Fulton "take one third, Mssrs Livingston, Clarke . . . one third, and that I retain the remaining third." When that didn't work, he pressed deeper into calumny. On January 16, 1809, returning from a stay in the country where he had retired for a few days to escape his creditors, he began filing a few patents on the steamboat's components in his own name. When he later claimed not to have noticed Fulton's patent until the following day, it was gently pointed out to him that the application had been on his desk for more than two weeks.

Thornton managed to be selfish even when committing acts of heroism. By the time the War of 1812 broke out, he had moved the Patent Office into a temporary location called Blodgett's Hotel (which, with history's knack for ironies, had actually served as a theater once). For some reason, he had also taken many of the Patent Office records to his farmhouse, which is where he happened to be, eating breakfast, when news of British troop movements reached him. He hastened down to the corner of Eighth and E streets in northwest Washington, where a certain Major Waters was readying to set the building ablaze.

"I was desirous not only of saving [a musical] instrument that had cost me great labor," Thornton wrote with remarkable pomposity, "but of preserving, if possible, the building and all the models."

Through an extraordinary brand of persuasion, Thornton was able to convince the major—whose orders were to destroy only public property—that burning "the public building containing models of the arts" would involve destroying private property as well, and, furthermore, that it would be tantamount to burning the library of Alexandria. The major, perhaps unaware that the library in Alexandria *had* been burned, ordered that the Patent Office be spared. It was the only public building in Washington to earn this distinction, and while the city was being rebuilt, Congress had to hold its session there.

Thornton may have earned a few favors as landlord to the statesmen, but the damage he did to a fledgling nation as its patent commissioner is incalculable. After Jefferson left office, Thornton was the center of the government's invention universe, and ostensibly, inventors could have sought his imprimatur by involving him in some kind of private show. But being ignored, overcharged, and possibly even robbed for their efforts could hardly have been an appealing prospect.

Where, then, was an inventor to go? There were as yet no public schools in America, very few private ones, and the government was simply not listening. If discreet, gentlemanly showings were no longer feasible, what was left? Could the public mechanical spectacle perhaps be elevated to a more respectable form?

At the time, there were reasons to believe that the answer was yes. But it was not a patriot who supplied those reasons. It was Benjamin Thompson, alias Count Rumford, traitor to his country.

## Chapter Three

# CROSS CURRENTS

In June 1798, as Eli Whitney was dotting the i's on his arms deal, Count Rumford sat down in London, dusted off the infamy that seemed to trail him wherever he went, and began to compose a letter to Thomas Bernard, a British philanthropist. What he proposed was nothing less than a permanent theater for exhibiting the major inventions of the age. Ultimately, his efforts paid off: his public forum allowed mechanical mayhem to be easily absorbed into society. But the country he chose for his theater was not America.

"A well arranged House of Industry is much wanted in London," Rumford wrote. "There must be something *to see* and *to touch* . . . otherwise people in general will have but very faint, imperfect and transitory ideas of those important and highly interesting objects with which you must make them acquainted." (Rumford's italics.)

Rarely have the forces of ambition and open-mindedness formed such an odd constellation as they did in Count Rumford. Born Benjamin Thompson on March 26, 1753, in what is now Concord, New Hampshire, he became an informer for the British in the early days of the Revolutionary War, writing letters in invisible ink to General Thomas Gage on the movements of the colonial troops around Concord, Massachusetts. When his neighbors got wind of his activities, he fled to England, where he rose to the rank of colonel and was actually permitted to command a legion of dragoons on Long Island in the last days of the Revolution. After the war, England had no more pressing military matters to engage him, so in 1784 he left for the Continent and ingratiated himself with the Elector (or prince) of Bavaria, Karl Theodor. Soon he had mastered both German and French, and worked his way up the social ladder to become the Elector's second in command. For this relentless politicking, he was awarded his noble title.

The change of identity seemed to mark a change in heart. Having exhausted his talent for deft maneuvering, Rumford returned to England in 1791 and made his first real contribution as an inventor by devising a fireplace based on the little-understood principle of radiant heat. Londoners soon grew accustomed to the sight of an inordinately tall man with a large proboscis and a sly grin, calling on local residences to maintain his own handiwork. If Benjamin Thompson coveted power, Count Rumford wanted to be remembered for his largesse.

Yet even at his best, Rumford found it difficult to shed his ego entirely. He justified many of his inventions during this period—chimneys, stoves, boilers—as boons to the poor, but he was just as quick to reward his own philanthropy. After establishing a prize for achievements in physics—the Rumford Medal—he took the first one home himself. And though he imagined his "House of Industry," which came to be known as the Royal Institution, as a showcase for poor audiences, he also tried to crowd all of the available exhibit space with his own inventions. Count Rumford was an apparently gifted giver.

The Royal Institution, as the first major public forum for the practical sciences, certainly boded well for the greater airing of inventions. That it came to be at all was due in large measure to Rumford's decision to leave America—and its wary regard of publicity—far behind. Nevertheless, it was not universally applauded by the inventors of Great Britain. Not least among the dissenters was James Watt, of steam-engine fame. Watt's patent claims were exceptionally broad, covering not only steam power but also such arcane details as the use of "oils, wax, resinous bodies, fat of animals" for keeping his machines airtight. These patents were due to run out in 1800, and by this time many inventors were anxious to make a steam engine—any kind of steam engine—if only they could be free of infringement worries. Wanting more than anything to keep his secrets to himself, Watt wrote a thorough paper on the subject—"Thoughts upon Patents, or Exclusive Privileges for new Inventions"—and letters to influential Londoners, urging them not to waste their money on the Royal Institution.

Rumford forged ahead anyway. His House of Industry, a long, impressive building on Albemarle Street with Corinthian columns abutting the sidewalk, opened its doors on March 11, 1800. The main lecture room, known as the Great Theater, seated 1,000 (today, fire codes have reduced the capacity to 400), with a steep rise in the house, such that charts and apparatuses were clearly visible to those in the back. Rumford himself built a dome into the ceiling for admitting greater or lesser light, depending on the lecturer's needs. Michael Faraday, the British scientist, later deemed the Great Theater the best lecture hall he ever saw.

Unfortunately, the same could not be said for Rumford's administrative skills. His dream of halls filled with models from every country in the world would have been difficult to achieve even if he had enjoyed the backing of all the crowns of Europe, which he did not. His despotic temperament also made him less than popular with his peers. As money got tight and things continued to go not entirely his way, he grew restless. In fact, his tenure at the Royal Institution lasted only until sometime in 1801, when he returned to Bavaria with the promise to start a similar organization there.

No Bavarian organization ever appeared. Sidetracked once again, Rumford instead married the widow of the French chemist Antoine Lavoisier, argued with her vehemently, and passed into relative obscurity on the Continent. In a final flurry of productivity, he invented an early version of the drip coffeepot and a method of steam heating. In 1811, three years before his death, he wrote to Robert Livingston from his home in Auteuil, France, recommending that steamboat technology be immediately applied to the development of a horseless carriage. "I have not the least doubt of the practicability of the scheme," he ventured, "and do much expect to live long enough to see it executed."

Clearly, Count Rumford was among the more far-seeing and talented inventors of his day. Nevertheless, his place in history owes less to his own innovations than to his efforts to bring the public in contact with the latest inventions. And even these efforts—indeed, the Royal Institution itself—might never have taken root except for the foresight he showed, just before leaving England, in appointing a young chemist named Humphry Davy to the position of lecturer.


Humphry Davy could easily have ended up in Drury Lane rather than Albemarle Street. As a boy in Penzance, he wandered the Cornish moors, composing ecstatic poetry in his head, then went home to read the works of chemist Antoine Lavoisier. In 1799, after working as an apprentice to an apothecary, he was hired by Thomas Beddoes to work in the Pneumatic Institute, an experimental institution in Clifton founded on the premise that certain gasses had therapeutic value. There, patients wandered the grounds after taking the "airs," and famous poets such as Samuel Taylor Coleridge and Robert Southey dropped in from time to time. Davy flourished in such an environment. In fact, when he isolated nitrous oxide, or laughing gas, he learned that his interests in science and art might not be so separate after all.

In the course of his experiments with nitrous oxide, Davy enlisted the help of James Watt, a family friend, to build a breathing chamber. The resulting machine resembled a misguided accordion, with a bellows and a gas holder formed of two cylinders, one sliding within the double walls of the other. Watt eventually built a more elaborate apparatus: a sealed breathing chamber, something like a sedan chair, inside which the patient was meant to sit and respire great quantities of nitrous oxide. (Watt also proposed a "beehive," perhaps never developed, to be made with oiled silk rolled in charcoal. When fitted around the head, he explained, this beehive would facilitate the breathing of exceptionally weak patients.)

When Davy finally sat in the chamber—despite Watt's caution about the strength of the gas—he emerged as one imbued with cosmic knowledge, exclaiming "Nothing exists but thoughts. The universe is composed of impressions, ideas, pleasure and pain."

Exalted, Davy pressed on, testing nitrous oxide on a host of other maladies, including syphilis and the "hysterical and nervous affections," even as he used it to further his own spiritual life. With Coleridge on one side and Watt on the other, it was a happy arrangement. At times, he breathed six quarts of nitrous oxide in a sitting. Another habit was to drink a bottle of wine in less than eight minutes, then switch to the gas. For a while, encouraged by the spirits, he contemplated writing an epic poem about Moses. It never materialized. He did, however, write an ode to nitrous oxide:

> Not in the ideal dreams of wild desire
> Have I beheld a rapture-awakening form:
> My bosom burns with no unhallowe'd fire,
> Yet is my cheek with rosy blushes warm;
> Yet are my eyes with sparkling lustre fill'd;

> Yet is my mouth replete with murmuring sound;
> Yet are my limbs with inward transports fill'd
> And clad with new-born mightiness around.

And so it was in a state of rapture that Davy stepped up to the podium of the Royal Institution's Great Theater in 1802 to deliver his introductory lecture. A slight but handsome man with a soft West Country accent, he transfixed his audience with his powers of poetic oratory. "[W]e do not look to distant ages," he declared, "or amuse ourselves with brilliant though delusive dreams concerning the infinite improveability of man, the annihilation of labour, disease and even death . . . we look to a bright day, of which we already behold the dawn."

Davy immediately became the darling of London's fashionable set. "The sensation created by his course of lectures," wrote one witness, "is at this period scarcely to be imagined . . . His youth, his simplicity, his natural eloquence, his chemical knowledge, his happy illustrations, and well-conducted experiments excited universal attention and unbounded applause." Women especially crowded in to see him, sighing that "those eyes were made for something more than poring over crucibles." On nights when he lectured, the traffic in front of the institution was so dense that Albemarle Street was made one-way, the first such street in the nation.

If Davy was part holy man and part sex symbol, he was also an able comedian. His nitrous oxide demonstrations, far from evoking the sublime, tended toward the ridiculous. Volunteer after volunteer grew stupefied with the amazing new air and began to spew forth nonsense. When the ladies held up their hands to declare themselves satisfied, the house thundered with applause.

The babbling of these volunteers was not so very different from a time-worn device of the commedia dell'arte troupes. Denied the right to use dialogue at fairground booths in the seventeenth century, the old masked players had devised a makeshift solution called *grummelot*—a succession of meaningless sounds that had no basis in language, yet managed to convey the sense of something being said, as if a chimpanzee were trying to speak.

Indeed, Davy's laughing gas lectures seemed to call commedia dell'arte back from the grave. In an etching by James Gillray published in 1802, a volunteer is shown blowing the gas out his backside as Davy administers the airs and a grinning Count Rumford looks on. The scene vividly recalled the Lazzo of the Enema, a widely performed gag that,

James Gillray's 1802 lithograph, *Scientific Researches!—New Discoveries of Pneu-maticks!—or—an Experimental Lecture on the Powers of Air.* Humphry Davy readies the bellows while Count Rumford (*at right*) looks on. *The British Museum*

however much it varied, centered upon the posterior of an unwitting victim. A world-class show inventor had arrived (in England at least), and with him came the intoxications of disorder—a bright day filled with comic possibility.

Davy's notebooks reveal just how disorderly he could be. Writing in carriages or in the midst of conversation, he would erase a line with a wet finger and then leave his inky fingerprints all over the page. He might enter his notes upside down, from the back to the front of the notebook, or directly over previous passages. The idea of dating his entries rarely occurred to him.

His imagination was no different: it would move laterally toward a goal he scarcely knew himself, then career the next week in another direction altogether. At one point, he introduced the "baking soda" experiment (reenacted by school children today when they ignite sodium bicarbonate inside a papier-mâché volcano) with the observation that "the globules flew with great velocity through the air in a state of vivid combustion, producing a beautiful effect of continued jets of fire." At another, he became interested in the "animal magnetism" of eels. He built an immense state-of-the-art battery, 128,000 square inches in area, and created continuous discharges of brilliant light in different shapes and colors. He invented a miner's safety lamp that earned him the gratitude of the nation's colliers. He sketched out the rudiments for the desalinization of water. Over the course of his career, he isolated potassium, magnesium, calcium, sodium, strontium, barium, chlorine, and iodine. Somehow, he also found time in this busy schedule to offer the first systematic geology course in England.

Part and parcel of this chaotic career was Davy's constant presence on stage. His Bakerian Lectures, delivered in the first decade of the nineteenth century, were so spectacular that they received an award from Napoleon, even though France and England were at war at the time. And at least once, he dabbled in theater proper. In January 1805, John Tobin's new play, *The Honey Moon*, had no prologue on opening night. A friend of Tobin's alerted Davy to the problem, and he scribbled a prologue on the spot. Performed by one Mr. Bartley in Drury Lane, it reveals the work of a show inventor in his prime:

> Hence Genius draws his novel copious store:
> And hence the new creations we adore:
> And hence the scenic art's undying skill
> Submits our feeling to its potent will;
> From common accidents and common themes
> Awakens rapture and poetic dreams;
> And, in the trodden path of life, pursues
> Some object cloth'd in Fancy's loveliest hues—
> To strengthen nature, or to chasten art,
> To mend the manners or exalt the heart.

Davy's immense renown drew many admirers into his orbit, one of whom was a pauper who worked in a bookbindery. A beneficent, thoughtful young man with lamb-chop sideburns, Michael Faraday came to represent the antithesis of his mentor in many ways. Where Davy basked in the glow of celebrity, Faraday abjured all social life for his work. Where Davy entered into bitter priority disputes, Faraday refused to patent his inventions. And when the time came, Faraday declined to follow Davy into knighthood.

Faraday did gain from Davy's performance methods, however. Studying at the flamboyant master's footstool, he consciously observed what might be called the mechanics of lecturing, then filtered them through his own, more cautious, sensibility. Eventually, this produced a demonstration style that was the very model of clarity.

"Every part illustrative of the lecture should be in view," Faraday wrote in a letter to Benjamin Abbott in 1813, the year he joined the Royal Institution, "no one thing should hide another from the audience nor should anything stand in the way of or obstruct the lecturer." Nor, by Faraday's lights, was the scientific performer to employ any sort of misdirection: "A lecturer falls deeply beneath the dignity of his character when he descends so low as to angle for claps, and asks for commendation." As Faraday came to employ such methods in his own lectures—including his Friday Evening Discourses, which were open to the public and scientists alike—he established the protocols for scientific presentation that remain in effect today.

This was a far cry from the egotistical maneuverings of Count Rumford. Even so, some of Faraday's performances were fairly spectacular. Lord Kelvin (William Thompson) once remembered the man in the midst of one his more arresting exhibits:

> We all know how Faraday made himself a cage six feet in diameter, hung it up in mid-air in the theatre of the Royal Institution, went into it, and as he said, lived in it and made experiments. It was a cage with tin-foil hanging all around it; it was not a complete metallic enclosing shell. Faraday had a powerful machine working in the neighborhood, giving all varieties of gradual working-up and discharges by "impulsive rush" . . .

Poverty, purity, a man in a cage—if Faraday's work suggested that an inventor might live the life of an electric hunger artist, it also represented one of the more successful transitions from disorder to order. Straitlaced as he was, Faraday had learned from Davy (who had learned from Rumford before him) that science was meant to be *shown*. And in the end, his commitment to clear, exacting performances bore ample fruit.

Moving from laboratory to lecture and back again on a regular basis, Faraday learned to apply his stage directions to his experiments—in a sense, his experiments functioned as rehearsals for the show. As a result, he tended to formulate problems in concrete, spatial terms that could be easily explained to his audience. When he came to the prospect of converting magnetism into electricity, for example, he did not reach for mathematical equations. Instead, he wrestled with physical configurations. Should he coil the wire more tightly around the magnet? Should the magnet be made in a different shape? Finally, in 1831, it occurred to him to move an iron rod back and forth *inside* the magnet. When the coils generated a current, the electric generator was born, and with it the Electric Age.

Faraday continued on as a public lecturer at the Royal Institution for the rest of his life, inspiring the careers of many British scientists, including Charles Wheatstone, James Clerk Maxwell, and Lord Kelvin. These figures, some of the most influential thinkers of their time, all had access to the public. Not all of them handled the stage well. Once when Wheatstone was scheduled to give a lecture at the Royal Institution, he got stage fright at the last minute and beat a hasty retreat, leaving Faraday to extemporize on his early ideas on the electromagnetic theory of light. But the opportunity to reach an audience was there nonetheless.

The English were able make the transition from Rumford to Faraday because they had been able to accept mechanical spectacles, even bawdy ones, as redeeming public events. Their cousins across the ocean were not so blessed, though they had had every chance to be. In fact, America produced its own Count Rumford, its own Humphry Davy, and its own Michael Faraday—who invented his own electric generator only weeks before his double. But because Americans had yet to blend theater and science into an effective whole, their version of the story took on a different cast.

A portly man who combed his black hair straight back, Amos Eaton was very much a man after Count Rumford's heart. Like the irrepressible count, he had a keen sense of his own self-interest even as he devoted himself to the public weal. And like Rumford, he had a habit of running afoul of the law.

In 1809, after a brief stint in law school, Eaton was indicted for forgery in connection with land deeds in Catskill, New York. The charge didn't stick, leaving him free to teach mathematics and botany on an informal basis, but trouble continued to come his way. Saddled with a second forgery count in 1811, he went bankrupt, lost his land, and was sent off to Newgate Prison in Greenwich Village. (He passed the time writing a 342-page tract on mineralogy while the War of 1812 raged outside the prison walls.) After his release in 1815, he went to Yale and studied under the American scientist and educator, Benjamin Silliman.

But life in prison had coarsened him, so after some unspecified confrontations, he packed his bags and fashioned himself as an itinerant teacher.

Eaton took to his new role like a religious evangelist, hoping to make converts to the spirit of scientific curiosity. For all his certitude, he quickly learned that a wandering teacher was essentially a performer, and thus in need of respectable credentials. "My principal patrons are ministers, doctors and lawyers," he wrote to John Torrey in 1818. "I always go recommended from one clergyman to another; and never set out for a place until I am invited by at least one minister, one doctor and one lawyer."

It was during this time that Eaton developed his explanation-demonstration technique. Taking a conversational tone, he would show in great detail how an apparatus worked, then invite audience members to handle it for themselves. The populist tenor of these demonstrations can be surmised from Eaton's own description to Torrey:

> I give most of the experiments . . . with about 50 dollars value of apparatus. A pewter sucking bottle is my fluoric gas bottle—a stone jug and a tin tube, my earthen retort—a teakettle with the cover luted on, is my iron retort etc. etc. . . . I have had in all my classes more than three hundred pupils. You will wonder why my lectures are so popular. I will tell you. I am perfectly acquainted with this sort of people. "I become all things to all men." Silliman, McNeven, Griscom or Davy would do nothing here. I turn everything in science into common talk. I illustrate the most abstruse parts by a dish-kettle, a warming-pan, a bread-tray, a tea-pot, a soap bowl or a cheese press.

The explanation-demonstration technique set an important precedent for the show inventors who came later. By making the public exhibition of scientific devices more than a passing sight in the American landscape, Eaton made it possible for the first time to imagine the inventor's show as an ongoing tradition.

Eaton also managed the trick—not a small one—of breaking the gender barrier. In Northampton, Massachusetts, his demonstrations drew crowds of up to sixty-five people, most of whom were women. When the crowds increased, they did so disproportionately in favor of the fairer sex. Did these women think of themselves as potential mechanics? As fascinated witnesses of a masculine display of power? It is hard to know, but their presence, along with Eaton's tendency to bend his English to the vernacular, suggests a certain amount of liveliness in what might otherwise have been fairly staid affairs.

Eventually tiring of what he called the "Tartar life," Eaton settled in Troy, New York, in the early 1820s. There, he met the patroon General Stephen Van Rensselaer and joined in establishing what today is called the Rensselaer Polytechnic Institute. When the fates again threatened to imprison him—this time handing him the charge of embezzlement—his new associations, which by now included New York State Governor De Witt Clinton, saw to it that he received an unconditional pardon before the facts were sorted out.

The Rensselaer School opened on a trial basis in 1825, according to the guiding principles set down by Eaton. "[S]tudents shall be exercised," he announced, "in the elementary principles of the sciences of chemistry, experimental philosophy, natural history, land surveying &c., with their daily application to agriculture, manufactures and the arts." Again, he promoted the welfare of women, proposing that classes be made up of mixed company.

By the middle of the decade, Amos Eaton, ex-convict and wandering zealot, found himself in relatively satisfactory straits. He had authority. He collected a steady income. He was often seen sitting with friends under an old Dutch gambrel roof, holding forth on the beauties of chemistry and geology. The sanctuary of the Rensselaer School had brought him what he most desperately needed: a measure of respectability.

Meanwhile, mechanics across America were beginning to realize that their fate was their own, and Eaton began to have company. An educational forum called the lyceum had already appeared in England, with Scotsman George Birkbeck as its prime mover. In 1810, the American lyceum movement was still a mere seedling. (Eaton himself joined the Lyceum of Natural History of New York in 1818, and the Troy Lyceum after that.) By 1826, it was large enough to warrant a manifesto, and a man named Josiah Holbrook duly provided one.

The express purpose of the American lyceum, according to Holbrook, was to "apply the sciences and the various branches of education to the domestic and useful arts, and to all the common purposes of life." Holbrook insisted that each branch have a president, a vice president, a treasurer, a correspondent, secretaries, five curators, and three delegates. Lyceums were also to be democratic: meetings could be held as often as members saw fit, and membership was open to anyone who paid the yearly fee of a dollar.

The young mechanic who joined one of these organizations had much to contemplate. Meetings could touch on most any subject, from pneumatics and mineralogy to political economy and history. Whatever the focus, practical demonstration was always on the roster. No lyceum could consider itself complete without an "apparatus for illustrating the sciences, a cabinet of minerals, and other articles of natural or artificial production."

Mechanics institutes evolved independently of the lyceums, but the difference between them was slight. The most abiding of these in America was the Franklin Institute, organized in Philadelphia in 1824. Dedicated to promoting and encouraging "the manufacture of mechanical and useful arts," it also offered lessons in mechanical drawing and a library for technical literature. In its first year, the Franklin Institute also put on a mechanical exhibition, which soon developed into an annual event—an odd tradition for an institution that bore the name of a man who had assiduously avoided exhibitionism, but there it was.

By the mid-1820s, then, the exhibiting of machines was no longer an uncommon sight. The question now was how to keep the proceedings above reproach, and the pioneers of these societies took such matters well into consideration. In laying out his manifesto, Holbrook in particular made a pitch for the lyceum as moral sanctuary:

> It may be questioned if there is any other way to check the progress of that monster, intemperance, which is making such havoc with talents, morals, and every thing that raises man above the brute, but by presenting some object of sufficient interest to divert the attention of the young from places and practices which lead to dissipation and ruin.

A scientific forum, as far as Holbrook was concerned, was just the thing to keep young boys from a life of dissolution. In practice, this approach was a bit self-defeating, because it meant that the lyceum movement appealed most strongly to those who were least likely to plunge into the more adventurous territories that machinery offered. Lyceums in New England soon became vehicles for the likes of Henry David Thoreau, who joined the Concord Lyceum and waxed eloquent on the virtues of the self-sufficient pastoral life, much as Jefferson had earlier.

When the Franklin Institute aspired to noble status, it also found itself at cross-purposes. A sizable faction of its members espoused the need for classes in Latin and Greek, but such things meant little to the mechanics in attendance. By 1829, Alexander Dallas Bache, grandson of Benjamin Franklin, had received a certificate from Eaton's Rensselaer School and was primed to arrive at the Franklin Institute as its guiding light. Bache managed to bring the high and low factions together, at least for the moment.

A final thread in the fabric was pulled through by Jacob Bigelow, who wasn't terribly concerned with the demonstration of devices but nevertheless gave them a name befitting their newly elevated status.

"To embody, as far as possible," he wrote in the *American Journal of Education* in July 1829, "the various topics which belong to such an undertaking, I have adopted the general name of Technology, a word sufficiently expressive, which is found in some of the older dictionaries, and is beginning to be revived in the literature of practical men at the present day."

And so a new word passed into the English lexicon: *technology*, from the Greek *tekhne*, meaning "skill." The lyceums and mechanics institutes were having their problems, but America was closer to having a public forum for inventions than ever before. All that was needed, really, were the thrills that a theatrical treatment might provide.

Such thrills were there to be had. In the 1820s, as lyceums from Maine to Pennsylvania were filling up with new members, American theaters were beginning to boast gala appearances by the latest British luminaries. Actor Edmund Kean stepped onto American shores in 1820 and commanded sums of fifty pounds plus a percentage of the take. Junius Brutus Booth arrived in 1821 as Richard III and started an illustrious dynasty, including a descendant who would murder Abraham Lincoln. Charles Mathews put a lighter spin on things by emigrating from England with a one-man show that featured his abilities as a ventriloquist. Fanny Kemble introduced audiences to her astonishing range of voices and fanned the flames of controversy by using her maiden name even after she was married.

But for all the grandeur of the British thespians, respectable Americans still held theater in wary regard. For one thing, the audiences tended to be coarse. Frances Trollope—mother of the author Anthony Trollope—moved to Cincinnati in the 1920s and was astonished to discover the state of theatrical culture there. Audience members nonchalantly rested their boots on the edge of the proscenium or spat straight onto the floor. "Gentlemen will be particular in not disturbing the audience by loud talking in the Bar-Room," read one list of injunctions, "nor by personal altercations in any part of the house." Naturally, an honest Yankee woman wouldn't even think of going to a play, much less gossip over the alternate purposes of a performer's eyes, as the ladies of London did.

Other signs suggested that Americans were, at best, ambivalent about the dramatic arts. Trollope herself tried her hand at a tasteful play and was quickly disabused of the project when her debut performance produced only a handful of spectators. Paradoxically, on another occasion, she watched even the tobacco spitters leave in disgust when the actresses made their entrance in risqué attire.

America's unresolved attitudes were perhaps best encapsulated by the reaction to *The Infernal Regions*. This prototypical haunted house took shape when Trollope encouraged a local friend, Hiram Powers, to recreate Dante's celebrated *Inferno* in mechanical form. Powers was something of an inventor (he had devised a mechanism for cutting clock wheels and a new kind of organ reed) and welcomed the idea as an opportunity to test his mettle. By the time he was through, *The Infernal Regions* included the "grand colossal figure of Minos, the Judge of Hell," skeletons, artificial flames, a frozen lake, a creature gnawing off the heads of its enemies, and myriad other animals twisted into grotesque forms—all made more disturbing by the "unearthly sounds, horrid groans and terrible shrieks" that seemed to come from everywhere. High above, lavish illustrations of Purgatory and Heaven mocked the fates of the visitors.

*The Infernal Regions* was, in a sense, too popular. A Bostonian who had occasion to witness this sobering scene reported that some of those groans were actually emitted by ministers who, having entered Hades, seemed unable to leave. "While the timid and ignorant were viewing this work of man's device," the tourist deadpanned, these marooned men of the cloth "would exhort them to flee to the ark of safety!"

By the third decade of the nineteenth century, Jeffersonian notions of privacy were on the way out, but American public life still suffered from a kind of moral confusion. Ladies eschewed high theater, yet marveled at Eaton's vernacular delivery. Mechanics remained disgruntled, while ministers protested too much. If anything, the sense of uncertainty was simply becoming more robust. Not surprisingly, when America's

Faraday appeared on the scene, this uncertainty worked its way into his psyche and left a lasting imprint.

Joseph Henry was uniquely situated to bring science and drama together into a single American idiom. Had he managed to do so, the effect on the culture might have been great. It is conceivable that some of his findings, if widely publicized, could have hastened radio into existence several decades early. But there was something terminally indecisive about this man from Albany, New York. Legend has it that when he was a boy, a local cobbler asked him whether he wanted round-toed or square-toed shoes. Unable to make up his mind, he procrastinated endlessly. Finally, the exasperated craftsman gave him a pair that split the difference—one toe was round, the other square. And so Henry proceeded through life, one step this way, one step that.

Yet for all his indecisiveness, Henry was also capable of exceptional enthusiasms. Anyone who knew him as a teenager, for example, would have confidently predicted a career in the theater for him. After he saw his first play, he went home and acted out all of the parts for his friends. Soon, his interest in the stage ran roughshod over everything else, no matter how much his Calvinist parents protested. Albany had a good company under the direction of the English comedian John Bernard, and Henry began to frequent it. Before long, he joined—perhaps even started—the Rostrum theatrical company, which met at the Thespian Hotel, on the corner of North Pearl and Patroon streets. There, he created stage effects, produced plays, acted in them, and became president of the society—all before he had turned sixteen.

In his later years, Henry generally played down his acting stint, but he did let slip once that he had written a play called *The Fisherman of Bagdad*, which he put on with the help of his friends. Though no copy exists today, Henry's young age and the materials at his disposal suggest that the play was an adaptation of "The Story of the Fisherman," from *The Thousand and One Nights*. This tale turns on a fisherman who finds a magic lamp. When he opens it, a genie appears and threatens to kill him. He soon tricks the genie back into the lamp, but the genie convinces him to uncork the lamp again. Even Henry's characters found it hard to make decisions!

There is no doubt that Henry was born to the stage. "His young Norval, Damon and even Hamlet," recalled childhood friend Thurlow Weed, "were pronounced equal in conception and execution to the personations of experienced and popular actors. His friends, charmed with his talents and genius, urged him to adopt the stage as a profession."

But already a second profession was calling. While conquering the local drama scene, Henry had enrolled in a private school and quickly established himself as an exceptional student. His talents soon came to the attention of one Romeyn Beck, a chemistry teacher at the Albany Academy. Beck was a charismatic lecturer, much like Humphry Davy, except for his lack of renown—and his attitudes about theater.

As Weed remembered, Beck "believed that there was a way opened to the young man promising usefulness and more enduring honors than the drama could offer. After consulting with the trustees, Dr. Beck invited young Henry to enter upon and complete a gratuitous academic course." Henry called upon his friends to help him decide, and "after a long and anxious mental struggle" one of them convinced him to take up Beck's offer.

So Henry quit the stage and began working as an assistant to Beck. In 1826, Beck had occasion to introduce his protégé to Amos Eaton, cautioning that this man, "though a pretty good fellow, is given to too much puffing." Puff or not, Eaton was a good enough fellow to give Henry a post in mathematics at the Rensselaer School. From that point on, he would stand or fall as a scientist.

As Henry told it, the change was more radical. At the age of sixteen, he recalled, he was confined to his bed with an illness and had occasion to read a book on natural philosophy, *Lectures on Experimental Philosophy, Astronomy and Chemistry* by George Gregory, an English clergyman. What he read there prompted him to renounce theater abruptly and completely. In fact, he described the moment as a *conversion experience.* "It . . . caused me to resolve at the time of reading it," he wrote, "that I would immediately commence to devote my life to the acquisition of knowledge." Given the choice, Henry decided that he did not want to go to hell.

There are reasons to believe that Henry's conversion, however permanent, did not come about overnight. By 1828, he was a professor of mathematics at the Albany Academy, with a stern countenance that gave him the appearance of a great abstainer. At the same time, he still relished the chance to show off his stage effects. On one occasion, he produced snow in a room that measured a temperature of 80 degrees. On another, he inserted an electric wire into a wall, shocking unsuspecting victims on the other side.

If Henry changed his mind in a flash, his heart was slow to follow. Yet unlike young Michael Faraday, who entered a vibrant public forum replete with gas gags and electric fireworks, he was certainly asked to *choose*—between the purity of the classroom and the glamor of the footlights. The effect was ultimately damaging. Unable to purge his dramatic flair completely, he was compelled to vent it in fits and starts.

Henry's embarrassing string of wrong moves began in 1828, when the British scientist William Sturgeon brought a powerful electromagnet to New York, and Henry took a trip down to see it. Impressed with what he saw, he cleared away all other responsibilities to make time for serious scientific experimentation. By October, he had constructed a magnet that was stronger and simpler than Sturgeon's colossus. This, like Faraday, he could credit to his belief in giving demonstrations. He had been trained to strive for simplicity, he said, because his models had to be easily understood.

Still, he wasn't satisfied. He began experimenting with larger coils and demonstrating them before larger audiences. In the end, he devised a spectacular magnet: wrapped with 60 feet of silk-covered wire coiled to 20 inches in diameter, it could lift 3,000 pounds. Nothing of the sort had ever been seen.

Or almost nothing. When Gerard Moll of Utrecht announced a similar magnet in 1831, Henry rushed to publish his own results, making sure to include his progress on an experiment involving "the greatest magnetic force with the smallest quantity of galvanism." That inclusion would come back to haunt him. At the moment, though, Henry hardly had time to think before moving on to the next discovery.

Years later, a student remembered one demonstration from that time:

> When classes resumed, Henry had reeled up his long wire and had carried it up to the third floor classroom. Here he strung the wire around the walls and even added to its length, for it is described as having reached a length of almost a mile. At one end the wire was connected to the plates in the Cruikshank trough [a primitive battery], and the other was connected to the magnet. Close to one pole of the magnet he placed a permanent magnet on a pivot so that it was free to swing. When the circuit was closed and the electromagnet was energized it instantly repulsed the permanent magnet and caused one end to swing sharply against a small office bell.

The import of this event was not lost upon Henry's students. Here was the first electromagnetic telegraph. All that was missing was a code to course through the wire.

This time, instead of hurrying, Henry *delayed* publication. The postponement in itself was a misstep, but it was not the worst of it. Sometime in August 1831, he discovered that he could convert magnetism into electricity by introducing motion into a coiled magnet. It was as amazing a moment as any inventor could hope for, since it opened up the possibility of the widespread use of electricity. But again he waited.

As Henry later explained it, he postponed publishing his papers on magnetic induction (the science behind the dynamo) because he was preparing a series of demonstrations on a much larger scale. Be that as it may, there he was, still frittering his time away when news came from England that Michael Faraday had achieved the very same results. Worse, Henry's notes were patchy, while his rival had documented everything. As far as the world was concerned, Faraday was the inventor of the dynamo, and that was that.

Joseph Henry had lost the actor's most important weapon: his sense of timing. When the moment called for waiting, he published. When the moment called for unveiling, he dithered until he could present as grand a spectacle as possible. Much to his chagrin, he was living out the role of the fisherman he had once portrayed on stage: the genie came out of the bottle, the genie went back in.

There were never any hard feelings between Faraday and Henry. As far as Faraday was concerned, these things were not contests; ego did not enter into it. Henry felt much the same, and then some: as one of the few world-class American scientists, he saw himself as the keeper of the Faraday flame. His job was to civilize the student, the mechanic, and the inventor. To pander to the baser nature of man was beneath him.

The people of his native land would not be civilized, however, and became disgusted with Henry for denying them their fame. Henry in turn became depressed. Seeing him in this state, his old friend William Dunlap, a one-eyed painter, diarist, playwright and erstwhile manager of New York's Park Theater, turned to him one day and exclaimed, "Albany will one day be proud of its son!"

Albany was not proud enough to keep him. In 1832, Henry took a position at Princeton University, where in 1836 he became the first to notice oscillatory waves radiating from Leyden jars. He pursued the matter and was again able to ring a bell from a distance, this time *without any wires at all*. There were no Franklinian strategies of apocryphal demonstrations here, no encomiums flowing in from Europe. In what had become a signature failing, Henry kept maddeningly few notes, and the world learned of the first demonstration of radio through a student's description in "Lectures on Natural Philosophy by Professor Henry," given on February 28, 1844, some eight years after the fact.

Sooner or later, a man who balked so often was bound to become a target for a more decisive showman, and for Henry that showman was Samuel Morse. During the 1840s, Henry helped Morse develop his own telegraph, going so far as to reveal his ideas for a telegraphic relay. When Morse later took credit for the entire project, Henry seemed incapable of fighting back. Ironically, Morse was able to use Henry's paper on the "greatest magnetic force with the smallest quantity of galvanism" against him, arguing that it described a different sort of telegraph from his own.

Frustrated and battle-weary even in his academic safehouse, Henry left Princeton in 1846 to become the first secretary of the Smithsonian Institution—appointed by Alexander Dallas Bache of the Franklin Institute, no less. There, as the years drew on, he continued on as a leonine force, respected but remote—and, like Jefferson before him, too strict. Thirty years after his "conversion" to science, the passage from childhood thespian to a lenten authority was complete.

Englishman Thomas Henry Huxley once had occasion to quiz Henry on his requirements for the Smithsonian and learned just how narrow they were. *The Critique of Pure Reason*, he learned, was out-of-bounds, on the grounds that its ideas were unproven. In fact, Henry didn't even want the Smithsonian to take on museums. If James Smithson hoped that his institution would "contribute essentially to the increase and diffusion of knowledge," but Henry thought only of the increase and dismissed the diffusion altogether.

Henry was ribbed for this bias at times. The *Atlantic Monthly*, in its "Washington City" article of January 1861, described the Smithsonian as "a Scientific Institute which does nothing but report the rise and fall of the thermometer." But for all his antisocial behavior, he did manage to marshall a team of like-minded scientists around him. To outsiders, this group was known as the Florentine Academy, and to its members as the Lazzaroni.

An informal organization, the Lazzaroni convened once a year—usually in January—to discuss matters of scientific policy. The atmosphere was convivial. Dining upon oysters and ale, the members told jokes and addressed one another by special pet names. Bache was "the Chief." Henry was "Smithson." Louis Agassiz was dubbed "Fossilary." These posturings created such an air of exclusivity that the group was accused of acting as a cabal.

Certainly, the Lazzaroni had some sort of power. Many members held high positions at the American Association for the Advance of Science at one time or another. In 1863, they achieved their longstanding goal of founding the National Academy of Sciences. After the Civil War, they managed to infiltrate the government itself. Bache reigned over the U.S. Coast Survey. Charles H. Davis was head of the Bureau of Navigation. Henry oversaw the Smithsonian, of course, and he was also in charge of the Lighthouse Board.

Whatever their respective positions, the Lazzaroni strove to keep order within and chaos without. In 1856, the American Association wrote a new constitution allowing the exclusion of papers, in hopes of keeping science from the hands of quacks. In 1860, Benjamin Silliman, Jr., expressed his outrage that a "crazy man from New York" had been allowed to read his "foolish speculations on Atomic theory" at one of these meetings. A man named John Warner presented a similar annoyance. Warner was involved in a plagiarism case with Benjamin Peirce, and repeatedly demanded that Peirce explain himself in print. "The public," insisted Warner, "could and would form a just opinion." Peirce, however, refused to "be drawn into a filthy court for trial."

As they gained in stature, the Lazzaroni came to occupy the position of the nation's economizing force, much as Jefferson had a generation earlier. They acted as a bastion of privacy and order. They served notice that wasteful fantasies would not be tolerated. And if they couldn't claim to be the founders of a new nation, they were still pioneers of something quite remarkable: the first community of American scientists.

How this community affected the culture at large was another matter. Clearly, Henry lost the telegraph and the radio to the drifts of time. But he also lost a much greater opportunity. As the nation's preeminent scientist, he might have enlisted his peers to shore up a middle ground between the lyceum and the theater. In another world, he might even have organized his own Royal Institution. One can only imagine that such an attempt would have sped the passage into a new order, just as Faraday's status gave rise to the brilliance of Maxwell, Kelvin, and others in Great Britain. Similarly, Henry's forays into wireless technology, if highly publicized, might have accelerated research and led to the discovery of radio waves well before 1888, when Heinrich Hertz first described them.

Instead, Henry withdrew from the public sphere altogether. His reasons for doing so are understandable. Unlike Faraday, who was encouraged to fuse stage effects and physics into a clear, public form, Henry felt compelled to choose between public and private, between showing and knowing.

Yet in the end, the results were exactly the opposite of what he intended. His "cabal," for all its loftiness, lacked the power of either the church or the Patent Office to enforce its authority. It might be imposing, it might be exclusionary, but it was also inward-looking to the point of irrelevance. Even the self-absorbed Dr. Thornton had managed to entangle himself in the affairs of other inventors; the Lazzaroni simply ignored what went on outside their doors, as if it didn't exist.

And as it turned out, they had an awful lot to ignore, because at the very moment Henry chose to turn away from the public life, the rest of the country was embracing it with a vengeance.

*Chapter Four*

# THE AMAZING
# TALKING NATION

In the days leading up to Andrew Jackson's presidential inauguration, ten thousand Americans descended on Washington. Many traveled by foot through the swamps that still covered much of the capital city. They slept in fields or four to a bed, and in anticipation of seeing their hero, Old Hickory, take power, consumed the city's supply of whiskey within days. On March 4, 1829, Jackson delivered his speech at the Capitol building, and the teeming crowd followed him as he rode on horseback to the President's House, where postinauguration festivities were traditionally held. Then, to the dawning panic of the Washington elite, these hordes of filthy journeymen and crude farmers continued straight into the President's House itself. Congressmen, dressed in their finest attire, found themselves jostled and crowded out. Satin-covered chairs, costing $150 a piece, were muddied by workmen's boots. Several thousand dollars' worth of china plates and dishes were smashed. Barrels of orange punch were toppled. After Jackson seized an opportune moment to escape out the back door, liquor was served on the lawn of the President's House to lure the minions outside. All day long, the party continued alfresco.

The inauguration of Jackson was not a political revolution, but it surely was a social one—the birth of the public life in America. In the first decades of the Republic, the aristocratic traditions of Europe still lingered on, and the language of important American events and ideas was essentially literary. What the 1830s introduced into the official culture was a sound—sharp, canny, intimating lurid pleasures—the sound of the crowd. The "times that try men's souls" were becoming a "first-rate disgusting, jab savagorous fix."

The effects of the Jacksonian era would be felt across the technological spectrum for many decades to come. In the early nineteenth century, the ritual passage from disorder to order had centered around a single invention—Evans's steam dredge, Whitney's interchangeable musket, Henry's electric dynamo—and an invention's fate could depend on a few brief moments in the public eye. The Jacksonian era, on the other hand, brought a *general* sense of disorder. That society might be fundamentally chaotic—and fundamentally public—began to seem like a possibility for the first time. Joseph Henry notwithstanding, the nation discovered that it liked spectacles, and show inventors, suddenly freed from the ethos of privacy, were able to act with an impunity they had never experienced before.

Jackson alone was not responsible for this change. In fact, the character of the Jacksonian era is almost inseparable from the brash and haughty invention that paralleled his rise.

The locomotive had its roots in England, and in the steam-powered, trackless Orukter Amphibolos built by Oliver Evans. It was Evans, too, who predicted that "the time will come when people will travel in stages moved by steam engines, from one city to another, almost as fast as birds fly, fifteen or twenty miles an hour."

By the time Jackson was sworn in, that prediction had come true, thanks largely to British inventors, whose locomotives began appearing in America in the 1820s. In 1825, Colonel John Stevens could exhibit a circular railway at his leisure resort in Hoboken, among his aerial walkways and wax works. On the Fourth of July, 1828, Charles Carroll, the last surviving signer of the Declaration of Independence, lifted the first clod of earth for the first rail of the Baltimore & Ohio Railway amidst floats, fireworks, and speeches. In the very hours that the last of the inaugural revelers were being led from the White House lawn, the Concord Lyceum, ever decorous, was asking itself "Whether it would be expedient for the State to construct a Rail Road from Boston to the Hudson River near Albany?" On August 8, 1829, the genuine article arrived when British pioneer George Stephenson's Stourbridge Lion was tested in Honesdale, Pennsylvania, on the Delaware & Hudson line.

The early British locomotives were grand and quite praiseworthy, but they suffered from a crucial drawback. Having been built with the geography of England in mind, they couldn't make the wide turns or mount the steep grades of the craggier American landscape. Locomotives had arrived in the New World, but when they got there, none of them could travel very far.

The New York City landowner and glue manufacturer Peter Cooper was one of the first to grasp this problem. Cooper had long been interested in the problem of converting circular motion into linear movement. Hoping to turn this interest to his advantage, he began building his own locomotive from the spare parts of other machines. By August 1830, he was able to set his Tom Thumb on the B & O line.

As the first American-built locomotive to travel on American rails, the Tom Thumb was already cause for interest, but to make its appearance even more exciting, Cooper arranged to race his jerry-rigged contraption against a horse. The B & O officials watched with bated breath as the horse took an early lead. When the locomotive pulled ahead, they cheered. Then somewhere along the line, a pulley connected to the engine's blower slipped, and the engine began to wheeze. By the time the error was corrected, it was too late.

Though Cooper lost the race, his Tom Thumb nevertheless conquered wide turns and steep grades that had thwarted the larger British locomotives. More important, he had hit upon a winning dramatic formula. After all, one of the benefits of the live spectacle was its ability to contain disorder within order, to provide a forum where nonsense could be rendered sensible, and a contest served this purpose quite well. His slapdash assembly of machine parts might have been laughable on its own, but when it was placed within a prescribed set of rules, its virtues could suddenly be understood.

That Cooper pitted his engine against an animal said a great deal about what those rules involved. In an earlier age, mountebanks had taken on the characters of animals as a way of embodying the mysterious powers of nature. After them the chapmen had engaged nature more directly, grappling with it on the frontier and perhaps going a bit native in the process. When John Fitch returned to the town square, he was a presentiment from beyond—a wild man. Cooper's race, on the other hand, made nature a rival—a respected rival, but a rival nonetheless. By pitting his iron horse against a real one, he dramatized the moment when humanity stood on the verge of breaking the cosmic order.

This possibility was too intoxicating to ignore. On June 1, 1831, the B & O executives who had witnessed Cooper's demonstration pitched a contest for the best locomotive America could produce, with the winner to be judged six months hence and awarded a prize of $4,000. Engineers jumped at the chance, and a spate of locomotives followed: the York, the Atlantic, the Arabian, the Mercury. Horatio Allen, who had imported the Stourbridge Lion, built the Best Friend and the West Point. In August of 1831, New York produced its first homegrown locomotive, the mighty De Witt Clinton, and set it bellowing on the Mohawk & Hudson Railroad. "Could they once be thoroughly persuaded that any point of the ocean had a hoard of dollars beneath it," observed Frances Trollope from her perch in Cincinnati, "I have not the slightest doubt that in about eighteen months we should see a snug covered rail-road leading directly to the spot."

In the excitement, money seemed to be no object. At least one investor planned to make his rails out of silver. Nor did anyone stop to ask whether their specifications matched those of their neighbors—the South established one gauge, New England another, Pennsylvania another again. The American locomotive was less like an iron horse than a runaway horse, with no single guiding force, much less a single inventor, to rein it in. No venue was safe from its rumbling prowess. In 1830, in Philadelphia of all places, George Washington Custis put on a play called *The Railroad*, in which a locomotive chugged onto the stage and had a delirious audience tooting along as it exited.

The burgeoning national sentiment could not have been better expressed. President Jackson himself had announced that "it is time that the principal events in the history of our country be dramatized, and exhibited at theatres," and a mechanically inclined nation had taken him at his word. As the rabble had penetrated the President's House, so had their machine penetrated the stage.

Respectability? Order? Morality?

*To hell with it all!*


The locomotive, besides appearing on stage, spread the spirit of the spectacle to the many whistle stops along its route. After Isaac Purdy and Rufus Welch of Westchester County, New York, initiated the tradition of the street parade sometime in the late 1820s, a figure known as the promoter began traveling by rail from one hamlet to the next, organizing parades for the locals.

This promoter had no credentials. He had nothing, in fact, but the persuasiveness of his pitch. Upon his arrival in town, he would convince the local merchants to sign contracts for a "street fair," to be held on their very own city streets. Then he would spend about three months convincing these same businessmen to buy space outside their very own stores. If he was doing well, he would sell them additional space in an exhibit tent, possibly even a float for the gala parade on opening day. Having staked the town as his own, he would put an ad in the *Clipper*— a trade magazine for like-minded individuals—announcing his intentions and requesting various attractions. All of these, which may well have included animals acts of one sort or another, would be well in place by the time the big opening parade marched down Main Street, with the ribbon cut by the town's very own mayor.

The street fair invariably won the townspeople over because it appealed to their vanity. At the same time, it made their daily lives more public. That may have wrinkled the brows of the local clergy, but it did wonders for the next itinerant who happened along. In the new noise-making society, a widening array of actors, wanderers, mountebanks, and peddlers felt all that much freer to come out of the woodwork to set up a stand or rent out a hall and hold forth on every conceivable subject.

The quacks, for their part, had never been entirely banished. In 1824, they were prevalent enough that the editors of a Portsmouth, Ohio, newspaper felt compelled to create a *fake* quack. Dr. Balthasar Beckar, a.k.a. the Unborn Doctor, had a nostrum that could change the shape of your nose, and betimes amused himself by distilling rosewater from his own breath. Outrageous as that may have sounded, readers would have been hard pressed to distinguish the Unborn Doctor from real quacks like Doctor Williams of Schenectady, who secured the testimony of a boy able to walk again after ingesting "Dr. Williams' Pink Pills for Pale People."

The mountebank was like a basso ostinato to the show inventors, sounding perennially from below. But the Jacksonian era saw more of them—and more "newfangled trumperies" that they could work into their acts. Magic lanterns had long been a staple item for the wandering show. Now there was the phenakistiscope, invented in 1832 by the Belgian scientist Joseph Plateau (who also discovered the phenomenon of persistence of vision); the kaleidoscope, invented by David Brewster in 1815; the zoetrope, or "wheel of life," which appeared in the early 1830s; the stroboscope of 1834; and Dr. John Paris's thaumatrope, a disc with an image on either side that, when spun, seemed to form a single image. If all these failed, the showmen could try to impress crowds with the old standby "ethereal fire," more commonly known as electricity. After Charles Poyer brought his own brand of mesmerism to the United

States from France in 1836, galvanic therapy—which Franklin had quietly attempted on a paralytic patient almost a hundred years before—became a commonly sought remedy.

These developments generally had their origins in serious scientific study—Faraday himself had created an optical device called the Faraday wheel, not to mention the electrical principle that gave the galvanic therapists their trappings—but the traveling performers weren't worried about that. Like the earlier European mountebanks, they subjected the crowds of the 1830s to a jumble of association, misdirection, and rhetoric, the main purpose of which was to entertain, or simply to bamboozle. In an age when science was a remote concept for most Americans (in part because their scientists were so inward-looking), neither purpose was difficult to achieve.

So associative was the new style of presentation that sometimes the inventions presented no longer related to the subject at all. Phrenology, for example, was not even remotely an inventorly discipline, yet mechanically minded showmen simply could not keep their hands off of it. Within the space of a few short years, they emptied this scientific discipline of its contents and stuffed its carcass with every gadget imaginable.

A long debunked science, phrenology espoused the doctrine that a person's character, as concealed in the brain, was revealed by the shape of the skull. The trained phrenologist would read a complex array of thirty-seven faculties and then diagnose the patient according to type. A person might be secretive, combative, amorative—any one of a wide range of types. Ralph Waldo Emerson, for example, as profiled by George Combe, turned out to be of the "idiotic" variety.

If such conclusions seem ludicrous enough today, the pioneers of phrenology saw themselves as a respectable lot, and they strove to keep it that way. In fact, George Combe's "On the Constitution of Man," which effectively introduced phrenology into print, appeared in the very same issue of the *American Journal of Education* in which Bigelow introduced the word *technology*.

By the time Combe got to it, phrenology was already two decades old. Its founder, Franz Joseph Gall, had tried to impress his ideas on Vienna and was hounded out of town for his troubles. On a lecture tour in 1800, he was joined by Johann Gasper Spurzheim, who coined the term *phrenology* and added science to what was essentially a philosophical pursuit. After Gall's death in 1828, Spurzheim assumed the mantle as phrenology's leading figure. Dying seemed to be a phrenological hazard, though; Spurzheim lectured in America so doggedly that he, too, met an untimely end.

It was at this point, though, that Combe stepped in, publishing widely and touring America, albeit on a more cautious itinerary—an eighteen-month tour limited to the territory east of Appalachia. Audiences ranging in size from three hundred to five hundred attended his lyceum demonstrations, which included spectacular brain dissections. Aware of the power of the press, Combe also saw to it that some of his lectures were serialized in the local papers.

For as much as he promoted his cause, Combe, like Gall and Spurzheim before him, wanted phrenology to retain its upper-class connotations as a science of human character, and his chosen venue to ensure as much was the lyceum. By now, however, the American public was more amenable to the practical phrenologists, who read your character for a small fee. In the 1830s, practical phrenology amounted to a craze. Soon, Combe was able to visit Hartford and find a practical phrenologist demonstrating his trade with a magic lantern. In 1839, he met someone who purported to be a phrenologist-magnetist. By 1842, a hybrid known as phreno-mesmerism incorporated the reading of bumps with a curative laying on of hands. Combe's beloved discipline had become a creature of show business.

No one understood the freak-show potential of phrenology better than the Fowler brothers Lorenzo and Orson. In 1835, the Fowlers set up at 135 Nassau Street in New York City; soon they had branches in Philadelphia and Boston under the partnership name of Fowler and Wells, with a self-appointed increase in the number of faculties to forty-two.

Increase was what the Fowler brothers knew. Recognizing that the reading of heads was a known quantity, they branched out into professional accessories, many of them on exhibit in their Phrenological Cabinet. They sold paintings and engravings of the brain. They sold forty different plaster casts, including those of Voltaire, Sir Walter Scott, and Aaron Burr (whose "secretiveness and destructiveness" faculties were "very large"). They sold animal and human skulls. And for twenty dollars, they sold a demountable model of the brain.

From there, the Fowler brothers expanded their offerings to include illustrations of women deformed by their Victorian corsets and of obstetrician's materials. It was only a matter of time before the pretense of category gave out altogether and they began selling galvanic machines, breast pumps, and self-acting gates. In the end, they opened a patent division, much like the invention submission companies of today, and charged for their services. Whatever inventions the Fowlers drew into their grasp were then sent back into the field with the traveling phrenologists who worked for them.

Everything about the Jacksonian era got the nation circulating, opening its imagination, and airing its clutter in public. Often, no purpose seemed to be served except to corrupt otherwise noble endeavors. But just as the general disorder could drag a dignified discipline down, so too could it yield results from below.

By 1832 or 1833, when Samuel Colt appeared on the streets of Lowell, Massachusetts, as a traveling "doctor" with a thinly veiled pseudonym, the leaflet he distributed had been refined and rewritten to his complete satisfaction.

## SCIENTIFIC AMUSEMENT—NITROUS OXIDE GAS

Dr. Coult (late of New York, London and Calcutta) respectfully informs the Ladies and Gentlemen of Lowell and vicinity, that he will lecture and administer Nitrous Oxide, or Exhilarating Gas, this evening, Nov. 29, at the Town Hall. The peculiar effect of this singular compound upon the animal system was first noticed by the celebrated English Chemist, Sir Humphrey [sic] Davy. He observed that when inhaled into the lungs, it produced the most astonishing effects on the Nervous System; that some individuals were disposed to Laugh, Sing and Dance, others to Recitation and Declamation, and that the greater number had an irresistible propensity to muscular exertion, such as wrestling, boxing &c., with innumerable fantastic feats. In short, the sensations produced by it are highly pleasurable, and are not to be followed by debility.

Dr. C. being a practical Chemist, no fears need be entertained of inhaling an impure Gas; and he is willing to submit his preparation to the inspection of any Scientific Gentlemen.

The persons who inhale the Gas will be separated from the audience by means of a network, in order to give all a better opportunity of seeing the exhibition. Dr. C. will first inhale the Gas himself, and administer it to those who are desirous of inhaling it.

Tickets 25 cents each, to be had at the principal Hotels and at the door.

Colt was heir to Humphry Davy's mantle by appropriation only. He had never met the famous British chemist, much less seen him lecture. But he understood Davy's sense of theater, and then some. A burly, hazel-eyed man who forever looked as if his wisdom teeth had just been pulled, Colt took the dramas of the Royal Institution and set them to a sharp American tempo. And he had the time of his life in the process.

Born in 1814, Colt was effectively on his own at an early age when his father, Christopher Colt, was widowed and had to put his children in foster homes. It must have been a life without much supervision, because young Sam was able to get his first pistol at the age of seven. He had a fondness for firing it on Sundays, a troublesome habit that soon had him hiding his weapon in a tree trunk.

At eleven, Colt was sent off to school in Glastonbury, Connecticut, more for discipline than for schooling, where he came across a copy of *The Compendium of Knowledge*. Among other things, this book described Robert Fulton's career, galvanism, and how to make gunpowder. While lounging around waiting to fire his pistol in private, he listened to the locals recount the military campaign at Saratoga and dream aloud about what they could have done with a repeating gun back then.

From Glastonbury, Colt moved to Ware and worked briefly in a textile plant. Taking the veterans' ponderings to heart, he made a gun that consisted of four revolving barrels tied together. But even with a galvanic battery to operate the firing sequence, the weapon was far too bulky to be practical. Frustrated, he turned his attention to his burgeoning knowledge of explosives, and soon afterward, handed out the first of what would be many leaflets.

"Sam'l Colt," it declared, "will blow a raft sky-high on Ware Pond, July 4, 1829."

The event drew a sizable crowd. Unfortunately, the fireworks at Ware Pond succeeded only in blowing mud onto the spectators, which made them visibly unhappy. The mob seized Colt and almost certainly would have drowned him had a stranger passing through named Elisha Root not interceded. Still, the townspeople were not mollified. Was it Colt, they wondered, who had set off the recent explosions that had scared off John Quincy Adams's horses when he had graced the town with his presence?

Colt was sent to school in Amherst before the question could be answered. He showed his gun off there, devised a submarine mine, and generally continued to make things explode. Again Independence Day did him wrong, and the faculty threw him out when his pyrotechnics started a fire. Like so many Melvilles of the day, there was nothing to do but go to sea.

Life on the *Corlo* bordered on the criminal. Sailors were required to show that their knives had been blunted before going aboard, and once they were on, fistfights were routine. Colt argued in favor of the steamship for seafaring, to the violent opposition of the other sailors. After a time, he learned to be silent, and practiced his knot tying. He noticed that the old seamen carved oddities out of wood—using, one assumes, the sides of their blunted blades—so he started whittling a few things of his own.

Somewhere in the Indian Ocean, Colt was watching the steersman when he noticed that whichever way the wheel was spun, each spoke came directly in line with a clutch that could be set to hold it. In a flash, the principle of a practical revolver became obvious. Like a crafty prisoner, he whittled his first one from wood, switching to a ship model whenever anyone came by. Then he assembled and dismantled it to make sure before disembarking that he had something to brag about.

Colt's father seemed to think he did. The captain of the *Corlo*, on the other hand, thought the boy had been swindled in some port and was boasting about a useless piece of wood. This was true in a way, since the first wooden protoypes, built early in 1832, failed to perform.

It was around this time that Colt, never one to sit too long when things were slow, took up the itinerant life. Soon the citizens of Ware and its neighboring towns noticed an adolescent boy pushing a nitrous oxide apparatus on a handcart down the local roads. He would set up his act on a village common or, failing that, a street corner. After he had attracted a crowd, he would demonstrate the use of the gas on himself and then invite spectators to try it for themselves. Inevitably, the volunteers amused the crowd, and Colt would take the opportunity to pass the hat.

So young Sam Colt wandered the towns of the Northeast, inciting hard-working citizens to break into animal tongues. Naturally, he didn't go far before he met with resistance. The local preachers required that he remove all vestiges of entertainment from his handbills and substitute the nomenclature of science. Surprisingly, after he did, they lauded his scientific "discovery" of nitrous oxide (not "laughing gas") and even considered his street show highly educational—a quiet but significant turning point for American show inventors, since Colt was now selling mayhem under the rubric of a respected worldview.

The wanderer's life proceeded apace. Colt had two revolvers made and tried them out to his satisfaction on the streets near Baltimore (whether he had an audience is unknown), then went to Boston intent on moving his nitrous oxide show into public halls, which he considered more "respectable" than his usual outdoor venues. He succeeded in booking the Masonic Temple in Boston for June 21, 1832, glamorizing his name with both a commedia dell'arte title and an extra vowel, as "Dr. Coult, of New York, London and Calcutta."

Not quite eighteen, this Dottore had nevertheless managed to grow a full beard and moustache. For added effect, he donned a frock and a high hat. He had bought plenty of ad space in the Boston papers, and the house was packed both nights. Some of the money earned from these performances went to a silver-embroidered black drape for the table that held the apparatus. The rest paid for a net to prevent sensitive subjects from falling into the orchestra pit. When the papers gave his subsequent performances superficial coverage, Colt protested that he had shelled out good money for the editors to write him up. The editors shrugged and went on with their work.

If an article published on October 26, 1833, is any indication, the editors at the *Albany Microscope* were better paid:

> We never beheld such an anxiety as there has been during the past week to witness the astonishing effects of Dr. Coult's gas . . . The museum was crowded to excess every evening; and so intense the interest which was manifested, that the doctor has been compelled to give two exhibitions almost every evening.
>
> The effect which the gas produces upon the system is truly astonishing. The person who inhales it becomes completely insensible, and remains in that state for about the space of three minutes, when his senses become restored, and he sneaks off with as much shame as if he had been guilty of some mean action.
>
> No person will begrudge his two shillings for the gratification of half an hour's laugh at the ludicrous feats displayed in the lecture room.

Around July 1834, Colt took his show to Cincinnati, where his brother John lived. There he met Hiram Powers, proprietor of *The Infernal Regions*—the very spectacle that Frances Trollope had inspired in the previous decade. At the time, Powers was looking to increase the draw with a fireworks act. Colt agreed to help out and parlayed his contributions into a slot for his own show on the bill. To keep the crowds coming, he kept changing the pyrotechnic routine. Oddly enough, when the show worked well, audiences tended to lose interest; when it went wrong, they could scarcely contain themselves.

A critical moment in Colt's laughing gas career came when he asked six Indians to take the stage, and, instead of entertaining the crowd with nonsensical yelps and stammers, all six fell asleep in their chairs. Fireworks that went awry were one thing, this was another. Thinking quickly, "Dr. Coult" asked for a volunteer to take his turn at the Exhilarating Gas and to see if he might be inspired to wake them up. A robust blacksmith came forward and greedily emptied the entire bag. When he reached for seconds, Dr. Coult pulled the bag away, but the man grabbed him and began bellowing violently, knocking over the Indians, and orating wildly, only to come to his senses in mid-speech, mortified. The audience roared.

Soon after this debacle, Colt left Cincinnati for New Orleans and, in a strange reversal of racial practices, began performing his act for slaves. When cholera hit the city, he found himself headed north on a riverboat filled with nervous passengers. Some of them, in fact, were already showing symptoms of the dreaded disease. Desperate, they turned to the good Dr. Coult for help. When he resisted, they began to suspect him of holding out for an exorbitant fee.

This put the young showman in a quandary. Should he expose himself as a fraud and risk being thrown overboard, or should he play along? In the end, he opted for playacting. He set up his apparatus and administered the gas to his patients, then made them exercise vigorously under the spell. Amazingly, when they came to, their symptoms had vanished. Dr. Coult had cured their cholera!

A guilty conscience prevented Colt from charging his usual rates, but this was only perceived as proof of his innate goodness. The news spread quickly, more quickly perhaps than the disease itself. Ailing patients approached him at every stop. Others cried out from rafts to be saved. Colt hid belowdecks and bribed slaves to keep quiet as to his whereabouts. This ploy didn't always work, as the slaves could sometimes fetch higher bribes for revealing him.

As soon as he could, Colt fled to Cincinnati, only to find his brother adamant about continuing the charade. Did Sam have any idea how much money he could make with this act? Eventually, a few cholera victims found him out and appeared on John's doorstep, pleading to take the cure. Colt stalled, assuring them that he would administer to them shortly. Then he fled out the back way.

In early 1835, Colt turned up in Richmond, by way of Canada, as the manager of a theater. At the time, the prospects for selling his revolver to the state of Virginia looked good—so good in fact, that he thought it might be the right moment to forsake his stage act. But he still needed the money that his "lecturing" brought, so he moved to Lynchburg, where he put on his show only a few miles from the farm where reaper-inventor Cyrus McCormick was living.

Meanwhile, Colt's theater partner back in Richmond, Joseph E. Walker, continued to dun him for money, and then to spend it as quickly as it was received. On April 5, a letter from Walker requesting twenty dollars disabused Colt of the stage life for good. From now on, there would be no more Dr. Coult. The following year, Colt received his first U.S. patent for a revolver and organized the Patent Arms Manufacturing Company in Paterson, New Jersey, at the ripe age of twenty-two.

Colt must have remained mildly enamored of outdoor commerce, because he sold his first revolvers on street corners and in general stores. He never turned these sales into street shows, though, and soon he was on his way to Washington in search of federal funding. The prospects looked promising there, and a deal probably would have been concluded without much delay if Colt's brother John, now living in New York City, hadn't interrupted the proceedings by being accused of murder.

One of John's creditors, Sam Adams, had been cut up with a hatchet, salted, packed in a suitcase, and shipped off to a fictitious New Orleans firm. When John confessed to killing the man in self-defense, Colt did everything possible, including retaining a team of lawyers, to keep his brother from going to the gallows. Found guilty, John was scheduled to be hanged on November 18, 1842, and certainly would have been except that a fire broke out in the prison. The official report said that John was found in his cell with a knife through his heart. Word on the street was that he escaped. The real story was never learned.

The murder case, combined with an economic depression, drove the Paterson company bankrupt in 1842 and forced Colt into a variety of pursuits. A waterproof bullet cartridge led to a waterproof cable, which in turn led to an improved underwater mine. This he used to spectacular effect, blowing up ships in demonstrations in New York Harbor and the Potomac River. When the government became squeamish about endorsing such hideous weaponry, Colt thought to capitalize on the underwater cable itself, and involved himself briefly in the fledgling telegraph business.

Indeed, Colt might have forgotten all about the arms business had the Polk administration not asked for a thousand of his six-shooters for $28,000, to be used in the Mexican-American War. Colt didn't have a single sample, but that was no problem. He whittled a new prototype from wood and enlisted the help of Eli Whitney's son, Eli Whitney, Jr., to build the production machinery. In the end, Colt lost $3,000 on the venture, but gained the machinery in the process. Moving to Hartford, Connecticut, he brought in a mechanic named Elisha Root—the same man who had saved him from the mob so many years ago at Ware Pond—to run the new factory.

Root was a proponent of making machines do the work, and at this the Colt factory was successful. As with the elder Whitney's New Haven factory, Root had one worker confine himself to boring barrels, another to chambering the cylinders, and so on. A measure of his success is that he became the hero of Mark Twain's biting satire, A *Connecticut Yankee in King Arthur's Court.*

Colt was not endowed with Root's mechanical aptitude, but he knew a thing or two about keeping people entertained. At the Hartford factory, he erected Charter Oak Hall, where his employees could get involved in fairs, exhibits, musicals, amateur theatricals, and a brass band that was eternally out of tune. A century later, many corporations would organize similar cultural activities, oblivious to the fact that Colt had been there first.

Colt was also a proponent of interchangeable parts, a goal that could only have been enhanced by teaming up with Eli Whitney, Jr. In what was beginning to shape up as a grand tradition, Colt claimed that his gun parts could be mixed and matched with ease, though in fact true interchangeability eluded him. Riches proved more attainable. Having set fire to schools, sailed the high seas, hypnotized Indians, cured cholera, and provided the classic weapon of the frontier, he spent the last fifteen years of his short but eventful life basking in the comforts of his success.

Colt's revolver was never closely associated with his fireworks and gas shows, so his celebrity did not represent the arrival of the full-blown show inventor. On the other hand, in pursuing theater long past the point when Joseph Henry would have broken rank, he provided strong evidence that serious inventions could arise from the street-show mentality. What's more, in moving from the stage to the lyceum with aplomb, he succeeded in blurring the line between science and entertainment.

That line was growing blurrier elsewhere as well. As the lyceums moved west, audiences in Ohio and Kentucky did not hesitate to razz a dull speaker or walk out on a condescending one. (Henry Ward Beecher seems to have been particularly singled out for his eastern airs.) Gradually, the midwestern lyceums developed a downright dramatic flair. By April 5, 1866, the *Cincinnati Gazette* could describe footlights as "accommodations generally required by professional lecturers." And Anna E. Dickinson, known as "Queen of the Platform," could insist on an additional set of them on either side of the podium before she would lecture on "The Assassination and the Suicide" without the use of notes.

Then, too, in the eastern cities, the lyceums and mechanics institutes had to vie with decidedly more lively forms of congress. In the first half of the nineteenth century, many a New York play pandered to the mechanics in the audience with the character of "the honest but poor printer" who "set actual type from actual cases." The rough-and-tumble Bowery crowd would even applaud arts-and-crafts demonstrations, perhaps effected by knitting machines, if performed with the right sort of brio. In the early 1840s, when the nation was pulling itself out of a severe depression, *The Earthquake*, with its vibrating and collapsing set, grossed $8,000 in its first week. Tank dramas also became popular, with ships set into huge pools of water to battle it out onstage. Whereas the early commedia dell'arte troupes had overcome the difficulty of many Italian dialects by emphasizing physical gags, American showmen appealed to their multilingual immigrant audiences with a dumbshow of machines.

As stage machinery eclipsed plot, characterization, and even dialogue, so too it eclipsed the mechanics institutes and the lyceums. Eclipsed them, that is, by subverting them and rendered their terminology meaningless. By the mid-1900s, mechanics were called mechanics, of course, but so were faro dealers and their fellow cardsharp kin. These "mechanics" often made use of a device known as the dealing box, invented in 1822 by an anonymous American. Made of brass and slightly larger than a deck of cards, the device had a thumbhole on its top that could be used to push the cards out through a slit while a spring held the rest of the deck in place. So successful was the dealing box that mechanics developed an entire cottage industry of variations whose particulars can only be imagined today: the gaff, the tongue tell, the sand tell, the top-sight tell, the needle squeeze, the horse box, the screw box, the lever movement, the coffee mill. Also popular in this milieu was an invention called the Money Maker, which churned out dollar bills until purchased by a gullible customer.

As for institutions, there was the Lyceum of Natural History of New York, with its courses in botany and the like, but there was also the Lyceum, run by John Brougham on Broome Street. Typical of his productions was a Christmas Eve, 1855 extravaganza that he dubbed the "Original, Aboriginal, Erratic, Operatic, Semi-Civilized, and Demi-Savage Extravaganza of *Pocahontas*."

If that bill sounds like the work of Phineas T. Barnum, there was reason for it. Of all the showman of the Jacksonian era, none was more powerful or more influential than the bulbous-nosed Barnum. During his lifetime, American newspapers devoted more column inches to him than to anyone else, except for the nation's presidents. His influence was so great as to garner a verb of its own—to be Barnumized.

Yet Barnum's reach was not just a general one; he too mingled science and entertainment. At various times in his life he became a business partner in companies that sold clocks, sewing machines, and fire extinguishers. He was called on to take over the New York Crystal Palace exhibition in 1854. Later, he called one of his caravans "P. T. Barnum's Great Traveling World's Fair," and later still gave advice on how the Columbian Exposition of 1893 should be run. Throughout the century, his exhibits would lionize or inspire important inventors. Cyrus McCormick, Elisha Otis, Isaac Merritt Singer, and Alexander Graham Bell would all cross paths with him in one way or another and learn the value of Barnumization for themselves.

His early days in show business suggest these connections in embryo. In 1835, after a brief stint as a newspaperman, Barnum considered buying a Hydro-Oxygen Microscope from Scudder's American Museum for exhibition purposes, but couldn't afford it. As it was, he began his ascent to legend by exhibiting Joice Heth—the putative 161-year-old nurse of General Washington. Soon after—while Colt was setting up his Paterson factory—Barnum became treasurer of Aaron Turner's Columbian Circus and went on the road. When his contract ran out on October 30, 1836, he left Turner's employ and opened what he called "Barnum's

Grand Scientific and Musical Theatre," which he operated until he returned to New York in 1838.

It seems there was very little that was scientific about Barnum's traveling show, which offered the usual crew of riders, clowns, and singers. It also seems not to have mattered. Upon the announcement of a permanent exhibition to be located in New York, Barnum was besieged by solicitors, among them, as he recalled, "inventors in large numbers, patent-medicine men, etc." One of these solicitors offered a perpetual motion machine, which Barnum turned down upon discovering its mainspring. Some of the offers must have piqued his interest, though, because Barnum soon started to make good on the "scientific" dimension in his advertising.

The famous American Museum opened its doors on the corner of Broadway and Ann Street in 1841, and by 1842, the attractions included the Lecture Room, or in wording reminiscent of the Royal Institution's main hall, "the great Lecture Room." At first, this stage was occupied by curiosities and ordinary show-biz fare, but gradually, as Barnum enlarged and improved the space, the bill was expanded to include the mechanical alongside the macabre.

The effect was to equate machinery with the "lower" limits of the human form—with the animal element of man. Among the many examples of bizarre physicality—the educated dogs, albinos, fat boys, giants, dwarfs, and rope-dancers—visitors to the Lecture Room could also see automatons, dioramas, panoramas, glass blowing, Physioscopes, Chromatopes, knitting machines, an Anatomical Venus, a clockwork Swiss village and—in a phrase of Barnum's creation—"other triumphs of the mechanical arts." Perhaps his most outrageous foray into invention came in the form of a "Negro inventor" who claimed to possess a weed that would turn black people white. Barnum, always quick to upend notions of the natural order, gave the man prominent billing and championed the physic as the solution to slavery.

There were certain rules of thumb to be observed, of course. As for the nature of the demonstrations, Barnum believed that they should not be perfect. Something should be slightly amiss about them, on the premise that a noisy automaton made for a noisier crowd. That was certainly in keeping with what Colt had discovered about fireworks that went wrong—fallible technology, by creating disorder within organized parameters, got the audience *involved*.

At the same time, Barnum made sure to appease the more correct members of the audience by introducing the "Moral Drama" as a regular item in his programs. *Harper's Monthly* remembered him specifically for this when he died, eulogizing that the "late Mr. Barnum, a generation ago, in his American Museum showed that a theater could be as innocent as a concert-room. . . . He eliminated the wickedness."

Here was a new order of demonstration, if it could be called an order. Where the lyceums had labored to make their lectures high-minded, and the mechanical institutes to make their members fluent in Latin, Barnum went straight to whatever was interesting, justifying it with a smattering of positive uplift. At the same time, he expanded on the one-trick-pony shows of the wandering showmen, and in the process, established the aesthetic of variety. In this sense, Barnum promoted an aesthetic that fit the way inventors actually thought. Rather than a hierarchy of values, his exhibits were, as he liked to say, "a wilderness of wonderful, instructive, and amusing realities."

Barnum was not averse to riding the coattails of the lyceums, either, if it proved expedient. Around the time that his Lecture Room opened, he wrote a series of letters to the press under the name Dr. Griffin, postmarked from points south. Purportedly an agent of the Lyceum of Natural History of London, Griffin claimed to be in possession of an anthropological find from the South Pacific. Barnum then had a man named Lyman check into a hotel in Philadelphia under this high-sounding name. Upon checking out, "Dr. Griffin" casually showed his Feejee Mermaid—the cadavers of a monkey and a fish sewn together—to the proprietor, who, predictably, ran to the press. The charade was repeated at a New York hotel, and ten thousand handbills passed out before Lyman, alias the esteemed Dr. Griffin, displayed the marvel before an astonished public in the great Lecture Room.

As if to cap his co-optation, right after the Civil War, Barnum was invited to go on his own lecture tour of the new, Barnumized lyceums. He made an extended run through Pennsylvania, Ohio, Indiana, Illinois, Wisconsin, Missouri, and Iowa under the auspices of the Associated Western Literary Society, speaking—naturally—on the subject of "Success in Life." Afterward, he quipped, "The curiosity exhibitor himself became quite a curiosity."

As if from nowhere, invention and showmanship had become inextricably entwined. In 1848, even Walt Whitman caught himself thinking of technology as sleight of hand when he wrote of the local ferryboat machine works. "It is almost a sublime sight that one beholds there;" he wrote in the *Brooklyn Eagle*, "for indeed there are few more magnificent pieces of handiwork than a powerful steam-engine swiftly at work! . . . We do not profess to understand the tricks—or rather the simplicities of machinery."

Meanwhile, holed up in his red-brick building in Washington, Joseph Henry continued to do everything possible to keep the tricksters from crashing *his* party, but he was fighting a losing battle. At one point, the Patent Office tried to pawn off its National Institute collections on the Smithsonian in order to make room for an increasing number of invention prototypes. This collection included among its curiosities a "Double-headed snake, found alive near Port Tobacco, Md.," a "Syrian Sarcophagus . . . removed from the elevated grounds near the rear of Beirut," and Benjamin Franklin's cane.

Henry was doubly aggrieved when it turned out that the Syrian sarcophagus had not simply been donated, but donated with the request that Andrew Jackson be buried in it when he died. Though Jackson politely turned the request down, his name continued to be associated with the wonder from Beirut. A Dr. Washburn, who worked at the Smithsonian, surreptitiously changed the label's literal description to the legend: "Tomb in which Andrew Jackson REFUSED to be buried."

Still, if Barnum championed the show inventors while Henry scoffed, there were aspects to their actions that suggested the possibility of a meeting ground. After all, Barnum, for all his disingenuousness, did back up his temperance lectures with his own sobriety. And Henry, for as much as he battened down the hatches, ventured into Barnum's camp on at least one occasion.

In December 1845, while in Philadelphia, Henry was invited to see a machine invented and being shown for profit by a German named Joseph Faber. The device was carved to look like a Turk sitting on a table, but the actual workings were a much more ingenious sight: a complex amalgam of pedals, bellows, whistles, tubes, diaphragms, pulleys, and shutters connected to a seventeen-note keyboard. When the keyboard was played, the machine spoke. The words were distinct, the voice a uniform drawl. It was said that the machine could manage entire sentences in "all the living languages of Europe."

Henry had expected to find a hoax and was delighted to be proven

THE EUPHONIA, OR SPEAKING MACHINE.

Both the austere Joseph Henry and the genial Phineas T. Barnum admired Mister Faber's Talking Machine, which prefigured the telephone. This is how it appeared in August 1846 at London's Egyptian Hall. *New York University Libraries*

wrong. He declared the automaton promising, and imagined that "words might be spoken at one end of the telegraph line, which had their origin at the other."

With a statement like that, it seems probable that Henry could have secretly invented the telephone, along with his secret inventions of the telegraph and the radio. Instead, he was content to imagine a device that would let preachers deliver their sermons to multiple endpoints. Perhaps he saw himself as rescuing a bit of technology for the pious side.

The automaton did not end up on a pulpit, however. Barnum, looking for new acts, obtained it a few months later and dispatched it along with sixteen American Indians to London, where it was exhibited as the "Euphonia." The advertisements at the Egyptian Hall suggested a more boisterous personality than the one Henry had in mind. According to the bill, the curiosity could say "anything and everything suggested by the audience in all languages, whispers, laughs, and sings all airs, including the air and the words to 'God Save the Queen.' "

If Barnum considered the device a middling success, it was probably because of Mister Faber's stage demeanor. An infinitely sad man, the inventor sat behind the automaton, never moving, never looking up. Future theater manager John Hollingshead, only nineteen at the time, recalled the scene vividly:

> The Professor was none too clean, and his hair and beard sadly wanted the attention of a barber. I have no doubt that he slept in the same room as his figure—his scientific Frankensteinian monster—and I felt the secret influence of an idea that the two were destined to live and die together . . . There were truth, laborious invention, and good faith, in every part of the melancholy room. As a crowning display, the head sang a sepulchral version of "God Save the Queen," which suggested, inevitably, God save the inventor.

Despite the gloom, the exhibit cleared a profit of $300 in its first week of exhibition and remained in London for several months. Thackeray, writing in *Punch*, imagined it being used for purposes that anticipated the phonograph. The Duke of Wellington saw it and signed his name in endorsement. A less moneyed witness who paid an extra shilling to see the Euphonia was Melville Bell, father of the telephone pioneer.

In the following years, the name *Euphonia* was shed for the more descriptive title of Mister Faber's Automaton Speaker, Professor Faber's Amazing Talking Machine, or sometimes simply the Wonderful Talking Machine. Whatever its name, it simply would not go away. Henry would see it again when its owner came looking for support. Barnum would take it on his "Traveling World's Fair." Melville Bell's prodigious son would hear of it, then see it, then hear of it again as he worked his way toward his own amazing talking machine.

Faber never amounted to much more than a footnote in the history of technology, but his automaton held out an important promise nevertheless. If both Henry and Barnum could see value in the same invention, then the Olympian scientists and the infernal show inventors might agree on something after all. And if that was true, then excessive gestures might yet lead to the greater welfare of society.

It would take another thirty years for the high and low visions of

Faber's machine to come together in the life and work of Alexander Graham Bell. Meanwhile, what there was of a middle ground was occupied by the sole figure of Samuel Morse, who labored hard to give the profession of show inventor a dignified face. And for a time, it seemed as if he might succeed.

## Chapter Five

# LIKE A GENTLEMAN

In many ways, Samuel Finley Breese Morse was Robert Fulton come back to life. Imperious and intimidating, he embraced a lofty vision of life in which politicians were all-important. Like Fulton, he appealed to the courts of England and France before succeeding in the United States. The two inventors even shared the same painting teacher.

Yet Morse lived in a different time. Outwardly, he may have evoked the stately discretion of the Founding Fathers, but he was also enough of a populist to crave the attention of the American public. The result was a curious hybrid. Higher than Colt but lower than the Lazzaroni, he held out the possibility that the American inventor's show, unruly as it was, might still be connected to a grand, orderly scheme.

Morse tried his hand at invention at an early age, devising a fire-engine pump and a marble-cutting machine, but soon decided on a career in art. Fresh out of Yale in 1811, he went to England and studied with Benjamin West, who favored him "with a sight of the sketch because I am an American." He also had a sight of the public event, and wrote home of horse races, theater shows, and a balloonist at Hackney who rose above a crowd of three hundred thousand people.

Under West's tutelage, Morse developed a passion for history painting. Throughout his artistic career, he gravitated toward the landmark events of his country and the heroes involved in them. To his mind, inventors belonged in the company of these noble figures; in the course of his life, he painted the portraits of both Eli Whitney and Eli Terry, the inventor of a wooden clock, using the lofty iconography generally reserved for statesmen.

Morse exhibited a few pictures when he returned to the States, but he found that his fellow countrymen did not hold painting in the same regard as Europeans did. The occasional patroon notwithstanding, Americans wanted painters to render their portraits for a fee. Morse didn't care for this kind of commercialization, and once boasted, "If I cannot live a gentleman, I will starve a gentleman." By his own lights, that meant that he ceased to be a gentleman fairly early in the game. Soon, he was traveling from Concord to Walpole to Hanover, earning fifteen dollars a portrait.

Hard times dogged him for a while. His *Congress Hall, or the Old House of Representatives*, completed in 1823, was taken seriously by its subjects—almost seriously enough to buy it, in fact, but not quite. In 1829, the painting was sold to Sherman Converse in London, and in 1849, it was found nailed to a partition in the Coates & Company store, covered with dust.

Eventually Morse, who was more talented than Fulton, came to be recognized as one of the important artists of his day. By the late 1820s, he was president of the National Academy of Design and he was earning the respect of his peers. Still, widespread success eluded him, to say nothing of riches. Hoping that another dose of European culture might lend cachet to his work, he returned to the Continent in 1829 to see the great masterpieces of France and Italy.

It was while returning home aboard the *Sully* in 1832, his head filled with da Vincis and Michaelangelos, that Morse conceived of his telegraph. He and a few other passengers were wiling away the hours when one Dr. Charles T. Jackson, an amateur conjurer, started pulling eggs out of hats and toying with an electromagnet. The conversation soon turned to André-Marie Ampère's recent experiments in France. Jackson remembered that Benjamin Franklin had passed a current through many miles of wire with no difference in time between the two terminals. Franklin had never done any such thing, but such misunderstandings were hardly unusual. By this time, most people knew for a fact that Franklin had conducted a kite experiment.

Thus misinformed, Morse replied: "If this be so, and the presence of electricity can be made visible in any desired part of the circuit, I see no reason why intelligence might not be instantaneously transmitted by electricity to any distance."

The language of this statement sounds oddly formal for such an impromptu discussion, suggesting a cleaned-up version of the facts. Other aspects of Morse's version of this moment show a similar transformation at work. Long after his passage aboard the *Sully*, he produced a drawing of the familiar Morse code symbols, which he claimed to have sketched out during the voyage. These symbols have often been praised for their elegance and efficiency. Yet two-element codes were not new. As early as 1605, Francis Bacon had devised one, and by 1832, a Baron Schilling had developed a dot-dash system for use in telegraphy. Morse himself drew on the work of three French brothers named Chappe, who had created a two-element semaphore system. Moreover, some historians believe that the dot-dash system that emerged from Morse's earlier notation was actually the work of his assistant, Alfred Vail. If this was the case, and if Joseph Henry deserved credit for most of the technical aspects of the telegraph, then Morse had little to claim as his own. How critical a piece of paper could be in such circumstances. How much, in fact, like pulling an egg—in this case, a very elegant egg—out of a hat.

Once he was back in New York, Morse put his telegraph aside to resume his career as a painter. In 1834, a Congressional committee had been assigned to commission artists to paint four huge panels in the rotunda of the Capitol building. Again, the prospect of recognition for a grand history painting beckoned. As president of the National Academy, Morse was in a position to nominate himself for the job, and he did so in a letter dated March 7, 1834. The painting he proposed to execute was of a typically high-minded theme: "The Signing of the First Compact on Board the Mayflower."

Unfortunately, John Quincy Adams, who was on the committee, decided that America did not have any painters worthy of the commission. When the field was opened to include Europeans, an anonymous letter appeared in the *Evening Post* protesting the decision. Many thought that Morse had written the letter. It had actually been penned by his friend, writer James Fenimore Cooper, but the rumor took hold and caused Morse to be excluded from the project.

When the committee decision became public in 1837, Morse was stunned and counted it as one of the major setbacks in his life. At the time he wrote: "Painting has been a smiling mistress to many, but she has been a cruel jilt to me." One of his last paintings shows New York University surrounded by a pink landscape of pools and castles—a Gothic phantasmagoria that his artistic admirers have tended to write off as a misguided experiment.

Perhaps it would be more appropriate to see this painting as a prelude to his most important phase because, having ventured to the edge of one artistic style, Morse made the leap into something truly new. "My first instrument," he later wrote, in describing his first telegraphic apparatus, "was made of an old picture or canvas frame fastened to a table." Onto the frame he attached an electromagnet that he himself had wound, the wheels of a wooden clock, a single-cell galvanic battery, a strip of paper, and a pencil. This was, in effect, an *electric canvas*— the first kinetic art, date 1835. Appraised as such, it would be at home in any twentieth-century art catalog.

The machinery was set up to create not the familiar dots and dashes, but a continuous line with identifying dips and lines. If that was a promising start, Morse still had no way of sending his messages over an appreciable distance. Dr. Jackson had been mistaken; the signal would behave sporadically or simply die out. When Morse approached Joseph Henry for help, the Princeton professor taught him how to set up an electrical relay, which allowed the signal to travel longer distances without losing its force (basically, by installing fresh batteries along the line to boost the power). Of course, this was hardly difficult for Henry, who had rung a bell over a miles' worth of wire way back in 1831.

With the technical obstacles effectively overcome, Morse made his first practical version of the telegraph in 1837. It was built in Morristown, New Jersey, and being heavier than anticipated, could not be moved right away. Thus, the debut demonstration was given to the locals at hand in the first days of 1838, using a cumbersome shorthand dictionary for transmitting messages. As soon as they could, Morse and his assistant, Alfred Vail, hauled it into New York and showed it to scientists and reporters on January 24 of that year at the New York University's Geological Cabinet on Washington Square.

Morse may have been like Fulton in many ways, but not when it came to demonstrating his machinery. Fulton had taken Fitch's invention and labored to show it more privately. Morse, on the other hand, took Henry's invention and tried to make it more public. After the NYU demonstration, Vail noted in a letter to his brother that Morse, in preparing for this exhibition, had "printed five hundred blank invitations in his own name at your expense." Of course, those five hundred people may have made for an exclusive audience, but had they all shown up, they hardly would have constituted an inner circle. Where Fulton preferred a private gathering, Morse liked a full house.

And after the New York show, he must have liked reporters. On January 29, the *Journal of Commerce* published an account:

> THE TELEGRAPH.—We did not witness the operation of Professor Morse's Electro-Magnetic Telegraph on Wednesday last, but we learn that the numerous company of scientific persons who were present pronounced it entirely successful. Intelligence was transmitted through a circuit of TEN MILES, and legibly written at the extremity of the circuit."

From there, the telegraph went on the road. The first stop was the Franklin Institute in Philadelphia, where it was demonstrated on February 8 before the Committee of Arts and Sciences. During this visit, Vail bristled when Morse referred to him as an assistant. By the time they had arrived in Washington, Morse had apologized and the tiff had been smoothed over. The contretemps may have been a simple clash of personalities. Or, since they were using a system of alphabetic symbols instead of a dictionary by this time, it may have been that Vail was feeling his rightful credit slipping from his grasp. Either way, the point was clear: Morse was publicity-minded enough to insist on top billing.

Morse might have taken the telegraph to any one of a number of entrepreneurs at this point. He might have gone into business for himself and become a tycoon. Yet he did neither of these things, largely because he believed that the telegraph, like the post office, belonged in federal hands. It is hard to separate this wish from his love of history painting. Trained in the ways of Benjamin West, Morse naturally looked to the government as his subject. And no doubt he still felt a desire to put his rotunda-mural defeat to rest, at least in his own mind. So after Philadelphia, he and Vail set their sights on Washington.

Morse fully expected a warm reception in the capital, and these hopes seemed to be justified when he was allowed to set up his telegraph in the room where the Committee on Commerce met. Unfortunately, the Panic of 1837—really a euphemism for the Panic of 1837, 1838, 1839, 1840, 1841, and 1842—had made money hard to come by even for the government, and Congress remained noncommittal.

Then again, America was not the only country in the world that had a government. In 1839, during a lull in the lull, Morse sailed to Europe in pursuit of a foreign patent. The British, who already had several other telegraphs either in operation or in development, were unimpressed, but the response in Paris was enthusiastic. Through the eminent scientist

François Arago, Morse was able to show the telegraph to a gathering of distinguished scientists, Baron Humboldt and Gay-Lussac among them. Upon seeing it in action, the scientists blurted out, *"Extraordinaire! Très admirable!"*

The telegraph immediately became the talk of the Paris cafes. Three flights up at No. 5 rue Neuve-des-Mathurins, Morse set up his apparatus—the register in the parlor, the batteries and the sending device (called the "correspondent") in the bedroom. In the small space between, he set up his telegraph model, and professors, dukes, duchesses, governors, editors, and directors all came to see it. But, as Fulton had discovered four decades earlier, the French did not always buy what they liked.

Encouraged but not enriched, Morse returned to Washington and continued his vigil. He received a U.S. patent on June 20, 1840, but still no purchase. He waited. He demonstrated. Then he waited again. And in the middle of all this waiting, he stumbled across an odd reminder of his past.

In order to string some wires between committee rooms for yet another demonstration, Morse had to go into a vault below them. Down he went, with a workman carrying a lamp, and found a statuette that he himself had made years earlier, called *Dying Hercules,* which had earned him the Adelphi Gold Medal. So at least one politican had appreciated his art work after all!

Back above ground, Morse again appealed to Henry, this time asking for an endorsement. Henry gave it and more: he taught Morse how to insulate his telegraph lines. That and the end of the economic depression finally turned the tides. When in 1843 Congress passed a bill including a $30,000 appropriation for a telegraph line between Washington and Baltimore, Morse had a fraction of a dollar in his pocket. In fact, he was preparing to quit Washington for good when Annie Ellsworth, a friend (and daughter of the patent commissioner, H. L. Ellsworth), told him the news. Elated, he borrowed enough money from one of his pupils to buy a coat and a pair of pants.

The high spirits soon wore off, however. As the first telegraph was being readied, Morse became moody, and again his relations with Vail became strained. "Professor Morse is so unstable and full of notions," wrote Vail. "He changes his mind oftener than the wind, and seems exceedingly childish sometimes."

One less-than-fruitful idea was that the lines be laid underground, an expensive undertaking that ate up $23,000 of his appropriation. The telegraph seemed to be dying yet another death until the foreman on the project, Ezra Cornell, convinced Morse that telegraph wires would work better if they were strung in the air. Morse acquiesced, yet he remained mindful that the telegraph had become an open-air show. He asked Cornell to stop work, cautioning him not to do anything that would give the public the impression that the project had failed.

Cornell understood perfectly. Doing Morse one better in the acting category, he shouted out, "Hurrah, boys! We must lay another length of pipe before we quit!" Then he stepped up to the mule-drawn plow that was being used to clear a path for the wires. Cracking his whip, he started the mules out at a lively clip and, waiting for the opportune moment, caught the plow on a rock, breaking it to pieces as Morse looked on. That was all the pretext that was needed to start building their line in the air, and by May 1844, the job was finished with the remaining $7,000.

Morse had worked long and hard to meet his goal, but it was Annie Ellsworth who chose the message that would ring through the ages. The phrase "What hath God wrought!" was perfectly in keeping with the tone of the event—stentorian, cosmic, noble. It also contained a hidden message for those who would hear. Drawn from the Book of Numbers, these famous words were first uttered by the soothsayer Balaam, who proclaimed himself unable to curse the Israelites, even though they had been ordered to kill him. So too did Morse aggrandize his country's leaders to the end, no matter how badly they had treated him over the years.

Of course, Morse, who was well versed in the ways of the showmen, gave himself the same hyperbolic treatment. "Nothing could have been more appropriate than this devout exclamation at such an event," his announcement crooned, "when an invention which creates such wonder, and about which there has been so much scepticism, is taken from the land of the visions, and becomes a reality."

The first official message was sent from the chamber of the Supreme Court in the Capitol building to Baltimore on May 24, 1844. A few days later, messages were again sent to and from Baltimore. For these, Vail sat in the third story of a warehouse at the railroad depot on Pratt Street; Morse waited in a room below the Senate Chamber, where he would post the news on a bulletin board in the rotunda.

The event being transmitted had considerable symbolic weight. The

Democratic National Convention, being held just then in Baltimore, was preparing to nominate its ticket for the upcoming presidential election. For Morse, however, there was an additional layer of symbolism: he was situated in the very building in which he had hoped to install his paintings. And now, in a sense, he *was* painting. Better still, the prospect at hand was no mere portraiture; he was representing a great historical scene of his country. The electric canvas clicked, the news came over the wire: Senator Silas Wright, nominated for vice president.

This news in itself was no cause for comment, but what followed certainly was. Wright, who was in Washington at the time, declined the nomination. When Morse relayed this information to Baltimore, the conventioneers distrusted the report and adjourned until more "reliable" information could be delivered by train. The following day, of course, Wright's decision was confirmed, and the voices of disbelief were silenced.

The significance of the Morse telegraph was now patently clear. Britain already had a telegraph for signaling the movements of locomotives. This, on the other hand, was a *live report*—the first in the world—and an example of the inventor's show at its best. After months of rising suspense, Morse had provided a surprise, then followed it up with a decisive confirmation. In Baltimore, hundreds of people besieged Vail for permission to enter his office, just to be able to say they had seen the telegraph. The newspapers waxed effusive, calling it the greatest invention of the age.

Perhaps most impressive, the telegraph demonstrations provided a rare moment in American life in which performers and patricians stood on equal ground. In Morse's hands, the telegraph was public, yet it was also high-minded. It was immediate, yet it was artistic. It was perfect, in fact, for making the new order seem like the old. Having failed at painting historical scenes, Morse succeeded admirably in creating a history painting "come to life" as a public performance.

Morse had rearranged every unruly detail in his path toward the establishment of this well-ordered realization. Battles with Henry and Vail, ill-fated decisions to lay underground cables—these things had been submerged into a unified, public display of power. Yet the conflicting elements in Morse's repertoire came together only when he electrified the world from his perch in the Capitol building. After that, everyone seemed satisfied to let high and low go their separate ways again.

The lofty connotations, it must be said, remained with the inventor. Morse quickly took his place among the likes of Robert Fulton and Benjamin Franklin. He needed no introduction to pay a visit to the crown heads of Europe. He was often called upon to make ceremonial speeches and to unveil statues, and in the end, lived to see a statue of himself erected in Central Park.

The telegraph, meanwhile, devolved into a chaotic enterprise. When the U.S. government declined to take on the invention (unlike the British Post Office, which oversaw another version of the telegraph), all hopes of an efficient, centralized order were dashed.

The fate of the telegraph might have been surmised by anyone who chanced upon the first issue of *Scientific American*, published in 1845 by an itinerant inventor (and as it turned out, a lowbrow painter) named Rufus Porter. In this inchoate publication, a modest announcement of Morse's invention ran on page two, while the center of page one was given over to livelier fare:

> EXTRAORDINARY PHENOMENON.—The inhabitants of the village of Moulton were greatly astonished on Saturday last, at observing a considerable quantity of hay (from a field where it was in cocks for stacking) rise rapidly into the air. There was not the slightest breeze of wind perceptible at the time: however the hay continued to ascend until it apparently passed through the clouds, which were sailing high at the time. After the lapse of a few minutes it again appeard [sic] like a small black streak in the cloudy vapor, where it continued to form a most novel and astonishing sight for ten or fifteen minutes, when it gradually descended again to the earth.

Thus Morse's invention entered the Jacksonian fray where improbabilities abounded. Rather than spreading in well-planned geometries, telegraph lines began to spring up willy-nilly, erected by anyone with half a mind to do so. One of the first to seize upon the telegraph, in fact, was the master of chaos, Samuel Colt.

Morse and Colt had met in Washington while seeking their respective audiences with the government. Thinking to turn his own underwater cable to new purposes, Colt developed an interest in the telegraph. In 1845, he joined forces with a book dealer named William Robinson of

208 Broadway to form the New York & Offing Magnetic Company, one of the first telegraph companies in the country. New York & Offing set up an observation tower on Coney Island, with the idea of communicating the movements of ships in the harbor to subscribers. Colt, wily as ever, became a wire supplier for his own company.

Others were just as quick to see the potential in the telegraph. On May 15, 1845, the Magnetic Telegraph Company paid Morse $30,000 for the licensing rights to erect a telegraph line between New York and Philadelphia. By 1849, Magnetic was being run by Henry J. Rogers and Zenus Barnum, president of the Northern Central Railroad and a fifth or sixth cousin of Phineas T. Barnum. Whether the two Barnums ever met is not known. Yet the fact remains that between 1860 and 1865, they were among the most powerful figures in the nation, one in show business, the other in telegraphy.

The lesser-known Barnum began building his empire with a new telegraph line between Washington and Baltimore. From then on, he did nothing but rise in stature. In 1860, when Magnetic was bought up by the American Telegraph Company—known as the Titan of the East because it controlled telegraphy all along the Atlantic seaboard—he became its president.

The American Telegraph Company was even more powerful for belonging to the North American Telegraph Association, which covered virtually the entire country. And since Zenus came to head the larger association as well, it was during his tenure that the telegraph achieved transcontinental status—on October 24, 1861, when two lines were joined at a telegraph office on Main Street in Salt Lake City, Utah. It was also during Zenus Barnum's tenure that a telegraphic spectacle on a global scale joined the words *cable* and *carnival* together.

The mastermind behind this spectacle was Cyrus Field, a paper manufacturer. By the time he was thirty-three, Field had made $250,000 and was able to retire. Unable to sit still, he immediately took a trip to South America and showed a bit of the animal tamer's pluck by returning with a jaguar, the remains of a South American tiger, and twenty-four live parakeets. He also brought back an indigenous boy of fourteen named Marcus, who enjoyed brandishing knives and laying snares around Field's Gramercy Park home. One story has it that Marcus managed to break the cook's neck. In any event, the Fields waited until Cyrus was away on business, then sent Marcus back to his bullfighter father. What became of the jaguar is not recorded in Field's personal notes.

Around this same time, a man named Frederick N. Gisborne began calling on Field. Gisborne had secured exclusive rights to erect telegraph lines in Newfoundland and was looking for backers in New York. After one of their meetings was over and Gisborne had left, Field gazed idly at the globe in his library. Suddenly it occurred to him that a cable might be laid from Newfoundland to Ireland. The following day, he sent a letter to Morse, currently residing in Poughkeepsie, and to his own neighbor, Peter Cooper, inventor of the Tom Thumb and, more lately, of the gelatin dessert. Then Field went directly to England, where he solicited the help of the electrical pioneer Michael Faraday and the shipbuilder Isambard Kingdom Brunel for the enterprise.

Soon the laying of the transatlantic cable became a drama very much on the scale of Morse's demonstration in the Capitol building, except that Field and his crew were struggling with the furies of nature rather than cavorting with angels as Morse had done. The first attempt to lay a line from Trinity Bay, Newfoundland, to Valentia Bay, Ireland, was cut short when a cable began to unreel during a storm. Newspapers reported the crew laboring in vain as the wire slithered into the sea. A second attempt, in 1858, brought momentary success before the transatlantic line went dead.

By 1862, Field had the active support of Zenus Barnum's North American Telegraph Association, and he was ready to try again. This time, after the cable was laid, New York City held a "General Celebration of the Laying of the Atlantic Telegraphic Cable."

The *New York Herald* announced the event in festive tones: "The Cable Carnival. Achieved is the Glorious Work. The Metropolis Overwhelmed with Visitors." A crowd gathered at the Battery at one in the afternoon, then proceeded uptown to the Crystal Palace. "The crowd upon Broadway," wrote one reporter, "was so great that the military had much difficulty in getting through it, and so the procession was somewhat retarded," all of which "gave to Broadway a carnvalesque [sic] appearance which it is almost impossible to describe." In Central Park, fireworks exploded above the colored lanterns "a la Chinois." A dinner in Field's honor at the Metropolitan Hotel feted six hundred with all the luxury a gourmand could imagine.

The following day, the cable again did not work, and landlocked cable operators sent perplexed questions back and forth. Not until 1866, in fact, did Cyrus Field succeed, but in the process he had taken the telegraph far from the painterly aspirations of Morse. A jaguar, a Barnum, a chaotic parade—the Atlantic cable had all the earmarks of the inventor's show writ large. Gentleman that he was, Morse had given his telegraph over to the unruly forces of Carnival.

Morse was never able to invest the telegraph industry with the grandeur he imagined himself to possess, but he did have the chance to dignify another invention that came his way. And as fate would have it, this other invention was also the work of a painter.

In 1839, when Morse was in Paris trying to sell his telegraph, he received word of a new technology that seemed to bear great significance for his profession. Morse fired off a letter and quickly received a reply. Yes, Louis Jacques Mandé Daguerre would be happy to receive him.

The two painters cum inventors met sometime between March 2 and March 9. Morse looked through a microscope at Daguerre's plates and was amazed to be able to read every letter of a street sign. "Rembrandt perfected" was his verdict.

And unfortunately, Rembrandt in ashes. Daguerre returned the favor a few days later and came to see Morse's invention at No. 5 rue Neuve-des-Mathurins. Morse recounted that "while thus employed, the great buildings of the Diorama, with his own house, all his beautiful works, his valuable notes and papers, the labors of years of experiments, were, unknown to him, at that moment the prey of the flames."

The labors of all those years had amounted to a great deal by then. Originally a specialist in trompe l'oeil effects, Daguerre became famous for the sunlit stage he painted for the Paris Opera's production of *Aladdin* in February 1822. Five months later, he unveiled his Diorama, a 350-seat theater at 4 rue Sanson that may have been inspired by Robert Fulton's earlier Panorama on Boulevard Montmartre.

If the Paris Diorama did not survive long enough to be described in English, Augustus Charles Pugin's imitation in Regents Park may serve as a reasonable substitute. This Diorama seated two hundred people in a house that pivoted seventy-three degrees, from one picture to another. The pictures were seen through a 2,800-square-foot window made of calico. Translucent from behind and opaque from the front, the window gave the illusion of being brilliantly backlit. A complex system of pulleys, shutters, cords, and slides varied the intensity, color, and placement of the light. The only drawback was it didn't work when the London fog rolled in. If it was any consolation, the pictures behind the window were painted by Daguerre himself.

An even more magnificent diorama was eventually produced by the land surveyor Thomas Horner at the Regents Park Colosseum. Using an optical telescope invented by the painter Cornelius Varley in 1811, Horner cast a projection that covered 24,000 square feet. The entire spectacle was contained in a building of stucco-covered brick with a dome 115 feet high—30 feet higher than St. Paul's Cathedral. A panorama showed London as seen from the Bull's Eye Chamber in St. Paul's, and could be viewed from below or from the Ascending Room, accessible by London's first hydraulic lift. The audience members were led by lamp-carrying usherettes to their seats, where they sat in darkness (an innovation at the time), and used binoculars to discern many of the details. Byron and Wordsworth acclaimed this spectacular invention and its replicants in other major European cities, encouraging tourists to see them at all costs.

Having revealed a show inventor's predilection for heights, Daguerre joined forces with photography pioneer Nicéphore Niepce on December 14, 1829, and turned his attention to smaller works. Together, the two men generated images exposed by the sun on bitumen, or asphalt, but Niepce never lived to see their collaboration bear fruit. Daguerre continued the effort after his colleague's death, and met with success only by accident. In 1835, he placed his plates in a cabinet, not knowing that a container of mercury inside had a leak in it and was emitting vapor into the enclosed space, thus creating the first daguerrotype.

With his first successful picture in hand in 1837, Daguerre paraded his invention by cart through the streets of Paris, hoping to solicit licenses for its use. The fifty-kilogram machine, which he loaded on a cart, fumed from the iodization process, and the images themselves were visible only under a cloth.

To Parisians already acquainted with the trumpery of Daguerre's Diorama, the daguerrotype seemed like little more than a cheap illusion—until the eminent scientist François Arago endorsed it in 1839, at which point it created nothing short of a sensation. Almost immediately, the Continent became peppered with gentlemen consulting their watches beside their three-legged boxes. Before a year had passed, Daguerre's instruction booklet, which included a description of the device, went to thirty editions and had been translated into eight languages. The description was pirated many times over before the booklet had even gone to press, making the workings of the daguerrotype available to all.

Admittedly, there were drawbacks. When Daguerre tried to take a picture of King Louis-Philippe, the results were disastrous. The king had sat with his face to the sun for five minutes with his hat off—not a discomfort that monarchs often suffered—and even then the image was unsatisfactory. Still, there was no mistaking the import of the invention. Upon seeing his first daguerrotype, the painter Paul Delaroche declared, "From today painting is dead." By 1845, Parisians apparently had been convinced of that, and were buying two thousand cameras and three million plates a year.

Meanwhile, Morse, feeling that his own career in painting was dead, had brought the bright news of the daguerrotype back to New York. In April 1839, he nominated Daguerre for honorary membership in the National Academy; the motion passed easily. Morse also tried his hand at improving the daguerrotype technology, recalling that he had dabbled with a camera obscura back in his Yale days—a desultory bid for priority perhaps. He never arrived at much and had to content himself with teaching the existing process while, though, waiting for his telegraph to be discovered. During this time, he took on a student who would become well known in the years to come. In the end, Mathew Brady may have absorbed more than technical information from Morse, as he was to begin the tradition of taking credit for photographs that others had produced.

Meanwhile, John William Draper, Morse's colleague at New York University, and Alexander Wolcott, a manufacturer of dental supplies, introduced changes that made portraiture slightly less time-consuming for the subject. Wolcott joined forces with John Johnson in March of 1840 to open what may have been the world's first public portrait studio, in rooms 21 and 22 of a building on the corner of Broadway and Chambers.

So far, so good. The daguerrotype had entered the culture with the outer appearance of dignity that Morse, its American godfather, was ever anxious to maintain. But then along came Jean Baptiste François Fauvel-Gouraud with another kind of show altogether.

Stepping off the *British Queen* on September 21, 1839, Fauvel-Gouraud had already spent some years sailing the world, or, as he put it:

> [I had] tasted the "ambrosia of Constance," and hunted the African ostrich at the Cape of Good Hope; breathed the perfumes of the incense upon the burning soil of Yemen; enjoyed the nectar of the coffee upon the sandy plains of Mocha; eaten the dates of Arabia in the tented streets of Muscat; languidly pillowed my head upon the downy carpets of Teheran in the kiosks of Bassora, while in-

haling the rosy attar of the harems beneath the shade of its perfumed acacias; admired the Asiatic splendors of Surat, Bombay, and
Calcutta; hunted the hydrocroax and the paraquet through the for-
ests of Malabar and Coromandel; attended the sacrifice of the Hin-
dostan widow upon the funeral pire of her husband; fished up the
pearls of the ancient Ormus upon the nacreous coasts of Ceylon;
mounted the elephant of Seringapatam; bathed in the sacred waters
of the Ganges; luxuriated in the gaudy palanquin of the rayahs of
Aracan; gathered the spices of the Moluccas in the perfumed groves
of Sumatra; drank the tea of the Celestial Empire at Canton from
the gilded porcelain of Pekin; smoked the exhilerating [sic] opium
in the gold and amber pipe of the conceited mandarin; pursued
the hyperbolical ornithorincus upon the desert shores of Van Die-
men; dreamed of the golden age of Cythera, Paphos, and Amathus,
beneath the Elysian shades of Tahiti; trod upon the silver mines of
Potosi; escaped the perils of Cape Horn; glided like a bird beneath
the beautiful sky of Buenos Ayres, Montevideo, St. Salvador, Rio
Janeiro, and the "faithful Havana"; paid homage to the glorious
shade of Columbus in his gilded chapel; furrowed the liquid tomb
which rolls its mountainous waves above the ruins of Atlantis; tasted
at the Fortunate Isles the honied orange of Teneriffe, and the nec-
tarine wine of Madeira; thrilled with pleasure at the voluptuous
dances of the voluptuous Iberia; and at last visited again the Penates
which I had quitted three years before, and which I was soon again
to leave to encounter successively the ices of two poles, before
visiting, in still happier days of my wandering existence, the ruins
of Carthage and the Colosseum; the antique mosque of St. Sophia;
the tumulus of Achilles, of Ajax, and of Patroclus; the column of
Pompey; the Pyramids of Cairo; the remnants of the Persepolis; the
ruins of Palmyra; the humble tomb of Christ; the palaces of Mon-
tezuma; the majestic ruins of Quito, of Uxmal, and Palenque; until
the time when, guided by a benevolent Providence, I came to burn
my roving wings in this focus of the future liberty of the world,
while awaiting the destined hour when at last, freed from its mortal
envelope, my spirit, taking its last flight, shall depart on its final
voyage.

And now here he was, not even remotely exhausted, "as the pupil
and friend of Daguerre . . . with the charge of introducing to the New
World, the perfect knowledge of . . . The Daguerreotype."

Morse offered Fauvel-Gouraud, who was known variously as Gouraud and even Fanvel-Gouraud, a rent-free room, and on December 4, 1839, the Frenchman gave his first exhibition, which included two images reputedly taken by Daguerre himself. Soon, he was charging one dollar for the public to see his exhibit and lecture. As with Colt's laughing gas comedies, these shows gave off a whiff of the mountebank's medicine. In 1840, while describing how to get as much light as possible into the camera, Gouraud was apt to refer to the daguerrotype subject as "the patient." Dark, sly, and charming, he was a hit with the press.

He was not a hit with Morse, however. As Gouraud continued to exhibit into the early months of 1840, the two came to loggerheads over the course the daguerrotype should take in America, and Morse ended up throwing him out. Gouraud turned around and trounced Morse in the papers, then left for Boston on February 26. When he got there, his exhibition materials were attached by court order. He borrowed money from a man in a hotel and failed to repay it. Somewhere in the midst of this chaotic schedule, he found the time to publish the first photographic manual in the country. Then he promptly left Boston, his rent unpaid, for parts unknown.

It soon developed that Gouraud had never been authorized to represent anyone, much less Daguerre. That did not stop him from resurfacing at 281 Broadway on January 16, 1844, after apocryphal visits to New Orleans and "the faithful Havana," presenting himself as the author of the *Phreno-Mnemo-Technic Dictionary*. While sitting at the edge of Niagara Falls, he declared, he had discovered "the golden key to the Kingdom of the Universe"—that the planets were "ANIMATED BE-INGS, *endowed with passions and feelings*."

This and other revelations provided the material for a series of lectures in New York and Philadelphia in 1844, dedicated to the likes of Horace Greeley, William Cullen Bryant, and Henry Wadsworth Long-fellow. While these lectures did not involve inventions per se, they offer a window onto what his daguerrotype lectures, which went largely undocumented, might have been like.

Night after night, Gouraud rattled off obscure dates from ancient history, solutions to complex mathematical problems, the longest word in the Greek language. A favorite device was to have a child climb onstage and reel off precocious sums. All this, along with tremendous powers of oration, routinely brought down the house. "One of M. Gouraud's lectures," gushed one reporter, "is, even from the point of amusement, a greater treat than many a fashionable drama." Eventually, he was compelled to move his act into larger auditoriums to accommodate the swelling audiences. At a head count of two thousand, these crowds— most of whom were women—were the largest to assemble for a lecture in America at the time.

The drama reached a high point near the end of the Philadelphia lectures, when Gouraud appeared on stage with a letter penned in red ink. This letter, he claimed, contained a threat to murder him—and his wife and children—as payment for his plagiarisms. Greatly distressed, he went on to read aloud from a letter of endorsement signed by numerous New York editors. "He was vehemently applauded," noted the *Philadelphia Spirit of the Times* on May 30, 1844, "after which he fainted from the agitation. Recovering, he went on with his lecture."

Morse and Gouraud would eventually make amends when they ran into one another at Niagara Falls. (Gouraud was taking views of the Falls and, according to Morse, making some improvements in the art.) But it was Gouraud who first popularized the daguerrotype in America, and it was his methods that prevailed.

While European countries required licenses for the taking of daguerrotypes, America placed no such restrictions on the profession. In rural areas, a daguerrotypist could go so far as to pose as a magician before the unsuspecting villagers, "especially," writes the photography historian Robert Taft, "if he had a smattering of phrenology." The cities were no different. Fowler and Wells, still plying their ferocious trade, offered to read characters "from daguerrotypes, ¾ pose preferred."

Gouraud, champion of the daguerrotype and of "phreno-mnemotechnics," had shown the way forward; phrenology, that great revealer of character, had a new partner in crime. By 1846, the association between the daguerrotype and Combe's corrupted philosophy had become so widespread that the general interest editor E. Littell could write, with a backward glance to Samuel Colt and Humphry Davy:

> . . . of all the advantages of this novel art, the aid which it affords to the successful study of human nature, is among the most important. Daguerreotypes properly regarded are the indices of human character. Lavater judged of men by their physiognomies; and in a voluminous treatise has developed the principles by which he was guided. The photograph, we consider to be the grand climacteric of the science . . . It has been said that the inhalation of exhilarating

gas is a powerful artificial agent for disclosing weaknesses of human nature. In reality, however, the sitting for a daguerreotype, far surpasses all other expedients.

What were the particular techniques of the daguerrotype mountebanks? While much of this information has been lost, the methods must have been determined to some extent by the technology itself. Taking from forty seconds to two minutes indoors, and from twenty seconds to a minute and a half in the noonday sun, daguerrotypes were a ready-made test of character. Unlike the snapshot of today, the daguerrotype demanded a great deal of participation from the "patient" to achieve satisfactory results, as Daguerre himself had learned with Louis Philippe.

The physical ordeal alone must have played into the charlatan's designs. The subject, having had the bumps on his head analyzed, would already be on the defensive. Then, sitting before the camera, he would have to ask himself what sort of facial expression and posture he could sustain. As he sat in great discomfort, he would have ample time to feel the lens probe into his soul, slowly drawing out his inner life. He would feel, quite literally, *exposed*. It couldn't be long before he began to question the courage of his convictions. Meanwhile, the "doctor" would disappear into his darkened chamber to perform mysterious functions. The suspense would build until, at long last, the doctor emerged with his nefarious illusion—not a nostrum as quacks had produced before, but a magic mirror, perfect in every detail.

During this procedure, the comic doctor became fused with an earlier figure from commedia dell'arte: the invoker of demonic powers. Understandably, his presence incited fear in some quarters. "The Magnetic Daguerrotype," published in the *New York Sunday Courier* in the early years of the daguerrotype, expressed this concern in a way that has since become a cliché. A Poe-like nightmare, this story involves a mysterious scientist who captures a woman's image through an "electro-galvanic" or "magnetic" action. From then on, the woman is haunted by the scientist's ability to see her innermost thoughts, even as the scientist becomes plagued by this seemingly living portrait. The power to steal souls had been born.

And yet people demanded to be robbed at the drop of a hat. By 1841, New York City boasted one hundred daguerrotype studios, each set up after the fashion of an elegant parlor. By 1853, there were thirty-seven parlors on Broadway alone, and a town on the banks of the Hudson, one mile south of Newburgh, had been named Daguerreville.

No doubt people liked the daguerrotype because it allowed them to indulge their fantasies. Photography brought realism to the world, to be sure. But posing for a daguerrotype also meant dressing up in exotic costumes and standing before fantastic backdrops. And as the subject overcame his initial trepidation, he did more than suspend his disbelief. He became *part* of the disbelief. With the daguerrotype, the lowliest citizen could suddenly become a zany (albeit a severely disquieted one) in the doctor's play. He could take part in the technological spectacle as one of its characters.

Daguerre's reaction to all this can best be gauged by a portrait of him taken by Charles R. Meade in 1848 and now on exhibit at the Smithsonian. It shows the Frenchman with long tousled white hair and a moustache, more bohemian than bourgeois. His hand is propping up his head, giving him a wistful appearance, but it is the eyes that captivate. Warm yet penetrating, with a frown of sadness framing them, they look back at the machine he has made, which in turn is making the image we see. Is he in our world, or are we in his?

As for Morse, his features gradually grew sterner as the wild daguerrists held forth, and he began to take on the appearance of a titan from an earlier age. His center had not held. Riches and fame were his, and his telegraph lines festooned the skylines of the nation, but the next generation of show inventors would not emulate him. They would follow instead in the footsteps of Colt and Gouraud, exalting the ways of the mountebank.

The final collapse into disorder was all too apparent by the 1850s, when this patent-medicine advertisement began running in the *New York Times:*

> MORSE'S INVIGORATING ELIXIR IS PRESENTED as a phenomenon in the materia medica hitherto unheard of—a stimulant without a reaction. . . . Dr. Morse, whose name is an undisputed authority in science, discovered the production in Arabia, where his attention was excited by the wonderfully invigorating effects it produced on the natives.

When Morse could be made over as an ordinary medicine man without his consent, the tradition of the noble inventor, like history painting itself, was dead.

## Chapter Six

# THUNDERING CARAVANS

In the middle of the night on December 15, 1836, a fire broke out in the Patent Office. It began in the cellar, where fuel was stored, and soon awoke a messenger who slept on the premises. But the alarm came too late. The flames spread quickly through the tinderbox of a building, and by the time the firemen arrived, an estimated 7,000 models, 9,000 drawings, and 230 books, not to mention countless applications, correspondences, and copies of issued patents, had been consumed.

Disastrous as it was, the conflagration was timely. In recent years, the government had taken stock of the prevailing patent practices and found them wanting. Dr. John D. Craig, who replaced Dr. William Thornton as patent commissioner in 1829, had proven to be a serious liability. After haranguing inventors for six years with a vehemence that would have shocked Jefferson, he stood accused of destruction of public correspondence, ignorance of the law, and rude conduct. He was dismissed from office on January 31, 1835.

Senator John Ruggles of Maine was among those who saw the moment as an opportunity, and at his prodding, Congress instituted what came to be known as "the American system," on July 4, 1836. There would be no more imperious patent chiefs. The three-man board of old was reinstituted, with a commissioner who would appoint clerks, draftsmen, a machinist, and an examiner. A thirty dollar application fee was fixed by law, and appeals by inventors would be permitted. To prevent another Jefferson from dominating the proceedings, the board was empowered to determine the feasibility of an invention's usefulness, rather than the certainty of it. Perhaps most important, patents would no longer be simply filed. If another invention already covered the claims, the application would be rejected.

The sum effect of this overhaul was to make inventors more competitive. For the first time, they had real incentive to innovate, and they could take their claims to the public with some assurance. Moreover, the new system encouraged them to improve on existing patents—to diversify and to create their own niches. No longer did they have to battle a stringent governmental authority. In effect, the Patent Office became transparent, leaving inventors free to pit themselves against each other.

Come the 1840s then, the gathering Jacksonian spirit and the revamped patent structure combined to create a new, grassroots breed. These show inventors had none of the timidity or archness of their predecessors. Even the shyest of them could emerge with the bellowing voice of the old commedia dell'arte character Pulcinella, who was wont to hurl such epithets as, "You brothel-bred shithead, you and your brother and your sister!" Indeed, the show inventors of the 1840s integrated theatrical tradition and invention more completely than any of their compatriots before them. In the process, they made the mechanical spectacle more vibrant, more diverse and more likely to wreak havoc on the existing order.

Cyrus Hall McCormick is a textbook study of a mouse who learned to roar. Certainly, there was nothing in his background to suggest that he would become a pioneer of the modern American business system, or that he would open the West by making its prairies arable. His native Walnut Grove was a sleepy hamlet typical of antebellum Virginia. Farmers generally sold their crops in nearby Staunton or Lynchburg. Occasionally, a Democratic politician would hold forth on the courthouse steps in Lexington, some eighteen miles away. Beginning in 1827, Rockbridge County began to hold county fairs that displayed unusual vegetables, merino sheep, and hogs "fit only for soap." Otherwise, the plantations produced tobacco; the seasons came and went.

As a child, Cyrus disliked field work, though he loved horses and was considered the best rider in the area. Sometimes, he would ride off to meet paramours, but his strict Presbyterian upbringing prevented him from straying too far afield. When his sister went off to school, he stayed home and helped his father, Robert, around the farm. Beginning in 1816, this work included a protracted attempt by father and son to build a reaper.

The need for such a machine was obvious enough. At the time, it took scores of workers and just as many sickles to reap grain at harvest time, and the workers tended to offset their hard labor with generous amounts of hard liquor. But the development of a practical reaper was also tough going. By 1831, no fewer than forty-seven versions of such a machine were on the market, all of them subject to glaring defects. When Robert McCormick added his to the growing list of failures, Cyrus took up the cause on his own. Perhaps his father had been exerting too much control over the project, because soon afterward—only weeks before Joseph Henry demonstrated his telegraph to a roomful of students—Cyrus was able to produce a working reaper.

In its time, the McCormick reaper was a bewildering visage, as if Oliver Evans's Orukter Amphibolos had been transported into the Appalachians and set loose in the fields. Drawn rather than pushed (as some other models were), it was attached to a horse by shafts, with a large wheel and a cacophonous array of gears, wire teeth, an eight-ribbed horizontal reel, and a vibrating sickled knife clattering behind.

Curiously, young Cyrus didn't run out and start promoting his new invention right away, even though it was ready to be used by the harvest of 1831. A full two years passed before he demonstrated it before a crowd of skeptical locals and got mention for his troubles in the *Lexington Union*. Even then, he didn't bother to patent it until he read about another reaper, invented by a man named Obed Hussey, in *Mechanics' Magazine* of New York.

McCormick wrote a public letter to the magazine, telling Hussey in no uncertain terms who the real inventor of the reaper was. That done, he again lost interest in his reaper and began developing a new kind of iron-smelting furnace with his father. This project occupied their time from 1835 until well into the 1840s. But by 1837, money had become a problem, and the McCormicks turned to family friend William Massie for help.

Massie was a pivotal figure for many people in the area, not least for the McCormicks. Living just over the Blue Ridge Mountains from them, he had an eight-thousand-acre plantation with a flour mill and 130 slaves, and was influential in Virginia politics. Eminent as he was, he also believed in McCormick. Early on in the furnace venture, he lent the inventor $600, which was repaid in six weeks. In 1839, he offered his own holdings as security when McCormick wrote a bad check for $2,500. He continued to offer his services after more drafts were protested. By 1841, Massie's security amounted to $4,600, yet his enthusiasm never flagged throughout their ill-fated venture.

It was during Massie's stewardship of the furnace project that Cyrus McCormick underwent a change. In 1839, he returned to the reaper and started promoting it with a vengeance. Suddenly, it was as if another man were going by his name. He advertised. He organized. He began to do things no one had thought of before. Within a span of fifteen years, he metamorphosed from a backwoods southern mechanic into a nationally celebrated inventor and a raging Pulcinella.

What caused McCormick to change so radically? No less an expert than his biographer was stumped when he wrote: "In view of his slight acquaintance with the world outside his own State, his small experience in salesmanship, and his meager capital, it is remarkable that Cyrus McCormick so soon worked out by trial and error a business practice which served him so well. His methods of publicity were so forward looking that they are in use to-day without essential change."

McCormick's rise can be credited in part to the nascent spirit of competition; even in such a remote terrain as Walnut Grove, the iron-furnace inventor would have known of the changes going on in Washington. But his transformation owed just as much to the long, circuitous train that carried the spirit (and very nearly the person) of Phineas T. Barnum to the Valley of Virginia.


In 1836, when Barnum quit Aaron Turner's Columbian Circus, he set out on his own for a while before returning to New York with a vow (broken many times over) never to go on the road again. Meanwhile, Turner continued on, taking his three master riders, two clowns, a juggler, and a duo of comic singers through the backroads of the South.

Turner was one of many farmers from Westchester County, New York, who, in the early nineteenth century, turned to show business rather than attending county fairs, and became rich in the process. The first of them, Hachiliah Bailey, set the trend in 1808 when, instead of buying a merino sheep, he bought an elephant—the second ever to walk on American soil. Bailey's exhibitions of Old Bet, as she was called, were so successful that his neighboring farmers quickly followed suit. Many were Bailey's kin, or putative kin, and the show world grew thick with Baileys. Among the illustrious founders of the Westchester dynasty were Lewis Bailey, Solomon Bailey, James Purdy Bailey, Joseph Todd Bailey, Fred H. Bailey, George Bailey, George Fox Bailey, and finally, the famous James A. Bailey, whose real name was James T. Mc-Guinness, but who was allowed to use the name when he moved to Westchester from Detroit. (James T. Nixon, who started as a groomer for Aaron Turner, continued this tradition by having his apprentices take his name.)

These Westchester farmers, like McCormick, were expert equestrians, and in joining this passion with their newfound career in show business, they were following in the footsteps of Philip Astley, founder of the modern circus, who raced his horses in chariots at the Royal Amphitheatre of Arts. But where Astley was happily settled in London, these showmen traveled. And traveled and traveled and traveled. By the early 1830s, when the source of the Mississippi was still unknown and Chicago was still a ragtag assortment of shacks, the farmers of Westchester had at least twenty "rolling shows" on the road, from Maine to Michigan, New York to Washington, D.C. A single tour in 1842 covered 2,482 miles and 85 stands, as the engagements were called, ranging from big cities to unmarked road crossings.

Especially popular among these shows were the menageries, which were not circuses, but exhibitions of caged animals and trainers renowned for their derring-do. The most famous animal trainer of the era was Isaac Van Amburgh, who was portrayed by one artist as an idyllic poet lazing about splendiferously among his bestiary. The image was somewhat disingenuous, though. As much as his menagerie act was depicted as gentility itself, the real story involved tremendous physical prowess: in person, Van Amburgh was quick to bash a tiger over the head with a crowbar if it misbehaved. He was also the first to thrust his head inside a lion's mouth, an act that soon became standard circus repertoire.

Specious as these early showbills were, the Westchester men had good reason for keeping brute force out of their advertising. Where circuses were considered immoral and met with resistance in their travels, the menageries were seen as educational, and as long as that view held, they could promote their acts freely in backwoods country towns. And so they did. Given the go-ahead, they saturated their routes a month in advance with immense posters, presaging an arrival that would be accompanied by musical bands and a great deal of commotion. The *Brattleboro Messenger* described the typical scenario:

Tremendous showbills, on which the whole array is set forth large as life (some animals it is said even larger) proclaim everywhere the coming entertainment; and to cap the whole we have a grand procession in which man and beast, some on foot and some on wheels, martial music, trains of carriage, cars and omni-buses; clouds of dust and oceans of popular amusement, all lend their aid.

The operative word is *everywhere*. There were twelve menageries on the road in 1834—enough to cause their itineraries to overlap by acci-dent while still leaving fertile territory uncovered. So in January 1835, after returning from their tours, five menagerie men sat down at the Elephant Hotel in Somers, New York (where Hachiliah Bailey had housed Old Bet and subsequently raised a statue in her memory), to draw up the articles of association for the Zoological Institute.

The stated purpose of the Zoological Institute was "to more generally diffuse and promote the knowledge of natural history and gratify rational curiosity." Outwardly, that sounded a lot like the charter of the Smith-sonian, but the reality was quite different. The Zoological Institute served to draw nine menageries under the control of one organization. One hundred and thirty-five signatures were collected from investors, for a capitalization of $329,325. The institute took over the lease of 37 Bowery, where winter shows were held. Most important, it worked out routes for the different menageries. One would take New York State, another Pennsylvania, and so on.

Nothing like this had existed in the United States up until that time. The *Gibbons v. Ogden* decision of 1824 had prevented any one steam-boat company from holding a monopoly. A man named Levi Pease had operated something of a postal network for the federal government in the first decade of the nineteenth century. The Yankee peddlers had covered the territories in a loose and leaderless confederation. But this centralized web—which moved right up to and beyond the frontier—was, for all intents and purposes, a cartel.

To secure its routes, the Zoological Institute, like acting troupes of the day, would send out advance men. But booking a play was one thing, housing a caravan of exotic animals another. The advance men had to secure contracts with local proprietors—innkeepers or whoever else might be likely to put up with the inconveniences involved. To them also fell the task of standing off against insurgent rival menageries. They were a persistent lot. On the road, the Zoological Institute crews came to be known as the Flatfoots, from such outbursts as "We put our foot down flat. We shall play New York State."

Getting a town booked almost always involved bringing a local in on the action—an informal agent of sorts to work as a liaison to the community. And as it turned out, one such agent for the Flatfoots was Cyrus McCormick's creditor, William Massie.

In 1836, states like South Carolina, Georgia, and Virginia had had only minimal exposure to the rolling shows when Waring, Raymond & Company, one of the Flatfoot subsidiaries, was given orders to descend upon the South. Starting from Maryland, the showmen papered the Virginian countryside with gargantuan posters announcing the "Grand Exhibition from the Zoological Institute, Baltimore," then thundered into the small towns—through Buckingham, Curdsville, Physic Springs, and Lynchburg. And on June 14, 1837, not long after Massie announced a visit to the McCormicks to see how their furnace was progressing, the Grand Exhibition came to a tiny stand, shown in their advertising records as Massie's Mills.

The moment would have been hard to miss. A caravan of thirty to forty wagons and ninety to one hundred horses, heralded by the Washington Military Band, rolled into Massie's plantation and erected a tent 100 by 300 feet wide near the mill at the center of the property. Locals who entered this big top could gawk at Solomon Bailey's collection of eight leopards, six lions, five panthers, two tigers, two elephants (Hannibal and Flora), and a rhinoceros.

The New York Travelling Museum and Exhibition of Fine Arts, an added attraction, was set up in a separate tent, displaying wax figures, paintings, stuffed birds, serpents, and mineral and fossil specimens for those who would pay the fee—satisfaction guaranteed or your money back. Aaron Turner's Columbian Circus, which officially joined up with this show by September, was very probably there as well. It was the biggest show on the road that year, the largest ever seen in the South, and an ostentatious display of the Zoological Institute's prosperity.

Who were these people, and what were they doing in a lazy backwater of Virginia in 1837? If Cyrus McCormick, who lived only a short ride away and owed this menagerie's sponsor thousands of dollars, did not ask these questions, he certainly did a good imitation of understanding the answers.

For starters, in 1839, he returned to his reaper, a horse-drawn oddity

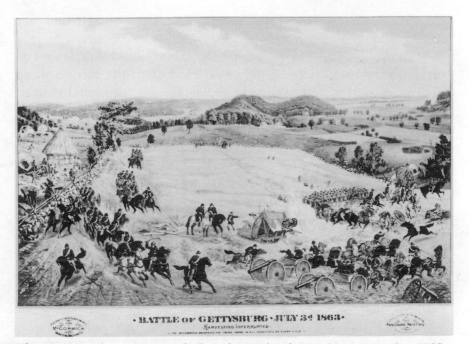

The McCormick reaper enmeshed in the Battle of Gettysburg. Printed in 1883, this poster was considered a new low in taste even by those close to the inventor. *The State Historical Society of Wisconsin (#S30535)*

that, like the menageries and unlike his furnace, featured an animal. He also began papering the countryside with posters, attaching them to snake fences and village tie-rails. McCormick took care in these posters not to show sweaty, disgruntled farmers picking stones out of their new-fangled contraptions, though this would have been a fairly accurate representation. Instead, he depicted top-hatted gentlemen undertaking reaping as if it were a pleasant diversion, much like the posters that showed Isaac Van Amburgh reposing among the wild beasts. It seemed to be an advantageous gambit, as McCormick sold his first Virginia Reaper in 1840.

By 1842, McCormick had introduced the money-back guarantee, another feature borrowed from curiosity exhibitors. "I warrant them superior to Hussey's and all the others," he trumpeted from his stronghold in Walnut Grove. "I have a reputation to uphold. Let a farmer take both and keep the one which he likes best."

As McCormick began to tread beyond the Valley of Virginia in his quest for publicity, he discovered he was not alone. Plenty of others had invented reapers. Not only that, but the spirit of competition—and the spirit of the rolling shows—had descended on them as well, and they felt no compunction in challenging one another to contests.

Such contests had much to commend them. If an inventor showed his reaper by itself, it could always be lumped in the merino sheep category of oddities. But given a choice between one reaper and another, the audience became involved; the contest, unlike a solo demonstration, had heroes and villains, favorites and outsiders. As with Peter Cooper's race, it gave disorder a structure. What's more, these contests were held every year, which made for an ongoing climate of competition. Inventors learned what worked and what did not, and attempted new variations accordingly. Audiences, meanwhile, were held in suspense as they waited for the next harvest ritual—enlivened now by the stamping and rearing of horses—to develop into a raucous farce.

The buildup to a reaper contest tended to be dramatic in and of itself. Challenges would be advertised in newspapers and agricultural journals long in advance of the event. The long pompous claims contained in these ads sounded very much like a ringleader touting his act, or like Pulcinella flexing his tongue. This was just as true of McCormick's rivals as it was of himself. "McCormick warrants his machine to cut 1½ acres of wheat in one hour," wrote one competitor, no doubt toning down his language for publication. "Will it? Yes! How? Have everything in the best of order, and then drive on as hard as you can for one hour. The next hour will have to take care of itself."

The contests invariably matched the tenor of these boasts. Often they were held under the auspices of an agricultural society, which provided a panel of judges. Food and drink could be expected by farmers turning up for the show, and it was by no means rare for contestants to hire musical bands (though probably nothing so fancy as the Washington Military Band) to rouse the sympathies of the crowd. The prize was usually money, a ribbon, or a medal, which could be announced in the next advertisement, with praises attached to the winner and rank insults to the loser.

As might be expected from the ballyhoo, a good amount of stylizing went on during the actual show. The demonstration reapers were highly polished and often better made than the ones the farmers would buy. With specially trained drivers (read riding masters) and horses trained to move swiftly when they heard the machine behind them (read animal tricks), the reaping was done at top speed, with an abandon that a farmer could never hope to achieve on his own. In Belvidere, Illinois, in 1854, some contestants went so far as to give brandy to their exhausted horses in order to keep them racing in hot weather.

Indeed, all kinds of trouble attended reaper competitions. They could only take place during the few short weeks when harvesting was done, and they were anticlimactic at times, since a rock could catch in one reaper and end the festivities in a moment. It was not uncommon for judges to be bought off, or to own a reaper that was represented in the contest. Even when that wasn't the case, they might disagree on the rules and take to arguing, and bring in volunteers to help settle the debate. One such ruling did not end until there were seventeen judges in the fray. In some areas, the judges gave up altogether and the winner was determined by the loudest ovation.

None of this boded much in the way of reliable outcomes, so contestants often looked for ways to prolong the excitement. One year, it was suggested in all seriousness that a marathon competition follow the harvest north, not stopping until the last oats were in the barns of Wisconsin. While this never happened, a six-day tournament did materialize in Geneva, New York, in which nine reapers and seven mowers competed with dynamometers attached.

As it turned out, one of the first adversaries McCormick took on was Obed Hussey, the man he had tried to warn away in print. The contest took place on July 27, 1843. McCormick drove his reaper through a field in Richmond just before a light rain fell. Faced with a stretch of wet wheat, Hussey lost badly. Two more contests held in better weather, although just as complicated by other variables, brought about the same result.

This was a big score for McCormick, who sold twenty-nine machines that year, and a big defeat for Hussey, who retreated from Virginia for the time being. But McCormick did not put all his stock in contests. On the contrary, he tended to avoid the scrutiny of dynamometers and corrupt judges whenever possible. He didn't win his first award until 1844—at a county fair in Hamilton, Ohio, on the basis of testimonials from New York and Virginia—long after others had brought theirs home. Yet in the end, he was more successful than any of his competitors, because to his braggadocio he added the *inner structure* of show business.

By 1845, McCormick had traveled the country widely—as widely as the Zoological Institute itself—and was advertising in farm papers in Chicago, Detroit, Columbus, and northern New York. In that same year, he hired his cousin J. B. McCormick to rove the lower Ohio Valley into Tennessee and Missouri, looking for local agents who could sell the Virginia Reaper. This unpleasant relative wrote letters back to Walnut Grove that were as vituperative as they were informative — fitting enough for the world's first traveling sales representative.

McCormick was soon employing regular traveling agents (though one is tempted to call them *advance men*, since they arranged both the advertising and the subsequent contests) to cover great portions of the United States. By 1848, H. G. Hubbard, A. G. Hager, and J. L. Wilson each had their allotted territory, in which they were responsible for finding and appointing local agents, and for coordinating their activities with those of the company back in Virginia. Like the Zoological Institute, McCormick had spread a centralized network across the nation, up to and beyond the frontier.

In the end, McCormick surpassed the menagerie men and established some business practices of his own. His local agents, for example, were responsible for considerably more than housing and hay. They had to maintain a sample machine, canvass wheat districts, deliver reapers and instruct in their operation, stock spare parts, do repair work and field operation when necessary, make reports, collect money on notes, and distribute advertising.

From this dizzying array of responsibilities grew McCormick's franchise system, in which retailers, having mastered the intricacies of the business, bought the territorial rights to sell his machines. In a nod to the Baileys of the menagerie world, McCormick also began to license out his name to manufacturers who made their own reapers, so that anyone could become a McCormick — with the essential difference that McCormick's name cost its bearer money.

In a curious twist on the painted caravans of the menageries, McCormick also began to paint the components of his machines in different colors, "showing the connection of the different parts with one another that they can be readily put together by the farmer." This practice — still used by many a manufacturer today — neatly fused flash with function, even as it reassured farmers that they were smart enough to do some of McCormick's work for him.

McCormick's marketing and promotional campaigns were just as sophisticated. Agents attached posters to fences as before, but they also distributed them from astride a horse and had them used as wrapping for the products sold at country stores. Eventually, they adopted the custom of riding up to the customer's gate in a horse and buggy, looking very much like the gentlemen in the company showbills. Farmers who became fixated on the exorbitant price (about $130 in the 1850s) were softened with an installment plan—a down payment for shipping, with the rest to be paid within the year—unaware, no doubt, that this beautiful horse and buggy had been procured from an unfortunate customer who had failed to meet the schedule.

By 1848, all of these tactics had made a quiet Presbyterian farmboy every bit as successful as the menagerie men of the North. Having at last paid off his debts to William Massie, McCormick was in a position to leave Walnut Grove for a more advantageous location. It makes sense that he chose Chicago, the geographic heart of the nation, as headquarters for the business known today as International Harvester. After all, a year earlier, two Westchester showmen named Ed and Jerry Mabie had moved to Delavan, Wisconsin, a small town only forty-odd miles to the northwest. Other showmen followed, and Delavan developed into the circus capital of the country, a title it kept until some years after the Civil War.

So the spiral turned, from menageries to business and back. In 1881, three rolling shows joined together and announced the fact as "Centralization of All That is Great in the Amusement Realm" and a "Trinity of the Three Grand Animal Collections of Earth—Eight Million Dollars Invested."

Meanwhile, much to the chagrin of those around him, McCormick celebrated the fiftieth anniversary of his first reaper demonstration with a showbill that depicted the armies at Gettysburg battling around his original machine. A rough equivalent today would be a television commercial in which a toothsome actress enjoys the beverage of her choice while the Vietnam War rages around her.

Here was the mountebank asserting himself with impunity. McCormick's spiritual ancestor, Pulcinella, had once closed his soliloquies by announcing that he was "Prince and lord of everything/Lord of the land and the main." McCormick, an equal champion of bad taste, chose the caption: "The McCormick Maintains the Front Rank in All Contests on Every Field."

A centralized network, poster saturation, local agents, money-back guarantees, musical bands, trained riders, and exaggerated claims— McCormick was not the only rural inventor to feel the draw of these methods. The campaigns of the Zoological Institute and the tempo of the times had breathed new life into the public demonstrations of the heartlands, and in the 1840s, agricultural fairs went considerably beyond the hawking of unusual vegetables. But inventors in such venues were markedly more successful to the degree that they incorporated the techniques of the menagerie men—and no one incorporated more of them than Cyrus McCormick did. Between 1839 and 1848, he wove almost every single method used by the Zoological Institute into his business.

The payoff was clear enough. Unlike his competitors, McCormick had not been content simply to demonstrate a device and be done with it; he had learned how the show worked—and then taken it a step further. His "deep" showmanship won over many a farmer who might otherwise have balked at this strange and noisy invention, and as the reaper cultivated the prairies of the West—before the arrival of the railroads—McCormick tamed nature just as surely as Isaac Van Amburgh pacified his errant tigers.

Indeed, the overwhelming impact of McCormick's methods begs the question whether he learned his tricks directly from the Flatfoots on Massie's plantation back in 1837, as they stood gossiping around the stake-and-chain wagon after the show. Both McCormick's and Massie's collected papers are silent on the subject, but the English critics seemed to be acknowledging his debt to the prototypical menagerie man, Phillip Astley, when they derided the McCormick reaper at the London Crystal Palace as "a cross between an Astley chariot, a wheelbarrow and a flying machine."

Barnum, too, seemed to be paying his respects in 1851, when he exhibited the Grand Moving Picture of the Crystal Palace (admission twenty-five cents), as "a brilliant chronicle of our success on the great battlefield of rural industry." This exhibit included a representation of the McCormick reaper, which had just defeated Obed Hussey's machine at the Crystal Palace to win the Council Medal, the highest honor of a highly honorable exhibition.

Of course, inventor's shows were good for Barnum, too, and by the early 1850s, he was increasingly relying on them to bolster his own career. In addition to exhibiting the Grand Moving Picture, he became involved in a clock factory and a sewing machine company. He took over six agricultural fairs in Fairfield County, Connecticut, where reaper contests were a staple feature. And in a stunt curiously reminiscent of the great reaper contests, he tricked up an elephant and had it pull a plow across one of his fields (making sure it was visible from the trains that passed nearby). In fact, Barnum had become so adept at promoting inventions that when a new director was needed at America's first industrial exhibition, he was the only real candidate for the job.

The Exhibition of the Industry of All Nations turned out to be a tall order even for him. Costing at least $600,000 to produce, it had brought in only $330,000 two months after opening day in the fall of 1853. The location—today the site of Bryant Park in midtown Manhattan—was then a good half hour from the center of town, out in the boondocks really. Admittedly, the overhead was low: the land had been rented for only a dollar a year. But the spending habits of the organizers looked fishy in other areas. For some reason, the architect had been unable to prevent his many-domed, Greco-American building from leaking when it rained. Then there was the name. Nobody even bothered to call the event by its official title. They called it the Crystal Palace, and unfortunately, there had already been one of those.

A royal affair in every sense of the word, the original Crystal Palace, held in London in 1851, was a tough act to follow. Its pedigree stretched back to 1760, when the Royal Society of Arts, Manufactures and Commerce held the first of many public art exhibitions. While these exhibitions were ostensibly meant only for the display of fine art, one exhibitor was Robert Barker, inventor of the panorama that Robert Fulton had shown in Paris. Barker's enormous paintings-in-the-round of the battle of Copenhagen, the fleet at Spithead, and the town of Constantinople hinted that art exhibitions might soon extend to more inventorly pursuits.

And so they did. After Francis Wishaw held two small industrial exhibitions in London in December 1844 and January 1845, the call went out for a much larger event, in which prizes would be awarded for "industrial products embodying artistic design." That remained the charter for the Crystal Palace exhibition. "To wed mechanical skill with high art," said the president of the Royal Society of the Arts, "is a task worthy of the Society of Arts and directly in the path of its duty."

Sir Joseph Paxton lived up to the standard when he erected the famous Crystal Palace building. An immense cathedral of iron and glass, it covered more than 20 acres, its length corresponding to the year—1851 feet. The roof was fitted with 18,392 panes of glass in one week by eighty men. When it opened its doors on May Day, it greeted the first international gathering in the West to be held for peaceful purposes, giving a powerful suggestion that industrial art could be an agent of peace.

The day was sunny and mild, and "a sea of heads extended over the whole of St. James's Park, along Constitution-hill, through Knightsbridge, and Rotten-row . . ." As the queen approached the main entrance of the exhibition, the scene

> became inexpressibly animated; the cannon stationed on the banks of the Serpentine, from their "brazen throats," sent forth a thundering welcome, emulated by the joyous shouts of the applauding multitude; while "the merry bells rang round," the union-jack was displayed in triumphant exultation, from every elevated point, to greet the entrance of her Majesty within the precincts of the glittering palace.

Inside, the hopes of its organizers were satisfied many times over. To be fair, the exhibition did have its share of absurdities. The Man of Steel, made of seven thousand pieces of metal, expanded from scale to gigantic proportions. A special set of twelve pairs of scissors, collectively weighing half a grain, could only be seen under a microscope. Those desiring a more civilized means of opening oysters could appreciate a device called an ostracide. But the general effect was one of Old World splendor, as Russia, France, and Italy all opened their luxurious stores of tapestries, sculptures, and paintings.

The American inventors who attended this munificent, magnificent, and otherwise transcendent event came off like rude relatives who were too smart to be ignored. Colt showed five hundred of his fabulous revolvers and doled out free brandy. A locksmith named Alfred C. Hobbs stunned crowds by picking the famous Bramah & Company lock, believed until then to be "as impregnable as the Gibraltar." McCormick's reaper, as noted, fought back ridicule to win the Council Medal. Morse was there to show off his telegraph, though presumably at a safe distance from Joseph Henry, who played an administrative role for the U.S. contingent. Providing backup for Morse was his Daguerreian student, Mathew Brady, who took home the prize for daguerrotypes.

By the time it was over, the London Crystal Palace was a success for everybody involved. "The philosopher and the savage stood side by side," wrote a chronicler of World's Fairs, "the accomplished artist and the rude boor alike were free to choose, 'a local habitation,' and might each with equal advantage, hope to acquire a 'name'; from the wondrous calculating machine, down to the simplest toy." More than 100,000 visitors a day came during its peak, and the total profit was 200,000 pounds.

The material legacy in England was evident in the institutions that grew out of the Crystal Palace: the Albert Hall, the Royal College of Music, the Victoria and Albert Museum. The philosophical effect, meanwhile, was to make everyone else want to hold an exhibition of their own. France learned to excel at such affairs, beginning with its Universal Exhibitions of 1855 and 1867. In 1853, Ireland gamely tried its hand at the exhibition business with a structure on the lawn of the Royal Dublin Society. Built mostly of wood, "the general idea it gave," wrote one wag, "was of five Brobdignagian vegetable marrows laid side by side." That same year, America jumped on the bandwagon, too.

If the New York Crystal Palace wasn't exactly Brobdignagian, it wasn't an exemplar on the order of the original Crystal Palace, either. Everything about the London show—from its aristocratic sponsorship to the carefully choreographed entrance of the queen—was coordinated to give a unified impression of national might. No such preparations had been made in New York. As the U.S. government failed to nationalize its railroads and its telegraph, so too did it leave its industrial exhibition to the cacophonies of the moment. Thus, while the pundits were busy comparing the New York Crystal Palace to its London counterpart, the common folk were comparing it to the other things they might see that day.

In the New York of the 1850s, this amounted to quite a lot. Tuttle's Curiosity Shop, a "resort of pleasure" at 345 Broadway, advertised itself as a must for anyone visiting the Crystal Palace. O. S. Fowler could be found lecturing on his inestimable phrenological findings at Houston and Allen streets, or at the corner of Hudson and Grove. "Jones' Pantoscope" promised "a magnificent painting from 1,500 daguerrotypes," and Godfrey Frankenstein's Panorama of the Niagara Falls was forever threatening to leave the city. Even more worrisome, in the early part of November, the Washington Circus opened on the corner of Thirty-ninth Street and Sixth Avenue, only *one block* from the Crystal Palace, and charged a mere quarter for admission, against the industrial exhibition's fifty cents. Of course, Barnum provided some of the competition, too, as his American Museum continued to put on "prize moral dramas" such as *Orphan's Dream* and the newly published smash sensation, *Uncle Tom's Cabin*.

But far and away the most serious rival was the Twenty-Sixth Annual Fair of the American Institute, which opened on October 10, 1853.

Filling the rotunda, galleries, stage, and dressing rooms of Castle Gardens with inventions and wonders entirely from the United States, the Fair threatened to steal the show entirely.

"It is generally understood," wrote a reporter for the *New York Times* on October 11, "that the present Fair will not be inferior to its predecessors, although a competitor with the Crystal Palace. Many ingenious inventors have reserved their models for the present occasion, more confident from the familiarity with the latter than the former." The writer, tipping his hand, went so far as to pronounce that, with the American Institute of that year, "[w]e may now call our great Republic the *Constitution Mechanique.*"

In the fall of 1853, while the Crystal Palace made the best of its furs ("these very beautiful inventions"), its furniture, and its china vases, the American Institute held plowing matches on the plank road to Coney Island and performances by the MacDougal brothers, who astonished crowds by assembling their portable houses in nine minutes, start to finish. Day after day, the *Times* favored the American Institute by many column inches.

So inventors were not the only ones to be pitted against one another in the pre–Civil War years. Entire exhibitions would have to vie for attention, too. Naturally, the organizers of the Crystal Palace adapted to the situation and, as time went by, began to emphasize excitement over efficiency.

The Southern Belle, a steam engine from Alabama that ran all the machines in the Hall of Machinery, was both the centerpiece of the show and the paragon of this tendency. One visitor described it as "very showy and (at present) very useless. No shop would ever dream of making or buying such an engine for use. It would keep one man busy the whole time just to keep it bright and clean." Other exhibits were criticized for their "extra gew-gaw show, such as some exhibitors seem to think make their articles more attractive." Rather than applying the lofty principles of painting to industry, Americans were inclined to apply the paint itself.

In years to come, this fetishizing of American machines would grow stronger. A semiportable steam engine put on display at the Centennial Exhibition of 1876 represented what may have been the apex of this garishness—its boiler was bright blue, its base maroon, its pipes black, and its rivet heads bronze. (A steam engine meant to be assembled at home perhaps?)

One reporter visiting from Great Britain summed up the puzzlement of other nations observing the phenomenon from afar:

> Ornament as a characteristic of engineering practice in America is one of which it is hard to speak comparatively. It is a peculiarity almost wholly their own, and it is extremely difficult to understand how in a people so practical in most things, there is maintained a tolerance of the grotesque ornaments and gaudy colors, which as a rule rather than an exception distinguish American machines.

When Barnum took over the Crystal Palace, he did anything but try to stem the rising tide of garishness. On the contrary, he designed the attractions to be even more exciting, and by extension, even more memorable. He made sure that the opening day of the "Reincarnation" filled the entire front page of the *New York Times*. He hired the balloonist John Wise to make an ascension and drop "News From The Skies" from ten thousand feet. He put on "Musical Congresses," more commonly known as the Monster Concerts, in which the popular French conductor Louis Antoine Jullien attempted to conquer fifteen hundred performers. As legend has it, he also introduced sex into the mechanical spectacle by setting a woman named the "Lady in Red" in the shadow of the "showy and useless" Southern Belle.

When none of this succeeded in drawing the crowds, Barnum brought the American Institute into the Crystal Palace, eliminating the major source of competition. Still, the receipts continued to dwindle. Finally, when the organizers tried to saddle him with their old debts, he got out altogether. His last recommendation—that the lavish structure be rebuilt on Boston Common, where robust walk-in traffic could be expected—was ignored.

Afterward, Barnum played down his involvement entirely, declaring simply that the "dead could not be raised." Others concurred, and the exhibition has been almost universally mourned ever since. Yet Barnum's show outshone the queen's in at least one respect: The London Crystal Palace, however glorious, did not unveil any new inventions; the fare under its fabled roofs was there to show off the established bounty of the civilized world. Barnum, on the other hand, was able to speed an invention into the world with an eye-grabbing debut.

In May of 1854, Elisha Graves Otis had been advertising his safety elevator for six months, with barely a ripple of interest from the public.

When Barnum engaged Elisha Graves Otis to demonstrate his safety elevator at the New York Crystal Palace in 1854, the inventor gave the audience their money's worth. The first commercial safety elevator was installed in 1857, in the E. V. Haughwout building on the corner of Broome and Broadway in New York City. *Otis Elevator Company Historic Archives*

People simply did not believe that elevators could be safe for human use. Barnum, wise to the ways of spectacles, gave him a chance to prove otherwise and allowed him to erect a 300-foot structure in the center of the main exhibition hall.

Some drawings from the time show Otis in top hat and tails; others give him more ordinary attire. In any case, he stepped onto the platform at the base of the structure and began to ascend into the air, then commanded that his assistant cut the rope holding him aloft. A gasp shot through the audience below. . . .

It was a becoming something of a tradition for show inventors to climb to great heights. Fulton had presented his panoramic view of Moscow in flames, Daguerre a vast stretch of the London skyline. Now, Otis's platform looked out onto another heady landscape—not a metropolis from history in this case, but a city of the future. It was, in fact, a city that show inventors would create in their own image—chaotic, daring, yet somehow productive in spite of it all. And perhaps its vertical outlines, teeming and endless, were almost visible to the spectators as Otis plummeted for a split second, then stopped in midair to deliver a courtly bow.

"All safe, gentlemen," the inventor cried out. "All safe."

*Chapter Seven*

# THE STAR SYSTEM

I saac Merritt Singer did not exhibit his invention at the New York Crystal Palace, but he may as well have. A theater man who had stayed on the stage much longer than his contemporaries, he eventually surpassed even the Southern Belle and the Lady in Red in gaudiness, and fully equalled Barnum in attention-getting techniques.

Born in 1811, Singer was the son of Adam and Ruth Reisinger, German-Jewish immigrants who shortened their name after arriving in America. In his early childhood, the family lived near Troy, New York, then moved west to Oswego, on the shores of Lake Ontario. When Isaac was ten, his mother divorced Adam and began a rootless trek through the wilds of upper New York State, settling for a time in Rochester. Soon, Isaac became yet another itinerant mechanic of the Northeast, and so he might have remained, had he not come upon an acting troupe in Rochester in 1830, led by Edwin Dean.

At the time, the stage was beginning to enjoy a style of celebrity that inhabitants of the twentieth century have come to think of as their own. The British theatrical headliners who stormed the New World in the 1820s had left American actors with a palpable thirst for celebrity, and out of this newborn desire grew the star system, which concentrated renown in a single name on the playbill.

William B. Wood, a stage manager in Philadelphia, Baltimore and, Washington for sixteen years, bemoaned the development in his autobiography. "The star is the light of everything," he wrote, "the centre around which all must move. He has his own times, his own pieces, his own plan of business, and his own preferences of every sort . . . The result is that when the star does come everything is to be done *impromptu.*" When a star took on a role, he could demand that his favorite scenery, no matter how incongruous, replace the existing set. Come opening night, he might order that an entirely different play be performed, whether his supporting actors were familiar with it or not. It was not unusual for Wood to overhear actors backstage trying to guess the name of the play they had just been in.

In joining Edwin Dean's troupe in 1830, when the star system was reaching its peak, the tow-headed, six-foot-tall Singer entered Joseph Henry's alternate universe, embracing everything that the scientist rejected—a world that encouraged sensation over sense at every turn. In fact, Singer seemed determined to champion showing over knowing, rather than the other way around. Later in life, he liked to boast that he was "one of the best Richards of his day," but this was true only after the curtain dropped. Critics outside Rochester thought him "crude and bombastical," and his peers knew him as a rough and sometimes violent man who consistently played to the crowd. Generally, he was forced to take whatever roles he was offered. When the pickings got exceptionally lean, he turned back to work as a mechanic or acted as an advance man for troupes.

No matter how he supported himself, life on the road agreed with Singer, because in addition to freedom of expression, it offered endless opportunities for sex. In Singer's case, this generally meant sexual complications as well. No sooner had he joined Dean's troupe than he married a fifteen-year-old girl named Catharine Maria Haley. When Catharine reached the spinsterly age of twenty-one and they had moved to New York City, he sped off post-haste to Baltimore with a troupe and became engaged to Mary Ann Sponsler. He and Catharine were separated, and Mary Ann came to New York, only to discover that he was already married. She overcame her horror and married him anyway. Soon enough, he was on the road again, and she was back in Baltimore, claiming desertion. The pattern varied little over the years. By the end of his life, Singer had married five times, spawned twenty-two children, and left behind a trail of heartache as long as his ego was large.

In 1839, several donnybrooks down the line, Singer produced his first invention—a drill to be used on the Erie Canal. But the idea of the inventor's life left him cold, so he sold the patent for two thousand dollars and moved to Chicago, where he started a theatrical company under the stage name Isaac Merritt.

The Merritt Players was a good-sized company, with twenty actors in the cast (Mary Ann, reconciled somehow, was enlisted to lend a hand). As might be expected, the troupe quickly met up with the religious opposition. The temperance movement, sounding very much like the Quakers in Franklin's day, was anxious to have the Merritt Players put on shows that were palatable for the whole family. Singer was contrite and soon found himself touring the country, performing morality plays that thundered against the evils of drink.

One imagines that these presentations were fairly intimate affairs at times. Once, the troupe arrived at a town on the Allegheny where they were scheduled to perform, only to find that its inhabitants had yet to build their first house. One also imagines that the pay was bad, even by actors' standards, because continued poverty forced Singer to stop touring in 1844 and to return to mechanical work. He took up a job carving wooden type and, out of sheer laziness, contrived a machine that would do the carving for him. If it worked, he could draw an image, and a set of "pantolevers" would mimic the motion of the pen, carving the image into wood. He continued to improve this invention as he moved from town to town, and finally was able to patent it on April 10, 1849. And so, at the age of thirty-eight, he moved to New York, intent on making a fortune.

Moving into a second-floor apartment on Third Avenue, Singer immediately went looking for buyers and found one in George B. Zieber, a publisher and venture capitalist. In late August 1850, the two of them rented a shop from Orson C. Phelps at 19 Harvard Place in Boston, where they put the machine up for review. Unfortunately, wooden type was becoming obsolete. Publishers yawned and walked on.

Then one day someone came in to the shop with a crude sewing machine based on the inventor Elias Howe's design. With much arm twisting, Singer was convinced to improve it. "I would have it move to and fro in a straight line," he told Phelps, "and in place of the needle bar pushing a curved needle horizontally, I would have a straight needle moving up and down."

Singer made a sketch, and on September 18, 1850, he and his two partners—Phelps and Zieber—drew up a contract for the manufacture of the Jenny Lind Sewing Machine, named after Barnum's famous singer, who had made a standing-room-only appearance one week earlier at Castle Garden in New York.

The creation of the Jenny Lind had a dramatic turn of its own: Singer later liked to relate how he worked for days on end, sleeping only three or four hours a night while Zieber held a lamp over him. After a long struggle, the machine still did not sew tight stitches. At the edge of despair, Singer realized that he needed to adjust the tension of the needle. He returned to his task and produced his first workable sewing machine.

This story was necessary if Singer was to succeed. The sewing machine was perhaps the most complex machine of its era, and many of the components could be improved or altered in such a way as to warrant intellectual property rights. Elias Howe, who patented a sewing machine in 1846, had priority only in the broadest sense. By August 12, 1851, when Singer received his patent, the field was littered with competing versions. Howe, Singer, George Corliss, John J. Greenough, Grover and Baker, Wheeler and Wilson, and Babson and Wilcox all had claims to originality. And where originality was in doubt, a myth was always in order.

Singer had no lack of mythmaking ideas. Like McCormick before him, he advertised and sent agents into the field. He put out his own periodical, called the *I. M. Singer & Co. Gazette.* Characteristically, he also exhibited his machine in hired halls, and at county fairs and carnivals, even as Barnum's flesh-and blood Jenny Lind was touring the same countryside.

In the end, Singer never did sell a sewing machine called the Jenny Lind. Fearful that the Swedish Nightingale would fall out of fashion, he dropped the name and, in true star form, put his own on the machine instead. If the pun was lost on anyone, he spiced up his demonstrations by singing "The Song of the Shirt," a popular tune from the stage. For those attuned to history, the sight may also have evoked a scene from the past: here was a man who rearranged theatrical fragments around his mechanical wonder, much as the mountebanks of old had used "bits" of plays to liven their pitch.

Soon Singer was back in New York, where he hit upon a more original method of promoting his invention: He put his son Gus and a seamstress named King in the store window of Smith & Conant's clothing shop on Broadway. There they stayed, from Thanksgiving 1850 until New Year's Day. This was one time when his exhibitionism did not hold him in good stead, though. Elias Howe, inventor of the machine Singer had modified back in Boston, first learned of Singer's existence on earth when he saw this display, and immediately began posting threats in various New York papers. Soon, the two inventors railed at each other in the pages of the *Tribune,* the *New York Times,* and *Scientific American.*

By 1854, Singer was going all guns. While Barnum tried to lure the crowds uptown to the Crystal Palace, Singer was trying to draw them to his shop at 323 Broadway, where his sewing machines—as he announced only lines away from the Crystal Palace ads—could be "seen in operation at all times." At the same time, Singer bayed like the quarrelsome Pulcinella incarnate that "Howe and all his associates devote their energies to abusing and vilifying I. M. SINGER & CO., and what is of more consequence, unscrupulously appropriate our inventions to their own use, without leave or license."

Howe triumphantly shot back in the space directly below: "CAU-TION.—SEWING MACHINES.—Last Wednesday I obtained an injunction from the United States Court in Boston, PROHIBITING THE USE OF THE SINGER SEWING MACHINES, and now have a suit pending against him here, which is soon to be tried, and without doubt will result in like manner."

It was true. What's more the court eventually ruled in favor of Howe, and in July of that year, Singer was forced to take out a license in order to continue manufacturing his own machines.

For a time, disagreements continued to break out among the many sewing machine manufacturers. But finally, the most prominent of them realized that the battles were taking up too much of their valuable time, and they decided to pool their patents together. According to the Albany Agreement of October 24, 1856—the first business agreement of its kind in America—Elias Howe would receive royalties on all machines sold by Wheeler and Wilson, Grover and Baker, and Singer, who in turn would allow each other to benefit from their respective patents. As with the Flatfoot cartel twenty years earlier, everybody benefited from this scheme, and the howls of priority disappeared from the journals of the day.

It was at this point that Barnum made his entrance into the sewing machine field, through the quarters of the Wheeler and Wilson Sewing Machine Company.

The year 1856 was by all accounts the low point of Barnum's career. Having been swindled by the principal of his clockmaking interest, a man named Chauncey Jerome, the showman had been forced to sell his various Bridgeport properties. He had even been compelled to give up his beloved American Museum. There was no other word for it. He was bankrupt.

But not for long. Barnum shrewdly encouraged Wheeler and Wilson to move into the idle Terry and Barnum clock factory, located in East Bridgeport. In return for this act of largesse, he received a five-thousand-dollar loan without security, and was able to buy back other properties he had lost in East Bridgeport and then some. "[T]he plan promised relief," he wrote, "and actually did succeed, even beyond my most sanguine expectations, eventually putting more money into my pocket than the Jerome complication had taken out."

The turnaround made for a rather genial situation. While Barnum had an interest in seeing Wheeler and Wilson do well, Wheeler and Wilson shared its patents with Singer, Howe, and Grover and Baker. Singer and Barnum, accustomed to playing opposite each other, were now effectively playing in the same cast.

As Wheeler and Wilson profited from the patent pool, Barnum's properties went up in value and he was able to buy back the American Museum. Singer, meanwhile, free to use the patents of his former competitors, took his business to new heights. In the year of the patent combination, his company manufactured 2,564 machines. By 1860, the number had grown to 13,000. Having started out on the Lower East Side in a single room where his son Gus had been born and progressed to East Fifth Street near Fourth Avenue, he now took up residence at the posh address of 374 Fourth Avenue. He had arrived.

With success, Singer's love for ostentatious display went into full bloom. In 1856, he threw the first of his Grand Invitational Balls for his company employees and his machine owners and operators, with attendance exceeding three thousand; these balls soon became a New Year's Day tradition. To keep the drama going, he also began to install sewing emporiums—which functioned as manufacturer's outlets—in cities and medium-sized towns across the nation.

The techniques of the mountebank remained very much in force at the Singer emporiums. While female employees gave personal demonstrations of the product to each visitor, company agents delivered a pitch that was carefully calculated to instill a sense of guilt. The Singer sewing machine, they said, freed up a woman's time for more important homemaking tasks. Conversely, any mother who continued to sew by hand did so at the risk of shirking her familial duties. Like Cyrus McCormick, Singer also instituted a layaway plan to offset his high prices (his machines went for a heady $125), which sometimes had the sudden effect of sending female debtors to prison, feeling swindled and misunderstood.

If the cruder aspects of Singer's business practices went unnoticed by many (until it was too late!), perhaps this was because the emporiums themselves were so inviting. High-ceilinged and elegant, they were the paragon of cleanliness and cheer, and expressly designed to put a woman at ease. Refreshments were served and, on occasion, presents given away. Like the daguerrotype studios of the era, they functioned as fantasy worlds, allowing hardworking customers to be someone else for a day and to play-act their way toward the all-important purchase.

Singer's personal effects were by no means less grand. In 1859, he built an amazing coach, in which servants, children, and beds could all be housed. The *New York Family Herald* called it a "steamboat on wheels, drawn by six and sometimes nine horses, three abreast." Its cavernous reaches contained a nursery, a smoking room, seats for sixteen on the outside (meant for musicians), and a baggage compartment capable of stowing a dozen or more persons—all aboard a moving house weighing 3,800 pounds, painted canary yellow, and edged in black. The passage of the coach along a New York City street, needless to say, was an event unto itself. Indeed, the fact that Singer took out a patent on its design (no. 25,920) made its appearance in public its own kind of inventor's show.

Endlessly profligate, Singer built another new home, threw more grand balls, and drove the streets imperiously until the 1860s, when he moved to Europe with a new wife—Isabella Blanche Singer. After some years, he settled on the South Devon coast of England and built his most monstrous residence yet, called the Wigwam. There, he proceeded to live the riotous life, throwing lavish parties (and according to legend, engaging at least one circus to perform on the grounds) until his death on July 23, 1875. A piece of promotional literature may serve as his eulogy:

## THE HERALD OF CIVILIZATION

MISSIONARY WORK OF THE SINGER MANUFACTURING COMPANY. At the close of the recent war, the King of Ou (Caroline Islands) came to pay homage to the Government of Manila. As the best means of advancing and establishing a condition of things that would prevent all future outbreaks, the King was introduced to the "Great Civilizer," the Singer sewing machine, and we have here his photograph, seated beside the Singer sewing machine, with his Secretary of State standing beside him. This is absolutely authentic. It is a half-toned plate made from an original photograph, which can be seen any day at the office of the SINGER MANUFACTURING CO., 149 Broadway, New York City.

By the beginning of the Civil War, the battalions of bombast were well in the ascendancy. Fitch and Evans, laboring without a context, had stumbled and fallen. Joseph Henry had shunned the stage life altogether. Colt had played the mountebank until his factory preempted the need. McCormick had given the language of the menagerie to rural manufacture. But with Singer, the rogue element had come out of the wilderness to assume the simultaneous roles of Great Civilizer, tycoon, and star—with his own plan of business and his own preferences of every sort.

The long march of the American show inventors into the mainstream had reached a climactic moment. The strolling player, now casually flaunting his carriage on main street, had taken control of the center of town.

*Part Two*

# CARNIVAL UNBOUND

HELEN:   I? To marry Goodrich the ventriloquist?

MR. DAY: *(aside)* Goodrich the ventriloquist. *(feels his whiskers)* Dear me! I forgot to take my whiskers off, after I called here this morning!"

—Alexander Graham Bell, *Play of Douglas*

## Chapter Eight

# A BIG BANG

According to the *Tampa Observer*, no fewer than five million people visited Florida on December 1, 1865. The crowd was densest on the plain around Stone Hill, where makeshift shanties housed members of every nation and class, some of whom had been camping out for days. The local barrooms and taverns did a record business in gin slings, brandy smashes, and Burgundy sangarees, and a festive atmosphere reigned throughout the day. Then, the moon rose, and the crowd grew pensive.

At about seven o'clock in the evening, three men appeared near a small enclosure in the center of the crowd. A cheer went up, and the Americans in attendance broke into a spontaneous rendition of "Yankee Doodle Dandy." Then a hush descended on them again as the three men walked over and stepped into the enclosure—a metal vehicle with a conical nose that pointed toward the sky.

The time was 10:46 P.M. The moon was just reaching its zenith, in the constellation of Gemini. When the countdown reached zero, a man pulled a switch that sent an electric spark into the base of the cannon, many feet below the earth.

As one observer recounted: "Instantly there was a terrifying, fantastic, superhuman detonation which could not be compared to thunder or any previously known sound, not even the eruption of a volcano. An immense spout of flame shot from the bowels of the earth as from a crater. The ground heaved, and only a few people caught a brief glimpse of the projectile victoriously cleaving the air amid clouds of glowing vapor."

That Jules Verne had witnessed this explosion—the launching of a lunar mission—in his imagination didn't deter his readers terribly much. On the contrary, when they read his account of it in the 1865 novel *From the Earth to the Moon*, they believed the fiction a little too readily. "Some of them," marveled Verne at the letters he received, "really want to travel in my projectile."

Such enthusiasms were typical of the times. By the end of the Civil War, the disorder of the Jacksonian era had given rise to a general suspension of disbelief, and America had come to be perceived as the repository of all possibilities. What was real and what was not were questions better left to academics. Americans *believed*. Even Europeans, looking on from afar, believed in their belief, and signed up for the next flight to the moon.

This credulity, it must be said, did not generate immediate results. Mark Twain once commented that he had seen many amazing things in his life, "but most of them never happened." He could easily have been talking about the aura of technological promise in the late 1860s. The show inventors of the 1840s and 1850s had pushed the mechanical spectacle to the point where there were no hoaxes, only inventions waiting to find their way into physical fact.

A sampling of postwar patents shows just how far the notion of reason had fallen. A bullet designed to travel "in curved lines with the same accuracy as in straight lines" received Patent no. 107,909. John McDonald's Patent no. 97,101 combined an upright piano with a pull-out bed. An endless rail device, patented by James A. Glenn of New York City in 1867, allowed a train to supply its own tracks A multitiered table rotated by steam power offered buffet-style dining without the nuisance of live servants. For the ultimate in Victorian pleasures, there was a rocking chair–bellows that blew air down on the fatigued sitter. Meanwhile, an automaton called the Steam Man, invented by George Moore, appeared at a location almost directly opposite Barnum's museum, exhaling steam from a cigar and wired into place so as not to walk off into the city streets—a gargoyle of the machine age.

In a climate where anything went, which would have been more believable? Richard Dudgeon's 1866 Dudgeon—a clattering, trackless

SCENE IN PRINTING-HOUSE SQUARE, NEW YORK CITY.—SKETCHED BY STANLEY FOX.

By the end of the Civil War, mechanical spectacles were commonplace. This scene of New York's Printing House Square in 1868 is typical of the times: lung testers and weight machines abound. *Author's Collection*

locomotive, with wooden seats astride the boiler—or the report from Lee, Virginia, on January 25, 1868, that three suns had risen at once? It was hard to say. The line between the preposterous and the plausible was all but nonexistent, the nation in some strange sort of trance.

Verne captured the mood perfectly in his 1865 novel. His imaginary mission to create a human cannonball begins when a band of limb-deprived Civil War veterans, disgruntled at the lack of demand for weaponry during peacetime, decide to turn their mastery of ballistics to novel use. When Impey Barbicane, their charismatic leader, formally announces the project, a torchlight parade is held spontaneously in his honor. The festivities last until two in the morning with drunkenness and revelry all around.

"Hesitations, doubts and misgivings," wrote Verne, "were out of the question." The news spreads at "248,447 miles per second," and is picked up by fifteen hundred periodicals the next day. Every American citizen comes down with lunar fever—infected, so to speak, by telegraph. "An artilleryman is like a cannonball," declares one enthusiast, "he can never go too far!" When an audience hears for the first time that the earth's axis is tilted, one of them hollers without compunction, "Well, then . . . let's unite our efforts, invent machines, and straighten the earth's axis!" This was not so different from the real-life theory, put forward in the pages of *Scientific American*, of Dr. D. Mortimer, who located heaven in the center of the earth and calculated the time it would take for a soul to arrive there from the planet's surface.

Such pronouncements were the height of absurdity, of course, yet they were also integral to the very real achievements of the last quarter of the nineteenth century. Without public moments in which mechanical fantasies could be entertained, the range of possibilities could only narrow down to the sure bet. But when inventors had immediate access to a credulous public, the implausible could flower, first as a mirage and eventually—perhaps—as a palpable reality.

Verne himself was more than a passive chronicler of this dynamic. So compelling were his accounts of fictitious inventor-adventurers that, in later years, many real show inventors credited him as being a guiding light. When Edison sent travelers into the Amazon and the jungles of Southeast Asia in search of a material for his light-bulb filament, he cited Verne as his inspiration. When the Wright brothers described what kept them going through the dark hours, Verne was on their list. Rocket pioneer Robert Goddard went so far as to use Verne's moon novel as a basis for his inventions. In a sense, Verne's writings were a mirage that came before the mirage, blueprints that show inventors could study and master.

This effectiveness was not sheer luck. If Verne wrote with such theatrical flair and such a keen eye for mechanical detail that he inspired others to action, it was because he was very nearly a show inventor himself.


Jules Verne was born on February 8, 1828, on an island in Nantes, the capital of Brittany, and grew up on the mainland, just across the channel. Childhood friends remembered his notebooks cluttered with drawings of flying machines and steam-powered engines. Though these notebooks have never surfaced, it is telling that he was perceived as an inventor during his lifetime: what he created on paper seemed too real not to exist.

Packed off to study law in 1847, Verne arrived in Paris a good-looking man with a broad forehead, fine features, curly hair, and intense, passionate eyes. He quickly discovered a taste for the lures and attractions of the capital city. One of the many lewd love poems he wrote during this period made its way to a literary society back in Nantes, where provincial eyebrows were raised in unison. The response from his family was much the same when, on May 8 of that year, he wrote his first play, a five-act tragedy called *Alexandre VI*. Between 1847 and 1863, he would write fifteen dramatic works and see six of them produced; his family disapproved of them all.

Verne took up permanent residence in Paris at the end of 1848, and through the graces of his uncle, a painter and a more liberal spirit than Verne's other relatives, he was soon mingling with celebrities, among them Alexander Dumas. When the Theâtre Historique reopened on February 21, 1849, Verne asked Dumas to have one of his plays produced there. Dumas chose *The Broken Straw* over *The Gunpowder Plot*, and it opened on June 12, 1850.

From the reviews, it seems to have been a fairly mediocre piece of work. Still, Verne continued to churn them out. He completed a three-act play, a music-hall sketch, a mime-play, and *The Castles of California*, a play about the gold rush. He also published his first short story during this period, "The First Ships of the Mexican Navy."

Verne clearly enjoyed the thespian life. As secretary to the director of the Theâtre Lyrique in 1852, one of his favorite activities was to loiter backstage. Once, he borrowed an actress's false-ermine property coat and paraded around in it, much to the amusement of the crew—and the consternation of the actress. (Of course, when such reports reached his family back in Nantes, the routine disgust was expressed.)

It was in this rambunctious context that Verne began to rediscover his interest in technology. A comedy about Leonardo da Vinci and the Giaconda, written in the early 1850s, shows him pondering the character of a mechanical genius. During the same period, Verne began to frequent social meetings at Jacques Arago's house. The brother of the scientist François Arago (who had championed Daguerre and influenced Faraday's electric generator), Jacques Arago impressed him with the possibilities of science.

Finally, the semiscientific writings of an American writer tipped the scale. On July 16, 1856, Verne wrote: "After reading Edgar Allan Poe. Something the critics have not noticed: a new literary world, pointing to the literature of the twentieth century. Scientific miracles, fables on the pattern A + B; a clear-sighted, sickly literature. No more poetry, but analytic fantasy. Something monomaniacal." This manifesto, as it were, led to all 103 volumes of Verne's *Voyages extraordinaires*, the collected works for which he gained his fame.

There were a few final episodes of debauchery. A comedy of manners sent Verne into the red-light district, which abutted the theater district, for "research," and a flurry of dirty love poems followed. But the carousing died down considerably on January 10, 1857, with his marriage to Honorine de Fraysse de Viane, a woman of high social standing.

Though he wrote two light social satires in 1860 and another play in 1861, Verne the husband began to turn away from the bohemian life. He stopped writing poems about his sexual adventures (though there is some evidence that he continued to have them) and took up a job as a stockbroker. He also stopped visiting the music halls, which, after all, were so close to the *maisons de tolerance* and so far from the hearth. Yet his dramatic activities had always been inseparable from the other pleasures of the demimonde. How then was he to satisfy his theatrical aspirations and still keep his marriage intact?

As if on cue, a solution presented itself. Félix Tournachone was known throughout France by his pseudonym, Nadar. A man-about-town who had spent time as both a political cartoonist and a journeyman spy, Nadar was most at home in the wide-open field of technology. When he wasn't photographing the Paris sewers by electric light, he was busy taking the first aerial photographs or arranging to have a model of a steam-powered helicopter demonstrated in his studio. Today, people know Nadar mostly through his photographic work, little aware that he is generally credited with coining the term *aviation*.

Nadar also had a voracious appetite for publicity, which led him to seek out anyone and everyone of note in Paris. In Verne's case, it was a technical detail from his first critically recognized novel, *Five Weeks in a Balloon*, that captured Nadar's attention: the principle of a heated coil, which made ascent, descent, and direction more controllable. Nadar contacted the author posthaste, formed the Society for Aerial Locomotion, and made Verne its secretary.

Having nothing else to do really, the society built a balloon named the *Giant* and launched it in October of 1863. Taller than Notre Dame, it rose from the Champ de Mars carrying "crates of champagne, food, guns, a princess or two, other famous people (at a thousand francs per head) and a Negro—who was presumably there to act as interpreter in case the balloon came down in Africa." For better or worse, the balloon landed not in Africa, but a few miles away from its launch site.

Meanwhile, *Five Days in a Balloon* was hailed as a landmark in its time. As one of Verne's friends put it, "An unknown writer had created the scientific novel." The praise kept coming as Verne produced more books. Apollinaire later praised his iconoclastic style as consisting of "nothing but nouns." Of another novel, a critic pronounced: "This fictional journey has all the colours and movement of reality; and if the author had not taken care to tell us himself, the illusion would be almost too complete. M. Jules Verne is a true scientist . . . and a writer of the greatest merit."

The plaudits were well deserved. If Verne was something of a hack at playwriting, he was a genuine innovator as a novelist. Others had written science fiction before, Francis Bacon and Mary Shelley being among the more noteworthy examples. But where Bacon's *New Atlantis*, with its predictions of "sound-houses" and "means of seeing objects far-off," had been essentially a treatise on morality, and Shelley's *Frankenstein* a powerful metaphor for creativity, Verne's *Voyages extraordinaires* put the very language of inventors into literary form. From him came the tradition, still in effect today, of science-fiction characters rattling off plausible technical jargon in order to make the story more believable. An incorrigible positivist, he all but placed scientific facts (or what he thought were facts) at the center of his tales.

This alone made it easier for readers to suspend their disbelief. Yet Verne hadn't really left the world of real-life spectacles behind; he had simply found a way of participating in them without jeopardizing his marriage. *Five Weeks* came out in December 1862—less than a year before the launch of the *Giant*—and the two events provided fanfare for each other. Indeed, any attempt by Parisians to distinguish Nadar's actual *Giant* from Verne's imagined *Victoria* quickly became a lost cause.

The simultaneous release of book and balloon, which today would be called a cross-promotion, made Verne's narrative and the technological spectacle inseparable. They were fables on the pattern A + B, where A was the novel and B was the demonstration of a real invention—and he could write them without scavenging the music halls for material.

Understandably, Verne followed the equation often in the years to come. *Twenty Thousand Leagues under the Sea* first took root in his mind when he saw the drawings for Jacques-François Conseil's submarine, which had made a half-hour dive in 1858. Another submarine, *Le Plongeur*, shown at the Universal Exhibition of 1867, provided the direct model for his literary fancy. Thinking more like an inventor than a novelist, he added the idea of an electrical engine to his version. And, of course, in calling his vessel the *Nautilus*, he was harking back to the days when Robert Fulton had lowered his own *Nautilus* beneath the Seine, a living memory for some.

Verne's most popular novel exhibited these same cross-promotional abilities. He was inspired to write '*Round the World in Eighty Days*— more a celebration of existing transportation technologies than a projection of future alternatives—after coming across an ad posted by Thomas Cook's, a travel agency that sponsored global excursion packages. In this novel, Phileas Fogg, a mysterious and perversely exact Englishman frequents the Reform Club, counting the number of steps from his house as he goes. One night, he makes a bet with another gentleman that he can circle the world in eighty days. With his French valet Passepartout at his side, Fogg proceeds to use every form of transportation on the planet—and one or two of Verne's own devising—to accomplish his end. He saves a few lives, winning the bet and a wife in the bargain.

Fogg was not spun from thin air, however. After the publication of '*Round the World in Eighty Days*, an American named George Francis Train came forward and described his own real-life trip around the world, made in eighty days (discounting time spent in jail) and completed just before the fictitious Phileas Fogg had set out. On top of this, there was also a real Fogg—W. Perry Fogg—who completed a global voyage in 1871 and had published a book called *Around the World* to prove it.

The real Fogg and Train could cry foul as much as they wanted; it was the imagined Fogg who provided the inspiration for others. As the book sold off the racks, the Cook agency was glutted with would-be travelers. Eventually, the journey developed into an official tradition. By 1949, editions of '*Round the World in Eighty Days* could include a history of the recordholders for traversing the planet, Verne style.

Fogg's peculiar walking habits became a source of interest as well. In 1972, S. J. Perelman attempted to retrace the trek from 7 Saville Row to the Reform Club—and deduced that Verne had miscounted! This same calculated gait, it can be assumed, provided the model for the inventor Nikola Tesla when he too insisted on counting every step he took. Like everyone else who read Verne, Tesla wanted to slip into the shoes of his hero and try the blocking for himself.

By the 1880s, Verne was a heartily celebrated figure, and he resumed his romance with the public life. (Presumably, after gaining an audience with Pope Leon XIII, he could behave as he wished.) He owned several houseboats and traveled from port to port throughout Europe, receiving accolades wherever he went. Twice he threw full-scale, fancy-dress balls. He returned to theater as an administrator and gave public talks at fairs. In 1889, he started the Municipal Circus in Paris. After the initial spectacles that paralleled his fictions were long forgotten, he dramatized many of his novels, which had the effect, in a sense, of making him a show inventor after the fact. The plays made even more money than the novels.

The desire to realize Verne's novels was also remarkably long-lived; in one case, it lasted more than a century. Although the publication of *From the Earth to the Moon* plainly did not coincide with a real lunar launch, those looking back from the twentieth century have been amazed at the number of details that coincide with those of the Apollo lunar missions. A contest between Florida and Texas to host the launch really did take place in the 1960s, with Florida winning, just as Verne imagined. The launch site that Verne picked, Stone Hill, has almost exactly the same latitude as Cape Canaveral. Three men traveled in both the first real mission and the imagined expedition. In 1969, astronaut Frank Borman wrote to Jean Jules-Verne, grandson of the author, pointing out that the Apollo 9 mission bore additional similarities: "It had the same weight and the same height, and it splashed down in the Pacific a mere two and half miles from the point mentioned in the [sequel] novel."

This was not so much a case of prophecy as of persistence. In the early 1900s, the American inventor Robert Goddard was already basing his ideas for rocketry on Barbicane's gargantuan gun. In the 1920s, Goddard then reversed the situation by accepting the editorial task of revising *From the Earth to the Moon* according to his own findings. Soon afterward, he developed America's first multistage, liquid-fuel rocket, thus laying the groundwork for the space program of the 1960s

The line is unbroken: when Neil Armstrong stepped onto the surface of the moon in 1969, he wasn't proving Verne right as much as he was finally *acting his vision out*. In fact, the essentially theatrical nature of the real lunar mission has grown increasingly apparent in recent years, as people have come to question what purpose a trip to our dusty satellite really served, except to generate a colossal drama.

In *From the Earth to the Moon*, Verne left his fictitious characters adrift in the heavens, circling the moon, but he still held out hope for them.

Ingenuity had put them there and ingenuity would bring them back. "We'll communicate with them," says one his earthbound heroes. "They'll hear from us and we'll hear from them! I know them: they're ingenious men!"

That cry had a special resonance for Americans in the years after the Civil War. Many people had someone close to them die in battle, and their inconsolable grief opened the way for the spiritualists, who promised to bring the dearly departed back.

By the late 1860s, spiritualism was a veritable craze, replete with table-rapping parties, self-made preachers, and best-selling inspirational books. Naturally, it didn't take long for inventors, who were ingenious men, to see their place in this. After all, if they could make bullets curve, sleep in piano beds, and tilt the world on its axis, couldn't they try to materialize a spirit or two?

Professor Henry Morton seemed to think so. In June 1868, Morton walked onto a stage at the Philadelphia Academy of Music and, placing himself and an apparatus on a platform that was secured to a stage trap, had himself hoisted fifteen feet from the floor. From this height, he burned a thick steel wire rope (as cables were then called) inside a compound blowpipe, causing a fountain of sparks and melted steel to cascade to the stage and roll "in a torrent of fiery hail" toward the footlights. Then he activated the largest induction coil in the world, belonging to the University of Pennsylvania, which fed electrical fire into a five-foot-wide wheel, "producing a dazzling star of constantly changing colored rays."

The curtain was dropped. When it was raised again, a troupe of masked figures marched onto the stage, illuminated in white limelight and bearing banners in all the colors of the rainbow. At a signal, the white light was replaced by a yellow one, which miraculously drained the banners of color. "The entire phalanx became a ghastly company of spectres," wrote one reporter, "bearing banners of black and white." So bright was the light Morton had invented that it illuminated the entire audience as well.

Others took their specters more literally, and entertained the possibility of speaking to them through mechanical intermediaries. Today, we have the Ouija board; in the 1860s, it was the planchette. Among those asked to render an opinion on this simple device was the staff of *Scientific American*. Still enamored of whimsies some twenty years after its debut, "The Best Mechanical Paper in the World" put aside its discussions of industry for several weeks in 1868 to plumb the matter.

The technical details were easily dispatched: the planchette was a toplike device designed to summon spirits and named after the woman who invented it. But eventually it arose that Planchette was an *invented* inventor. Long before a single planchette was sold, the magazine *Every Saturday* reprinted a piece of fiction from an English magazine, which described both the woman Planchette and her self-named spiritualist device. The author furnished a drawing along with his story and, showing some cunning, identified America as the place of the invention's origin, so as to make it more believable to English audiences. It was another mirage before the mirage; even so, the spiritualist's aid was soon to be found "in every stationers' in England and America."

*Scientific American* was by no means the only authority asked to hand down its judgment on the ghost machines of the day. No less an eminence than Michael Faraday was imposed upon to comment on planchette-like devices. (Ever the experimentalist, he publicly defended an empirical approach to the subject.) Even Joseph Henry, that great resister of nonsense, found himself caught up in the controversy when Mrs. Mary Todd Lincoln, a close friend of his, cornered him and introduced him to a ventriloquist. As the man began to work his wiles in the name of the hereafter, the First Lady tried with some enthusiasm to solicit Henry's approval. He could only hedge and wait for the moment to pass.

As for John Roebling, hedging was out of the question. This wire-rope inventor had leanings toward the afterlife that simply could not be quelled. After his wife, Johanna, died on November 22, 1864, Roebling sought succor in the teachings of Andrew Jackson Davis, known as the Poughkeepsie Seer. Born of an alcoholic cobbler, the teenage Davis underwent a spiritual conversion in 1844. From then on, he traveled the Atlantic seaboard with a hypnotist in tow, getting "magnetized" before rapt audiences, a latterday phreno-magnetist. His own personal scribe wrote down every word and turned the transcripts into best-selling books.

Upon becoming a widower, Roebling, formerly an intensely rational man, became an intensely irrational one, embracing Davis's techniques in hopes of communicating with his deceased wife. Neighbors around his home in Trenton, New Jersey, looked on with silent curiosity as the seances commenced with the Roebling children in full attendance. In the winter of 1868, contact was made, and Johanna was able to provide the answers to a number of pressing questions, among them the all-important information that there are no Bibles in the afterlife.

Eventually, the fever passed; even Roebling couldn't suspend his disbelief forever. On the other hand, if he couldn't build a bridge to heaven, he might still build one to Brooklyn. Soon, he began producing drawings, plans, blueprints. He held business meetings and got the backing of major investors. To hear him talk, it would be the greatest bridge ever built.

There are many today who would still give the Brooklyn Bridge that honor, but Roebling did not live to see it completed. On June 28, 1869, he was working out on the Fulton Ferry slip, trying to determine where the Brooklyn support tower should be erected, when he stepped backward and caught his foot between an incoming boat and the dock. The boat dragged by, crushing his toes.

Laid up at his son Washington's house, Roebling immediately took charge of his treatment and fired one doctor after another. When the local preacher suggested it was a case of hard luck, Roebling, paraphrasing Prospero, shot back: "All is wisely ordered."

None of this did anything to stay the signs of tetanus. From July 13 on, his life was an unending torment. He first complained of headaches, then of terrible thirst. Family members watched his face, neck, and jaws lock tight, forcing his expression into a macabre grimace, his eyebrows permanently raised. Then the seizures began, during which his chest would be frozen hard. In one of his moments of lucidity, he commanded that a lifting device be built to help him out of bed. But soon he began to issue technical orders, thinking he was at the bridge office. On July 21, he had a seizure so violent that he was thrown out of bed. A few minutes later, he was as taut as one of the wire ropes he manufactured.

As in the bell-making tradition, which held that the death of a worker during the forging process would make the bell ring true, folk wisdom deemed the demise of Roebling a good sign for the bridge. But no one tried to contact him.


In the national pursuit of fantasy, the tangible and the intangible could intersect in peculiar ways—spiritual aids could be spun from fictions, bridges could stand in for the less reliable pathways to the hereafter. But of all the developments of the period, the most peculiar by far were the inventions designed to avert premature burial. The fear of premature burial was an old one; an old comedian's gag, called the Lazzo of the

Dead, had once satirized this very predicament. But the greater frequency of trances, combined with the growing zest for mechanical solutions, changed matters somewhat. If people were being buried alive, it was no longer enough to bemoan the fact. Something had to be done about it.

In France, the matter was solved with the Respiratory-Advertising Apparatus for Precipitate Inhumations, a device with a funnel-shaped mouthpiece, to be attached to the possibly living body and fed from the coffin to the air above ground. This invention, however promising its name, seems to have vanished fairly quickly. The Germans, meanwhile, developed a more durable variation in the coffin alarm.

According to standard German practices of the time, bodies were placed in mortuary houses until an official could pronounce them dead. To span this interim safely, the proprietors at cemeteries in Frankfurt am Main and Munich attached bracelets to the corpses-in-waiting, with wires leading to an alarm box. Each bracelet was numbered, indicating the location of the potentially revitalized party. Various electrical apparatuses were set up in an adjoining room to revive any body that showed signs of life. The bodies, set in a sitting position on cots, were generally surrounded by flowers and a band of glum watchmen.

In Munich, the alarm went off once; in Frankfurt all remained silent. In Wentz, where this practice also obtained, a surgeon once heard the alarm when someone's abdomen, "having subsided from the discharge of a large quantity of fluid, allowed the arms to fall lengthwise beside the body."

The Germans persisted in this program all the way to Newark, New Jersey, with a characteristic increase in bravura on American shores. In September 1868, a Mr. Vester enacted his own burial with the help of a cord and ladder, contained in a tube near the head of the coffin. The cord provided air from the surface, the ladder allowed him to climb out. Vester also had plans for alarms to be connected to interested parties—exactly how that was to be accomplished, he didn't say.

At the appointed hour, Vester appeared and climbed into his casket, an elaborate affair covered with flowers and a cross. The coffin was then nailed shut with four screws and lowered into a grave. A second box, containing a staircase, was lowered in an upright position into a square that fit in the coffin. Earth was thrown over the lot, and the crowd settled in for a suspenseful wait. When one wag took it upon himself to look down the upright box and ask the inventor if it was warm down there, the other spectators made it perfectly clear how they felt about the gesture: "He narrowly escaped being put from the grounds," wrote a reporter, "by the excited Germans present."

The reemergence took about an hour. When Vester surfaced at last, some members of the crowd kissed him. Vindicated, he pitched his invention as a boon to loved ones who might be accidentally buried while in a trance state.

The father of a famous inventor joined the ranks of the coffin improvers under less comical circumstances. In the fall of 1864, Immanuel Nobel suffered a stroke from the emotional shock of an explosion at the family nitroglycerine factory in Heleneborg, Sweden, that killed his son Oscar-Emil and others. An eyewitness account, printed on September 4, 1864, could not have made the impact of the disaster plainer:

> More ghastly was the sight of the mutilated corpses strewn on the ground. Not only had the clothes been torn off but on some the head was missing and the flesh ripped off the bones. These formless masses of flesh and bone bore little or no resemblance to a human body. The effect of the explosion could be judged by the fact that in a nearby stone house, the walls facing the factory had split open, and a woman who had been standing over a stove cooking had part of her head crushed, one arm torn off, and one thigh terribly mauled. The unfortunate victim was still alive and was carried to the hospital on a litter, looking more like a bloody mass of meat than a human being.

In April 1865, six months after the Heleneborg disaster, Immanuel Nobel gained enough strength to lift a tremulous hand to paper and embark on a seven-year communique. He became fixated on an invention that would give him "dictatorial powers in matters of war and peace in the whole world for at least several centuries." When that didn't occupy his time, he contemplated "pipes for the transport of coffins from the cities to the burial sites outside them." More tellingly for a man who was all but paralyzed, Immanuel described coffins constructed such that "someone apparently dead but actually in a state of suspended animation could himself lift off the lid, which would be provided with necessary air holes for breathing and connected by way of a pulling cord or signaling bell."

So it went until he died on September 3, 1872—eight years to the day after his son Oscar-Emil's death. The all-powerful invention he hinted at never came to light, but his nature was fully expressed through his son, Alfred Nobel, who was known to refer to his time on earth as "half a life" and who forever feared being buried alive.

In many ways, Alfred Nobel was the mirror image of Jules Verne. Like the French celebrity, he was lured to Paris in the 1850s by the attractions of the bohemian life, and like Verne, went on to become a playwright with a penchant for explosions. But the similarities end there. Nobel's explosives were all too real, and rather than celebrating life, he existed in a near-permanent state of melancholy. While Verne's adventures in the demimonde had him rifling off lascivious odes, Nobel's night with a prostitute produced a lament that bordered on self-mortification:

> When youth has lost its faith in love
> When we have known the soul and heart to rot
> In woman long before her charms are gone
> We pay for that experience a price.

Soon after this tryst, Nobel fell in love with a Parisian waif who died quite suddenly, further stoking the furnace of his suffering:

> . . . my love is with the dead
> Nor was I there to soothe her last hours
> But came to gape upon a putrid corpse
> . . . From that hour
> I have not shared the pleasures of the crowd
> Nor moved in Beauty's eye compassion's tear . . .

Nobel never did share the pleasures of the crowd. He was much too gloomy for that. While other inventors treated the world like their own personal turkey shoot, Nobel was endlessly plagued by his conscience. He seemed eternally caught up in the trappings of despair and self-abnegation—the Ingmar Bergman of his day. Nevertheless, in the wide-open 1860s, even such a man as he was tacitly encouraged to become a performer and a personality. And so, rather than renouncing the public life, he stepped into it, his face turned away in a wince.

Late in life, Nobel wrote an autobiographical play called *Nemesis*, which he considered among his most important achievements. It was also a highly public revelation of his internal hell. Based on *The Cenci*, by Percy Bysshe Shelley (who had in turn been influenced by Humphry Davy), the story centers on a father's incestuous desire for his daughter. When the father's feelings become known, the family plots his murder. The treachery is soon discovered, whereupon the family is tortured, then condemned to death by the pope. Ironically, the Nobel family did its own share of plotting against Alfred by destroying every existing copy of this play, save one that eluded their grasp.

Then again, this was nothing new to Alfred: Immanuel pressured his son to give up writing from the very beginning and to take up inventing instead. The elder Nobel was something of an inventor himself, and by the time Alfred reached his majority, he had developed a practical sea mine and found commercial success with it in St. Petersburg. It only made sense, he thought, for his son to quit his wanderings and join the family business.

So in 1863, having traveled to St. Petersburg, Paris, and America, Alfred returned to Sweden at the age of thirty as a trained chemist and a fluent speaker of five languages. Before long, he invented the blasting cap, which made nitroglycerine reasonably safe for the first time. Along with his subsequent inventions, which included dynamite, blasting gelatin, and smokeless blasting powder, this advance became the basis for all blasting technology until the 1920s.

Nobel clearly had drama in his blood, but nitroglycerine was one item that defied the suspension of disbelief. Even as Verne's fictitious detonations were being lauded, the press called him "the devil in the guise of a man," a "mass murderer," and a "traveling salesman in death." As far as the public was concerned, Alfred Nobel was an exceedingly dangerous man. He made personal visits to mining villages to quell the public's fears, and safely blew a hole in the side of a mountain in the presence of Sweden's Prince Oscar. But Nobel was not in the position of a Colt or a Singer to exaggerate his claims. When he admitted that lives would invariably be lost, he met with resistance. And of course, the 1864 Heleneborg disaster, known locally as the "Nobel bang," did nothing to further his public-relations cause.

Seeing the expansive frontier of America as a market with great potential, Nobel applied for a U.S. patent on his blasting cap technology, and it was issued on October 25, 1865. He himself was issued onto American shores on April 15, 1866, a traveling bag filled with nitroglycerine firmly in his grip.

His reception was no more welcoming than it had been in Sweden. The press, always on the lookout for disaster stories, was happy to supply the public with tales of the latest nitroglycerine catastrophes. One told of a German guest at a Greenwich Street hotel who had left a mysterious crate at the reception desk. Employees took to sitting on it, the report said, until someone noticed that it had started smoking and threw it onto the street—only moments before it exploded. The report of a ship that exploded while transporting nitroglycerine near Panama, killing forty-seven, caused worldwide condemnation of Nobel's invention. Shortly thereafter, a German boat bound for New York exploded in its Bremerhaven port when its load of nitroglycerine detonated, and again there was a general outcry.

To win approval for his invention, Nobel followed the dictates of his time: he obtained permission from Mayor John T. Hoffman to demonstrate his blasting technology on the streets of New York City. Before he could go ahead with the show, however, Congress called him to Washington to prove the safety of his substance. When Nobel proved only what *wouldn't* make it explode, the government sent him packing. Nobel went ahead with his New York performance anyway, knowing full well that he risked the death penalty in the event that anyone was killed.

On May 4, 1866, a crowd of nervous onlookers appeared at the quarry on "the mountainous slopes between Eighth and Ninth Avenues, near 83rd Street." The inventor poured nitroglycerine on a rock and put a match to it. The substance burned like tar. He threw a cannister and a bottle containing nitroglycerine into the quarry. Nothing happened. In fact, there were no explosions at the quarry that day.

Nobel made some attempt to enliven the proceedings. "In a variety of entertaining and graphic ways," a *New York Times* reporter wrote, "he kept experimenting with the explosive and convinced those present that, during the conditions there presented, nitroglycerine is safer to handle and transport than both gunpowder and cottonpowder."

Nevertheless, for as much as Nobel put on a game face, there was a dramatic flaw to his demonstration that couldn't be helped. Ever since the days of Samuel Colt's pyrotechnic displays, Americans had exhibited a fondness for fireworks, especially fireworks that went awry, and this was one show that dared not satisfy that demand. The *Times* coverage notwithstanding, the press continued to censure Nobel, and the Merchant of Death epithets lived on. In the end, it was only through the efforts of a genuinely unscrupulous figure that Nobel's fortunes began to change.

Colonel Taliafero Preston Shaffner was a dyed-in-the-wool mountebank whose title was entirely self-styled. He had first inveigled his way into Nobel's life on the very site of the Heleneborg disaster, quite literally while the remains were still smoldering. Soon after that, he invented a casing that made nitroglycerine safer to transport. He then took his invention to the U.S. government and, his path smoothed by Nobel before him, succeeded in getting the penalty for causing a fatal nitroglycerine explosion reduced from death to imprisonment.

That was all Shaffner needed to set out across the country, blithely boasting that he had fired "ten thousand blasting shots," much as Gouraud had run away with Daguerre's invention twenty years earlier. To the endless vexation of Nobel, he ultimately tried to claim the invention of the blasting cap as his own, and even attempted to transfer the patent rights into his own name without Nobel's knowledge. Nobel retaliated by making a large investment in the United States in the form of the Atlantic Giant Powder Company, which excluded Shaffner. The colonel sent out rumblings about a lawsuit, but it never materialized.

With this mitigated sort of assistance, the future of Nobel's invention in America was secured, and the world began to wake up to nitroglycerine's potential. Between 1865 and 1873, Nobel and his business partners built fifteen plants throughout the world to manufacture his explosives. By the end of that period, he was one of the wealthiest men of his day.

Free to go where he wished, Nobel returned to Paris, glad to be done with America and its churlish mountebanks. He moved into a four-story house at 53 avenue Malakoff, and soon made his entrance into the Parisian salons. He met Victor Hugo, and the two became good friends. On a trip to Baden bei Wien, he met a flower girl named Sofie Hess. In another echo of his incest play, he moved her into a separate apartment in Paris, explaining her away as his niece. She remained his mistress for ten years, until she finally caused his "heart and soul to rot" through a host of imagined transgressions.

That Nobel put on inventor's shows at all is more a measure of the times than of the man. He seemed to flee from the chaos of life—to jump to the role of penitent—as early as he could. Yet even after dynamite became more accepted, his conscience seemed unresolved. The Nobel Prize, with its commitment to peace, was one form of penance. Another was the odd manner in which he internalized his success.

In his old age, Nobel affected a stern, bearded countenance, except for his eyes—deep blue beneath a heavy brow—which invariably betrayed an inner world of infinite sadness. Yet that inner world had its own share of explosions. In 1895, he began to suffer from angina pectoris and had to take nitroglycerine internally to soothe the tremors. Surely, he must have seen the irony in this—the Merchant of Death prolonging his life by ingesting the substance he had done so much to promote. Tormented and melancholy, the inventor ate his supplies.

Nobel had come to America intent on convincing the public that his invention provided nothing to see, and in this he was oddly in step with the times. Between the spiritualist mechanics and the fictitious machines, invention was becoming an increasingly nebulous business. Small wonder, then, that many inventors of the post–Civil War era turned their attention to the most nebulous subject of all: the ether.

A subtle substance thought to pervade the universe and to allow light to travel through space, the ether, first postulated by Descartes, suggested both the Beyond and some fairly exciting machinery. And since the best scientific minds of the day, Michael Faraday among them, could neither confirm nor deny its presence, the field was open to anyone with an eye on the main chance.

The most important explorer of the ethereal realm in the Reconstruction era, Mahlon Loomis, might have done better manufacturing coffin alarms, as he has been all but buried by history. A dentist from Oppenheim, New York, Loomis produced the first commercial version of wireless telegraphy, or radio, at the age of forty. In 1866, he sent signals between the Cohocton and Beorse Deer mountains of Virginia—a distance of fourteen miles—and later, between ships separated by a distance of two miles in Chesapeake Bay. The aerials he used were "kites covered with fine light gauze of wire or copper, held with a very fine string or tether of the same material, the lower end of which formed a good connection with the ground by laying a coil in a pool of water."

This was a few years before Heinrich Hertz identified the principles of radio waves, so Loomis was left to work out the theoretical underpinnings for his invention as best he could. As he conceived it, his aerials could either radiate or receive by disturbing the electrical balance of the atmosphere, which he described as "the static sea" surrounding the globe.

On May 21, 1872, the Loomis Aerial Telegraph Bill came before Congress, with the inventor soliciting fifty thousand dollars for further work. In his appeal, Loomis explained that his invention caused "electrical vibrations or waves to pass around the world, as upon the surface of some quiet lake one wave circlet follows another from the point of disturbance to the remotest shores, so that from any other mountaintop upon the globe another conductor . . . may be connected to an indicator." The Patent Office found this explanation sufficiently convincing to issue Loomis Patent no. 129,971 on July 30, 1872.

On close inspection, this document contains some extraordinary information. Loomis claimed to have discovered not just a method of communication but also "a new and Improved Mode of Telegraphing and Generating Light, Heat and Motive-Power." In other words, his kites prefigured the attempts of others to produce television, the wireless transmission of power, and robotics—obsessions that, a generation later, Nikola Tesla would make his own.

Moreover, the basis for Loomis's invention was not very far from the theory of "free energy." "I also dispense with all artificial batteries," he wrote, "but use the free electricity of the atmosphere, in cooperation with that of the earth, to supply electrical dynamic force or current for telegraphing and for other useful purposes, such as light, heat and motive power."

The Patent Office may have let these claims through, but Congress did not want to subsidize them, and the experiments in Virginia and on Chesapeake Bay failed to garner big headlines. When the Loomis Aerial Telegraphy Company went public, no one bought any of its stock.

Why did Loomis fail to break the acceptance barrier in an age when oddities like Planchette were taken seriously? Loomis's personality may have played a role. That his very existence has survived in only the barest of outlines (even the mysterious François Gouraud left a better paper trail) lends credence to the notion that, if he could generate light without wires, he failed to generate many witnesses. A "Professor Loomis" does appear in the June 6, 1868, issue of *Scientific American*, advancing the theory that the earth is like a giant steam boiler waiting to explode, sending "the fragments careering through space as small planets or meteors, each bearing off some distracted member or members of the human family, to make, perchance, new discoveries and new acquaintances in other parts of the planetary system now revolving with us." Then again, Loomis was a common name at the time, and whether this was the same man who communicated across the mountains of Virginia remains a mystery.

If the exploits of John E. W. Keely are any indication, etheric inventions fared better when presented as viscerally as possible. Certainly, he never had any trouble finding stockholders, even though he stretched the laws of physics well past their breaking point.

Initially a musical composer, Keely trod into the world of invention after purporting to discover a connection between sound waves and the disturbance of the molecules of matter. By studying the behavior of drops of water, he developed a theory of adhesive attraction based on the magnetic currents of the earth. From there, he deduced that acoustics could break water into its components, releasing a force related to magnetism. This was no penny-ante force. "I once drove an engine 800 revolutions per minute of forty horse power with less than a thimbleful of water," he boasted, "and kept it running fifteen days with the same water."

Rousing interest through such bold claims, Keely was able to organize the Keely Motor Company in New York in 1872—the same year that the Loomis bill came before Congress. After his miraculous engine failed to materialize, he announced (sounding Whitney's old chestnut) that he was on the verge of his greatest discovery, thus raising the stakes for investors anxious to stay in the game.

Keely did produce something for people to see. He first demonstrated his "vibratory generator with a hydro-pneumatic-pulsating vacue machine" on November 10, 1874. In his Philadelphia workshop, he began the festivities by nonchalantly pouring a pint of water over a cylinder. When the needle on a gauge indicated 50,000 pounds of pressure per square inch, all hell broke loose. A tuning fork sent a brass ball running at 600 revolutions per minute. The stroke of a violin bow raised a heavy weight at a force of 2,000 pounds to the square inch. Ropes were torn apart. Iron bars were mangled or broken. Bullets flew out of nowhere and pierced foot-thick planks.

This complex of devices would soon work more comprehensive wonders, if the ballyhoo was to be believed. Mrs. Clara Jessup Bloomfield-Moore, a Philadelphia matron and enthusiastic supporter of Keely's project, said of it that the "divine element is shown by the laws of the etheric force to be like the sun behind the clouds, the source of all life though itself unseen." Keely himself spoke of having discovered "a new substance; a new force, altogether unknown to science." More concretely, his machine was supposed to pull a train of thirty cars from Philadelphia to New York at sixty miles an hour, using no more than a quart of water for fuel.

Around 1886, Keely changed tacks and began demolishing the air.

At the Sandy Hook Proving Grounds, his "inter-etheric liberator" used vacuum tubes to fire guns and move tons of matter. Sly to his bones, he also built a good many mechanisms to show how the principle of this machine worked, as if perpetual motion might be effected by adding more and more accessories.

Inevitably, some of Keely's stockholders lost their taste for the incessant predictions and brought suit. On November 17, 1888, Keely was found in contempt of court for refusing to explain his secrets to a committee of experts and landed himself in jail. The effect was negligible. Upon his release, he picked up right where he left off and continued wreaking his special brand of mechanical havoc until he died in November 1898—leaving behind a company capitalized at five million dollars.

After Keely's death, two University of Pennsylvania professors and Clarence B. Moore, an electrical engineer, became curious about the long trail of bravado and visited the famed Philadelphia laboratory. In the basement they found a compressed-air apparatus that fed into his hydro-pneumatic-pulsating vacue machine through a hole in the floor. So much for liberating the ether. They found no secret stash, though; to his credit, Keely had sunk all his money into improvements on his fabulously theatrical machines.

On November 22, 1875—just a year after Keely had first blasted bullets through wooden blocks—another inventor joined the "ether rush" after he observed a strange phenomenon in his Newark, New Jersey, lab. He had been training his attention on acoustic telegraphy—the transmission of tuning-fork tones over a telegraph wire—and had set up "a vibrator magnet consisting of a bar of Stubbs steel fastened at one end and made to vibrate by means of a magnet." In the midst of this experiment, he noticed a spark coming out of the core of the magnet.

The spark behaved mysteriously. It had no effect on an electroscope and thus was seemingly not electric. When the device was connected to a gas pipe, it generated a spark from other gas pipes in the room. Furthermore, the spark ignored the rules of insulation. To its discoverer, such properties indicated a new force. Rather than continue his investigations, however, he ran to the press with a breathless announcement. The scenario proposed was not so very different from those conjured up by Keely: Houses would soon receive this "etheric force," as he dubbed it, through the system of common gas pipes already in place.

The reporter for the *New York Herald* story of December 2, 1875, was respectful in tone about this unknown up-and-comer. "Mr. Edison," he wrote, "whose name promises to become famous as the discoverer of a new natural force, was at his laboratory in Newark last evening attended by his assistants and surrounded by a little company of interested persons, among whom were several expert electricians and a representative of the *Herald*. Mr. Edison is a young man, of about medium height, with full oval face, a large head, and a manner that bespeaks the utmost devotion to his business."

To give this discovery a context, the reporter compared it to the work of Baron Reichenbach, who some years back had discovered that electromagnets emitted light when placed in the hands of "sensitive persons."

In the age of the human cannonball, that was a logical inference. Mr. Edison moved directly to inform the scientific community that the world would soon be conversing through its stove pipes.

**Chapter Nine**

# HOW THE GOLDEN AGE WAS MADE

Traditionally, Carnival was a momentary celebration, a release from the social order before the rationing of food began. An ongoing Carnival, however, was something else again. The years between 1865 and 1875 were spectacular, yes, but they were also relatively uneventful as far as solid results were concerned. Rockets did not explode, the center of the earth was not reached, the dead did not return. For America to fulfill its promise, indulgence and industry had to be combined.

In 1875, Thomas Edison was not yet up to the task. Had he been more levelheaded, he might have researched his discovery more carefully and delivered a sound explanation of his findings. (What he called etheric force was, in fact, evidence of high-frequency electromagnetic waves, which Heinrich Hertz described more fully in 1888, thus laying the groundwork for radiotelegraphy.) But he did no such thing. In thrall to the spectacular, he ran to the scientific community blathering on about unknown forces and gas pipes. Naturally, they were only too happy to heap contempt on his head.

In England, where scientists were considered public figures, the response was full-throated. "He called it 'etheric force,'" groused Sir Oliver Lodge, "which rather set our teeth on edge." Lord Silvanus Thompson, a physicist, followed in the best Faraday tradition and gave a demonstration to his colleagues that was meant to prove Edison's claims false.

The American response, if less direct, was no less damaging. The Lazzaroni had always done their best to ignore any madman who appeared at their gates, and this time was no exception. Neither Joseph Henry nor any of his aging peers bothered to refute Edison. The younger generation of scientists, on the other hand, were not so inward-looking, and when *Scientific American* opened its pages to the etheric-force debate, Elihu Thomson, nominal heir to the Lazzaroni throne, chose the moment to demolish Edison in public.

Thomson's biographical profile contains only the faintest glimmers of the show inventor's character. As a child, he read *The Magician's Own Book* and learned to perform magic tricks such as the "electric kiss." Once, he saw fit to surprise his father with an electric shock. But in 1866, he entered Central High School—a public school in Philadelphia founded by Alexander Dallas Bache—and put away childish things. While there, he started a scientific society called "Scientific Microcosm," patterned after the staid lyceums of old, and made a desultory attempt to follow up on Henry's radio experiments in 1836.

By 1874, Thomson was teaching at Central High and belonged to the Franklin Institute, which Bache had headed so ably in the Jacksonian era. A grown man with a look of plain sense in his eye, he was a prime candidate to carry on the Lazzaroni tradition. But he was also anxious to prove himself, and so, risking his standing among Henry's circle, he published a refutation of Edison's etheric force in the *Journal of the Franklin Institute*. To his idols, he justified his decision on the grounds that he was acting in the interests of the truth.

In the decades to come, Thomson would again walk a thin line between the forces of order and disorder, with more complex results. For the moment, however, the article served its purpose: it painted Thomson as a careful scientist, Edison as a spurious mountebank. Edison's dream of the ether was roundly defeated.

Having been cast among the quacks, Edison resolved to stay well away from theories and to train his sights exclusively on inventions from then on. This decision would serve him well in the long run, but in 1875, it left him at an impasse. Telegraphy, his only area of real expertise, had been taken about as far as it could go. The etheric-force fiasco had made him even less credible than he had been in his days as an unknown roustabout. What he needed to find was a groundbreaking invention that already passed muster with the scientists, yet still offered room for improvement.

Ironically, if Edison had not been possessed of such a thoroughly unpredictable nature, he might have provided that invention himself. Before he discovered his etheric spark, he had been trying to send acoustic tones over a telegraph wire. Acoustic telegraphy would prove to be an important link between the telegraph, which transmitted a single tone, and the telephone, which could carry almost any sound. As it was, Edison interrupted his work in this area, and it took a more balanced inventor to follow acoustic telegraphy to its logical conclusion.

Photographs of Alexander Graham Bell invariably suggest a man who could be comic without sacrificing his dignity. His biography bears this impression out. Bell took advantage of the star system, but avoided the tendency of stars to rearrange reality on a whim. He derived much of his thinking from the stage, but worked out his equations with the diligence of a Faraday. It was Bell who mended the age-old division between the Lazzaroni and the show inventors, and Bell who brought the best of both worlds together. In the process, he transformed a creaky nineteenth-century automaton into an invention that continues to define the modern world.

Born in 1847 in Edinburgh, Scotland, Alec Bell grew up in a family that had much to offer in the way of both science and the arts. His mother, Eliza Bell, introduced him to painting, drawing, and music. He learned to sight-read quickly and at times was so excited by music that he couldn't sleep. His father, Alexander Melville Bell, was an elocutionist who developed a phonetic alphabet called Visible Speech. Melville also had a darkroom and encouraged all three of his children to put on homespun dramatic performances, so he could photograph them in striking poses. A pair of glass-plate negatives from the 1850s shows one of the Bell children, perhaps Alec, mimicking the famous masks of the dramatic arts—one smiling, the other weeping.

Towering above everyone in the Bell family was Alec's grandfather. The original Alexander Bell started out as a stage comedian and made a splash with a part in an Edinburgh production of *Rob Roy*. When he was subsequently demoted to the role of prompter, he opened a tavern to make ends meet. Modest success came when he transformed himself into a lecturer on elocution. Eventually this led to a position at the University of Edinburgh, where he gave one of the first public readings of Charles Dickens. When his church complained that Dickens was improper reading, he changed churches.

In 1846, Grandfather Bell published a 1,232-line poem in blank verse, titled *The Tongue,* a love song to his organ of choice. A year later, he published a five-act play called *The Bride,* which he passed down to his grandson Chichester, and was subsequently seen by Chichester's friend, George Bernard Shaw. As might be expected from Grandfather Bell's predilections, the play concerned itself with matters of elocution. The valet, a character named Allplace, opens the proceedings with the remark: "How much I have improved the manners in this family . . . Polishing a prosy lawyer into a tolerable baronet is a task to break a man's back." Allplace may well have been the inspiration for Shaw's Henry Higgins, though the original preface to Shaw's *Pygmalion* gives praise to "Alexander Melville Bell," thus confusing the generations along with the issue.

In any event, Grandfather Bell took it upon himself to play a real-life Pygmalion to young Alec during a stay in London, making him memorize speeches from *Hamlet, Macbeth,* and *Julius Caesar.* The training was hardly bohemian. The stern grandfather used theater as an iron rod to turn a boy, as Bell himself later said, "somewhat prematurely into a man." Later, however, these soliloquies would aid the inventor in his mechanical spectacles.

During his teens, Alec moved freely between the worlds of theater and technology. In 1862, he undertook a play of his own, calling it *Play of Douglas.* Filling fifty-six pages of a four-by-six-inch notebook, this five-scene drama employs puns, Irish laborers, impersonations, and unlikely coincidences to secure the requisite double marriage of a romantic comedy. Hoping to wed a fair lady, the protagonist disguises himself as a well-to-do ventriloquist with a speech impediment. The wedding takes place on April Fool's Day—an occasion when, as with Carnival, the ordinary rules are suspended. One of the laborers (who collectively act as the zanies) delivers the culminating logic:

PAT:        Ach! You're a pack of fools. Oi could put your brains in a nutshell. If the Captain and the Missus were married first, then Masther and Miss Helen would be brother and sister. And how could brother and sister marry, d'ye think. Eh? But if the Masther and Miss Helen married first, then the Captain & Missus would be their own mother and father, and of course, the mother and father should be married.

ALL
LABORERS:   Yes, you are right Pat.
PAT:        Of course oi is.

Alexander Graham Bell, 1876, posing with his cousin Frances Symonds in the habiliments of his friend Mohawk Chief Johnson. *Library of Congress*

In this play, one can see a budding comic playwright perhaps, but also a real-life ventriloquist beginning to find his way. The following year, Alec and his father visited Sir Charles Wheatstone, a colleague of Michael Faraday. Wheatstone had invented "an enchanted lyre" in 1821, which connected tuned rods to a source of vibration by an inconspicuous sound conductor. Melville, remembering Mister Faber's automaton from Barnum's exhibit in 1846, was interested in learning what Wheatstone had to say about mechanical-voice machines.

The visit clearly inspired the young Bell; back in Edinburgh, he and his siblings made a talking head of their own. Whether the automaton was to be a child of theater or of science was a matter of debate. Alec wanted to give it a face and a wig, but his father insisted that this was a serious scientific effort, and Alec's plan to design soft lips and cheeks was approved only because there was functional justification for it.

The finished product did not aspire to "Turkishness"—perhaps because of these negotiations—but its interior fully rivaled Faber's machine. It had a bellows for lungs, a tin-tube throat, nasal cavities, a larynx, gutta-percha jaws, and a soft palate made of rubber stuffed with cotton. Of course, in a family where the grandfather had composed a poem on the subject, the tongue received special attention. Designed by Alec, it consisted of a series of wooden cross sections covered in rubber and controlled by levers, which, much like Faber's version, could be made to rise and fall at any point along its length.

When the Bell children started working their homunculus—Alec moving the lips—it gave off a falsetto that reminded them of Punch and Judy. Before long, it uttered the word *mama* (admittedly, the odds favored such a word), and mother Bell came running to the stairs to see what the baby needed.

Melville was pleased and encouraged further experimentation. Alec was happy to oblige: by April 1865, he had begun work on a tuning-fork experiment, in which he tested the musical pitches of vowels to see if there were any consistent pattern to be found. Still, his thirst for theater had not been slaked. Around this time, his brother wrote him a letter discouraging his literary efforts—much as his father had discouraged the idea of a wig for his automaton—bemoaning "the extreme poverty of thrilling ideas which you manifest in most of your prose and dramatic works."

Arriving in Boston by way of Canada in 1871 (and taking in a play, *The Octoroon*, on his second day), Bell found work at the Pemberton Avenue School for the Deaf. Soon he was teaching his students to point to parts of their faces as a way of building up symbols. He also got them talking—an astounding achievement at the time, and an intriguing reprise of his efforts at teaching an automaton to speak.

Meanwhile, Melville Bell, who had also come to America, commanded that his son take part in a Visible Speech lecture tour. These lectures were not without their fringe benefits. By speaking at what became known as the Thursday Night Meetings, Bell got to know some of the leading scientists of the city. In return, he gained access to two inventions—the Revolving Mirror Apparatus and the Phonautograph—that helped him explore the possibility of incorporating the Visible Speech system into a telegraphic code.

While living in Boston, Bell again felt the presence of the Amazing Talking Machine, if only indirectly. In 1871, the Euphonia resurfaced for a one-week engagement at the Horticultural Hall, not far from where Bell worked. By this time, the original Mister Faber had died, bequeathing the invention to his niece. She in turn had joined up with her husband, and, styling themselves Madame and Professor Faber, they had taken the show back on the road.

If the new owners clung to the hope that their outlandish possession might still be taken seriously, they were in an increasingly small minority. A year or so after the Boston engagement, the reborn Professor Faber approached Joseph Henry for a loan, only to be politely but firmly turned down. And so once again the machine returned to the realm of curiosities. From the scientists' office in Washington, it went on to appear in Barnum's Traveling World's Fair, first in 1873, and again in the 1874–75 season, along with scores of Indians. For the Amazing Talking Machine, the division between science and sideshow seemed as wide as ever.

Bell was able to navigate between these shores more deftly. By 1875, he was making significant advances in musical telegraphy—the same technology that Edison was exploring simultaneously down in New Jersey. He also began to avail himself of the technical services provided by the Charles Williams shop at 109 Court Street—where Edison had worked briefly in 1869. Bell was not distracted by sparks, however. His account was assigned to Thomas A. Watson, a shop employee, and together they began working on a device that could transmit the human voice along a wire.

The two made a good team—so good, in fact, that Watson has some claim as coinventor of the telephone. Still, progress was not as fast as it might have been. On May 5, 1875, Bell employed Manuel Fenollosa, a friend and former traveling bandleader, to send the strains of piano music along a wire. Unfortunately, the piano was attached to a metal frame, causing the experiment to fail. Bell did not realize his error even after checking things over. He wondered if he should remove certain clauses in his patent, but he wasn't sure. It was becoming obvious that he needed more help than his peers could provide, so in 1875 he too he paid a visit to Henry, just as Faber had before him.

The aging Lazzaroni listened sagely as Bell stammered and ran his hand through his hair. This young man, though unkempt, was not like Faber or the smooth-talking John Keely, who had come knocking earlier that year. Rather than making strident claims, Bell actually expressed doubts about his project. Of course, Henry knew something about the subject, too; he had thought of sending the human voice over telegraph lines before Bell had even been born. He was willing to hear more.

When Bell described what he had achieved thus far, Henry's icy composure fell away and he promised to publish the findings. Bell then confessed that he had little knowledge of electricity, to which Henry replied, "Get it!" Bell did get it, and on March 10, 1876, the famous first words, *Watson—come here—I want you*, were spoken over a telephone line.

As has been commonly noted, Bell's patent application arrived only hours before Elisha Gray, an inventor under contract with Western Union to make improvements in telegraphy, filed an almost identical one. This story, although true, reveals more about cultural attitudes than it does about legal facts. Bell's telephone was ready for the Centennial Exposition a few months later; Gray's was not. Moreover, the Patent Office awarded its patents to the first to invent, rather than the first to apply, which suggests that the dead-heat finish was played up from the beginning by a public eager for a dramatic inventor's contest.

This was only natural, though, since the telephone was first imagined as a dramatic device. In the first months after the invention was a fait accompli, the common speculation was that it would allow performances to be transmitted into homes. "By means of this remarkable instrument," wrote the *New York Times* on March 22, "a man can have the Italian opera, the Federal Congress, and his favorite preacher laid on in his house."

All things considered, it seemed appropriate for Bell to put on a public demonstration; indeed, everyone was waiting for one. At the time, the Centennial Exposition was about to be held in Philadelphia. Bell, no longer the uncertain neophyte who had appeared at Henry's footstool, but a tall young man with jet-black hair, side whiskers, a mustache, and "black eyes that could look through a water commissioner" moved directly to secure an exhibit there.

He might as well have been swallowed by a whale. Grand and rambling, the Centennial defied inventory. A common joke of the time made a butt of the yokel who thought he had "done the exposition" after seeing the three-headed cows and the manatees. But in truth, even sophisticated types missed most of the show, because it was impossible to see it all.

Illustrations of the time typically show the larger exhibition buildings disappearing into the vanishing point, so as to suggest infinite size. Compared to what the United States had produced in the way of exhibitions before, this was very nearly the truth. The Main Building was 1,880 feet long and 464 feet wide. The Machinery Hall was 1,402 feet long and 360 feet wide, built of wood and glass on masonry. A total of 30,684 exhibitors plied their wares, among them a dental machine (run by foot power, water, steam, or electricity), Sir William Crookes's radiometer, Langen and Otto's atmospheric gas engine, the newest Gatling gun from Hartford, looms, boilers, a steel exhibit, brick-making machines, newspaper-folding machines, lighthouse lighting systems, the arc lights of Moses G. Farmer, and the first practical typewriter. Credulity was more than strained. It was all but overwhelmed. With few exceptions, even the most ostentatious show inventor could not hope to stand out from the crowd.

This enormity of scale served a definite purpose. The Centennial was not a local affair, as the New York Crystal Palace had been. It was a patriotic occasion designed to illustrate national might. The exhibition opened on May 10, 1876, to the parading of troops and the strains of eighteen national anthems. The keynote speech was delivered by President Ulysses S. Grant, who then headed a legion of dignitaries through areas representing different regions of the world, as if demonstrating his global dominion.

In much the same vein, the exhibits were arranged around the Corliss Engine, built by Rhode Islander George H. Corliss and delivered right on time on April 17, 1876. The Corliss Engine dominated all the other exhibits and, so to speak, gave them life. With 1,400 horsepower (and an option to boost it to 2,500), it rose 39 feet in the air, weighed 680 tons, and powered everything from the weaving exhibits to the foundry.

The nationalist overtones of the Corliss Engine became clear on closing day, when the president again made an appearance, this time to turn the machine off. The Honorable D. J. Morell described these two giant powers—the man and the machine—in glowing tones:

> When these our ceremonies are ended, the President of the United States, by the motion of his hand, will make the lightning his messenger to stop the revolution of its wheels, and at the same instant to tell the world that the International Exhibition, which marked the Centennial of American national life, is closed.

And so it was. At 3:37 in the Judges' Hall on November 10, 1876, before a crowd of 450 select audience members (and an orchestra of 110 members, who had played Wagner to commence the ceremonies), the president rose and turned to the left to give the signal to a telegraph operator, who transmitted the signal "7-6" to the main telegraph office. The same current caused a gong to strike, which was repeated by a forest of gongs, and the machines ceased running.

The Corliss Engine and the president provided the center of the Centennial, orienting everyone and everything else in relation to them. By one measure, this approach made for a successful exhibition. John Welsh's closing speech indicated as much when he declared, "The International Exhibition is to be regarded as a reverential tribute to the century which has just expired . . . Its memories are hallowed."

Yet because the exhibits were meant to serve as ornaments to the overarching spectacle of American political power, many inventions deserving the keen attention of the public went by unnoticed. Indeed, rarely have the achievements of the past been so poorly couriered into the future.

The Difference Engine of George B. Grant, for example, was nothing short of a miracle. Finished only a few days before the exhibition, this engine was able to produce tables of logarithms, sines, tangents, reciprocals, and square and cube roots. "When the machine is worked by hand," wrote Joseph Miller Wilson, "a speed may be made of ten to twelve terms per minute, and from twenty to thirty when power [sic] by the attachment at the rear end." It was, in other words, a computer.

The Difference Engine was new, yet it was not new. Charles Babbage, an English economist, had begun work on a machine with the same name and the same function in the 1820s, based on the sophisticated Jacquard loom, which used prerecorded designs on punched cards to produce patterns in silk. At his London home, Babbage took immense pleasure in holding weekly soirees, during which visitors could behold his invention as it computed tables of numbers according to finite differences.

In 1831, Babbage began work on a much grander machine called the Analytical, or Great Calculating Engine, which would have been capable of analyzing information rather than simply calculating within given parameters. For this project, he joined forces with Augusta Ada Byron, Lady Lovelace daughter of the poet Lord Byron.

They met when he was lecturing on his Difference Engine at the

Mechanics Institute in London. With a radish-shaped face and the build of a small bird, Lovelace captivated Babbage, though the relationship never became romantic. On the contrary, she soon demonstrated her intellectual mettle and began assisting him on his project. By 1836, they had devised a system of punched cards that gave instructions to the Great Calculating Engine. "We may say most aptly," wrote Lovelace, "that the Analytical Engine weaves algebraic patterns just as the Jacquard loom weaves flowers and trees."

Both of them were doomed, however—Lovelace tragically so. A longtime opium addict, she found it increasingly difficult to focus on the project at hand. On November 15, 1844, she described a vision worthy of her predecessor in Romantic inventions, *Frankenstein* author Mary Shelley:

> I have my hopes, & very distinct ones too, of one day getting *cerebral* phenomena such that I can put them into mathematical equations . . . In order to get the exact effects I require I must be a most skilful manipulator in experimental tests; & that, on materials difficult to deal with; viz. the brain, blood and nerves of animals.
>
> In time I will do all I dare say . . . I hope to bequeath to future generations a *Calculus of the Nervous System.*

Lovelace was a compulsive gambler who bet on horses often. In the late 1840s, she compounded this problem by becoming the mistress of a track companion, John Crosse, who may also have been her bookie. It was a singularly unhealthy relationship. By 1852, she was in debt to the tune of 3,200 pounds. Unable to explain herself to her husband, she managed to pawn some of her diamonds through Crosse. When she was diagnosed with cancer of the uterus, her mother weaned her off opium, and she died in a torment of disease and withdrawal.

For his part, Babbage suffered from a more prosaic malady: lack of funds. Left to fend for himself by the British government, he postponed his work on the Analytical Engine and undertook various ventures, including a foray into arc lighting for a theatrical production at the German Opera House in 1845. At the time, stages were lit by gas, which was effective in its way, but not as effective as colored electrical lights. Michael Faraday offered Babbage his assistance on the project, remembering perhaps that his mentor Davy had astonished audiences with an experimental arc light at the turn of the century.

Babbage sketched out a vignette for demonstrating the lights, called *Alethes and Iris.* Scene one opened with "The Temple of the Sun. Alethes a Priest of the Sun determines to search for the book of Fate." Events progress along glaciers, through a marble palace to a circular rainbow, where at last Alethes unites with his love. Limelights illuminated this odyssey in blue, yellow, purple, and red, while two fire engines waited at the ready outside the performance. Afterward, an educational epilogue made use of a diorama depicting the earth's crust, with animals preserved in the various levels.

Whatever the aesthetic value of Babbage's forays into drama, they had no discernible connection to his computer, and he seemed never to realize the impact that an inventor's show could have. Toward the end of his life, he came across the work of George Boole, who introduced the Boolean algebra of zeroes and ones, and remarked the arrival of "a serious thinker." In 1869, Charles Peirce, son of Lazzarone Benjamin Peirce (and sometime producer of plays), took Boolean algebra one step further and assigned the values of *on* and *off*—the first expression of today's familiar binary code. But Babbage was in no position to capitalize on the idea; after years of effort, his Analytical Engine existed only on paper. When he died in October 1871, the funeral gathering was small.

Historians have generally assumed that Babbage's advances were lost until the twentieth century, thus accounting for the enormous gap in the development of the computer. Yet five years after Babbage's death, there was George Grant showing his version at the Centennial. The chroniclers of the exhibition also mention a successor to Babbage, a printer from Stockholm named George Scheuz. (Grant may or may not have known of either inventor, though given the parallels, it seems that he did.) Observers thought Scheuz's computer was slow, but they remained hopeful and considered it better than Babbage's machine. These observations didn't really matter, however, since the invention was dwarfed by the larger show of the Centennial itself.

Another forward-looking device at the Centennial was the Map Fac-Simile Telegraph—a fax machine—which transmitted weather maps to a point about 150 miles away for the Signal Service. These maps produced isobaric lines—a notation showing the divisions in barometric pressure. "This invention produces the map entire, with its lines and figures," explained one witness. "It is then lithographed and printed for distribution on the presses with which the signal office is supplied . . . It is believed that this invention will prove a valuable adjunct to the

present systems of telegraphy, or may, with further improvements, su-
percede them."

The fax machine, like the computer, also had a distinguished past by
the time it appeared at the exhibition. Alexander Bain, who ran a successful telegraph business of his own until the American Company (with
Zenus Barnum at the helm) bought it out, had begun work on one as
early as 1850. Bain devised a rotating cylinder on which the sender
could write. This cylinder, when turned, would break a circuit wherever
it encountered the ink and close the circuit wherever blank spaces appeared. The result on the other end was a negative of the original: white
writing on a black background.

Telegraphers were generally aware of Bain's invention. Alexander
Jones, author of *Historical Sketch of the Electrical Telegraph*, complained in 1852 that it was too slow and ruminated on his own plans
to improve it. "By our method, we proposed to send 600 to 1000 words
per minute," he wrote. "Besides, our plan like Bain's and Bakewell's,
can be made to send small maps, plans of houses or vessels, &c., or the
full length outlines of the human figure."

Fax technology took a further leap forward in the 1860s, when an
Italian named Giovanni Caselli tried his hand at it. Caselli's pantele-
graph used the motion of a pendulum on both the sending and receiving
ends. It could also reduce images and send simultaneous messages along
the same line. On May 16, 1865, two of these six-foot-tall devices were
installed by order of Napoleon III, one in Paris, the other in Lyons.
Faxes of beautiful quality were sent back and forth for the next five
years. In 1867, a Marseilles leg was added. By 1868, the line could
accommodate 110 telegrams per hour. While ornate messages, such as
a calligraphic message to Emperor Xian Feng of China, were sometimes
sent, the majority were stock quotations.

Like the computer, Caselli's fax machine is generally thought to have
vanished into history. But that didn't stop a similar machine from churning out maps for the Signal Service in 1876.

The forgotten accomplishments of the Centennial give the lie to the
idea that technology advances in an inexorable, linear fashion. We may
think of computers and fax machines as products of the information
age, but in fact they appeared long before airplanes, movies, or television. The failure of these inventions to take their rightful place in the
march of progress was a cultural phenomenon as much as a scientific
one. It was the story of Oliver Evans and his automobile all over again—
a case of ineffective promotional techniques.

There was one difference, though. Where Evans had behaved like a star years before audiences were ready for one, the purveyors of the Difference Engine and the Fac-Simile Telegraph failed to recognize that the star system had matured into the most effective means available—and that the large-scale exhibition format would bury them.

As it turned out, feminist inventors attending the Centennial made the same mistake. Even though they did everything possible to be recognized—and in fact, succeeded quite admirably in being recognized—they consistently underestimated the importance of the star system.

In the opening ceremonies, Reverend Bishop Matthew Simpson included a special blessing for "the women of America, who for the first time in the history of our race take so conspicuous a place in a national celebration. May the light of their intelligence, purity and enterprise shed its beams afar, until in distant lands their sisters may realize the beauty and glory of Christian freedom and elevation."

This bit of praise may well have been an attempt at appeasement. As Richard Henry Lee took the podium and read from the Declaration of Independence, two women stormed into the hall and walked up the aisle to protest the exclusion of women from this portion of the exhibition. One of these women was Matilda Gage, an ardent suffragette and writer for the feminist newspaper *Revolution*. The other was Susan B. Anthony, manager of that paper, who three years before had been proposed as commissioner of patents by *Scientific American*.

Shouts of "Order! Order!" rang out, but the women would not be stopped. They continued right up to the stage, delivered their Woman's Declaration into the hands of a startled Lee, then turned on their heels and left. Outside, they stood on a platform and read this declaration, one woman shielding the other from the sun with an umbrella.

If the nature of this incident seems contemporary, the reaction by the official chroniclers was, too: they failed to mention it. But women inventors were not a new phenomenon, either. Ada Lovelace, as noted, was one important contributor. Katharine Greene, who at the very least coinvented the cotton gin with Eli Whitney, was another. Women had also appeared in the audiences of inventor's shows throughout the Industrial Revolution, often in greater numbers than men. They had turned out to see Humphry Davy and Michael Faraday, and they had been encouraged on the American side of the Atlantic by such figures as Amos Eaton and Elkanah Watson, the originator of the agricultural fair. Having been such devoted observers, it only made sense that they

would eventually want to try their hand at mechanical matters themselves.

Come the Civil War, Munn & Company, the patent agency that grew
out of *Scientific American*, was actively encouraging women inventors
from its branch office in Washington, directly opposite the Patent Office. "Women can also apply for and obtain patents upon the same terms
as the sterner sex," it announced in 1861. "We frequently take out patents for the ladies; but they do not exercise their ingenuity as much as
they ought. If the woman-patentee is of age she can transfer a patent
legally, and enjoy all the rights and privileges of any one."

That married women in many states still had to assign their patents to their husbands was an undeniable obstacle. Still, as Anne L.
Macdonald persuasively argues in her groundbreaking book *Feminine
Ingenuity*, women took up the mechanical arts with a new vigor during
the Civil War while their husbands were off fighting. The number of
patents issued to women in the 1860s was 441, a huge leap from the
28 patents they received in the 1850s.

By opening day at the Centennial, the feminist movement was large
enough to support a fair amount of infighting. These arguments may
resonate in the twentieth-century ear. One contingent, represented by
the likes of Mary Livermore of Illinois, was in favor of representation
for its own sake, even if the majority of the inventions to be displayed
were domestic, and therefore backward, in nature. The other side, represented by the voices of Matilda Gage and the writer Antoinette Brown
Blackwell, felt that women should show only inventions that tran-
scended the confines of the home. The women inventors, for their part,
did not really care about the finer points of the suffragist movement, so
long as they had a venue for exhibiting their wares.

Livermore, having chaired the committee for the Great Western Sanitary Fair in Chicago, was a likely candidate to lead the new female
exhibitionists. But the prime mover behind the Women's Pavilion at the
Centennial was to be Elizabeth Duane Gillespie, organizer of the 1864
Sanitary Fair in Philadelphia.

Gillespie went at it like a true promoter, sponsoring "concerts and
art shows, nationwide benefits, bazaars, and patriotic 'Martha Washington' tea parties"—a bit of theater in which women dressed up like their
great-grandmothers and sold memorial teacups for twenty-five cents
each. Radicals who had at first opposed a separate pavilion (preferring
women to take their place among the other exhibitors) relented and
bought stock. In the end, Gillespie raised more than $100,000.

Gillespie may have believed in her nickname—"The Imperial Wizard of the Centennial"—too earnestly. A large crowd assembled to watch the opening of the Women's Pavilion. Gillespie arrived late with the empress of Brazil, spoke in French, then pulled a golden cord, causing the many looms to spring to life.

As it was in the Centennial writ large, this ceremony succeeded in establishing the high standing of its leading figure, but little had been done to aggrandize the exhibit itself. William Dean Howell remarked that the needlework offerings were "no better than if men had made them," thus damning both sexes in a single blow. True, there was a smash hit in the butter sculpture made by the Arkansan artist-inventor, Caroline Brooks. But on the whole, the effect of the Women's Pavilion was one of "mottoes worked in worsted on cardboard."

Then again, given the purpose of the Centennial, the Women's Pavilion was probably meant to show (as the Reverend Bishop put it) the conspicuous place American women occupied in a national celebration, rather than to promote individual examples of mechanical excellence.

By and large, women inventors embraced this approach both at the Centennial and in the years to come. While they continued to be productive through the nineteenth century, they consistently favored the dubious benefits of statistical representation over the brash remonstrances of the men's star system. In the 1890s, Charlotte Smith prevailed upon the Patent Office to publish a list of all women patent holders, and even put out two issues of a magazine in an effort to give her constituency a voice. But far from descending to Pulcinella's boasts or Arlecchino's tricks, *Woman Inventor* implored women to behave in a "ladylike" fashion, and illustrated their presence at the Patent Office Centennial as a study in genteel comportment.

The effort to "clean up" the public appearance of women inventors muted their success considerably. Perhaps this was inevitable in an age when women were assumed to be crazy and men had to prove it. Nevertheless, the most popular woman inventors were still those who cast gentility to the winds.

In the case of the Centennial, there was only one such female zany of note, Dr. Elizabeth French, and she was forced to hold court outside the exhibition gates. At her electric clinic on 1609 Summer Street, French had her students read her vanity publication, *A New Path in Electrical Therapeutics*—and schooled them at a tuition of $500 for women ($1,000 for men). Her patented "Improvement in Electro-Therapeutic Appliances" came straight out of the Mesmer school, with a personal touch: she applied three metal alloys to the patient's body rather than two. Her treatment for nervous headaches was three to five minutes of electrical current, during which time the patient suffered a suction cup at the base of the skull and an electrode between clasped hands. Adding her own unique mark to the field of electrotherapy, French complemented this spectacle with a liberal supply of "Dr. Elizabeth French's Anti-Dyspeptic Electric Baking Powder," which could be used to bake "electrified bread."

In the sea of anonymity that constituted the Centennial, Bell could hardly have hoped to make headlines. Still, he tried. On June 25, 1876, Emperor Pedro II of Brazil, who looked something like a subtropical Santa Claus, and the British scientist Sir William Thomson (later Lord Kelvin) attended an impromptu demonstration, in which Bell set up a receiver before a few chairs, then ran wires past the Hook and Hastings organ exhibit to a point several hundred yards away, in the northeast corner of the Main Building.

Bell described the intricacies of his harmonic telegraph, or telephonic organ, and allowed the two dignitaries to send and receive "messages" on the device. After this, he removed himself to the sending area and began singing into the telephone. Thomson listened to this song through a receiver, enthralled. Then, out of nowhere, he heard the instrument speak with the inventor's voice. Startled, he ran over to confirm what he had heard.

Turning his upbringing to advantage, Bell began to recite Hamlet's "To be or not to be" soliloquy. When the Brazilian emperor, taking his turn at the receiver, heard the words of the tragic prince, his regal bearing dissolved. He ran over to Bell—his entourage bustling after him— shouting, "I hear, I hear!" Meanwhile, back at the receiver, onlookers jostled to hear snatches of the disembodied Hamlet. Among them was Bell's fiercest competitor, Elisha Gray, who put his ear to the receiver and heard the immortal words, "Aye, there's the rub." "I turned to the audience, repeating those words," Gray related afterward, "and they cheered."

The telephone was demonstrated again at the Judges' Hall, with stricter requirements: the transmitting and receiving apparatuses were placed in different buildings. The performance went off without a hitch, and Bell's esteemed advisor, Joseph Henry, saw to it that the telephone received the Certificate of Merit.

Bell demonstrating his invention. "As I placed my mouth to the instrument," he remembered, "it seemed as if an electric thrill went through the audience, and that they recognized for the first time what was meant by the telephone." *AT&T Photographic Archives*

This was a critical turning point in the history of American invention—the moment when the values of Barnum and Henry, excess and economy, converged in a single device. In Bell's telephone, the unlikely dream of the mournful Mister Faber and the scientific constraints of the ascetic Lazzaroni were completely intermingled. It was a gag with meaning, a lazzo in which the New World was made real. The conditions for a golden age were satisfied.

Nobody knew it yet, however. Pedro II may have been overwhelmed by the telephone, but his enthusiasm was short-lived. When he offered his impressions two weeks later, on July 8, 1876, it had already slipped his mind. The Walter press used to print the *New York Times*, he declared, "astonished him more than all else."

That was the big lesson of the Centennial for show inventors like Bell and Watson. For the telephone to receive more than a passing notice, only a demonstration that put them at the center of attention would suffice. Fortunately, the point was not lost on them. After a brief hiatus, during which Bell improved upon his telephone and generally tried to make ends meet, they achieved their first two-way conversation. Two days later, on October 11, 1876, they gave the first of their "star-billing" demonstrations, at the American Academy of Arts and Sciences.

Sir William Thomson had said that people would whisper secrets to each other over telephone lines, and eventually they would. But for the moment, technical limitations required that the performers shout, much as commedia dell'arte actors had on the outdoor trestles of yore. In fact, Bell and Watson seemed very much like an acting team supported by scientific fact.

A peak dramatic performance came in Massachusetts on February 12, 1877, when Bell and Watson held forth between the town of Malden and the Lyceum Hall in Salem (where Nathaniel Hawthorne had once been secretary), in a series sponsored by the Essex Institute. After explaining the principles of his device, Bell produced the sound of an intermittent current. This was meant simply as a test; it met with applause anyway. Building the expectations, the inventor had his telephonic organ play "Auld Lang Syne" and "Yankee Doodle." Then, he picked up the box.

"As I placed my mouth to the instrument," Bell remembered, "it seemed as if an electric thrill went through the audience, and that they recognized for the first time what was meant by the telephone."

Watson sang a ditty, reported on an engineers' strike that had just begun, and offered a few comments. Then a number of audience members were allowed to speak with him. After the show, the stage was mobbed, and it remained so even after the gas was turned down and the phone taken offstage. By popular demand, the lecture was repeated on February 23.

True to form, the star approach resulted in press coverage where the demonstration at the Centennial had not. On March 4, the *Springfield Republican* suggested that music could be broadcast by telephone. *Scientific American* picked up the story. So did *Leslie's Illustrated Weekly*, the *New York Daily Graphic*, the *Athenaeum* in London, and *La Nature*

in Paris. After hearing "The Last Rose of Summer" sung over the telephone at one performance, a correspondent for *Scientific American*
reported: "The effect was simply charming. The sound of the voice
penetrated the Boston end of the telephone with a distinctness equal to
that attainable in the more distant parts of a large concert hall, and a
unanimous vote of thanks was sent by the handy little instrument which
had procured for the assemblage so agreeable an hour."

As time went on, the demonstrations became more elaborate. Bell
employed, variously, the Boston Cadet Band, a Brown University quar-
tet, and Italian opera singers to deliver their strains through his invention. The sound quality being what it was, however, the shows were
eventually scaled down to songs and remarks by Watson. Tone-deaf, the
formerly small-time assistant to Charles Williams of Boston tore through
"Hold the Fort," a Moody and Sankey hymn, at a mighty volume.

The reactions to the telephone shows varied. Bell's mother-in-law-to-
be invoked the name of Barnum, as well she should have, given the
telephone's theatrical roots. James Clerk Maxwell, inheritor of the Faraday mantle in letter if not in spirit, scowled that Bell, "to gain his
private ends, has become an electrician." Inevitably, others intimated
the work of dark powers and seances. In an exchange reminiscent of the
days of the planchette, audience members at one of the Salem-Malden
performances asked not only, "Is it thawing or freezing in Malden?" but
also "Who will be the next President?" In any case, Bell was constantly
besieged for his autograph and signed it with the punlike "A. Bell" until
his fiancée, Mabel, insisted that he render his full name. The idea
seemed to stick: it is because of this show-business decision that he is
known today as Alexander Graham Bell.

As the spring turned to summer, the pressures of the intense performing schedule were building. By April 1877, Elisha Gray was giving Bell
and Watson some competition with his own series of lectures. Bell was
experiencing a mysterious rash all over his body, perhaps from stage
fright, or perhaps from the strain his activities were creating in his relationship with his fiancée. Still, the show drew an audience of two to
three thousand in Providence in the midst of a snowstorm and outdrew
Oliver Wendell Holmes on May 4. Bell pressed on, taking his act to
Hartford, New Haven, Boston, and New York.

*Scientific American* watched his approach with considerable interest.
"We await, with much pleasurable anticipation," wrote a reporter, "Pro-
fessor Bell's introduction of the telephone to a New York audience."
When it arrived, however, the editors were disappointed. Bell and

Watson spoke between New York and New Brunswick, New Jersey, a distance of thirty-two miles, but "the sound produced was not generally audible throughout the hall."

A second demonstration was needed to save the day, and Bell effected some fancy stagecraft to do so. The June 9 issue of *Scientific American* describes a performance that sounds for all the world like science as ventriloquism. "It is a most bewildering sensation," it read, "to hear a song faintly emitted first from a box on the stage, then from another suspended overhead, and finally from a third across the room, as the operator switches the current from one telephone to another." Privately, other critics in New York—Cyrus Field and the presidents of New York University and Columbia among them—weighed in with equally high praise.

Finally, the lectures came to an end in Lawrence, Massachusetts, when so many telegraph operators cut in on the line that they obliterated Watson's voice coming in from Boston. Bell took the opportunity to live out the plot of his childhood play in a flesh-and-blood romantic comedy. Trading in his "ventwiloquist's whiskers" for love, he and Mabel Hubbard were married on July 11, 1877, and the newlyweds absconded to Niagara Falls.

There was no mistaking it. The year had been a resounding success.


The phenomenon of the telephone shows had a galvanizing effect on American technological culture. As a personality, Bell served notice that work and play need not be mutually exclusive. He did not lie or exaggerate his claims but laid bare the fruits of his meticulous research for all to see. At the same time, he fully understood the power of theater and capitalized on it without reservation. As a result, he was able to humanize science even as he dignified the inventor's show. This cultural achievement, as much as anything else, was responsible for bringing about America's golden age of invention.

Of course, every new era also supplants an old one, and inevitably, as exchanges sprang up and people learned to shout at their neighbors from the comfort of their own homes, the older generation felt its moment slipping away.

Five months after Bell's marriage, Joseph Henry awoke in his office at the Light-House Depot on Staten Island and found his right hand paralyzed. A dagger of pain struck at his heart. Returning to Washington, he consulted his neurologist, Dr. S. Weir Mitchell, who diagnosed kidney trouble.

"Am I mortally ill?" asked Henry.

Mitchell admitted he was.

"How long do you give me to live?" Henry persisted. "Six months?"

"Hardly that," came the reply. Henry had Bright's disease, at the time a terminal malady.

Henry offered his resignation to the National Academy of Sciences in April 1878. At the suggestion of Professor George Barker of the University of Pennsylvania, a telephone was installed in his Smithsonian office, and on April 18, the man who had done so much to make the telephone possible listened on as an old friend in Philadelphia recited a nursery rhyme. Less than a month later, he died in his sleep. "But for Henry," said Bell by way of eulogizing him, "I would never have gone ahead with the telephone."

As for Faber's machine, by 1877 it was in Paris, in an exhibition at the Grand Hotel. Two years later, it had moved to a room adjoining magician Robert-Houdin's theater. In 1885, "Professor Faber," still threadbare and trying to promote his wonder, came to Bell for financial assistance. Bell remembered the talking machine he had built in his youth and lent the showman $500. After that, the Amazing Talking Machine slipped beyond the horizon of history.

## Chapter Ten

# ESCAPE FROM
# MENLO PARK

In Royall Tyler's 1787 play *The Contrast*, Jonathan, the rustic zany, is asked by a sophisticated city woman if he went to the "playhouse" the previous night. Jonathan recoils at the idea, saying that he went to the "hocus-pocus place," where every night a man displays his ability to eat a case knife. As he describes the "green cloth" that was raised on "the next neighbor's house," however, it becomes clear to everyone but him that he was at the playhouse after all. It also becomes clear that he failed to appreciate the niceties of the stage. "I paid my money to see the sights, and the dogs bit of a sight I have seen," he complains, "unless you call listening to people's private business a sight."

Edison could have delivered that line with ease. A hayseed in the big city himself, he once declared that "[p]lays and most other 'entertainments' became a bore to me, although I could imagine enough to fill in the gaps my hearing left. I am inclined to think I did not miss much." There was a fair amount of coyness in that statement. Like Tyler's Jonathan, Edison was undeniably an entertainer himself, and fully capable of capturing the public's attention.

The only question was how to turn this flair for publicity to advantage. In 1876, Edison was still a gangly upstart, distinguished mostly for his practical jokes. He had a respectable number of telegraph patents to his name, but the etheric-force episode had hurt his chances for achieving anything grand. For all intents and purposes, his future looked busy but not bright.

Then came the telephone, and with it, as the editors of *Scientific American* noted, "a new business sprang into existence almost in a day, with no end of scientific and practical problems to solve." Suddenly Edison's haphazard imagination had a wide berth in which to operate. Seeing his chance, he said good-bye to his life as a wanderer and began to build a new kind of theater—a permanent site that would allow him to dramatize the telephone in his own idiosyncratic way.

The first building to go up in the open pastures of Menlo Park, New Jersey, was a barnlike structure 100 feet long and 30 feet wide, with white clapboard sides, tall windows, and a porch. On the lower floor were a library, an office, and a drafting room. The second floor was a single room stocked with electrical apparatuses, chemicals, materials of every sort, batteries, and a variety of brass and steel instruments. By the end of May 1876, Edison was open for business.

The Menlo Park laboratory did not generate attention merely by its existence; at the time, the Centennial Exposition taking place some two hundred miles to the south overshadowed its christening. Nevertheless, Edison boasted a great future for it. To Dr. George Beard, who had rallied to his side during the etheric-force episode, he predicted he would turn out "a minor invention every ten days and a big thing every six months or so." It was an ingenious solution for a man who could not brook the rigors of abstract science. What he lacked in method he would make up for in sheer volume.

If Menlo Park was designed to reflect Edison's copious brain, it also allowed him to play different dramatic roles as circumstances demanded. He could sound the outrageous claims of a John Keely, or throw down a challenge worthy of Singer. He could play Jonathan the zany, Napoleon the conqueror, even the lone hero on the verge of death. He could be epic, comic, terrifying, brutal. In a sense, Menlo Park acted as a focal point in which the many traditions of the show inventors could converge.

There was, however, one role that framed all the rest. It was Edison's habit to announce his intentions boldly and then retire to Menlo Park as if into a secret chamber. While cloistered away, he seemed to grapple with the very laws of physics. Time passed and the suspense grew—would he fail this time? Often it seemed so. But when at long last he emerged, his results were almost always breathtaking. Concealment, suspense, surprise—the master role that controlled all of Edison's many faces, and the one he added to the tradition of the mechanical spectacle, was that of the escape artist.

Escapology had seen a recent vogue in the 1860s, when the Davenport brothers introduced a cabinet into the usual props of handcuffs and ropes. Known as the Indian Mail Trick, the Davenport's act demanded that the brothers be tied up in full view of the audience, then locked into a cabinet. After the door was shut, the audience heard a variety of bells and buzzers. When the door was opened again, there they would be, still bound as before. How had all those sounds been made, if not by supernatural spirits? The Indian Mail Trick was soon modified by others, but in every case, the drama was heightened by the concealment. Inside the cabinet, the rules of physics were suspended; the audience could only wonder how. If the trick took longer than expected, so much the better—this only built suspense.

Such shows were well known in late 1876, when an escapologist named Commandeur Cazeneuve took America by storm. By the looks of his resume, Cazeneuve was a multitalented man. A promotional poster boasted 111 items in the "Repertoire of Le Commandeur's Original Inventions," including "Dovetailed Atoms," "Photography of the Thought," and intriguingly, "Telegraphy a thousand years hence." Most impressive was his Double Indian Mail Trick, in which a reporter tied an empty trunk with ropes, then wrapped it in sheets of paper and sealed the paper with wax. The assemblage was slid inside a cloth-sided cabinet and placed behind a curtain. Within three minutes, Mrs. Cazeneuve had been miraculously transported into the trunk, in a bag, with the top tied and the wax seal unbroken. In admiring Cazeneuve a generation later, Harry Houdini noted that this show compared favorably with such competing acts as "the Moody Sankey meetings at the Tabernacle."

Though there is no evidence that Edison patterned himself after Cazeneuve, he would have recognized a kindred spirit. As Le Commandeur peppered his escape acts with visions of millenial telegraphy, Edison began doing much the same at Menlo Park. Both announced their intentions *in advance*, then vanished into their cabinets, where they defied the laws of physics. Both laid claim to a prolific repertoire (though Edison would do much better than 111 inventions), and both became more spectacular in the face of competition, producing new acts to keep the audiences coming.

The difference was that Edison actually made good on his boasts. Three times in a row, in fact, he escaped from Menlo Park with an invention based on Bell's telephone. In the process, he defeated all the major enemies American show inventors had known to date—the church, the government, and the scientists—and put an entirely new set of rules into play.

In the spring of 1877, while Thomas Watson was belting out "Hold the Fort" on stages throughout the Northeast, Edison announced the success of his own telephone to his investors. "As yet it is not sufficiently perfect for introduction," he crowed. "It is, however, more perfect than Bell's." Then he vanished into his Menlo Park, to do battle with the mysteries of winding coils and carbon.

But Edison surprised even himself with what he produced. In February 1877, he had been toying with the idea of a machine that could record the dots and dashes of a telegraph message on a revolving disc of paper when he thought to apply this same principle to the telephone. To illustrate the diaphragm of the device to his daughter Marion, he made a little paper man connected to a cord, a pulley, a ratchet wheel, and a funnel. If Marion shouted, the little man sawed the wood.

In effect, this was a voice-activated automaton, much like the one Thackeray had predicted for Mister Faber's machine thirty years earlier. As Edison worked on it, he discovered that some of the dots and dashes produced the faintest sound of the human voice. It was an accident, but once he was onto it, he kept going.

The disclosure of this invention followed a pattern that would become standard Edison procedure. He kept the project secret for a while, allowing a few leaks to slip out to intimates such as George Barker (the man who had arranged for Henry to have a telephone conversation just before he died) and a few others. Like the sounds of the spirits inside the escape artist's cabinet, these leaks generated a sense of mystery and, more important, suspense. By November 5, 1877, at least one newspaper was ruminating over Edison's possible movements.

Then Edison issued forth a mighty boast. His "stage manager" of the time, Edward H. Johnson, sent out a formal announcement of the phonograph on November 17, proclaiming that a practical version would be ready by the end of the year. The announcement showed remarkable nerve, since only after making it did Edison give his revised sketches to one of his "muckers," John Kruesi, with the order that "the machine must talk." Kruesi had never even heard of the project.

It was a gamble, but it paid off. When Kruesi delivered the prototype, Edison shouted the first verse of "Mary Had a Little Lamb" into it, and the machine dutifully played it back. The entire crew spent the night talking into it and playing it back, floored by this surprise invention. By December 6, the talking machine was sufficiently improved so that Edison felt he could take it to the offices of *Scientific American*. So many people crowded around it that the paper's editor, Alfred Beach, worried that the floor would collapse. The Patent Office was excited, too; in an age when patents often took months or even years to be awarded, Edison received one a mere twenty-three days after filing his application.

Edison called his invention a phonograph, a word that at the time referred to stenography, so the early visitors to Menlo Park beheld a "secretary" that inquired as to the editors' health, declared itself well, and then bid all a good night. Even after seeing it, many considered the phonograph a ventriloquist's trick. Among the doubters was Bishop John Vincent, a cofounder of the high-minded Chautauqua Association. Vincent gave the machine a hell-and-brimstone sermon at breakneck speed. When it was played back to him verbatim, the bishop became a believer. So much for the religious opposition to the Edison juggernaut.

The phonograph gave integrity to the phrase *overnight sensation*. Morse had created a craze with his telegraph, then slipped into lofty inaccessibility. But people knew where to find Edison, and from the moment the existence of the phonograph became known, he was a celebrity. Reporters, scientists, and tourists alike flocked to Menlo Park to see the wonder of the age. The Pennsylvania Railroad organized special excursions with the express destination of a certain six houses in the backwoods of New Jersey. Visitors were allowed into the sanctuary, where they gawked at wires and flasks of every variety, like audience volunteers looking over the magician's apparently empty trunk. People who lingered past nightfall remarked on the spectral figures passing from one building to the next, likening them to dark powers with knowledge beyond the normal ken.

Edison never "cared much for the theater" and got stage fright at the thought of a lecture, yet on his own turf, he was master of the show. For visitors, he had his phonograph whistle, cough, ring bells. Singing badly, he worked the heckling of the onlookers into the act. The machine played back his errant tunes along with the cries of "Go away, if you can't sing any better!" and "Help! Police! Murder!" He even went so far as to anthropomorphize the invention, calling it his "little feller." (Most stenographers of the day were men.)

In a bid at mythmaking, Edison also supplied interested parties with a quote from *Richard III*, written in his own hand, in a circle so as to loop back on itself: ". . . now is the winter of our discontent made glorious summer . . ." Oddly, this choice echoed the conflict between winter and summer represented so long before in the meeting of Carnival and Lent. Like so many show inventors before him, Edison was transforming absurdity into order, and from there into a new abundance.

For the moment, Edison was content to let chaos rule the day. When the Edison Speaking Phonograph Company was formed in January 1878 (with Bell's father-in-law Gardner C. Hubbard as a member), James Redpath of the Redpath Lyceum was appointed to give the phonograph a real tour—and one that out-Barnumed Barnum. Five hundred phonographs were exhibited in entertainment halls around the country in a bang-up revue, with barkers reeling in the people to hear music-hall comedians tell jokes and singers warble popular airs from the grooves. One week's receipts alone produced royalties of $1,800. En route, the phonograph stopped in Washington, where it talked to Joseph Henry shortly before he died and received what was at this point a perfunctory blessing. Then it went on to the White House on April 18, 1878, where it greeted President Hayes. So much for the opposition of the Lazzaroni and the U.S. government.

The phonograph craze finally died down after almost every American had heard and seen one, and, it must be said, after it became apparent that the invention gave, at best, a "burlesque or parody of the human voice." Edison's fame, meanwhile, was still expanding. In March 1878, Edison finally demonstrated his "more perfect" telephone, which contained his patented carbon microphone. The new telephone satisfied expectations all around when it transmitted a human voice loudly over a distance of 107 miles. Edison blithely remarked that he had "cured" Bell's invention.

With the success of the phonograph and the carbon microphone, rumor became an essential part of Edison's dramaturgy, and in fact, it was a rumor that resulted in his famous sobriquet. As has often been recounted, a reporter covering the phonograph craze once asked Edison whether he was "a bit of a wizard," to which the inventor replied that he didn't think much of that sort of thing. What is less widely known is that another reporter—or perhaps the same one—used the shower of publicity to paint a picture of a truly wizardly Edison.

On April Fools' Day, 1878, the *Daily Graphic* ran a story with the headline "A Food Creator: Edison Invents a Machine That Will Feed the Human Race, Manufacturing Biscuit, Meat, Vegetables and Wine

Out of Air, Water and Common Earth." In this article, the reporter described his visit to Menlo Park, where he was treated to a tour of the place and an explanation from the inventor.

"Lavoisier dismissed it, and Davy, Liebig and Farraday [sic] overlooked the simplicity of this thing," Edison was quoted as saying, "I was led on by Dalton's great discovery of the law of multiple proportions . . . the law of isomorphism . . . the general formula of $axnb$ . . . I can make cabbages that have never felt the rain."

When the reporter, W. A. Croffut, revealed his ruse in a letter, Edison was far from annoyed. On the contrary, he enjoyed the prank immensely. "I am receiving letters asking for the lowest prices for food-machines," he wrote back, "and asking when they will be ready for the market." Whether or not Edison intended to continue the charade by claiming to have received orders, the magical connotations continued. On April 10, an anonymous writer in the *Graphic*, the same paper that had run the food hoax, dubbed him "The Wizard of Menlo Park." On July 9, the *Graphic* went so far as to dress him in sorcerer's robes. From then on, the image was permanently embossed on the public's mind.

This marvelous food-producing machine had an unofficial ancestry in the Lazzo of the Magic Book, in which Pantalone and Coviello use a magician's book to make food appear—and succeed only in setting the book on fire. Why such a lazzo would be popular is perfectly understandable. After all, what better subversion of the prevailing order on the eve of Lent than a device that could produce endless supplies of food? One also begins to see where the twentieth-century notion that technology could feed the world originated: in the anointing of a food-producing wizard on April Fools' Day.

Edison, having shocked the world past all expectation, did not rest on his laurels. Immediately, he turned to the telephone a third time, hoping to fulfill his mission of turning out a "big invention" every six months or so. While working on the carbon microphone, he had noticed that some of the prototypes produced odd squeaks and tones. These tones had to be eliminated from the final microphone, but ultimately they became the basis for his micro-tasimeter, which measured infinitesimal variations in pressure and could allegedly detect the moisture added to a piece of paper two or three inches away.

The way Edison publicized the micro-tasimeter shows how far he had come. An article in *Scientific American* had "Professor Edison" pontificating on his discovery of "molecular music," with which he expected "to indicate the heat of the stars, and to weigh the light of the sun." This was not so very far from a pronunciamento on "cabbages that have never felt the rain." Yet Edison felt confident enough about his standing by this time to mail these newspaper reports directly to physicists such as Sir William H. Preece. For the moment, the British scientists were silent.

Around this time, the ubiquitous Professor Barker invited Edison for a viewing of a solar eclipse in Rawlins, Wyoming. Edison considered the unusual conditions of an eclipse to be ideal for testing his microtasimeter and accepted the invitation. When the celestial event gave uncertain results, Edison showed no signs of discouragement. He simply hopped the next train to California—riding on the cowcatcher the entire way—and met up with Barker again in Sacramento. As always, Edison's haphazard course led him to something auspicious: During this meeting, Barker persuaded him to test his mettle against the incandescent light.

The idea of a workable incandescent light—which, unlike the arc light, had to burn in an enclosed globe—was considered preposterous at the time, much as perpetual motion machines were. The commonly used name for the principle encapsulated the pessimistic attitude toward it. It was called the *ignis fatuus*, literally, the "fatuous fire." Ever since Humphry Davy had caused a brief illumination with an arc light in the first years of the century, many inventors, notably Englishman Joseph Swan, had labored in vain to achieve long-lasting incandescence. By 1879, incandescent lights were appearing here and there, but the results were still inchoate.

Edison knew a good dare when he saw one: trying to tame the electric light meant playing brinkmanship with known science. This approach had not worked well for him before, when he had espoused the wonders of the ether. But in a mere two years, he had risen from obscurity to worldwide fame, thanks to his prodigious aplomb. Perhaps it was time to leave the telephone behind and to forge again into new terrain. Perhaps it was time to pay the British scientists back.

Edison launched into the project in typically cavalier style. Upon returning to the East, he went with Barker and Grosvenor P. Lowrey to visit the shops of William Wallace, coinventor of a dynamo with Moses G. Farmer. When he beheld the glory of eight arc lamps burning brightly there, he grew animated and made a great show of calculations. Then he told Wallace point-blank, "I think I can beat you making the electric light." The two men shook hands, and Edison signed his name on a dinner goblet with a diamond stylus, along with the date: September 8, 1878.

Cyrus McCormick had made similar boasts when taking on his rivals in the 1840s. But this was no mere challenge to see who could cross a wheat field faster. It was a contest to see who could *invent* something faster. Edison continued to make this contest exciting at every turn. Shortly after meeting Wallace, he told a reporter that he would have electric lights ringing a miniature village around Menlo Park *in six weeks*. He had not even begun work on his first bulb. To the reporters who dogged him, he made even more sweeping claims. Sounding for all the world like that emperor of the ether, John Keely, he bragged, "I can produce a thousand—aye, ten thousand lights from one machine."

The British scientists, William Preece among them, spied their chance and leaped down Edison's throat. The idea that light could burn with the same brilliance no matter how many bulbs were used, they said, defied all laws governing the conservation of energy. As far as they were concerned, Edison was playing fast and loose with science again.

In fact, there was some substance to his audacious boasts. Edison had realized that a single light bulb meant nothing. If he was to stand out from the crowd, he would have to invent a light bulb that was commercially viable. To this end, he had begun to devise an electric lighting *system*, which could support enough lights to illuminate a city block. Of course, he didn't reveal that this system adhered to known electrical laws—not when he had a contest to win.

But the truth of the matter was that Edison no longer cared if the physicists mocked him. To demonstrate as much, he had hired a physicist of his own, a man named Francis Upton, whom he nicknamed "Culture" and gleefully treated like an underling. More important, he had identified an economizing force that had no connection to science. Having silenced bishops, presidents, and Lazzaroni, he was setting his sights on the financial titans of the day.

Grosvenor Lowrey was largely responsible for the shift. A New York corporate lawyer with business connections that ran wide and deep, Lowrey worked out a deal with some of the nation's most powerful financiers, including Western Union, W. H. Vanderbilt, and—operating the strings behind it all—J. Pierpont Morgan. The terms stipulated that Edison would receive $50,000 for his lighting project and stock in the Electric Lighting Company, while the investors retained the rights to his lighting patents for five years.

The Electric Lighting deal showed considerable nerve on the part of the backers. Many an investor had sunk his cash into a mechanical project before, but rarely had anyone done so without seeing some kind of working prototype, even if it later turned out to be deceptive or faulty. Edison's investors, on the other hand, were entering into a business that did not yet exist—and that scientists said could not exist.

To a robber baron, however, this was no cause for alarm. The tycoons of the Reconstruction era were, after all, kindred spirits to the show inventors in many ways. The infamous Wall Street overlord, Jay Gould, actually began his career selling a mousetrap of his own devising on the streets of New York. Others like Carnegie and Vanderbilt had built their empires on the telegraph and the railroad. They were acquisitive and unafraid of new technologies. And most acquisitive and fearless of them all was Morgan. A phlegmatic, towering figure, he had flourished as a profiteer in the Civil War, then enlarged his coffers as a money changer and a banker. By the time Edison came along, his company, known as the House of Morgan, controlled vast stretches of the American rails and much of the country's gold.

So it was very simple really. The principals of the Electrical Lighting Company, newly appointed as an economizing force, saw that there was a percentage in nonsense. And if this Edison had turned histrionics into history before, the odds were fair that he could do it again.

From Edison's point of view, the arrangement was even more promising. In fact, it could not have been better. Rather than bellowing discouragement and disgust at him, the House of Morgan actually underwrote his *unfinished performance*, in the hope that it would result in an invention that reorganized society.

Grosvenor Lowrey—the intermediary between excess and order—did a great deal to hasten this performance to its completion. It was at his bidding that Edison had made his Keelyesque claims, and it was at his bidding again that Edison held a public press conference on October 18 to demonstrate the state of the light bulb thus far.

Edison gave reporters a good look at a bulb powered by a Wallace-Farmer dynamo, then turned the light off. This show left the journalists impressed, but the truth was, he had yet to come up with a light that burned for more than a few minutes. Had he not turned the power off, the light would have gone out anyway. The sleight-of-hand proved to be an effective stalling technique. Soon afterward, Lowrey prevailed upon Edison to close Menlo Park's doors to visitors. The inspection of the empty trunk was over; the escape artists would be left to the spirits for almost a year.

Edison's muckers worked harder than ever on the lighting project through the winter. But even when three new buildings were added to accommodate them, results were slow in coming. When Edison's backers began to show signs of disenchantment, Lowrey once again stepped in and organized a demonstration.

In April 1879, Morgan arrived with an entourage at a new reception building on the Menlo Park grounds designed to mimic the cherry-panelled club rooms of Wall Street. Unfortunately, while the upholstery performed admirably, the light bulbs did not. The first burned out quickly. Mucker Charles Batchelor replaced it, but the second and third burned out, too. The investors retired to the library for a while, then solemnly returned to New York.

The situation deteriorated rapidly from there. In the summer of 1879, Edison announced the invention of the Long-Waisted Mary Ann, his own version of the dynamo. He claimed that this dynamo performed at ninety percent efficiency, but to the public it seemed like a form of misdirection, and it was widely ridiculed. Meanwhile, news of the failed demonstration for Morgan leaked out and the press began calling Edison a charlatan, or simply a doomed man. One reporter observed that he was "close to death."

Then, to add salt to the wound, word came in October that a man named William E. Sawyer had patented a light bulb of his own. Ultimately, this light bulb proved impractical, but the mere announcement of it was enough to send a bolt of panic through the offices of Edison's backers. Quick as they were to stab each other in the back, the financiers of the Gilded Age had no interest in seeing their vassals do so; it was far more prudent to hedge their bets. Using Lowrey as a go-between, the Electric Lighting Company proposed a merger between Edison and Sawyer.

But even the robber barons could not control a show inventor in his prime. Edison believed in the star system, and he believed in inventor's contests, no matter how wasteful they might be. He sent back a vehement reply, toned down by Lowrey en route, that under no circumstances would he consider consolidation with Sawyer. It would be a fight to the end.

This was a theatrical experience that was hard to match. Unlike Cazeneuve, Edison did not actually know the secret of his own trick. He was like a bound man first learning his knots while all the world watched, with no choice but to try out every possible combination. Sleeping hardly at all, he set about testing more than 1,600 materials for his filament. He read scientific journals day and night, searching for the secret that would finally turn the tide. One mucker invented what was called a "corpse-retriever," in effect, an extremely loud alarm clock to bring drowsing mechanics back to their task. It was Edison against the scientists, Edison against his own record, Edison against time.

Yet at times, the mood at Menlo Park could be almost sanguine. Edison had often encouraged his muckers to tell stories and listen to the music they had made on a phonograph. In the current siege, the atmosphere became more like that of an actual theater. One assistant rewrote H.M.S. Pinafore, with Edison playing the lead: "For I am the Wizard of the Electric Light/And a wide-awake Wizard, too." Boehm the glass blower played the zither and sang lonesome melodies; "My Heart Is Sad with Dreaming" seems to have stood out as a favorite. Early in 1878, an organ had been installed in the lab, and Edison himself was sometimes wont to improvise on it, though he could hardy have heard much of what he was doing.

This "hidden" theater would be further embellished in the years to come, when luminaries like Sarah Bernhardt came to sing into Edison's phonograph, and later still when muckers hammed it up for Edison's movie cameras inside an enclosed building on the grounds. For the moment, it turned the struggle into a drama obscura, in which Edison was accorded the position of star, to whom all others deferred. Such powers of direction allowed him considerable berth in his own narrative, so much so that, as far as anyone knows, it was the Wizard himself who on October 21, 1879, tried out the piece of carbonized thread that finally met the test.

For once, Edison did not run straight to the press. Perhaps Lowrey had advised against it. More likely, Edison wanted first to establish some aspects of the more elaborate lighting system that he had espoused all along. In any event, even his own investors did not learn of his success until early November. Meanwhile, those passing by Menlo Park at night could only guess what the strange illuminations emanating from within might portend.

The official disclosure was something else again. When the New York Herald finally got its story on December 21, 1879, the concealed drama became a powerful success story, with all the elements a playwright could want. An account from the muckers made the filament a character in its own right. When the light had already burned dimly for hours, they said, Edison tested it to see how brightly it could shine. "For a minute or more," one wrote, "the tender thread seems to struggle with the intense heat—that would melt diamond itself—then at last succumbs and all is darkness. The powerful current had broken it in twain, but not before it had emitted a light of several gas jets."

The cabinet was open. The light bulb was a reality.

A public demonstration was planned for New Year's Day, 1880, and again excursion trains were put on the rails. Far from the magnificent spectacle envisioned, there was little to see but an ad hoc improvisation involving a Long-Waisted Mary Ann and some forty lights. Two bulbs were attached to the library entrance: eight were set up on poles around the grounds, and another thirty inside the lab.

This display was enough for the spectators to behave as if Carnival were on anyway. At least three thousand spectators descended on Menlo Park in the days between Christmas and New Year's. Come the demonstration, they turned the lights on and off incessantly. Eight globes were stolen. A vacuum pump was smashed. In the dynamo room, pocket watches were magnetized. A lady bending over to pick up something she had dropped had her hairpins summarily removed by a dynamo magnet.

William E. Sawyer, the now-defeated rival, showed up inordinately drunk, shouting and cursing at Edison until the crowd shut him up. Then, hoping to discredit his competitor, he tried to short-circuit the lights. The bulbs were connected in parallel, however, and Sawyer managed to extinguish only four of them before some of the heartier members of the crowd threw him out with no uncertain turn of phrase. Two years later, Sawyer, still drunk, shot a man in a New York boardinghouse and died while awaiting his prison sentence.

And so the electric light entered the world, threatening to reel out of control, then put to rights by a crowd anxious to believe in the spectacle of it all. This was the inventor's show at its most powerful, the fulfillment of the many mountebanks' promises for so many years.

Of course, the complete lighting system, which promised to power many lights at once, was still far from completion, and most any other inventor would have concentrated all his energies on this untested idea. Not Edison. He pressed forward, as always, following the myriad impulses of his imagination. He developed one of the first electric trains, which he enjoyed driving around the grounds at forty miles an hour. He began work on a talking doll. One day muckers came across a brand of patent medicine called Polyform, with a label that sported the image of their leader's face and a promise to cure "sick headaches, neuralgia, and other nervous diseases." Edison, good mountebank that he was, saw the nostrum as a chance to make good money, and changed his mind only after repeated appeals from his associates, who thought it would tarnish his image in business circles.

But Edison did not recant his roots often. In the course of bringing his lighting system to fruition, he built a powerful dynamo capable of lighting 1,200 lamps, called the Jumbo generator, after Barnum's famous elephant. Behind schedule for its debut at the Paris Electrical Exposition of 1881, he imposed upon Tammany Hall to clear the roads between his office and the port, and have a fire bell and a police escort lead the horse-drawn procession of iron Jumbos, in pure Barnum style, through the New York City streets.

By this time, there was no doubt that Edison was as big a star as Barnum himself, and he could be every bit as ostentatious as the Great Humbug if he so desired. That is to say, he was a superstar. His story—the earthy practical joker from Milan, Ohio, who ran a printing press on a train and grew up to change the world—achieved mythical proportions. Reporters bore down on him to learn not of his plans for his next invention, but his sleeping habits, his thoughts on longevity, tobacco, progress—anything that held the slightest bit of mystery for the human mind. When the usual stories no longer sufficed, Edison was put upon to write down his idle thoughts for the curious minions. He dutifully complied and laid bare his personal musings. In his internal world, he converted churches into "heavenly fire escapes." He rearranged his wife and two daughters in his "mental kaleidoscope to obtain a new combination." He dreamed that "in the depth of space on a bleak and gigantic planet the solitary soul of Napoleon was the sole inhabitant." And, of course, he revealed that he didn't care much for the theater.

Edison's achievements between 1876 and 1879 were nothing short of revolutionary. Walking into the world of technology during its most implausible phase, he made good on its fantastic promises by churning out one outlandish invention after another. Show inventors had long exhibited a penchant for diversity, of course. Colt had tried his hand at the telegraph when the revolver business was slow; McCormick had returned to his reaper when his furnace failed. But no one had made variety part of their plan.

After Edison, no one could do otherwise. The principle of planned variety put robber barons in the seat the scientists had occupied, and from this vantage they scoured the field for inventors whose antics might yield the best percentage. At the same time, Edison, in staging his spectacles as challenges, embroiled his competitors in what amounted to an ongoing contest. Anyone remotely interested in keeping up with him had to build up an inventory of new machines or risk falling by the wayside. They had to become variety inventors.

This was true even for those who considered themselves above such things. As late as 1875, Elihu Thomson, schooled in the ways of the Lazzaroni, had relished his refutation of Edison's etheric force. But the spectacle of Menlo Park ultimately proved irresistible. In 1879, when the light-bulb fever was at its height, Thomson invented a three-coil dynamo with an automatic regulator, which greatly enhanced the practicality of direct-current electrical systems. Then, in 1880, he visited Edison's Menlo Park labs. What he saw at his adversary's lab must have been impressive, because soon afterward, he shocked his scientific peers by resigning from his teaching position at Central High and embarking on a full-time career as an inventor.

From then on, variety was most certainly Thomson's preferred mode. The list of his accomplishments came to include a method of welding that used electrical resistance to produce heat, an electric motor, a repulsion motor, an alternating-current distribution system, a cream separator, improvements in x-rays, high-frequency radio, an oil-immersed transformer, and various inventions in trolley cars and train control. By the time he was awarded his last patent in 1935, he ranked third in number of U.S. patents issued.

The barrel-chested Hiram Maxim learned the Edisonian virtues of planned variety by a harder route. A native of Maine at a time when this state was essentially a forest with legal borders, Maxim was a rough-hewn, ebullient character of the sort that Verne had characterized so well in *From the Earth to the Moon*. He loved wrestling and boxing. When asked by Russian imperial authorities to state his religious persuasion, he declared himself Protestant, "because I protest against the whole thing."

Maxim first made his mark in the 1870s as an inventor in the field of power systems, devising machinery for the gas and electrical industries, with a specialty in lighting and power distribution. By the time Edison announced his light bulb in 1879, Maxim was already two years into the race with his own incandescent light. Though this lamp was impressive, it availed him nothing. Whenever he displayed it, he invariably heard passersby praising this latest evidence of the Edison marvel, even though the Menlo Park inventor had yet to produce one.

But if Maxim suffered from the appeal of Edison's escape act, he also benefited from the presumption of diversity it created. Sometime between 1879 and 1881—after Edison had already emerged as the winner in the light-bulb race—Maxim was called upon by A. T. Stewart and Company, for whom he did consulting work, to pay a visit to a carpet factory. The resulting conversation, recounted by Maxim in the first person, reveals just how much the expectations placed on inventors had changed.

> I said, "If it is anything that relates to the machinery of boilers or a waterwheel I can attend to it."
>
> "No it is not any of these; it is trouble with the weaving of carpets."
>
> I replied that I had never been in a carpet mill in my life, and knew nothing of it.
>
> "But it is our orders that you go there and straighten it out."
>
> Still I protested, saying: "Suppose I should apply and say I have come up to straighten things out in the carpet factory, he would naturally ask me what experience I have had, I should have to say 'None.' What would he think or say?"
>
> "We don't care what he would say."

In other words, an inventor was someone who could invent on demand. Maxim acquiesced, then surprised himself by solving the problem in about five minutes. After inspecting the offending steam machine on the premises, he decided that it required nothing more than a shutoff timer. The manager at the carpet factory was amazed.

From that point on, Maxim was unyoked from the narrow confines of his field. First, he noticed that the dynamos employed in lighting exhibitions often magnetized the watches of onlookers, and devised a device for demagnetizing them. Then, on his trip to the Paris Electrical Exposition of 1881, he made the first drawing of the machine gun that would make him famous.

Maxim understood the nature of his departure quite well. When he approached a London barrel maker, he was told to go back to electricity, because the gun-making industry was rife with competition and failure. His reply was a veritable motto for variety inventors. "I am a totally different mechanic from any you have seen before," he thundered, "—a different breed."

In 1884, Maxim patented his machine gun—a belt-driven, water-cooled weapon capable of firing six hundred rounds a minute—and began manufacturing it at the Vickers-Armstrong munitions works at Erith in Great Britain. Then, settling in as an expatriate, he proceeded to demonstrate that he really was of a different breed. Over the remainder of his life, he extended his expertise to curling irons, riveting machines, locomotive headlights, fire extinguishers, a cathedral-sized flying machine, and, throwing in a touch of the mountebank, a medical inhaler—an output that ultimately earned him knighthood.

Edison's multifarious career also provided the blueprint for Alexander Graham Bell's post-telephone activities. In the late 1870s, seeing what Menlo Park had done with his invention, Bell established his own Menlo Park, a powerhouse called Volta Laboratories (which eventually became Bell Laboratories) in Washington, D.C. Then, he too began his own exercise in planned variety.

In 1879, as Edison's light-bulb drama progressed, Bell began to investigate whether echoes from the ocean floor could determine depth: a rudimentary version of sonar. It was a compelling notion, but he was no longer the tenacious inventor who followed an idea to the bitter end; there seemed to be too many other ideas to pursue. Before long, he became engrossed in something he called a photophone.

Bell knew from scientific journals that selenium changed its resistance in relation to changes in light, and he had once spoken to an audience at the Royal Institution about the possibility of "hearing shadows." His interest rekindled, he delivered a sealed envelope to the Franklin Institute containing information on "seeing by telegraph." Then he hired Watson and a man named Charles Tainter, who had also worked at the Charles Williams shop, to join him in his effort to send sound through the medium of sunlight.

On February 19, 1880, in their laboratory on L Street in Washington, Tainter produced a workable model. Using a selenium cell, mirrors, a system of lenses, and a telephone circuit, the mirror was vibrated by the voice: a kind of optical microphone. Bell was elated as he imagined the photophone's many applications—for wireless communication between ships, for sonic transmission of lighthouse signals, for determining the sounds of stars. Betraying his motivation, he declared that the photophone "would prove far more interesting to the scientific world, than the Telephone, Phonograph, or Microphone."

Bell managed to transmit messages a distance of 213 meters, from the Franklin School to the L Street lab. He also tried to transmit the sounds of cigar smoke, fried eggs, and a stick of sugar candy—of which, oddly enough, only the cigar smoke was audible. After these initial experiments, he convinced William Forbes, president of the National Bell Telephone Company, to back further development. Chichester Bell, the cousin who exposed George Bernard Shaw to Grandfather Bell's play, was brought onto the project for his knowledge of chemistry.

By April 1881, the invention had evolved into the Spectrophone, an early foray into spectrum analysis. No one seemed to be paying much attention, however. The photophone was exhibited at the Philadelphia exhibition of 1884, and given passing notice by *Scientific American* as an entirely theoretical development. Bad press or no, the device failed when subjected to fog, rain, snow, or clouds.

Another distraction presented itself to Bell on July 2, 1881, when President James Garfield was wounded by an assassin named Giteau. For weeks, Garfield valiantly clung to life in the White House (as the President's House had come to be known) as doctors delivered reports three times a day and the nation hung on tenterhooks, unable to act.

Bell looked on, too, and wondered how far his new, problem-solving powers extended. He had been on good terms with the White House ever since one of the first telephones had been installed there in December 1878 for emergency use by President Hayes. On July 26, then, he exercised his entrée and, along with Tainter, slipped in through a side entrance, eluding reporters. He had brought with him an apparatus dubbed the Induction Balance, which we would recognize today as a metal detector; when the device passed over metal, a circuit breaker indicated a change in tone. With it, Bell hoped to locate the bullet in the president's body.

Garfield was awake by the time they had set up. Unfortunately, the condensers made an indecipherable spluttering sound when passed over the President's body. Bell made another attempt on August 1, but again the Induction Balance didn't work. (He had placed the device on the right abdomen, but the bullet was lodged elsewhere.) Garfield was moved to Elberton, New Jersey, where he suffered his last terrible days.

Bell might not have been up to saving a president, but from the acoustic telegraph and the telephone, he had expanded his palette to include sonar, spectrum analysis, and metal detection. In the following decades, he would take an interest in flight, air conditioning, heat conservation, solar heating, hydrofoils, and potable seawater, among other things. He was not averse to the occasional scientific theory, either. On November 13, 1883, he presented a paper to the National Academy of Sciences titled "Upon the Formation of a Deaf Variety of the Human Race."

At the time, Darwin's theory of natural selection was becoming widely known, and Sir Francis Galton's newly minted notion of eugenics was achieving currency. Applying these ideas to his own experience, Bell came up with a novel theory. Deaf people, he pointed out, constituted one of the few handicapped groups that tended to intermarry. From this, he surmised that the deaf might one day spawn their own separate race. "Having shown the tendency to the formation of a deaf variety of the human race in America, and some of the means that should be taken to counteract it," he concluded, "I commend the whole subject to the attention of scientific men."

Medical inhalers, audible cigar smoke, a deaf species—by the 1880s, inventors were daring to publicize a wide variety of odd notions, even in such high-flown venues as the White House and the National Academy of Sciences. But none of them dared more or revealed a greater knack for diversity than Nikola Tesla.

In the spring of 1881, as Edison's caravan of Jumbos proceeded triumphantly through the streets of New York, this twenty-five-year-old Serb failed to show up for work at the Central Telegraph office in Budapest. Tesla had suffered from bizarre maladies before. When his brother Daniel died, the five-year-old Nikola began to have hallucinations. "When a word was spoken to me," he remembered, "the image of the object it designated would present itself vividly to my vision and sometimes I was quite unable to distinguish whether what I saw was tangible or not." At twelve, he learned to dispel the intruding visions, but he continued to see flashes of light throughout his life.

Now, the spirits raged in him again. He claimed to be able to hear a housefly land on a table and a ticking watch from three rooms away. His pulse boomeranged from 260 beats per minute to a sluggish pace. Years later, he remembered the episode vividly:

> The sun's rays, when periodically interrupted, would cause blows of such force on my brain that they would stun me. I had to summon all my willpower to pass under a bridge or other structure as I experienced a crushing pressure on the skull. In the dark I had

the sense of a bat and could detect the presence of an object at a distance of twelve feet with a peculiar creepy sensation on the forehead.

When his health returned, Tesla began taking constitutionals in the city park with his friend Anital Szigety, a mechanic and reportedly a handsome man except for his large, misshapen head. One evening, as the sun set, Tesla recited to Szigety some of his favorite lines from Goethe's *Faust*:

> The glow retreats, done in the day of toil;
> It yonder hastes, new fields of life exploring;
> Ah, that no wing can lift me from the soil,
> Upon its track to follow, follow soaring!

Here he stopped his oratory abruptly, and stood dumbfounded. Szigety thought his friend might be having a relapse and urged him to sit on a bench to recover. But Tesla had experienced a revelation and would not rest until he had found a stick and drawn a diagram in the dirt. "See my motor here," he said breathlessly. "Watch me reverse it." What he sketched out was a schematic for an alternate-current motor. With it, the long-distance transmission of electrical power would become possible for the first time.

Having discovered his most important invention and his most captivating role in a single stroke, Tesla went to Paris in 1882 and tried to sell his idea to the Continental Edison Company, which was then headed by Charles Batchelor. Though Batchelor turned down the invention, he saw promise in Tesla and hired him as a regular employee. Tesla applied himself diligently, and on his own time built his first alternating-current induction motor, which he tried, and failed, to sell to the mayor of Strasbourg.

For a while, Tesla contented himself with his work as an engineer and his nocturnal appetite for gambling at billiards and cards. But eventually he prevailed on Batchelor to write a letter to Edison, recommending his transfer to New York. At the age of twenty-eight, he donned a bowler hat and a cutaway coat, caught a moving train, talked his way onto the *Saturnalia*, and sailed to America. In his pocket, he had his notes for the ac motor, a few poems and articles, and a diagram for a flying machine.

Tesla stepped off the boat, bypassing the Immigration Department thanks to his letter of introduction to Edison, and proceeded directly to the offices of 65 Fifth Avenue. By this time, he had developed all the key elements of his persona. He had learned to dress the part of the hypercorrect *mitteleuropean*, honed his psychological game in billiard halls, and learned long passages from the classics. He was the poet of the dark transit, the captivating orator, the self-measured man.

Introducing himself briskly, Tesla launched directly into his alternating-current scheme. Edison scoffed at the idea, having bet everything on direct current, and put him to work that day on a lighting plant on the USS *Oregon*. Tesla dropped all pretenses and assumed an Arlecchino-like attitude: part servant, part magister, he worked feverishly and completed the task by dawn. Returning to the office in the early morning, he met his employer outside the office. Edison saw his bedraggled mucker and suggested to his entourage that their "Parisian" had been "running around at night." When Tesla calmly informed Edison that the job was done, he received a blank stare. Edison walked away shaking his head and muttering, "That is a damn good man."

As legend has it, Edison then turned a cruel screw on Tesla. He had given his new mucker free reign in the shop—as he did everyone—and Tesla routinely worked from 10:30 in the morning to 5:00 the next morning. Soon he found a way to improve Edison's existing dc systems, and reported as much to his boss. Edison allegedly answered, "There's $50,000 in it for you—if you can do it." When Tesla made the improvements, however, Edison laughed in his face, saying, "You don't understand our American sense of humor." Edison's side remembered a different story with the same ending: Tesla offered to sell his ac patents for $50,000, and Edison turned it down with a laugh.

Whichever story is the correct one, Edison would live to regret losing Tesla's ac patent, which fell into the hands of a competitor and brought grief to his doorstep some years later. And he would live to regret losing Tesla's intellectual capital as well. As the years progressed, the spurned young protégé would grow into a full-blown variety inventor, staking serious claims to inventions as diverse as radio, robotics, fluorescent lights, and turbines, thus warranting the dedicated attention of robber barons and scientists alike.

Then again, that was the price Edison had to pay for turning the mechanical spectacle into an ongoing pageant of new technologies. Before the Civil War, show inventors had waged their wars over a single invention; Singer and McCormick, for all their bluster, had never had cause to battle it out with each other. Once planned variety became the order of the day, however, the combinations of contestants were potentially endless. By inspiring so many prolific followers, Edison effectively created an entire army of competitors.

The first to strike was Alexander Graham Bell. In 1885, Chichester Bell and Charles Tainter, working under Bell's supervision, invented the graphophone, which used wax instead of tin foil as a recording substance. The invention was not yet perfect, but in making recordings more durable, it already showed marked improvement over the original phonograph.

Edison, who had long put his own phonograph aside, was caught totally unawares. Forgetting that he had once done something similar to Bell and openly mocked him for it, he fell into a rage. In 1886, the Bell team approached him with an offer to promote the new machine together; he flatly refused. To his English representatives, who had also been approached by the Bell team, Edison commanded in telegraphic style that they "have nothing to do with them. They are a bunch of pirates."

For the next two years, Edison trained his sights almost exclusively on besting the besters. And since the graphophone was still being perfected, that meant that a new contest was on. The escape artist was at it again.

# Chapter Eleven

# ANATOMICAL MUSEUMS

I am large," Walt Whitman declared defiantly in 1855, "I contain multitudes." By the 1880s, the American show inventor could say much the same. One day he might produce a machine gun, the next a curling iron, and the day after that a flying machine. In an age when the great determinist tracts of Marxism and Darwinism were being fitted to every circumstance, he was a free agent who had no idea what he might do next, except that he would be doing a lot of it, and that the public would take a keen interest.

Not surprisingly, American theater was exploding with vitality at the same time. From his place on the margins of society, the actor had moved to a central position in everyday life, and theatergoing amounted to a national pastime. Conventional plays toured the country with large casts and elaborate sets, and played to record houses. The minstrel show, with its current-events parodies, had become an institution. Scantily clad can-can dancers filled the stages in M. B. Leavitt's burlesques, or "burleycues." In 1881, Barnum merged his circus with two other shows to create the "Trinity of the Three Grand Animal Collections of Earth." In 1885, Benjamin Franklin Keith and Edward Franklin Albee began staging their first vaudeville acts, which, like Menlo Park itself, ran from early morning to late at night and used every possible advantage to maximize diversity.

The fortunes of mountebank and player moved in parallel as they always had, in boom times as in bust. So abiding was the connection between them, in fact, that a brief look at the theatrical forms of the 1880s may serve as an instantaneous history of the show inventors, from the remote past to the faint glimmers of the future.

The patent-medicine shows of the era, if nothing else, proved that the theatrical ancestor of the mechanical spectacle was alive and well. More nostrums were being sold in more varieties than ever before, and in the heat of the competition, the trestle stages of old were giving way to extravagant entertainments, with entire troupes of jugglers, hypnotists, ventriloquists, actors, and Indians supporting the mountebank's pitch.

By far the most successful of these large-scale events was the Kickapoo Medicine Show. Founded in 1881 by John Healy and Charles Bigelow, this act centered around the imaginary Kickapoo tribe and its arcane herbal remedy. Healy and Bigelow—who claimed to be ignorant of their own secret ingredient—employed banks of Sioux Indians to stand on the stage while they, as masters of ceremony, doled out the legendary brew.

By the second half of the 1800s, American mountebanks had also begun to move their operations indoors. Some set up dental parlors, in which the Lazzo of the Tooth Extractor, dating to Rome in 1560, lived on in the practice of "painless dentistry." (Few terms have ever been more misleading. Generally, painless dentistry involved pulling the tooth without anesthetic or art, then stuffing a rag in the victim's bleeding mouth.) Other mountebanks, such as the Reinhardt brothers, used their indoor spaces to house anatomical museums, luring customers inside with automata exhibits, such as the Dying Custer, which suffered the unfortunate general to breathe his last again and again.

At an anatomical museum in Gary, Indiana, a doctor and a nurse holding a syphilitic baby provided the bait. If a passerby were sufficiently intrigued by this sight to go inside, he would find a door marked "For Men Only." The door opened onto an antechamber, which contained numerous pâpier-maché depictions of venereal disease victims, and a few live monkeys, snakes, or birds. The lighting was low, the acoustics hushed. A particularly intriguing display case stood in the darkest and most remote corner of the room. When the visitor stopped before it, a light momentarily flashed, illuminating a drooling idiot boy inside, with the placard below reading "Lost Manhood."

At this point in the tour, a floor man would appear and ask the stunned visitor if he were all right—implying, of course, that he was not. The man would then be ushered upstairs to an office where a doctor would draw his blood, inspect it under a microscope, and summarily inform him that his sexual organs were in terrible disrepair. The blood was filled with "animalcules." Rare was the man who escaped without buying five or even twenty dollars worth of patent medicine.

Historically, many early American mountebanks had entered the world of invention by proffering electrical devices, and the stages of the late nineteenth century contained remnants of this transition as well. In the 1750s, Ebenezer Kinnersley had arranged to have artificial lightning avoid hitting a woman and instead strike "a Negro standing by." By the 1880s, manmade lightning was illuminating dramas—including the most-produced drama of the nineteenth century, *Uncle Tom's Cabin*—as a matter of course. One method of creating lightning was to place magnesium powder and potassium nitrate on a small metal stove—a popular choice, despite the discouraging rate at which theaters burned down. No more faith-inspiring was the magnesium flash pistol, which created stage lightning with alcohol-soaked asbestos, a blower, and a slotted barrel.

Samuel Colt's love of pyrotechnic dramas also lived on in the 1880s, though by this time stage managers had learned to take the precaution of separating the audience from the stage with an artificial pond some 300 feet wide. The acting, as usual, was considered less important than the fireworks. Albert Hopkins, a theater writer for *Scientific American*, went so far as to call this form "Fireworks with Dramatic Accessories."

*The Burning of Moscow*, which Fulton had exploited to such success at the turn of the century, was among the most popular of these pyrotechnic shows. The narrative, such as it was, opened on the Kremlin, with docks, quays, stone bridges, and walls "faithfully represented." Guards marched back and forth on the walls, exhibiting their considerable acrobatic skills to the sound of Russian hymns and Greek priests playing somber classical music. As Napoleon approached, the Russian army simply fled without further ado. The French prisoners were then released and ran to light the fires that set the fireworks bursting into the air.

Those who remembered Elisha Otis's 1854 performance at the Crystal Palace could see his invention put to dramatic use again in 1879, when P. T. Barnum engaged all-around theater man Steele Mackaye to build an elevator 55 feet high, 22 feet wide, and 31 feet deep, weighing 48 tons, into the stage of Madison Square Garden. This "elevator stage" had its own trapdoor and lights, and could move a total of 25 feet, 2 inches, giving new meaning to the notion of *deus ex machina*;

when the set needed to be changed, it was simply raised out of view.

Reprising the imaginary expeditions of Jules Verne in theatrical form was the *Trip to the Moon*, produced in New York as a recreation of a solar eclipse that took place near Berlin in 1887. The show began with a morning view of a lake as a crescent sun rose. Gradually, a series of screens and lanterns caused the sun to disappear and the waves on a lake to ripple. Similarly, the scenery itself transformed from the initial pastoral setting to a lunar landscape, giving the audience the thrill of seeing an eclipse of the earth, dimmed to a muted glow through the use of phosphorescent paint and muslin.

American theater also proved itself capable of capturing current events, as in 1883, when Edison's light bulb became the subject of a revue at Niblo's Garden. *Excelsior,* described as a "great Mimical Dramatic Ballet," honored Edison's invention with five hundred small lamps applied to various purposes. A major attraction was an electrically illuminated model of the brand-new Brooklyn Bridge that shone from the stage. For the grand finale, a troupe of dancers appeared with lights strapped to their foreheads and wands tipped with electric lights. One night, Edison himself appeared onstage, tucking a battery into a dancer's cleavage here, adjusting a corset there, in an effort to keep the dancers from breaking the circuits.

All of these theatrical uses of technology, as always, blunted the impact of technological change through the use of make-believe. And, as always, in making invention a public spectacle, they gave show inventors greater credibility in the public eye. But the steady addition of sophisticated mechanical props had another effect as well: as stages grew dense with pulleys, screens, and electric lights, theater was gradually becoming increasingly technology-oriented. This trend had been in effect, however imperceptibly, ever since the days of commedia dell'arte. The mask of eighteenth-century Venice lent the character of a specific animal to the actor. Over time, the actors took off their masks, stopped improvising their lines, moved indoors, and incorporated more and more stage machinery into their shows. The gradual move away from nature continued unchecked, and by the 1880s, technology stood on the verge of overtaking the stage altogether. The moon could be rendered in phosphorescent muslin; dancers could be decked out in incandescent bulbs. In the pages of *Scientific American*, writers discussed the possibilities of an entirely "scientific stage."

So despite the general unpredictablity of the showman's metier, a certain amount of determinism was at work after all. No matter what other developments arose, the mechanizing of the stage pointed inexorably to the day when audiences would sit down to enjoy a wholly artificial theater.

An important contribution to this new form was John Banvard's panorama. In 1848, Banvard, an American painter, constructed scrolling screens and stretched gigantic landscape paintings across them. These paintings resembled grand history paintings in a sense, except that they were not meant to edify viewers with the glorious achievements of their leaders. As they rolled past, they encouraged audiences instead to imagine that they were on their own exotic voyage. Barnum himself tried his hand at the panorama on April 16, 1866, when he presented *The Earthquake, or the Spectre of the Nile,* at his new museum.

Elsewhere, Neilson Burgess's play *The County Fair* introduced a stage invention that, rather than simulating motion, pretended to stop it. Burgess's complex arrangement used three treadmills, hidden from the audience by a picket fence. As a trio of jockeys rode live horses onto the stage at a full clip, the lights were dashed, the picket fence and the treadmills began to move, and a wind machine blew gusts of air from the wings. When a set of strobe lights began flashing, the horses could be seen galloping in place, their manes caught in the flashing glare.

Moving screens and horses frozen in mid-gallop—these two developments came together on a warm night in San Francisco . . .

A small crowd had gathered in a room at the Art Association on Pine Street. The lecturer's appearance, it must be said, did not inspire immediate confidence. With his hat pulled down almost to his beard, he looked more like a prospector than the inventor of a new medium— and, in fact, that was what he had been some years back. After a few moments, this odd-looking man made some introductory comments in a British accent, then turned down the lights and started working a machine with an even odder-sounding name.

What happened next was difficult to explain. For a split second, a photograph appeared on the wall. But it was not a photograph. It was a photograph . . . that moved. A one-second, moving picture of a horse, fleeting, but instantly recognizable in its animal grace.

The crowd demanded to see it again.


That Eadweard Muybridge chose the motions of an animal to demonstrate his zoopraxiscope holds no small amount of irony; in the same moment that the stage was transformed into a mechanical chimera, he made nature its primary subject. This paradox followed Muybridge throughout his career, as he used increasingly complex photographic techniques to investigate the mysteries of life in its natural state. Then again, most other subjects would have been alien to him, since by 1879, when his demonstration in San Francisco took place, he had spent much of his life in the American wilderness.

Born Edward Muggeridge on April 9, 1830, in Kingston-on-Thames, Muybridge added the extra vowels to his first name as a child, inspired by the exploits of Eadweard the Elder, a Saxon king crowned in 900, and Eadweard the Martyr, who ascended to the throne in 975. He changed his last name around the same time, presumably for equally romantic reasons.

Having marked himself from the start as an unorthodox personality, Muybridge spent the rest of his life making up the rules as he went along. In 1852, he sailed for America, following the scent of California gold, and worked at a string of obscure jobs until 1860, when he was injured in a stagecoach accident and had to return to England. By 1867, he was back in the States, studying with the photographer Carleton E. Watkins in San Francisco. Soon he was selling his photographs in sets of twenty for twenty dollars. Frustrated that exposures for the sky and the earth varied so greatly, he developed a method of painting clouds onto photographs, his first invention.

But city life never kept Muybridge long. An inveterate explorer, he spent the next decade of his life on one frontier or another, photographing sights that were beyond the pale even for most pioneers of the time. In 1867, he organized a mule train into Yosemite Valley, at the time largely uncharted, and captured the grandeur of El Capitan and the Bridal Veil Falls on whole-plate negatives and stereoscopic slides. A year or so later, he received a commission from the federal government to photograph the newly purchased Alaskan territory. In 1873, he photographed the Modoc Indian War, a gruesome conflict with the whites in which this tribe virtually perished from the face of the earth. The mid-1870s saw him in Central America working under the "pseudonym" Eduardo Santiago Muybridge, documenting the cultivation of coffee, the ruins of great Mesoamerican cultures, and the local life of Mexico, Guatemala, and Panama.

All of these expeditions required tremendous physical endurance. A photographer in Muybridge's day had to stand inside a small opaque tent and pour collodion—a solution containing potassium iodide—onto a sheet of glass. After tilting the plate until the liquid was evenly distributed (taking care not to cut himself on the glass), he dipped it in a bath of silver nitrate, placed it in a dark slide, and exposed it in the camera for ten to ninety seconds. Developing was done in either pyro- or protosulphate of iron, fixing in potassium cyanide, a highly poisonous substance. The plate was then washed and dried. There were no enlargers; a large picture required a large camera. In Muybridge's case, the hardships were aggravated by the challenge of carrying this cumbersome load into the wilderness: on muleback through Yosemite Valley, or aboard a steamer off the coast of Alaska.

These expeditions qualify Muybridge as one of the frontiersmen of the Wild West, and like many others who plunged toward the Pacific, his rough-and-tumble life yielded double-edged results. For one thing, his time in the wild turned him to something of a wild man himself; it was not always easy to say whether Muybridge had gone native or not. A similar ambiguity surrounded his photographs, which, in depicting the unprecedented beauty of Yosemite and the lives of the Modoc Indians, celebrated the strangeness of the frontier even as they tamed it for city-dwelling viewers. In this sense, Muybridge was already fulfilling a function similar to that of a show inventor, who brought disorder to an orderly world. And as he became a show inventor in his own right, this unresolved attitude toward nature would become more pronounced.

Throughout his expeditionary phase, Muybridge maintained his headquarters in San Francisco, where he achieved modest popularity under the cryptic moniker, Helios the Flying Camera. Reviews of his work, which included a photograph of him peering over the edge of the precipitous Glacier Point, were good, and he seems to have been fairly well known among local photographers.

It was in San Francisco too that Muybridge met the two people who had the greatest impact on his life. One of them was Flora Stone, née Flora Shallcross, a woman many years his junior. They married in late 1871 or early 1872. A short time later, he met Leland Stanford. The ex-governor of California, president of both the Central Pacific Railroad and the Pacific Mail Steamship Company, Stanford was a classic robber baron, who owned two hundred horses, a palatial Palo Alto estate, and his own private race course. Stanford also had some experience with mechanical spectacles. In 1869, he was one of the two men who drove in the last four stakes that linked the rails across the continent. (Actually, Stanford and another dignitary fought over this privilege as the crowd in Promontory, Utah, looked on. In the end, they split the difference and each man drove in one silver stake, one gold. Stanford swung the first blow and missed. Then he brought the hammer down again—and missed again. The duties were passed on to someone else.)

According to popular legend, Stanford and a fellow equestrian named Fred McCrellish made a bet one day as to whether a horse ever raised all four hooves into the air at once. More likely, the two men simply disagreed and the bet was tagged on retroactively by a public eager to think of inventions in terms of contests. There is some evidence, however, that both McCrellish and Stanford had read about the experiments of Dr. Etienne-Jules Marey.

A Parisian doctor, Marey had begun experimenting with methods of measuring animal motion in the 1860s. In one of these experiments, he attached four rubber bulbs to the hooves of a horse. Pneumatic tubes connected these bulbs in turn to four pens. When the horse's hooves hit the ground, the air forced the pens onto a revolving drum of paper, which was strapped to the saddle. This suggested to Stanford that his horse-hoof debate could be settled decisively, so he commissioned Muybridge to apply his photographic skills to the task.

The first experiments took place in May 1872. For a backdrop, Muybridge borrowed all the bed linen he could from the houses around the Sacramento race course. To maximize visual information, he left his shutter open for a long period of time. Unfortunately, the resulting silhouette pictures, while indicating something of the horse's motion, were too blurry to settle Stanford's question.

Muybridge might have progressed more quickly toward his goal if life had not intervened. Returning from his stint as a photographer of the Modoc Indian War, he discovered that Flora was pregnant. Not long after that, he found her out in public with one Harry Larkyns. He instructed Larkyns to get out of town; Larkyns obeyed and took a job as manager of a traveling circus. Apparently, this was not enough to quell the strife between the Muybridges, because in October Flora and their newborn son went to Oregon to stay with friends.

Then the truth slipped out. Muybridge discovered a picture of the child he thought was his own, sent from lover to lover through Flora's maid. The writing on the back identified the boy as "our little Harry." And so the photographer, undone by a photograph, responded to the affront in classic frontiersman style: on October 17, 1874, he found Harry Larkyns at a party and shot him dead.

In jail, Muybridge gave at least one interview, looking gaunt but relaxed. When the trial convened in February 1875, his lawyer urged him to plead insanity, but he insisted on pleading not guilty. His counsel continued to build an insanity defense anyway, showing a photograph—perhaps the one taken at Glacier Point—of Muybridge looking out over the precipice of a mountain peak into Yosemite Valley. It was another case of an inventor revealing his love of heights, although this time, the inference was less than flattering.

In any event, Muybridge was acquitted in short order and returned to normal life, his hair and beard suddenly an even shade of white. Flora, not content with this show of suffering, sued him for divorce on the grounds of cruelty. Her claim, it turned out, was based on a time when Muybridge looked through the bedroom window, saw her sleeping there, came inside, and went to bed. She made a second attempt to divorce him, but died (apparently not by Muybridge's hand) during the proceedings.

Freed from the demands of the courtroom at last, Muybridge went to Central America, on Stanford's bill, where he became the first to document the indigenous methods of coffee cultivation. When he came back, he made a number of panoramic photos—including one of San Francisco that was almost twenty-seven feet long. This monstrosity, cobbled together from smaller photos, was mounted on linen, folded accordion style, and covered with leather boards—inspired perhaps by the Mayan tradition of making folded books covered with jaguar skin.

With all these distractions, it wasn't until 1877 that Muybridge found time to resume his horse-motion experiments. On August 2 of that year, he took a picture with a shutter speed fast enough to capture the outlines of a horse in motion. This was a significant advance, because it allowed photographers to freeze the action of fast-moving subjects. For Muybridge's purposes, it also meant that he could take a succession of photos that broke down a horse's gait into its component parts. It seems he failed to gather the importance of his breakthrough, though, because another year elapsed before he was ready to give Stanford his answer.

The June 22, 1878, issue of *Pacific Life* described the press conference, held near Menlo Park, California (the other Menlo Park), at Stanford's Palo Alto farm. The first part of the demonstration involved a wheel, drawn by the horse, that would complete the circuit in each of a series of wires laid across the track, setting off a phalanx of fast-shuttered cameras in turn. "The horse trotted by, the wheel passing over the wires with a noise 'like the wings of a woodcock,'" read an eyewitness account, "and the press crowded into the darkroom to see the pictures developed. The result, seen by the light of the yellow window let into the side of the shed, looked almost magical."

In the second half of the demonstration, a second horse—the Kentucky racing mare Sallie Gardner—was trotted out, to break a set of trip wires. The broken threads showed up on the plates, and with this, even the skeptics became excited. Indeed, that the horse was entirely aloft during one phase of its stride was almost forgotten in the heat of the moment. Once again the horse and the machine had come together in an inventor's show, and once again the machine had stolen one of the animal's secrets.

Muybridge was excited too and, within a matter of weeks, had fashioned himself as a performer in order to spread the news. For his first lecture, given on July 8, 1878, at the San Francisco Art Association on Pine Street, he held forth for several hours, using a projector fitted with limelight. (Edison's light bulb was more than a year from completion.) Half of the screen was taken up by his photos of horses, the other half by artist's renditions of same. Muybridge used the opportunity to show that his high-speed photography was more accurate than the artist's eye; painting, this night, was deader than ever. He also engaged the audience with anecdotes from his exploits in Alaska, Yosemite, and Central America—stirring tales of his conquest of nature. After a slow first night, the next two engagements were packed.

By 1879, Muybridge's work in Palo Alto was over. He continued to lecture at the Congregational Church Hall in Sacramento, the Mechanics Fair in San Francisco, and on Pine Street. Then on May 4, 1880, in the same rooms in San Francisco, he projected moving pictures of animals onto a screen. He called his invention the zoogyroscope at first, then changed the name to zoopraxiscope.

The zoopraxiscope employed a revolving disk, much like a phonographic disk, on which images were recorded in concentric circles. Muybridge also devised a second wheel moving in the opposite direction. Made of metal with periodic slits, this wheel acted as a shutter and allowed viewers to experience the illusion of continuous motion known as persistence of vision. Though these discs showed extremely short visual passages—which Muybridge repeated, as he put it, for "a period limited only by the patience of the spectators"—they nevertheless opened onto a new world of sight. They were movies.

Such an invention could hardly remain a local phenomenon for long, and in April 1881, Muybridge set off on a grand tour of America and Europe. At the Royal Institution, his audience included Lord Tennyson, William Gladstone, T. H. Huxley, the Prince of Wales, and princesses Alexandra, Victoria, Louisa, and Maud. From England, he went to Paris, and in September 1881 put on a show for Hermann von Helmholtz, Sir William Crookes, and the ever-present Nadar at the laboratories of Dr. Etienne-Jules Marey.

At the time, Marey was making his own strides in motion photography. A month before Muybridge arrived, the Paris Municipal Council had given him a larger space in which to work, at the Parc de Princes near the porte d'Auteuil on the outskirts of Paris. Here, he was constructing what he called the Physiological Station, where he would continue to work along much the same lines as Muybridge.

Over the years, Marey had come to concentrate on the motion of birds, a choice that presented unique difficulties. For one thing, he could not rely on trip wires to freeze motion, as Muybridge had. Yet he was intrigued by Muybridge's results, so after their meeting, he began casting around for solutions to this problem. He soon came upon the work of Pierre Jules Janssen, the director of the Paris astrophysical laboratory and president of a Paris photographic society. Janssen had invented something called an Astronomical Revolver, which he used to track the planet Venus in its transit close to the earth in December 1874. Using a telescope, a mirror, and a revolving photographic plate, he had captured seventeen pictures of the heavens in a single glass-plate photograph.

The Astronomical Revolver was just what Marey needed. As 1881 turned to 1882, he wrote to Janssen asking for details of his machine. The astrophysicist, apparently not a selfish man, told him everything he wanted to know. Marey then modified the Astronomical Revolver to resemble a rifle, which allowed him to track birds as they moved. The invention was loaded with a disk, which recorded images of birds around its rim. In fact, it was very much like Muybridge's zoopraxiscope, with one important distinction: rather than projecting images, it captured them.

After testing the photographic rifle at the Bay of Naples in 1882, Marey turned his attentions back to his Physiological Station, and what had been a nondescript locale began to evolve into a kind of clockwork laboratory. There were two circular tracks, one for horses and another for humans. In the center, a darkened chamber on wheels contained the camera and experimenter, with a short train track running up to the screen. At regular points around the track, a telegraph recorded the moment when a subject passed, determining the speed of travel. The subject was photographed at one point along the track, in multiple exposures that broke down their motion into isolated poses. To integrate the time element, Marey gave his human subjects luminescent clock dials to wear, and eventually had them dress in black with silvered lines. The resulting photographs revealed not humans but abstract, multiple images of lines in motion.

Marey's work inspired a wide range of experimentation. His early investigations into bird flight prompted an assistant, Victor Tatin, to build a bird automaton, and later found avid enthusiasts in the Wright brothers. His investigations into human motion, meanwhile, found their way to the studios of the young Marcel Duchamp and were transformed into the famous Futurist painting, *Nude Descending a Staircase*. In an interview with Pierre Cabanne in 1967, Duchamp explained: "I saw . . . a book by Marey, where he showed men who were fencing, or horses in a gallop with a system of dotted lines delineating the different movements. . . . That is what gave me the idea for the execution of the nude descending a staircase."

Marey, in popularizing Janssen's invention, could also be said to have laid the groundwork for, of all people, Sigmund Freud. In 1899, Freud sought to prove the existence of the subconscious in his *Interpretation of Dreams*. This proof was made by way of an analogy, in which the mind acted as a combination telescope and camera. Freud was taken to task for the analogy by his mentor Josef Breuer, who pointed out that a telescopic mirror could not simultaneously be a photographic plate. Freud responded by devising an even more elaborate system, in which the "mirror" and the "plate" were separated, one involving naked perception, the other "permanent traces," or memory.

This description of the mind at work is surprisingly similar to the construction of Janssen's Astronomical Revolver. Did Freud, who visited Paris to study with physiologists in the year the Physiological Station was built, pattern his theory directly after this invention? Or did the Astronomical Revolver simply suggest an idea that could not be fully articulated by any other means? Either way, the motion study clearly had far-reaching implications for many disciplines. In the age of planned variety, it seemed to offer a limitless number of applications of one invention.

Indeed, the only application that seems to have eluded Marey was the dramatic one. A doctor by trade, he undertook his studies without fanfare and kept so resolutely to himself that biographers have despaired of describing his personal life. So it was left to Muybridge, who by this time had become an avid performer, to establish the potential of the motion study as its own kind of show.

The *Boston Daily Globe* of Saturday, October 21, 1882, announced Muybridge's return to American podiums, where he began demonstrating "His Queer Zoopraxiscope" with the ever-sudden title of professor. Then just as quickly as he had started, a disagreement with Stanford forced him to change tactics temporarily. When The *Horse in Motion* was published, Muybridge was credited only in the preface and appendix. Feeling slighted, he brought suit against Stanford for $50,000. The case was never taken to court, perhaps because Muybridge realized that Stanford had already underwritten his experiments at considerable expense. But the die was already cast. The two were not to be business partners again, and Muybridge began looking for work in an academic setting.

A viable prospect presented itself when the artist Thomas Eakins saw Muybridge's photographs of horses and struck up a correspondence. Their subsequent meeting, sometime in the spring of 1883, led to Muybridge's engagement by the University of Pennsylvania to pursue his study of motion, under Eakins's supervision. With initial funding from a new backer, J. B. Lippincott, Muybridge built an outdoor studio on the grounds surrounding the University Hospital and, in March 1884, began to generate what amounted to material for future performances.

That performances were still on Muybridge's mind can be seen in his choice of method. Where Marey preferred to produce multiple images on a single plate, Muybridge continued to create sequences of plates, each containing a single image, which could be converted to zoopraxiscope disks and projected for audiences at a later date. His subjects reflected much the same interest. Over the course of the next two years, he took ten thousand photographs, and while these expanded on his lifelong obsession with nature, they also drew on many themes from the theatrical world.

Of course, the theatrical world had its own connections to nature, and *The Horse in Motion* had already given pride of place to the showmen's time-honored favorite. In Philadelphia, Muybridge went further and began photographing the kind of species generally seen in circuses or menageries—tigers, lions, jaguars, baboons, gazelles, kangaroos, cockatoos, and ostriches, among others. When photographing domesticated species, he seemed intent on enlivening their appearance, placing mules

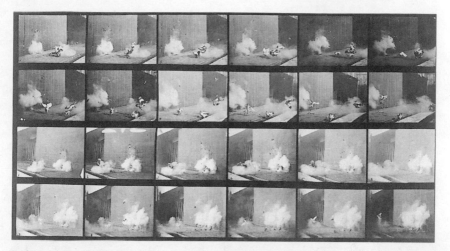

Eadweard Muybridge took some ten thousand photographs between 1884 and 1886 to study the range of motions among living creatures. Among them were such rousing subjects as *Legless Boy*, *Woman Dancing Nude*, and this one, *Chickens Scared by a Torpedo*. *Courtesy Addison Gallery*

on swings, making horses leap hurdles, and giving their antics captions such as "Denver in various performances." Perhaps his most eye-popping animal "trick" was one that came to be titled "Chickens scared by a torpedo." Adopting the crude comic techniques of the old zanies, he placed one or two firecrackers near or under a flock of chickens, then photographed the unfortunate birds as they rose from the smoke in alarm. From the plates, their fate is uncertain.

When it came time to photograph humans, Muybridge exhibited much the same flair for the profane. Back in Paris, Marey had devised a system that reduced human motion to geometric patterns and so inspired a generation of abstract artists. Not Muybridge. In a time when an exposed ankle was cause for scandal, he chose to photograph his subjects—most of them drawn from the ranks of the university's student body—in the raw. Perhaps the photographs of the men, who engaged in wrestling matches and equestrian feats, were acceptable enough. But the women appeared in poses that, without the benefit of clothes, made them look almost burlesque: they danced naked together, shared a cup of tea in the nude, poured pitchers of water over one another *au naturel*. More salacious still was the motion study of a naked woman, lounging provocatively as she smoked a cigarette.

If, in Muybridge's hands, the experiments at the University of Pennsylvania came to resemble an authorized peep show, they took on a more sinister cast when Dr. Francis X. Dercum arrived on the scene. An instructor in nervous diseases at the University of Pennsylvania Medical School, Dercum was a mixture of doctor, hypnotist, electro-therapist and would-be eugenicist. In his *Rest, Suggestion and Other Therapeutic Measures in Nervous and Mental Diseases*, he asserted hereditary causes for both insanity and neuropathic disorders such as hysteria. Though he prescribed rest for most every ailment under the sun, his preferred treatment for syphilitic and alcoholic insanity was sterilization.

Dercum had harsh prescriptions for criminals as well. "The baneful effects on the community from the free propagation of insane, defective and criminal stocks," he wrote, "is so well recognized that it hardly seems necessary to point out that isolation should be carried out as effectively as possible."

As for hysteria, Dercum believed it to be a degenerative, if less devastating, condition. He did not ask himself what hysteria was. He simply observed that motor disorders in hysterics did not follow the disorders observed in organic diseases. And if the movements of horses could be accurately perceived with Muybridge's equipment, he reasoned, so perhaps could the movements of hysterics be revealed.

Under the guidance of Dercum, then, Muybridge recorded a series of "abnormal movements," published in 1888, which sent him into terrain only one step short of an actual freak show. Or so the viewer must have thought when coming upon plates detailing a legless boy trying to get out of a chair and a paralytic child walking on all fours.

Most likely, the Muybridge-Dercum experiments also led to the development of posture photos. A phenomenon that peaked in the mid-twentieth century, posture-photo programs appeared at Harvard as early as the 1880s and, even in their later years, bore a striking resemblance to the activities at the University of Pennsylvania. By the 1950s, the practice involved the compulsory appearance of college students—men and women—at a special office, where they were required to strip down and have their bearing documented. In some cases, a series of rods were attached to the student's back, the more clearly to illustrate the curve of the spine. A camera was then used to photograph front, side, and back views of students on a single piece of film. From the resulting photographs, the posture-photo specialist categorized his subjects as endomorphs, mesomorphs, or ectomorphs, much as the Fowler brothers had analyzed daguerrotypes for phrenological clues a century earlier.

The posture photo was a far-flung relative of the motion picture, to be sure, but the connection is telling nonetheless. Where Marey and

Janssen had articulated the human pysche for the founder of modern psychiatry, Muybridge was left to pave the way for a consortium of Ivy League quacks.

Of course, this outcome is hardly surprising, considering Muybridge's interest in live performance. Between naked women and exploding chickens, the results of his experiments—published in 1887 under the title *Animal Locomotion: an electro-photographic investigation of consecutive phases of animal movement*—contained the same kind of material that was on exhibit in burlesque shows, menageries, and anatomical museums throughout the land. At the height of the theater's popularity in America, the same familiar acts were present in all their diverse splendor.

Yet Muybridge, in following his particular obsessions, also managed to introduce a disorienting ambiguity into the equation. Part of this had to do with his peculiar relation to nature. What, after all, was the viewer to make of a wild beast captured in successive attitudes? Did it glorify the animal kingdom perhaps, or did it signify the opposite—the final domination of nature? Muybridge had spent years of his life on the frontier; ironically, only a few short years after the publication of *Animal Locomotion*, that frontier was closed. Was his fabulous bestiary a memorial to the wilderness, then, or a celebration of its containment?

More important, in concentrating so heavily on the dramatic dimension of movies, Muybridge cast doubts about the future of theater itself. By its very nature, drama had always gained from its willingness to risk failure. With the high wire and the lion-tamer's act, just as much as the reaper that might not reap and the light bulb that might not light, the live performance provoked suspense, and by averting disaster, a heartfelt sense of success. This was especially true of the inventor's show, where success promised so much beyond the performance.

The zoopraxiscope, while it could fascinate endlessly, did not offer the familiar element of disorder, at least not in the sense that Barnum's imperfect machines or Samuel Colt's misfiring fireworks did. Each time Muybridge projected an image, the result was exactly the same. Instead of an expression of daring, it presented an infallible spectacle—and infallibility left little room for heroics.

The effects of this change were not immediately recognized. A generation would pass before D. H. Lawrence, sounding like a disenchanted Walt Whitman, bemoaned the replacement of the "carnal body" and "the bright circus flesh" with "personalities, that are best seen flat, on the film, flat personalities in two dimensions, imponderable and touchless." And it took another generation again for the motion picture to outstrip the live show in popularity.

The zoopraxiscope did raise a more immediate question about the relation of the show inventor to his drama, however. Until Muybridge, the inventor's show had focused on the inventor and his machine, and the test had been to see whether the invention would pass into general use. When Singer sang "The Song of the Shirt," or Watson sang Moody and Sankey hymns, the hero was inevitably the inventor, and his subject the machinery at hand. With the motion picture, however, the spectacle began to exist on two levels: the inventor was still the master of ceremonies, and the projector was certainly an object of fascination, but now there was also a drama contained *within* the technology. Who, then, was the hero of the cinematic experience? Was it the flesh-and-blood figure manning the projector—a failed prospector with a colorful personal life—or was it the artificial horse streaking across the screen?

In the end, there could be only one answer. All along, theater had been moving toward the completely scientific stage. One technological advance after another had found a place in the theater, and with each addition, the prospect of a controlled event became more plausible. The elevator became an elevator stage, and suddenly set changes could be effected with precise results. Torches gave way to light bulbs, and suddenly new subtleties in stage lighting could be achieved. Movies were the culmination of this trend, the ultimate in the controlled drama. They offered a dramatic event in which every element could be predicted.

Every element, that is, except for the show inventor himself. Descended from masked characters and wandering peddlers, the show inventor was still a wild man, unpredictable and all too real—an interruption of the total artificial experience. And so, after a brief transitional period, during which movies kept some of the trappings of the live show, he was destined to cede his position to the characters who filled the screen.

Muybridge, for his part, was too much of a performer to give up his place in the spotlight. When the university experiments were over, he took his zoopraxiscope back on the lecture circuit and continued to make his own disorderly person, an acquitted murderer with a quizzical name, the star of the program. But in the midst of this tour, he crossed paths with Thomas Edison. And Edison, having already changed so many rules of the inventor's show, was ready to change them again.

## Chapter Twelve

# THE BIRTH OF
# THE GRID

It had been eight years since Edison opened his grounds to the drunken minions for his New Year's celebration of the light bulb. In that time, his first wife, Mary, had died, prompting him to leave both her memory and Menlo Park behind. Now he had a new wife, Mina, and a new laboratory in West Orange, New Jersey. He still worked as hard as before, still had as many ideas. More than that, he enjoyed an unparalleled renown. His electric lights studded the night air of cities across the world, and people everywhere strained their ears to hear his phonographs sing.

But Edison's triumphs were also bringing him troubles. The Thomson-Houston Electric Company—Elihu Thomson's organization—was constantly vying for a bigger piece of the utilities market, as were Hiram Maxim and others. The phonograph was under attack by the Bell team. Amazingly, Edison was still mired in litigation over both his light bulb and his carbon microphone. Like a general extended on too many fronts, he was no longer fighting to advance but simply to hold on to territory already won. And like a general, he sought the master plan that would answer his many woes in a stroke.

Such was the state of affairs in February 1888 when Edison and Eadweard Muybridge—who was visiting Orange, New Jersey, to deliver a lecture—crossed paths. The potential for combining the phonograph and the zoopraxiscope must have been obvious to both of them, but it was Muybridge who broached the idea. Edison agreed, and together they worked to capture the glory of actors Edwin Booth and Lillian Russell in the world's first talkies.

The experiment, it must be said, left a good deal to be desired. Synchronization amounted to starting the two machines at the same time, and the effect was laughably crude. Then, too, the phonograph had yet to be adapted for large audiences. For Muybridge, that was enough to abandon the idea on the spot and continue on his way.

Edison was not so quick to give up. In fact, he absorbed far more from Muybridge than the rudiments of motion pictures. As in his dreams, where he rearranged the faces of his family into new combinations, he broke down Muybridge's entire body of work, then incorporated its various components into his own in unexpected ways.

From the outset, there was Muybridge's observation that the phonograph was not loud enough. Edison knew this to be true. He had been struggling to improve this invention ever since 1886, when Chichester Bell and Sumner Tainter announced their graphophone. After his meeting with Muybridge, he added the problem of volume to the list. But Edison also saw a novel application for motion studies in his competition with the Bell team: a new approach to the show itself.

By June 1888, the phonograph contest was reaching high pitch. A hundred muckers had been rounded up and assigned to some sixty different experiments. J. B. Lippincott, who had financed Muybridge's early experiments at the University of Pennsylvania, was already marketing the competition's version. With the graphophone about to be introduced, Edison told his men that they would be on round-the-clock duty until their new phonograph was a reality.

Predictably, when this order reached reporters, they rushed to West Orange to interview the inventor, expecting the riveting copy he had always supplied. But this time there would be no interviews. No one, they were told, could see Edison, not even his wife. For the next five days, journalists could only speculate as to the meaning of the fitful music and wild cries—the sounds of the spirits in the cabinet—emanating from behind closed doors. What kind of show would Edison put on? Would he make his "little feller" do tricks, as he had a decade ago? Would there be another barnstorming tour?

There would not. When the doors finally opened on June 16, Edison had a phonograph that, among its various improvements, did indeed project at higher volumes. Yet he choose not to show this new invention at all. Instead, he produced a photograph.

*Brown Bros.*

*Brown Brothers*

After three days without sleep in June 1888, Thomas Edison produced this photograph for the public instead of revealing his improved phonograph in person, as he had done with the first phonograph and the lightbulb. *Author's Collection*

Taken at five in the morning by mucker William Laurie Dickson, the original portrait shows Edison, head in hand, seated beside the new phonograph after three days without sleep. (The rumor mill soon turned three days into five). With him are muckers Dickson, Fred Ott, John Ott, Charles Batchelor, and one Colonel George Edward Gouraud, dressed in spanking cravat and absurdly shiny shoes. Eventually, the photograph was altered to show Edison alone, looking imperiously into the camera lens. Fatigue ravages his face, revealing the terrible cost of his heroic attempt. Many who saw it noted his resemblance to Napoleon.

Yet there was more to this photograph than Edison's expression. Where Muybridge had replaced live subjects with photographs, Edison replaced *himself*—with a packaged souvenir that could be presented again and again without variation. The significance of this substitution was great. Disconnected in time and space, the sleepless-vigil photograph was perhaps the first pseudo-event, as Daniel Boorstin defines the term: an infinitely reproducible image that comes to stand in for the reality of an event. And in this case, it stood in for an inventor's show that never happened.

That Edison was moving away from live performances became doubly apparent in his treatment of Colonel Gouraud in the aftermath of the phonograph race. The dandy in the original 1888 photograph, Gouraud had been Edison's representative in England since 1873, when he helped him promote a high-speed telegraph. And a well-trained representative he was at that. If in posing for the famous photograph in natty attire, Gouraud seemed not to be taking Edison's suffering seriously enough, he was only following in the footsteps of his father, François Fauvel-Gouraud—the mountebank who arrived in New York in 1839 claiming to represent Louis Daguerre.

Very little is known about George Gouraud's childhood. He was born in 1840 or 1841 in Niagara, New York, right around the time his father had his revelation about the passions of the planets by the thundering falls. When François stood on a Philadelphia stage in 1844 and interrupted his lecture on "phreno-mnemo-technics" to produce a letter that threatened the assassination of his family, one of the children marked for death was George.

François died in 1847, leaving George at large but not at a loss for bearing the family standard. After serving in the Civil War and receiving the Congressional Medal of Honor for bravery in battle, he appeared in New York City as a seller of sponges. From there, he went to England, where he cultivated an image that became more presumptuous with every passing year. Not content to be an agent for the Pullman Palace Car Company—or Edison's representative, either, for that matter—he amplified his wartime rank of aide-de-camp into that of assistant to General Sherman, and was soon using this title to wangle meetings with lords, princes, and emperors, and to otherwise make himself foremost in every Englishman's mind.

Immediately after the phonograph race was over, George sailed back to England with the first prototype of the new phonograph and a copy of the auspicious photograph. For anyone who was interested, he had the apparatus introduce itself as Mr. Edison, then go through a series of identity changes as William Gladstone orated, Robert Browning fumbled through lines of his own verse, and Sir Arthur Sullivan added a few self-effacing witticisms. One writer remembered this phonograph "performing" audibly before an audience numbering in the thousands. Echoing the morose Mister Faber's performances thirty years earlier, it then bid the crowd good night with a rendition of "God Save the Queen."

But apples don't fall far from the tree, and the junior Gouraud soon overstepped his authority. When he sent word to the inventor of his plans for an advertising poster in which the sleepless-vigil photo would be used, Edison barked back, "I don't propose to be Barnumized."

This was a novel request from the ranks of the show inventors, who typically wanted nothing more than to be attached to Barnum's name. It was doubly strange coming from one who had paraded through the streets with a caravan of Jumbo generators. But so it was. Gouraud seemed to be interpreting the sleepless vigil as an extended daguerrotype sitting, with all the attending histrionics that such things required, and Edison, no longer enamored of such stunts, put him at an arm's remove.

In 1896, Gouraud reappeared in his hometown of Niagara to demonstrate Edison's phonograph to the Chinese viceroy Li Hung Chuang, and caused a minor scandal by kissing the leader's hand. After that, accounts of his peregrinations fail to mention his connection to Edison. Eventually, the American Society of London issued a letter to the press stating that Gouraud had no authority to speak for anyone but himself.

The ban was as nothing to Gouraud. As Francis B. Keene of the American Consulate in Geneva observed some years later:

> Gouraud is a man of majestic stature and grandeur. He does not go; he proceeds. He wears his white hair long, down on his shoulders. His mustachios are twisted, and stick out fiercely, at irregular right angles from his lips. His eyes are not in tune. He wears a costume which, with his long hair, makes him look like Buffalo Bill gone stark, staring mad . . . If he ever writes a book, the title ought to be EMPERORS WHO HAVE MET ME.

At last sighting, the perambulatory colonel was insinuating himself into the company of "Lebaudy, otherwise known as Jacques I, Emperor of the Sahara," his connection to Edison long severed.

The two Gourauds, father and son, frame the history of American show inventors. In the 1840s, François wreaked havoc on Morse's dignified approach and helped establish the tumultuous public performance as the rule of the day. By the late 1880s, the tide had reversed. Edison was no longer looking backward to his own live demonstrations, but forward, and inward. True to his word, he would not be Barnumized anymore.

The public discovered this soon enough. As Edison readied the updated phonograph (called, oddly enough, "the Spectacle") for commercial production, the activity inside the West Orange labs was as frantic as always, but the view from outside suggested that all was calm. There were no rumors, no dramatizations at all. No one mentioned anything about barnstorming tours. Soon, his compound became more secret than ever. The public, which had generally been allowed in during the "open" phases of Edison's escape acts, was banished entirely. Reporters increasingly were barred as well. As the frontier was closing in the West, so were Edison's doors.

Meanwhile, behind those doors, the experiments in pseudo-events were evolving into something more complex. William Laurie Dickson, the house photographer, worked deep within the West Orange labyrinth, at first in the locked and darkened Room 5, then in a compound building that was closed to everyone but Dickson, Charles Batchelor, and Edison himself. There, one photograph was turning into two, then three . . .

Edison's master plan was taking shape. If all went well, it would solve his problems once and for all. Even the latest threat, which appeared only three weeks after the sleepless-vigil episode, was no cause for alarm. Gouraud, though out of the picture, had bequeathed his secretary to Edison some years earlier. And lately Samuel Insull was coming into his own.

In 1884, when Edison laughed in Tesla's face and refused to buy his ac technology, the Slavic inventor wasted no time mourning. He simply turned his back on his hero and set out on his own. Forming the Tesla Electric Light Company in Rahway, New Jersey, he developed a lamp that worked on a pyromagnetic principle: it derived electricity from heat. Temporary hardship came when he was eased out of his own company and had to work on street gangs (which presumably means that somewhere in the underlayers of New York City, his handiwork can still be seen). But as it turned out, the foreman of the crew was intrigued by his ac motor and took him to meet A. K. Brown, then manager of the Western Union Telegraph Company. Brown saw potential in the idea and helped Tesla set up another company, the Tesla Electric Company, which was organized at 33-35 South Fifth Avenue (now West Broadway) in April 1887.

Tesla received his first ac patents in 1888, and on May 16, was invited to lecture at the American Institute of Electrical Engineers. There, he proved his talent for addressing the highbrow crowd on its own terms. Of his paper, "A New System of Alternate Current Motors and Transformers," Dr. B. A. Behrend said, "Not since the appearance of Faraday's 'Experimental Researches in Electricity' has a great experimental truth been voiced so simply and so clearly . . . He left nothing to be done by those who followed him." Suddenly, Tesla—until recently a billiard player without portfolio—was a force to be reckoned with.

One member of the audience that day was George Westinghouse, a tycoon of portly eminence who knew something about showmanship from personal experience. In 1868, as a lanky twenty-two-year-old from Schenectady, Westinghouse had approached the Panhandle Railroad with a new kind of railroad brake. At the time, bringing a locomotive to a halt required a mile's notice and a large crew of brakemen, one for every car. Westinghouse believed he knew how to stop a locomotive more quickly than that.

The Panhandle executives agreed to let Westinghouse try his brake on a passenger train going from Pittsburgh to Steubenville, Ohio. In April 1868, the inventor climbed aboard a train equipped with his brake and ascended to the observation car. At first the run was nondescript, but fortune turned oddly in his favor just outside of Pittsburgh when a frightened horse threw its rider onto the track. The engineer, Dan Tate, engaged the brake and stopped a mere four feet short of manslaughter.

Once again, a locomotive met with a horse and made legend, but this time the message was different. In 1930, Peter Cooper raced against a horse to prove that his *Tom Thumb* could outdo nature. The Westinghouse brake demonstration said something else again: that the Iron Horse could be restrained, that life could be protected despite the advance of technology.

In July 1869, encouraged by the executives' reaction, Westinghouse organized the Westinghouse Air Brake Company. Five years later, ten thousand locomotives and cars were using his brake. A rich man, he moved out of Pittsburgh and into Breeze Point—home of Heinz, Carnegie, Frick, and Mellon—as a successful capitalist in his own right. And soon, like his new peers, he became interested in the activities of America's many inventors. By the time of Tesla's AIEE lecture, he had bought the ac distribution patents of Gaulard and Gibbs, and his engineers were working on a transformer. But only Tesla had produced an ac motor.

On July 7, 1888, Westinghouse paid a visit to Tesla's Greenwich Village lab, found the machinery to his satisfaction, and struck a deal. For the moment, Tesla would receive $2,000 a month to act as a consultant and to work on Westinghouse's burgeoning ac system. Then, when the time came, Westinghouse would pay him the incredible rate of $2.50 per horsepower sold.

With this bargain, Tesla could look forward to a handsome income for some time to come. Soon he was to be found in the Palm Room of the Waldorf-Astoria, rubbing elbows with the high-powered financiers in Westinghouse's circles. The press discovered him, too, and he learned to hold forth with journalists such as John J. O'Neill of the *New York Herald Tribune*, Julian Hawthorne (the only son of Nathaniel) of the *Philadelphia North American*, Franklin Chester of the *Citizen*, and Arthur Brisbane of William Randolph Hearst's *New York Journal*.

But Tesla's fate was not yet assured. Another man who had witnessed the AIEE lecture was Harold Brown, and Harold Brown did not like what he saw. Fearing death in the wires, Brown wrote a letter to the *New York Post* on June 5, 1888, to let the world know that alternating current could "be described by no adjective less forcible than *damnable*." If it had to be used, he recommended that it never exceed a capacity of 300 volts, else others share the fate of such unfortunate linesmen as "the poor boy Streiffer, who touched a straggling telegraph wire on East Broadway on April 15 and was instantly killed."

Believers in ac criticized the article, but this didn't stop Brown. He appeared at the gates of West Orange, where he had worked briefly, asking for the assistance of the Edison team. As it turned out, no persuasion was necessary. Edison had invested all of his capital in his direct-current system and perceived alternating current as a threat that had to be quashed. To this end, he had already begun demonstrating the dangers of his competitor's system in the most emphatic manner possible.

The field general in this crusade, which came to be known as the War of the Currents, was Samuel Insull. Perhaps as early as 1887, Insull had begun paying neighborhood boys a quarter to round up stray dogs and cats. Then, in the presence of newspaper reporters and other invited guests, these unclaimed pets were lured onto a tin sheet and subjected to 1,000 volts of alternating current. Various names were floated for this type of execution: *ampermort, dynamort, electricide*. After the Tesla-Westinghouse agreement was struck in June 1888, the verb suggested to the press was "to be Westinghoused."

Newly empowered by his alliance with the Edison team, Brown began conducting a series of experiments with mucker Arthur E. Kennelly to verify his assertion that ac should never exceed 300 volts. Brown then asserted his mastery of the stage. On July 30, 1888, he gave a demonstration at the School of Mines at Columbia University, before an audience of electricians, reporters, the superintendent of the Society for the Prevention of Cruelty to Animals, and a handful of public observers.

Falsely declaring himself a disinterested party, Brown compared and contrasted the effects of ac and dc on a large Newfoundland mix that had been attached to a pair of cables. First, he administered dc in increasing doses. The caged dog's whimpers turned to yelps, then to expressions of surprise, anger, fear, and agony. At 1,000 volts, it had not yet died. Some members of the audience had already left the room by the time Brown promised to make the dog "feel better." With a quick jolt of no more than 330 volts of alternating current, he killed it.

In keeping with a grand tradition, Brown rigged this show to ensure maximum effect. When administering the dc current, he made use of a relay that shut the juice off as soon as it was delivered; the ac current, however, had no such relay. Though no one in the audience discovered the trick, one skeptic suggested that the dc doses had simply worn the dog out. Showman that he was, Brown called down to the basement for another victim. At this point, the superintendent of the SPCA stepped in and prevented a second execution.

That was round one. Meanwhile, the New York State legislature had been considering proposals for a humane method of capital punishment and, out of some thirty-three choices, had settled on electrocution as the way of the future. (One method that was ruled out early on was "the illuminated body," in which numerous small holes were drilled into the doomed prisoner, then filled with oil and lighted.)

The Medico-Legal Society of New York chose Brown and his assistant at the Columbia gala, Dr. Peterson, to perfect a method. Under the watchful eye of Edison, the two men electrocuted and dissected about two dozen dogs, two calves, and a horse. According to the *New York Times*, the calves' meat was pronounced "fit for food." The society's report, delivered on December 12, 1888, came out in favor of the electric chair.

EXPERIMENTS IN KILLING ANIMALS BY ELECTRICITY, AS CONDUCTED AT ORANGE, N. J.

By the late 1880s, Edison was trying to discredit the technology developed by Nikola Tesla in a savage campaign that involved the killing of animals with alternating current before reporters and other public observers. *New York University Libraries*

Throughout all this, Westinghouse was in much the same position that Alfred Nobel had been in. He could not deny that ac posed some dangers, but handled correctly, he maintained, it was perfectly feasible for general use. The position was hardly a strong one: "alternating current will kill people, of course," he said, "so will gunpowder and dynamite and whiskey." (Curiously, no one had considered execution by dynamite.)

Yet Westinghouse kept at it, because he knew what the stakes were. The upcoming Columbian Exposition would provide the ideal showcase for whichever electrical system turned out to be the winning one. What's more, the Niagara Falls Commission was considering the benefits of each system for its new electrical plant. Though the battle was putting him in dire financial straits, Westinghouse doggedly tried to set the record straight.

Meanwhile, Edison had joined Elihu Thomson—the same man who had once demolished his etheric-force fantasy—in his most dramatic attempt yet to demolish the Westinghouse system. It was a masterpiece of industrial espionage. Brown, now an electrocution "expert" for New York State, wrote to Edison, asking him to foot the bill for the generators that would electrocute a human being at Sing Sing penitentiary. As Westinghouse would clearly not be quick to sell the necessary equipment to his adversaries, Edison worked with Brown through the Thomson-Houston Company, which worked through a third party to procure a few Westinghouse generators that were being sold to make way for upgraded models. Cryptically, Brown boasted that the generator he purchased "already had a record as a man-killer."

The privilege of being the first human to die in the electric chair fell to a convicted murderer named William Kemmler. After Kemmler's lawyer exhausted every avenue of appeal, the date was set for August 6, 1890. The event turned into a melee. People tried every form of persuasion to get one of the twenty-five witness seats. The Whitechapel Club of Chicago expressed a desire to buy Kemmler's body when the ordeal was over. A Dr. Southwick, who had first recommended electrocution some nine years earlier, offered his preferred method of applying the current: without straps, so as not to panic the victim.

Before the execution, the witnesses were locked into the chamber. By the time it was over, they no doubt wished they had never come. Kemmler entered dressed for a day at the track, wearing a gray jacket, a checkered shirt, a bow tie, yellow pants, and polished shoes. After he was seated and strapped in, the executioners discussed how long the voltage should be applied. Hastily deciding on ten seconds, they threw the switch. A Dr. MacDonald started the stopwatch. Kemmler's body went taut against the straps.

Fifteen seconds later, MacDonald cried "Stop!"

The prisoner had no pulse. But when the doctors began to remove him from the chair, someone noticed that a cut was still sending out a trickle of blood. Kemmler's heart was still beating.

The audience let out a mixture of groans and sobs. The prisoner was strapped in again and subjected to a considerably longer dose, causing bloody sweats, gurgles, a heaving chest, burning skin, and the smell of feces. Afterward, the body was hot to the touch. One of the physicians offered the simile "like overdone beef."

Years later, the chair (or what was touted as the chair) in which Kemmler perished turned up at Huber's, a dime museum in New York. In 1910, it was purchased by none other than Harry Houdini, who had it installed in his house. Houdini's wife, Bess, couldn't stand the sight of it and kept moving it to the basement. Missing it, Houdini would bring it upstairs again.


As a mechanical spectacle, the War of the Currents was a curiously inverted proposition. Show inventors had generally made a point of lessening the shock (so to speak) of inventions through dramatic techniques in order to hasten their acceptance. Edison, on the other hand, did everything possible to *heighten* the sense of alarm, so as to prevent a rival's invention from passing into general use. To electrocute animals, and eventually humans, was to destroy any suspension of disbelief Tesla and Westinghouse hoped to generate, and so to decrease the overall diversity of inventions existing in society. If Edison had prevailed, dc electricity alone would have survived, and ac—at least as a consumer technology—would never have flourished.

Negative publicity in itself was not new to inventors. Edison himself had been smeared by the gas companies when he first introduced his dc electrical system. Nor were the other elements of his spectacle without precedent. Animals had been subject to experimentation before (Benjamin Franklin himself had once electrocuted a turkey), and humans had been executed in public too many times to recount. The execution of animals in public, however, *was* new, and in the end this drama proved to be *too* alarming.

To understand how it must have felt to watch a Newfoundland meet its death on a stage, it is important to remember that show animals (as distinct from animals in general) had always added a sense of life to the mechanical spectacle. From the highly trained horse to the prize-winning merino sheep, they were synonymous with excitement and emotional identification. As a rule, they were given names and human attributes. Only a few brief years before the War of the Currents commenced, the death of Barnum's famous elephant, Jumbo, had been met with condolences from around the world, and his "elephant wife" Alice depicted in newspapers wearing a widow's cap. In fact, show animals were the *sine qua non* of Barnumization. To make such a deliberate display of electrocuting animals, then, was far more heartrending than doing the same thing in a laboratory. It looked like an attempt to kill the circus.

Edison seemed to recognize as much when he delivered a half-hearted apology in newsprint. "I have not failed to seek practical demonstration," he insisted. "I have taken life—not human life—in the belief that the end justified the means."

So here was a spectacle that seemed to run at cross-purposes for Edison, turning him into a villain rather than a hero. Yet his role in the War of the Currents did make a certain kind of sense given the larger context of the times. In 1888, while the three major electrical leaders of the time—Elihu Thomson, Westinghouse, and Edison—waged their internecine wars, J. P. Morgan had begun working behind the scenes, trying to break each of them in turn and bring them under his dominion. And his success would mean considerable loss of control for all the inventors involved.

Thomson was the first to go. By initiating price wars, Morgan weakened the position of the Thomson-Houston Company, then put Charles A. Coffin at its helm. Coffin then proceeded to Westinghouse's office, but he met with less luck there. After Coffin described what he had done to Thomson, Westinghouse replied, "You tell me how you treated Thomson and Houston. Why should I trust you?"

Edison, too, had outgrown his means, but he was no more willing to sell out than Westinghouse was. He had fended off Morgan before. In the 1870s, the Electric Lighting Company had tried to pair Edison with his rival, William Sawyer, and he had refused. Now, when the idea of a merger with Thomson-Houston was broached, Edison wrote to the president of Edison General Electric, Henry Villard, "I can only invent under powerful incentives. No competition means no invention."

In this context, the War of the Currents can be understood as a desperate attempt by Edison to salvage what he could of his independence. Unfortunately, it failed even on that level. Villard, acting against Edison's wishes, secretly signed Edison General Electric over to Drexel-Morgan, and on April 15, 1892, the company merged with the Thomson-Houston Company to form a new entity called General Electric. When Edison learned that even the Edison Lamp Company had fallen under Morgan's sway, he turned pale and sent out a statement that he had been "gulled."

By the time the War of the Currents was over, Edison was in a perilously weak position. His direct-current system paled beside its alternating-current counterpart, which could cover vast distances. He was overextended and short on capital. Though he was the world's most famous inventor, he had been ousted from the helm of one of his own companies. And on a deeper level, he was a changed man. For as much as the press kept his earthy image alive, the inventor himself was no longer the spry wisecracker he had been. From the mid-1890s on, he no longer oversaw every project under his authority. He experimented less. He began to voice caution. And though he would continue to churn out invention after invention, he would never put on another live spectacle. The escape artist had gone into his cabinet with the idea that he was not going to come out again.

Perhaps Westinghouse saw poetic justice in that. Thomson and Edison had conspired against him, and Morgan had broken them. Meanwhile, Westinghouse had done his best to extricate himself from the whole sordid spectacle and, lo and behold, emerged with his independence intact. What's more, it was becoming clear that alternating current was the way of the future. And this left his protégé—the man who had made alternating current possible—free to stage his own electrical dramas with renewed vigor.

All his life Tesla had suffered from inexplicable disorders—bizarre flashes of light, unstable pulse rates, an uncommon sensitivity to nearby objects. This particular genius of psychic trauma had presented him with the ac motor in 1882, and in the aftermath of the War of the Currents, it had new, more outrageous gifts to offer.

In fact, it could be argued that Edison's high drama encouraged Tesla to become more expressive in his lectures than he might have been on his own. Prior to the War of the Currents, he had been but one more colorful inventor in a parade of colorful inventors. After it, he seemed to take on the role of a shaman, hiding out to receive his visions, then appearing in public to present his outlandish visions like electricity's monster child.

A lecture delivered to the American Institute of Electrical Engineers at Columbia College on May 20, 1891, showed just how outlandish those visions had become. Earlier that year, Tesla had invented what is known as the Tesla coil, which could produce high voltage at a high frequency. Now he used it to create a luminous streaming discharge, changing its shape according to whim. In the same lecture, he demonstrated a carbon-button lamp—twenty times brighter than Edison's incandescent globes—that prefigured the point electron microscope, the atom smasher, and the discovery of cosmic rays.

Even more astounding was his proposal for a wireless light. "The ideal way of lighting a hall or room," the inventor explained, "would, however, be to produce such a condition in it that an illuminating device could be moved and put anywhere, and that it is lighted, no matter where it is put and without being electrically connected to anything. I have been able to produce such a condition by creating in the room a powerful, rapidly alternating electrostatic field."

Understandably, Tesla's colleagues were unsure what to make of him. Aside from his mastery of electrical engineering, he had already produced a valuable technology—the ac motor—and so could not be easily discounted. Then, too, Tesla was still cleaving to the high Faraday style. Except for his long-windedness, his exposition belied the utmost lucidity. Eying him warily, the English scientist John Ambrose Fleming, a co-inventor of the vacuum tube, dubbed him "a magician of the first order. Say the Order of the Flaming Sword."

Had Tesla's audiences been privy to one more fact, they might have been less ambivalent. Throughout his lectures in 1891 and 1892, he was able to retrieve the details of his present work more easily than ever, but he could not remember anything of his past except for his very earliest years. Once again, his was a psyche in crisis. But this time, he would emerge with something even more spectacular than the ac motor. In 1888, Harold Brown had dared Westinghouse to "take through his body the alternating current while I take through mine a continuous current . . . We will begin with 100 volts and will gradually increase the pressure 50 volts at a time . . . until one or the other has cried enough, and publicly admits his error." Westinghouse had ignored this challenge. Now, Tesla was ready to take it up, and then some.

Just before embarking on a lecture tour in England and France, Tesla cured himself of his amnesia by willing himself to concentrate on childhood memories. This task reawakened thoughts of his mother, who was gravely ill at the time. Then in England, he received a letter from Sir William Crookes, inventor of the radiometer and erstwhile champion of spiritualism. The two spent an evening together, and Tesla used the opportunity to test his telepathic abilities.

"I thought that if my mother died while I was away from her bedside," Tesla recollected later, "she would surely give me a sign . . . I [was] in London in company with my late friend Sir William Crookes, when spiritualism was discussed, and I was under the full sway of these thoughts. I reflected that the conditions for a look into the beyond were most favorable."

A few months later, Tesla was so exhausted from overwork that he had to be carried home. He slept fitfully, and early that morning dreamed of a cloudborne angel, which slowly transformed itself into a vision of his mother. Glowing radiantly, she floated across the room and vanished. Tesla awoke to the sound of a heavenly choir, convinced his mother had died. She had.

The shaman takes a journey, undergoes a crisis, and then waits for a sign. When he receives it, he is ready to rejoin the clan and deliver his testimony. So it was with Tesla. In August 1892, he returned to America but gave no lectures until February 1893, when he was invited to present a lecture at the Franklin Institute in Philadelphia. Springing lightly up to the podium on cork-lined shoes, he looked out at an audience of esteemed engineers and scientists. His hair and moustache groomed to the very last follicle, his attire in perfect array, he was a famous man at the peak of his career. For a moment, his eyes shone brightly.

"When we look at the world around us," he began in his meticulous English, "we are impressed with its beauty and grandeur. Each thing we perceive, though it may be vanishingly small, is in itself a world."

With this, Tesla dove into a long digression on the importance of vision. "How could I think and how would I know I exist," he asked, "if I had not the eye?" He refreshed the audience's memory—or more probably, revealed to them for the first time—that Hermann von Helmholtz had once seen his arm in the dark by the light that emanated from his own optic nerves. Vision, he said, was the key to all understanding.

Having breezed through more philosophy than the ordinary engineer could digest, Tesla moved to a demonstration table, beneath which was an induction coil submerged into a trough of oil. A secondary wire, which ran through a hard rubber column, a brass sphere, and a brass plate, was connected to the coil. This last detail was necessary, Tesla explained, obviously reaching for maximum effect, "in order to enable me to perform the experiments under conditions, which, as you will see, are more suitable for this experiment."

Taking a metallic object in hand, Tesla approached the working coil. As he came within eight or ten inches of it, sparks 200,000 volts strong leaped from his hand. A few minutes later, this same equipment caused feeble streams of light to play throughout his body.

"Were the potentials sufficiently high and the frequency of the vibration low," Tesla informed the stunned audience, "the skin would probably be ruptured under the tremendous strain, and the blood would rush out with great force in the form of fine jet or spray so thin as to be invisible." But this was a mere trifle. At three million volts, he said—defying everything Edison had claimed about alternating current—he could envelop his body in a sheet of flame without causing injury to himself.

During the remainder of this lecture, Tesla touched on many phenomena. In a repeat performance in St. Louis shortly thereafter, he added a particularly important demonstration: he presented the technology that, many decades later, would establish him as the inventor of radio. But surely it was that first image that stayed with the onlookers after all else faded. *Sprays of invisible blood? A body covered in flames?*

Tesla sang the body electric. The sign was upon him.

Tesla had reason to be bold in February 1893. A month before, he had learned that the Columbian Exposition, scheduled to begin in May, would light up its fairgrounds and exhibition halls using his ac system. The White City would be white by his hand. He would be its undisputed hero.

There were other reasons to think that the exposition would exalt the likes of Tesla. P. T. Barnum, for one, had been advertising his thoughts on how it should be run to anyone who would listen, and his ideas were much the same as those he had applied to the Crystal Palace exhibition forty years earlier. Hold it in New York, he said, and exhibit the sarcophagus of Rameses II (in which, no doubt, Andrew Jackson refused to be buried).

But Barnum never had the chance to wield his influence. Acute congestion of the brain struck in November 1890, confining him to his home, and his death on April 7, 1891, ended the matter conclusively. The fair would not be Barnumized any more than Edison would. In fact, in many ways, it turned out to be an exercise in de-Barnumization. As with the Centennial Exposition, its primary purpose was not to aggrandize individual inventors but to glorify a larger power. And at the Columbian Exposition, that purpose would be achieved by bringing inventors into a spectacle of order that purged them of their colorful personalities.

In the 1890s, Europeans and Americans alike were growing alarmed at the violent tendencies of large crowds. The French vividly remembered the horrors of the Paris Commune, and by 1892, writers such as Gabriel Tarde were anticipating Gustav Le Bon's 1895 landmark study *The Crowd,* calling the average assembly of citizens a "female savage" and a "monstrous worm."

Meanwhile, Chicago, the site chosen for the Columbian Exposition, had been experiencing its own waves of civic unrest. On May 1, 1886, a strike at the McCormick reaper works, now headed by Cyrus's son, had ended with the death of six workers, killed by Pinkerton agents. Six days later, the Haymarket Riot left seven police dead and seventy others injured. Eight anarchists were found guilty of inciting the riot, despite flimsy evidence.

The delegates of the Chicago Exposition Company, concerned about incidents of this sort breaking out at the fair, decided to commission a private security force to patrol the grounds. For the chief of the Columbian Guard, they hired a former army officer, who promptly started conducting daily drills in the summer before the opening. When the fair opened, a battalion of 1,750 guardians, dressed in bluish-gray uniforms and yellow-lined capes, were on hand to discourage dubious behavior and, if necessary, remove unsavory characters from the premises. An additional 250 plainclothes detectives helped further their task. The guard apparently served as an effective deterrent: on opening day, only 6 out of the 100,000 visitors who poured through the gate were arrested.

From a show inventor's perspective, this experiment in crowd control could only have a negative impact. Even crowd theorists admitted that an unregulated mob, while volatile, existed in a state of heightened suggestibility, and show inventors had long taken advantage of that fact to give their inventions greater mystique. At the Columbian Exposition, however, mystique was in short supply. Frederick Law Olmsted, designer of the grounds, groused that the exhibition lacked "incidents of vital human gaiety." Photographs taken at the fair support this sentiment, revealing a gathering that is surprisingly somber for being such a monstrous worm.

Perhaps even more effective than the police presence in establishing order was the decision to divide the exhibition into two distinct sections: the Midway Plaisance and the White City. The purpose of the division was overtly stated by Harlow N. Higinbotham, president of the board of directors, who described the creation of the Midway as an "opportunity for isolating . . . special features, thus preventing jarring contrasts between the beautiful buildings on the one hand, and the amusing, distracting, ludicrous, and noisy attractions." As the organizers hoped to mute the excitement of the crowd, so too did they hope to keep the din of entertainers from overpowering the more "important" exhibitions.

What this meant in effect was that those inventors who purged the impure live performance from their promotional schemes were permitted to exhibit in the White City, while those who did not were lumped among the "ludicrous" attractions of the Midway. With this arrangement, inventors who chose to segregate themselves from their thespian counterparts were expressly legitimized.

The Midway, named for its location halfway between Washington Park and Jackson Park, certainly lived up to the standard of being impure. Housing the outrageous and the odd in a space about one mile long and two hundred yards wide, it positively teemed with attractions — and won what emotion there was to be had from the crowds. The famed Little Egypt (or women who later claimed to be her) performed the *danse du ventre* with all the authenticity needed to "deprive a man of a peaceful night's rest for years to come." Samoa's Village of South Sea Islanders, fresh off the boat and "recently rescued from cannibalism," sang the wildly incongruous "Yankee Doodle Dandy." Sterilized water costing one cent was ladled into unsterilized glasses. The Moorish Palace and its Startling Wonders featured palm gardens, sultans, harems, and a labyrinth of torture scenes.

Every now and then, genuine mayhem broke out on the Midway. History records a dwarf getting an elephant drunk on several buckets of beer and setting him loose. And on closing day, after night fell, the crowd finally made its passions felt. "The rabble let itself loose," wrote a reporter, "and marched up and down the broad street blowing horns, tearing away awnings and becoming more boisterous by the minute. Finally, an attack was made on the Chinese theater with a view to looting it, but the Columbians guards called a halt, and the crowd was dispersed."

This was just the kind of environment that had always attracted show inventors, and there were a few exhibits where their presence still could be felt. The Monster Kaleidoscope fractured reality into larger-than-life bits. The Electric Theater took visitors on "A Day in the Alps," where an electric fan provided an alpine breeze, peasants sang through an electric gramophone, a red light created a sunset, and artificial lightning brought on a storm. And of course, towering above the other exhibits, near the center of the Midway, stood the Ferris Wheel.

When George W. Ferris invested $25,000 into his project, he was hoping to one-up the Eiffel Tower, which had been built for the Universal Exposition of 1889. By the time he turned an additional $250,000 from investors into a structure that weighed more than 1,000 tons and spanned a diameter of 264 feet, his great iron circle could certainly claim parity with the French wonder. Just for good measure, he erected a 20-foot replica of the Eiffel Tower by its side.

The Ferris Wheel was something new, a monument to pleasure. Romances were kindled routinely on the 20-minute ride. Many chose to ride it all day, bringing their food with them and eating it at the built-in counters provided for that express purpose. Though the attraction was perceived as dangerous, it was actually quite safe. The statistics show no accidents, even after 15 million passengers had taken their turn. One summer day, when gusts up to 100 miles an hour wailed through the grounds, Ferris and his wife proved the soundness of his engineering more conclusively by ascending in the invention themselves, much the way Elisha Otis had at a different exhibition, in a different age.

But for all its magnificence, the Ferris Wheel was not a groundbreaking invention, and no one pretended otherwise. In fact, the only arguably "useful" invention to appear on the Midway was Eadweard Muybridge's zoopraxiscope. Whether or not Muybridge preferred the honky-tonk atmosphere, the fact that he was still presenting his invention in person classified him as a performer, and therefore as a "distraction." The distinction was not advantageous. After six months, his Zoopraxographical Hall made only two hundred dollars, and with that his career essentially came to an end. (His last notable contribution before his death in 1904 was to return to England and tend a garden with pools in the shape of the Great Lakes.)

The White City, meanwhile, presented visitors with a very different experience. Where Midway exhibitors staked a claim wherever they could, the architecture of the White City was carefully planned to create "a chaste and modulated" harmony. Where the Midway raged with drunken elephants, the White City offered a sober array of stuffed and mounted animals. And while Little Egypt taxed the fidelity of husbands with the *danse du ventre*, Stanford White's statue of Diana in the nude (borrowed from the roof of Madison Square Garden) remained in the White City only under vigorous protest from the Women's Temperance Union.

Nothing illustrated the masterful composition of the White City better than electricity, which by night diagrammed the grounds in incandescent light. Or, as one writer put it, losing himself in the breathlessness of it all, the "pervasive loveliness, its beauty born of color and form, and around whose lineaments the radiance of light, shining with all the luxuriance of modern electrical design, has spent an aureole of surpassing joy, are molding anew our requirements in art."

In fact, ac electricity was the central subject of the White City. Within the space of a few years, it had gone from killing force to crowning achievement—the invention that provided the framework for all the other important inventions of the exposition.

The major figures from the War of the Currents seemed to understand the change. Formerly alternating current had been a weapon in their hands; now it was proof of their ability to throw in together. In the Electricity Building, Edison's Pillar of Light shone with the power of five thousand incandescent bulbs. General Electric, at the time Elihu Thomson's employer, supplied the three-ton searchlight that swept a brilliant beam across the unexpressive minions. By this time Westinghouse, too, had entered the fold and licensed his ac patents to his sworn enemy, Samuel Insull, newly ascended to head of Commonwealth Electric, to provide the power for the grounds, the fountains, and the waterways.

Gone were the accusations, the outrageous claims, the subterfuge. And gone were the inventors themselves. In order to distinguish themselves from the barkers on the Midway, they chose not to appear beside their inventions. No ballyhoo, no pitch—that was the price of admission into the White City.

Even Edison's Kinetoscope obeyed the general rule of contrition. Ostensibly, this invention was an anomaly at the Electricity Building, since it offered viewers a chance to peer into a box and see a ninety-second motion picture of circus animals, the dancer Carmencita, the boxer Jim Corbett, or the showman Eugene Sandow, who expanded his torso from 47 to 61 inches while bearing a platform and three horses on his chest. Indeed, the Kinetoscope would probably have ended up on the Midway, except for the fact that Edison failed to appear in person to deliver it to the world.

Historians have generally glossed over Edison's absence from his own display at the White City. Yet for those who stepped back and took a longer view, the Kinetoscope offered signs of a farewell. For almost two decades, curiosity seekers had lingered on the outskirts of Menlo Park or West Orange, hoping to catch a glimpse of a mucker moving from one building to another, and in more recent years, to hear the likes of Edwin Booth or Lillian Russell orating grandly into a phonograph. In a curious way, the Kinetoscope resembled this moment in miniature. An enclosure containing fleeting images of legendary figures, it held the same voyeuristic pleasures that Menlo Park once had. Edison himself seemed half-aware of this souvenirlike quality when he confessed to Muybridge that "These Zoetropic devices are of too sentimental a character to get the public to invest in."

The truth was, in substituting a peephole box for his peephole laboratory, Edison had completed the transit first set in motion after his meeting with Muybridge in 1888. He had replaced himself with the ultimate pseudo-event: a continuous series of photographs that could be presented in lieu of a personal appearance. With the Kinetoscope, he no longer had to take part in draining and costly public contests, or to venture into the public arena at all for that matter. His celebrity assured beyond all doubt, the man who didn't care for the theater could sit inside his movie studio at West Orange—a completely enclosed, light-tight structure nicknamed Black Maria—and churn out dramas that were entirely unrelated to the obstreperous world of inventions.

It was a brilliant piece of maneuvering by a brilliant man, but it came at a heavy cost. In eliminating himself from the mechanical spectacle, Edison had also eliminated himself from his own career. Though he continued to invent with unceasing vigor, never again would he produce a revolutionary invention. Most of his subsequent ventures led nowhere, and those that succeeded were either imitative or trivial. He could try his hand at prefabricated houses, storage batteries, synthetic rubber. It didn't matter, because, in the theatrical sense as much as the moral one, he had lost his character. His master plan had worked, but it had also failed.

The message at the White City was clear. The star system, which had glorified the individualist ever since Isaac Singer flaunted his oversized carriage on the streets of New York, had come to an unseemly pass with the War of the Currents. Inventors who wanted to continue in that vein were free to do so. Those who forsook their bawdy acts, however, could join in the effort to build what is known today as the Grid, a network of electrical power lines capable of spanning the nation—a hugely profitable venture.

The offer was too tempting for most inventors to resist. Nevertheless, there was one party in the Electricity Building who refused to give up his egocentric, performing ways. Visitors who stumbled onto a modest space allotted to the Westinghouse Company beheld a dark-eyed Nikola Tesla, smiling before a set of electrical tubes that spelled out the greeting, "Welcome, Electricians." Those who lingered longer to admire the eggs that spun at high speed or any of the other unusual exhibits might have caught the inventor's latest act, test-played before engineers, and now being given to the public direct. As one witness at the Electricity Building described it:

> Mr. Tesla has been seen receiving through his hands currents at a potential of more than 200,000 volts, vibrating a million times per second, and manifesting themselves in dazzling streams of light . . . After such a striking test, which, by the way, no one has displayed a hurried inclination to repeat, Mr. Tesla's body and clothing have continued for some time to emit fine glimmers or halos of splintered light.

By way of conclusion, Tesla predicted that one day he would cover himself completely with such a light. Someday soon, his inventions would allow a man to stand naked at the North Pole, swathed in lambent flames.

How did Tesla come to put on such a disruptive show in the White City? Didn't a man who spoke of flaming nudists roaming the Arctic belong among the rabble of the Midway? Perhaps, but for the moment, nothing much could be done; he was, after all, the man responsible for making the White City a reality. If he wanted to set himself alight with the same power that illuminated the grounds, this was one time it would have to be tolerated.

For his part, Tesla might have worried that his self-electrocutions risked alienating his peers. But in fact, he had nothing to lose, because a year or so earlier, he had given up any chance of taking part in the building of the Grid. And he had done so in his customary histrionic style.

With the success of alternating current, Westinghouse had come to realize that he had struck a bad bargain. The 1888 contract stated that Tesla would earn $2.50 for every horsepower sold. By 1892, it was estimated that these royalties already amounted to $12 million, and it was looking all but certain that Westinghouse would be awarded the contract for the Niagara Falls power plant. In order to honor his agreement with Tesla, he would have to bankrupt himself.

Reluctantly, Westinghouse called Tesla to his office and explained his position. Tesla listened carefully, then posed a question: "And if I give up the contract," he asked, "you will save your company and retain control? You will proceed with your plans to give my polyphase system [of ac] to the world?"

Nikola Tesla, dubbed by Sir John Ambrose Fleming "a magician of the first order," effectively won the War of the Currents when he took 200,000 volts of alternating current into his body before stunned audiences in 1893. *New York Public Library*

When Westinghouse assured him that this was the case, Tesla tore up both contracts and urged him to move forward. With this, he was no longer beholden to commercial restraints. And if that put him at a financial disadvantage, it also left him free to be as exhibitionistic as he pleased.

Thus at the Electricity Building, a new conflict found tangible expression. On the one hand, there were the corporations, which had already begun the process of depersonalizing inventors. On the other, there was Tesla, visionary, public figure, and—having become a citizen in 1891—the first American inventor who could be seen as a David, defying the Goliath of the system.

By the end of the decade, the corporations would emerge as a powerful, new economizing force, determining the fate of inventions according to their own stringent needs, and Tesla would be largely discredited. But not before he gave them a run for their money.

*Chapter Thirteen*

# CENTURY'S END

In October 1893, just after the Columbian Exposition closed, George Westinghouse called Tesla with momentous news. The Niagara Falls Commission, he said, had chosen alternating current to power its new electrical plant. Westinghouse would fire its new ac generator with 15,000 units of horsepower. General Electric, meanwhile, would provide the distribution lines, using Tesla's patents through a licensing agreement.

Another inventor might have taken pause at having given away his financial interest in the first permanent expression of the Grid. Not Tesla. Elated that his patents were finding such magnificent application, he returned to New York and immediately plunged into his work. Soon, he was able to invite the elite Waldorf set to his laboratory at 33-35 South Fifth Avenue—located in what was then the red-light district of the Latin Quarter—for performances that seemed closer to magic than to science. He caused his lab to be illuminated with no discernible light source. He rolled an electrical fireball in his hand before slipping it into a wooden box. Mark Twain had occasion to stand on a vibrating platform, which had the summary effect of evacuating his bowels. The Lazzo of the Enema had never been more sophisticated.

No doubt Tesla also took this opportunity to tell his audiences of the many plans still germinating in his mind. Someday, he would control automatons at a distance and send electrical power across many miles. His inventions would pull energy from the air itself. Fluorescent lights, bladeless turbines, jet aircraft—it could hardly be long before he mastered the secrets of transferring human thought onto a screen.

Tesla enjoyed a fair amount of credulity for his predictions. After all, he had already demonstrated radio and harnessed the roar of Niagara, and predictions notwithstanding, it was hard for his witnesses to dispute what they had seen with their own eyes. Inevitably, they leaked their escapades to the press, which painted them as modern renditions of Faust's royal masquerade.

But acclaimed as Tesla was, the ground was already beginning to shift beneath his feet. As his potential backers got to know him, they discovered a man riddled with quirks. He required exactly eighteen napkins whenever he sat down to dinner, and like Phileas Fogg gone electric, counted every step he took. The sight of a peach gave him a fever. Dropping small squares of paper into liquid would produce an awful taste in his mouth. He was deathly afraid of earrings, and could not touch another person's hair, as he put it, "except, perhaps, at the point of a revolver."

That Tesla was a man apart became painfully obvious in the area of romance. While his new acquaintances quickly learned that he was not a joiner, they couldn't pass up the chance to play matchmaker for such an accomplished figure. Robert Johnson, poet and publisher, and his wife, Katharine, were among the most anxious to see the inventor paired up. They met him in 1893, and forthwith began to introduce him to some of high society's most eligible debutantes.

One of these women arrived at a party at the Johnson residence turned out in a stylish French gown with a flowery neckline. After assuring Tesla that this woman was in love with him, Robert introduced her simply as "Miss Anne Morgan," then left the two to their own devices. Tesla took the opportunity to observe how beautiful Morgan was, and very likely to ponder how rich her father, J. P. Morgan, was as well. Unfortunately, her pearl earrings made it impossible for him to remain in her presence, and he extricated himself at the earliest possible moment. Rumor had it that Morgan suffered terribly from the rejection.

Socialites were not the only ones urging Tesla toward matrimony. An editorial in the August 14, 1896, issue of the *Electrical Review* of London made it clear how important the matter was to the public: "Whatever may be the cause of the abnormal condition in which this distinguished scientist finds himself, we hope that it will soon be removed, for we are certain that science in general, and Mr. Tesla in particular, will be all the richer when he gets married."

Of course, Tesla hailed from a long line of show inventors who exhibited quirky behavior. Yet his quirks were more intimately bound up with his creativity than most. In order to maintain his star status, he had to offer up ever more spectacular visions, and for each one, he had to undergo the requisite breakdown. By the mid-1890s, his prolific vision-seeking had him in a state of perpetual breakdown, and thus in a state of perpetual isolation from the world.

This insistence on keeping his own unusual counsel, while lifting his imagination to untold heights, ultimately proved disastrous. On March 13, 1895, a fire broke out in his lab and quickly spread out of control. The following day, the headlines announced the "Fruits of Genius Swept Away." Tesla's acquaintances tried in vain to locate him as he wandered the streets of New York in a state of shock.

Nothing was insured, but it hardly mattered. Tesla never kept notes, relying instead on his photographic memory—a power inescapably related to his breakdowns—to realize his inventions. His closest assistants knew of his work on robotics, wireless transmission of power, possibly even a form of liquid oxygen, but he often formulated new ideas too rapidly to inform them of every detail. Under such circumstances, an accurate appraisal was impossible for actuaries and historians alike.

Though Tesla was in a more precarious position than ever, he still showed no sign of surrendering his freedom. Shortly after the fire, Edward Dean Adams, the financier behind the Niagara Falls Commission, offered him a partnership in a company capitalized at $500,000 that could compete against the House of Morgan. Tesla accepted the offer of $40,000 to set up a new laboratory at 46 Houston Street, but declined the offer to join the company. He needed backing, to be sure, but to enter a partnership, he felt, could only mean the subjugation of his character.

Ironically, Tesla learned of one invention that he lost in the fire when someone else invented it instead. Edward R. Hewitt, an experimental photographer and Peter Cooper's grandson, remembered Tesla conducting an experiment with the help of Mark Twain, not long before the German scientist Wilhelm Conrad Roentgen announced his discovery of x-rays. "Tesla took a picture of Mark Twain under a Geissler tube," Hewitt wrote, "which proved to be no picture of Twain but a good one of the adjusting screw of the camera lens."

Tesla realized that this was an x-ray photograph only after the fact and, as usual, couched his oversight in mystical terms: "I had hardly finished the work of reconstruction [of his lab]," he wrote, "and resumed the course of my ideas when the news of Roentgen's achievement reached me. I hurried to repeat his incompletely reported experiments and there I beheld the wonder myself. Then—too late—I realized that my guiding spirit had again prompted me and that I had failed to comprehend his mysterious signs."

The x-ray burst upon the world with no warning and, because Roentgen sought no patent on it, set off a riot of applications. *Science* wrote on March 3, 1896, that "the rays were used to reflect anatomic diagrams directly into the brains of advanced medical students, making a much more enduring impression than ordinary teaching methods of learning anatomic details." George Johnson from Jefferson County, Iowa, professed to be able to change metal into gold with x-rays. On April 17, the *Electrician* related the exploits of Mr. Ingles Rogers, who "produced an impression on the photographic plate by simply gazing at it in the dark." Dr. S. H. Monell of New York, writing in the *American Medical Journal,* described a fluoroscope as "Roentgen's spectacles," and even went so far as to price this item—from five to twenty dollars, depending on the size. Assemblyman Reed of Somerset County, New Jersey, introduced a bill prohibiting the use of x-ray opera glasses in theaters. In London, there were ads for x-ray–proof undergarments. A gambler wrote Edison asking for an x-ray apparatus that could give him the edge at faro.

Tesla did not enter into this celebration but regarded it from afar. "Speculations, mostly unfounded," he observed, citing his beloved Faust, "increased to such an extent that, despairingly, one would exclaim with the poet: 'Oh happy he who still hopes to rise/Out of this sea of errors and false views!' "

Yet he had been so close to inventing the x-ray himself. Puzzled by his failure to heed the "mysterious signs," he threw himself into research in his typical fashion: he applied it to himself. Using his own apparatus, he exposed his hand to a Lenard tube (similar to an x-ray, or Roentgen tube) until it became red and swollen. Not content to leave it at that, he again subjected his hand to the invisible rays. This time, he instantly recoiled in pain. It took several days for his fingernails to grow back. In later writings, he described how the skin tightened on exposure, turning black in severe cases, forming ugly lesions and coming off in layers. On another occasion, he exposed his own head to x-rays for forty-minute intervals from a distance of forty feet, but surprisingly, suffered nothing more than sleepiness and a feeling of warmth. Only when an assistant received a terrible burn in the abdomen did Tesla begin to seek precautions.

Others soon discovered that x-rays were not ideal for casual experiments. A man named Hawks, after demonstrating x-rays in a New York department store, started feeling a painful "sunburn"; his fingernails stopped growing, his eyelashes fell out. An infantryman named Thomas McKenna, treated for a wound sustained in the Spanish-American War, developed large ulcers on his arms and chest after six days of exposures. In Edison's lab, an assistant named Clarence Dally exposed himself to so much radiation that, after a similar outbreak of ulcers, he had to undergo several amputations and eventually died.

All of these episodes bore witness to the fact that it was sometimes the invention and not the inventor that was to be feared. But in a climate where independent inventors were already suspect, it was easier to assign blame to a person—especially the sort of person who already trafficked heavily in histrionics. In a sense, the very tradition that insisted on giving inventors a pronounced character came back to haunt them in the guise of the "mad scientist."

H. G. Wells, writing in the midst of the x-ray craze, was perhaps the first to evoke the specter of the mad scientist in all his glory. His novel *The Invisible Man*, published in 1897, tells the story of a man named Griffin who arrives in an English hamlet bundled from head to toe, asking for a room. He is obliged, and his baggage arrives after him—a melange of curiosities and bottles. As time passes, Griffin begins to reveal a highly unpleasant personality, and the villagers grow to dislike and even fear him. When they question him about a burglary, they learn what is really happening: Griffin has invented a potion that has rendered him invisible. Enraged at being found out, he flees and embarks on a self-pronounced reign of terror, killing as many people as he can. When he is finally caught and killed in turn, he slowly becomes visible again.

Compared to tales of inventors before it, *The Invisible Man* represents a sharp turn to the dark side. Mary Shelley, contrary to film adaptations of her book, depicted both Dr. Frankenstein and his monster as essentially good characters caught in a tragic situation. Verne's Captain Nemo, despised as he was, continued to nurse his noble aspirations as he cruised the ocean depths. Even Robert Louis Stevenson's Dr. Jekyll wrestled with the demon he had created. But Griffin wastes no time with ethical dilemmas. He is evil from the very beginning and undergoes no moral transformation.

Griffin's particular sin is an overweaning pride, which makes him unwilling to publicize his invention even before he has incriminated himself. "I had no refuge, no appliances," he confesses when relating the events of his first invisible days, "no human being in the world in whom I could confide. To have told my secret would have given me away—made a mere show and a rarity of me!"

The result is a form of madness. Of the novel, Wells's son Anthony West wrote, "the story does not deal with an invisible man's interactions with a world we know, but with what befalls an invisible madman, a person impenetrably concealed within his own special frame of private references, resentments, obsessions, and compulsions, and altogether set apart from the generality of mankind." No longer a lovable rogue embroiling audiences in unlikely scenarios, the inventor in Wells's hands is a man apart, a man whose magic actually separates him from others—an inhuman character.

Perhaps Tesla saw the outlines of his own image in this portrait. Certainly, he too operated within a murky network of private obsessions, and certainly, he was just as defiant of normal society. When the Invisible Man describes his invention, it sounds very much like the man who had missed inventing the x-ray: "No, not those Röntgen vibrations," he says dismissively, "I don't know that these others of mine have been described." What is harder to countenance is why, while readers thrilled to the image of the evil Griffin, Tesla chose to become *more* like him, rather than less.

From 1896 on, Tesla acted like a man who prized his reputation over his record. Where once he had gladly revealed his inventions to the public, he now began merely to assert their existence, offering ominous descriptions in place of hard proof. This had the automatic effect of making the second half of his career apocryphal, since almost all of the claims he made in the "post-Griffin" era have resisted substantiation. More immediately, however, it allowed him to cultivate the image of a proud and powerful genius.

As Tesla himself liked to tell it, for example, he went to the cellar beneath his Houston Street lab one day in 1898 and, on a whim, attached a tiny electromechanical oscillator to one of the iron pillars that supported the building. He had often used this device to make various objects in his lab vibrate according to the frequencies he selected. On this day, however, more was at stake: Unbeknownst to Tesla, the pillar was connected to the substructure below Manhattan. Within minutes, buildings throughout Little Italy started vibrating, windows were shattered, and frightened residents ran into the street, convinced that an earthquake had struck.

The police appeared on the scene just as Tesla became aware of his mistake. Grinning impishly, he told them they had just missed his performance. When reporters arrived, he dismissed the contretemps as a trifle. If he wanted, he said, he could destroy the Brooklyn Bridge within minutes.

Tesla intimated his terrible powers again that year when he introduced a radio-controlled, submersible torpedo boat at the Electrical Exposition in New York. While this automaton—the first example of robotics—was surely an impressive invention, he withheld essential aspects of it. The public did not know, for example, that it contained technology designed to prevent radio interference, or that its antenna could be completely submerged. Rather than give a demonstration, Tesla gave only the *threat* of one, claiming that his invention could "attack and destroy a whole armada—destroy it utterly in half an hour, and the enemy never have sight of their antagonists or know what power destroyed them."

To do more, perhaps, would have been to make a "show and a rarity of him." In any event, such techniques were not well received. *Scientific American*, among others, took Tesla to task for pandering without bothering to demonstrate his claims:

> Judging from the comments of the scientific and technical press, we are not alone in our expressions of regret that any one of Mr. Tesla's undoubted ability should indulge in such obvious and questionable self-advertisement. That the author of the multiphase system of transmission should, at this late day, be flooding the press with rhetorical bombast that recalls the wildest days of the Keely motor mania is inconsistent and inexplicable to the last degree.

It must have been quite a sight, this oracle of the Electric Age—who had been imbued with hundreds of thousands of volts, who had bathed in a torrent of lightning—mouthing predictions of swift and terrible victories. Like the Invisible Man, he could strike without warning, destroying bridges, armadas, anything he desired. But there was more, so much more. . . .


On May 18, 1899, a carpenter named Joseph Dozier noticed that the Alta Vista Hotel in his hometown of Colorado Springs was unusually alive with reporters. Soon, a mysterious man arrived by buckboard. The reporters barraged him with questions. Dozier thought he heard a few phrases, something about Paris, something about the famous financier Mr. Astor.

The world just couldn't get any stranger, Dozier thought as he returned to his work. But later that day, it became stranger again when he looked up to see this mysterious visitor at his doorstep. Introducing himself in a slight European accent, Mr. Tesla showed the carpenter an array of blueprints for a building to be erected one mile east of town. Construction was to begin immediately.

Dozier soon learned what sort of man had hired him. At night, Tesla ordered his customary eighteen napkins for his meals, then retired to Room 207, acceptable because the number was divisible by three. He spoke of hearing beyond the mountains, seeing farther than normal men, and wrote in his diary of nights when "immense objects appear dwarfed, while small objects as horses, carriages or men assume unnatural gigantic dimensions." He carted machinery of every shape and size to the site, then began ordering more in daily frenzies of telegraphic communication. Every day he traveled back and forth from the hotel, dressed improbably well, his long legs sprawled over the side of the buckboard in case of a sudden crash.

The laboratory quickly began to take on the semblance of a ship. From the roof sprouted a tower some 80 feet high. Above it, a metal "mast" extended another 122 feet, crowned with a copper ball three feet in diameter. A fence went up around the grounds bearing the warning "KEEP OUT—GREAT DANGER." Later, a more ominous sign appeared on the building itself: "Abandon hope all ye who enter here."

Dozier had a great deal to absorb in the six months that Tesla remained in Colorado Springs. Once the laboratory was fully equipped, the inventor began his experiments. At night, the sky around the tower grew bright with sparks. Lightning arresters in a 12-mile radius created earthbound lightning bolts. Butterflies flew in the vortices of transmitter coils 52 feet in diameter and met their doom. Grounded metal objects drew sparks from as far as 300 feet away. Grazing horses felt the earth shiver with current and bolted. Locals reported seeing sparks in the imprints left by their heels in the dirt. Others said they had seen Tesla roaming the area and planting hundreds of 50-watt light bulbs in the earth, some 26 miles from his station, then causing them to light up from afar. The roar of the station could be heard 10 miles away. Finally, the voltages overtaxed the electrical plant in Colorado Springs, causing a citywide blackout.

Few had ever seen such a display of electrical power. It seemed as if the inferno itself was being loosed upon the earth. But to what end?

In fact, Tesla was after his most ambitious project yet: the wireless transmission of power. He hoped to draw energy from the resonant frequency of the planet using extremely high voltages at extremely low frequencies. If he could achieve this, it would mean unlimited power for everyone on earth. With a simple thrust of a rod into the ground, the current would flow.

Tesla believed he succeeded in obtaining this goal. When he sent a stream of electrons at 150,000 oscillations per second into the earth, he said later, they converged on the opposite side of the earth, in the Indian Ocean, and created a resonance sufficient to light 200 incandescent light bulbs. The very earth bent to the will of the shaman.

And perhaps the planets did as well. In the last months of 1899, the Colorado Springs experiments reached an unexpected climax. Mr. Dozier, apparently fully assimilated into the inventor's team, was on duty late one night when the inventor became excited by rhythmic sounds emanating from a receiver. Tesla listened expectantly, his eyes trained toward the heavens, and concluded that the sounds came from no known source within the earth's atmosphere.

Many untoward events had taken place in this lab, but Dozier, a carpenter raised in a frontier town, could only wonder at the limits of the human experience as Tesla sat down, plucked up a pen, and began firing off a letter to Julian Hawthorne, his reporter friend at the *Philadelphia North American* . . . to let the world know that he had received messages from Mars.

Tesla had drifted a long way from his 1888 lecture, in which he introduced alternating current with such clarity that "he left nothing to be done by those who followed him." If anything, he seemed intent on filling out the visage of the mad scientist described by Wells. And yet for all his dubious ventures, he continued to attract followers. Hugo Gernsback, an inventor and the father of American science fiction, saw in Tesla "a personality of a high order." A young Lee de Forest, who would go on to invent the first practical vacuum tube, found his first inspiration in Tesla's "weird, almost frightful results" and determined to follow him "into that tenuous realm that is the connecting link between God and mind and lower matter."

Indeed, the ranks of the freelancers did not seem to be thinning. By 1898, an editorialist at the *Electrician* could derogate them as a type, and in the process, reveal the bias of the public:

> It is popularly, yet quite illogically, assumed that the individual who is dissociated from, say, the telephone or telegraph enterprise, must be more worthy of a hearing than anyone whose attainments and experience have perforce placed him in the position of an *ex parte* advocate. The choice, in fact, generally lies between the well-informed individual whose valuable services have been retained, and the badly informed person whose futile assistance is required by no one.

The popularity of independent inventors presented more of a dilemma than this writer admitted. Often enough, their ideas really were futile, in which case, they threatened at worst to slow the work of others by filling the public's head with nonsense. But who could tell? Here and there, the occasional madman might stumble onto something truly valuable and, by winning the public over, leave even the most alert corporation out in the cold.

Given this state of affairs, it no longer made sense to give inventors a wide berth for their oddball performances. Tesla's inclusion in the Electricity Building alone was ample testimony that today's worthy contributor could become tomorrow's problem child. Nor was it enough to control one project, as Morgan had done with the electrical industry, because new inventions seemed to spring up without surcease. The inventor's penchant for planned variety, where possible, had to be *permanently* entrained into the corporate structure.

Few inventors had any inkling that such movements were abroad, least of all Tesla. Yet they *were* abroad, even he wound down his experiments at Colorado Springs and prepared to return East.

In December 1899, American Telephone and Telegraph employee George Ashley Campbell had reason to be jubilant. He had recently completed a series of laboratory tests in Boston and was preparing to unreel a set of telephone cables in a circuitous maze that stretched from Jamaica Plain to Newton, Massachusetts. If the experiments of this sharp-eyed man with a salt-and-pepper moustache proved right, the world would soon have its first long-distance telephone line.

At the same moment, a bespectacled Michael Pupin closed the door to his office at Columbia University. Pupin had come a long way from his childhood in rural Serbia. A graduate of Columbia with a doctorate from Cambridge University, he had earned a place in American society as a respected professor and a leader in the x-ray field. In March, he had made a speech at the American Institute of Electrical Engineers that portended even greater rewards in store for him—like Campbell, he had figured out how to build the world's first long-distance telephone line. But as a friend advised him after the lecture, there were dangers in revealing his ideas so publicly. Now, he was heeding his friend's advice and filing for a patent.

Campbell and Pupin were well on their way to one of the great contests in the history of invention. At the time, telephone communications were largely limited to regional calls because messages quickly became distorted as the distance between points increased. A practical long-distance line would offer an advance almost as significant as the leap from direct to alternating current—not to mention an opportunity for the winner to step into the spotlight. In fact, Oliver Heaviside and Sir William Preece had already proven just how much was at stake in the 1880s, when they fought the first, messy rounds in full view of the public.

A gaunt man with a grim expression, Heaviside liked to work alone in his room with the windows shut, even when it became hot and smoky. Typically, he would begin around ten at night and continue to the early hours of the morning, asking that his food be left outside his door so that he could eat when the urge struck him. Sometimes he experimented in these disheveled quarters, filling the house with the stench of battery acid. His only sustained contact with the world came through his brother, Arthur.

When Heaviside did make his presence felt in public, he never failed to add a touch of the zany. At scientific gatherings, he inevitably lent a cantankerous note to the otherwise decorous proceedings. To honor his hero, James Clerk Maxwell, he once suggested that a unit of energy be called the *mac* (plural, the *max*). Additional recommendations were the *tom* for William Thompson (Lord Kelvin), and "bob and dick also at some future time." His papers on electromagnetic theory, published in the *Electrician* in 1882, began at maximum ellipsis. "The daily newspapers," he mused, "as is well known, usually contain in the autumn time paragraphs and leaders upon marvelous subjects which at other times make way for more pressing matter. The sea-serpent is one of these subjects."

But for all his truculence, Heaviside also had a frightening ability to make math do his bidding. Rivaling the calculating power of early computers, he routinely peppered his notebooks with figures filled out to seven decimal places. What's more, his *Electrician* articles were essential to the electrical industry. Particularly important was an article published on June 3, 1887, which described the first distortionless circuit.

A man with such a temperament was bound to find a nemesis, and Heaviside found his in William Preece, the British scientist who a few years back had scoffed at Edison's subdivided lighting system. Heaviside and Preece waged a blood feud in print, restoring the vitriolic style of Pulcinella to a level not seen since the days of Isaac Singer. Without naming him directly, Preece referred to Heaviside as "a very arrogant and dogmatic individual" and "a little monarch in his own laboratory." Heaviside, holding his own, retorted by calling Preece a "scienticulist" and "The Nameless One." (In commedia dell'arte, it will be recalled, the equivalent exchange was only slightly more direct—Pulcinella: "Donkey dropping!" Capitano: "Pox on you!" Pulcinella: "Snivelling drunkard!" Capitano: "Gutless dog!")

So it went until 1891, when it became clear that Heaviside's theories on the distortionless circuit, also known as the loaded coil or the loading-lumps system, were correct. With this, all that remained was to apply his theories, and AT&T set its sights on the goal right away. In 1893, the company hired the doubly reliable John Stone Stone, a Johns Hopkins graduate, who in turn hired George Campbell in 1897. Stone left the company two years later, but Campbell continued on, all the while championing Heaviside to those who worked inside the company.

In September 1899, the matter seemed to be solved when Campbell's loaded lines passed the test in his Boston laboratory. Then Pupin's patent was filed, and the question of priority was thrown into court. As interference proceedings were filed, the two parties geared up for full-scale battle.

By all rights, it would have been logical at this point for AT&T to back its employee in this contest. After all, this was the company that had emerged from the great performances of a consummate show-

inventor team. Had they been on hand, Bell and Watson themselves would no doubt have played up the battle like seasoned veterans.

But they were not on hand. Though Bell was a major stockholder in American Bell Telephone and lived quite comfortably on his income, he had little say in business decisions by this time. Nor did he have any inventions to offer his company. A desultory attempt at an automatic telephone switchboard between 1895 and 1897 marked the end of his contributions to the company he had created. On the cusp of the new century, the most pressing issue on his mind was the magazine currently under his directorship, *National Geographic*.

As for Watson, he had worked out of the Charles Williams shop until 1881, then left to pursue a host of interests, including shipbuilding and geology. None of these ventures proved lucrative, however, and he eventually realized that, in the unraveling skein of the inventor's show, he was following the wrong thread. His heart belonged to theater. In 1910, he joined Frank R. Benson's Company of Shakespearian Actors in England and quickly progressed from spear carrier to a role as the clerk in *The Merchant of Venice*. In 1912, he started his own Shakespearian troupe, and even took it upon himself to adapt *A Tale of Two Cities* and *Nicholas Nickleby* for the stage.

In effect, Bell and Watson resumed the old twin trades, one as an amateur inventor, the other as a summer-stock actor. Their absence from the company boardroom changed the nature of the loaded-line contest considerably. From the perspective of the AT&T executives, the imminent court case between Campbell and Pupin raised the prospect of *both* patent claims being overturned. And if that happened, priority would go back to the truculent Heaviside, who had made his invention free to the public. It was too big a gamble. As long as the contest continued, the monopoly on the loaded line could be lost.

And so a decision was made. Rather than risk controversy—the lifeblood of show inventors for some fifty years—AT&T decided to quash it as quickly as possible. The contest would be a silent one. As a measure of how imperative it was to keep the matter quiet, Pupin received $445,000 for his patent, while Campbell, the company's own inventor, received nothing at all. That, apparently, was his reward for aligning with a pariah like Heaviside.

The legal proceedings dragged on for a few years until Pupin was finally awarded the patent, but by then the entire affair had been drained of its dramatic content. Even scholarly descriptions of this episode fail to name the company administrator who charted its course, resorting instead to the passive voice. In silencing the gibes of the contestants, AT&T successfully turned the invention of long-distance phone lines into a non-event.

While the great telephone-line contest barreled toward nowhere at all, Elihu Thomson, the former head of the Thomson-Houston Company, had his own non-events to worry about. Somewhat heavier, somewhat grayer since the War of the Currents had been waged, he sat at his desk in Lynn, Massachusetts, and reviewed his past few years at General Electric. The results were disquieting. He had approached the organization of the company as its own kind of invention and tinkered with its various structures. But lately the structure seemed to be tinkering with him.

Like so many others, Thomson experimented with x-rays when they first appeared, and before long he had devised an improvement, called the double-focus tube. As an employee of General Electric, however, he couldn't simply announce his success to the public, as he had done as the head of the Thomson-Houston Company. First, he had to confer with Edwin Wilbur Rice, Jr., supervisor of manufacturing and engineering, to establish its marketing potential.

By April 1896, GE was able to announce the double-focus tube, but its organizational methods proved to be slow. While the marketers had debated strategy, the L. E. Knott Company, an outfit considerably smaller than GE, had brought its own double-focus tube to market. What's more, the glasswork was superior to Thomson's model. Rice declaimed, "We certainly cannot afford to have a small manufacturer excel us in a matter of this kind." The inventor would simply have to turn out his product faster—under the same budgetary constraints.

This put Thomson in a bind. A believer in planned variety ever since Edison's glory days, he was simultaneously exploring technologies as diverse as x-rays, automobiles, and light bulbs, and he was eager to introduce any or all of them. To his friend Frederick Fish he wrote:

> [M]y opportunities to work for General Electric are and have been . . . so restricted in various ways that there is little satisfaction to me in continuing my present relations, and I feel too that it may be that the Co. cannot afford me to do so. . . . My regret is that under present conditions, I can be useful only in a limited way. New work in new fields is not to be attempted at Lynn on any

considerable scale as the tendency is to let manufacture at lowest cost absorb all facilities.

In other words, scarcity had become the principle that dictated the inventor's every move. Still, Thomson continued to follow his multifarious muse. His interest in high-efficiency engines soon led to a steam-powered car, which he developed jointly with Hermann Lemp. This enterprise fared no better than the x-ray tube had. The Thomson-Lemp car was operational in August 1898 and ready to market in May 1899, when Charles A. Coffin, the controlling power at GE, decided to scuttle it; the company attorneys had deemed the patents were too weak to warrant commercial introduction. When Thomson suggested that the patent department should have assigned a lawyer specifically to automobile patents, the department replied that there was no reason to take such steps until it was known that the company would make a serious move into the field. Disappointed, Thomson and Lemp assigned their patents to GE, which promptly turned around and sold them.

At this point, another inventor might have felt a pang of nostalgia for the star system, with its scattershot, impromptu agenda. Thomson himself might have remembered the excitement he felt years ago, when he entered the public fray to refute Edison's etheric force. But the Lazzarone in him would not be moved; the problem, he was convinced, had to be in the organization of GE itself. And so, sitting at his desk in December 1899, caught in a vortex of circular reasoning, he began writing a letter to Coffin:

> [I]t has grown upon me strongly within the last four or five months that what is needed is a department at the Works especially for the development of [high efficiency engines]. We should have men and machinery wholly devoted to work in this field—together with the automobile field—and they should be separated out as if it were in a building or department by themselves . . . I find it extremely difficult with the work as scattered as it is . . . Things move at an exasperatingly slow rate, and the only cause for it that I can discover is the lack of concentration in one place of draftsmen, men and tools.

Thomson got his wish, and the first American research-and-development laboratory was born. Henceforth, General Electric would hire specialists, led by Willis R. Whitney, to work full-time under one roof in

Schenectady, New York. Inventors had been employed by corporations before, of course, but as a rule they had been commissioned to accomplish specific tasks. In Schenectady—and in the many corporations that initiated R & D labs of their own—they would be bankrolled on an ongoing basis, in hopes that they might contribute in unforeseen ways.

The effect of the R & D lab was enormous, and ultimately not at all what Thomson desired. That Whitney and his team were not public figures was probably of no concern to him. But it soon became clear that they were even less free to act on their impulses than Thomson had been. Developing a car on company time without prior approval, as he had done, was no longer acceptable. Whenever an inventor stumbled upon a new and unexpected idea, he was expected to submit a report to higher-ups, who determined its importance according to a highly structured economic scheme.

For nearly a century, show inventors had asserted themselves with impunity, holding forth on street corners as if the mechanical Carnival would never end. In that time, they had beaten the church, beaten the scientists, and, for a brief moment, stood on equal ground with the robber barons. On the threshold of the new century, however, the lenten powers had dealt them a withering blow. AT&T had proven itself capable of quietly removing a technological debate from the public arena. General Electric, meanwhile, had done something even more auspicious. In the past, the forces of order and disorder had always appeared as separate and opposing communities. With the R & D lab, however, an economizing force absorbed the inventor's anarchic spirit into itself, collapsing these two communities into one. And to the degree it succeeded, it meant a more permanent end to meaningful public discourse over the future of technology.

Tesla could talk about Martians all he wanted. The wild dreams of inventors were passing into the hands of cautious, faceless men.

### Part Three

# CARNIVAL CONTROLLED

PLAYER KING: But orderly to the end where I begun,
Our wills and fates do so contrary run,
That our devices still are overthrown
Our thoughts are ours, their ends none of our own.

—*Hamlet*

## Chapter Fourteen

# A NEW UNIVERSE

In 1900, the writer Henry Adams visited the Paris Exposition and came away perplexed at the tumultuous changes that had taken place since the Columbian Exposition of 1893. "In these seven years," he wrote, "man had translated himself into a new universe which had no common scale of measurement with the old." Adams, who harbored a lifelong interest in understanding the cultural effects of technology, was determined to find this common scale himself. But in the end, the goal proved elusive. He stayed up late at night, filling "thousands of pages with figures as formal as though they were algebra, laboriously striking out, altering, burning, experimenting, until the year had expired, the Exposition had long been closed."

Few could have done better. At the time he was writing, technology was outdoing itself admirably. Automobiles, x-rays, wireless telegraphy, and motion pictures were all well on their way to becoming viable commercial forms. Yet the story of technology had momentarily broken down for lack of a coherent dramatic structure. Tesla had clearly become an outsider, but no one had really seen the insider's view as of yet. In 1900, AT&T and General Electric were just as inward-looking as the Lazzaroni had been, and as far as they had come in stripping inventors of their dramaturgy, they had yet to substitute any dramaturgy of their own.

A full quarter of a century would pass before the corporations devel-

oped a spectacle capable of replacing the show inventors and their theatrical mode. This new show came into being piece by piece—perhaps
even by accident—and when it was finally in place, it would prove far
more effective than anything a playwright could hope to offer. Indeed,
this new show, more than any other development (including the widespread establishment of R & D labs), would ultimately ensure the
permanency of corporate culture in America.

In the meantime, however, Adams was right in choosing the Columbian Exposition, the birthplace of the Grid, as the first value in his
equation. Where the veterans of the Electricity Building had reached
an impasse, a younger generation came to the fair with fresh eyes and
saw new possibilities. Looking at the grounds lit up by alternating current, they did not see histrionic inventors pitted against faceless corporations. They saw that for the first time it was possible to create
permanent, large-scale spectacles—technological environments, which
could stretch out to the limits of the power lines themselves.

Despite the bewilderment of Adams, these environments did not develop in random, undifferentiated fashion; here, too, they followed a
logic laid down in 1893. After all, the Columbian Exposition had been
cordoned off into two distinct fairs based on the opposing principles of
wild debauchery and serious purpose, and in trying to make sense of
the "new universe" it had inherited, the new generation took this sep-
aration as a given. And so, from the ashes of the Midway and the White
City rose the first large-scale mechanical spectacles of the twentieth
century: the amusement park and the modern factory.

When George C. Tilyou moved to Coney Island in 1865, it was little
more than a forlorn spit of land at the edge of Brooklyn. It had been
twenty years since Samuel Colt left his telegraph behind to rust in the
sea breezes. Most of the people who considered the island home were
outlaws and prostitutes, but the years passed, and gradually Coney Island
began to develop its own genius loci. In 1875, the Coney Island Railway
was completed. In 1880, the first sideshow arrived, bringing with it a
gang of unemployed freaks. Four years later, the spirit of Coney Island
materialized more definitively, in the form of the Elephant Hotel.

Billed as the Colossus of Architecture, the Elephant Hotel was 122
feet tall, a behemoth of wood sheathed in tin, with long tusks and a
howdah at its peak. An advertisement touted it as "a whole seaside resort

in this unique giant," and it was no lie. One of the hind legs led to an observatory in the howdah. In one of the front legs, a tobacco shop put out its shingle. At night, the four-foot-tall eyes blazed with electric beacons. Paying customers could spend a night in the trunk, or—elsewhere in the pachyderm's capacious interior—rent rooms for shorter periods of time. A rendezvous with a prostitute in this unlikely hotel became known as "seeing the elephant."

As Coney Island found its stride, so too did Tilyou. For a time, he satisfied himself with putting on shows in Tilyou's Surf Theater. Then, in 1893, a trip to the Columbian Exposition opened his eyes. He was especially impressed by the Ferris Wheel and promised himself that he would have this great iron circle transported to Coney Island. When he learned that it was already scheduled to go to the St. Louis fair, he had his own wheel built. The Pennsylvania Steel Company took the contract, and he sold enough concession space to break even in advance. Though the wheel was smaller than the original, he availed himself of Ferris's liberal use of superlatives and billed it as the largest in the world.

Once infected by the spirit of the Midway, Tilyou never looked back. He observed the activities of his neighbors at Boyton's Sea Lion Park, and saw how popular a ride like Shoot the Chutes could be. In 1897, he did them one better and opened Steeplechase Park, with its famous ride that took customers down a wavy groove on mechanical horseback. The immense popularity of Steeplechase allowed Tilyou to expand and, in scouting for new rides, to discover the future titans of Coney Island: Frederic Thompson and Skip Dundy.

Frederic Thompson hailed from Ironton, Ohio, where his father built steel works. At eighteen, Frederic went to Nashville and found work as an architectural draftsman. Thanks to the success of the Columbian Exposition, industrial fairs were blooming like so many wildflowers, and when Tennessee decided to put on a small one, Thompson designed several buildings for it. When his client failed to pay, he took over one of the buildings and ran a show of sorts. From there, he set out on the exhibition circuit.

At the Omaha Trans-Mississippi Exposition of 1898, Thompson met Skip Dundy, a court clerk and financial wizard. The two men immediately hit it off and became business partners. By the time Tilyou met them at the 1901 Pan-American Exposition in Buffalo, they were running an illusion ride called the Trip to the Moon and making more money than anyone else at the fair. Recognizing their potential, Tilyou invited them to join him at Coney Island. They did, and before long, their rides did so well there that they were able to buy Boyton's Sea Lion Park and refashion it in their own image.

At first, Thompson and Dundy advertised Luna Park—renamed for Skip's sister, Luna Dundy—as a World's Fair. But they quickly realized that the enterprise was a departure from ordinary expositions. Savage and giddy, it was an "Electric Eden," a technological playland that seemed to have no end.

For an hour or a day, Luna Park's mostly poor visitors could involve themselves in most any aspect of the human experience. They could ride electric trains through fantastic foreign lands, take trips to the moon, or appease their curiosity in any one of number of demonic habitats. An education could be had in the "electric plant," where dynamos, engines, and portraits of Franklin and Morse in gold-studded frames were duly explained by a "college-educated professor" in white gloves and a brass-buttoned, duck-white jacket. If a military tour was more to their liking, there was the War of the Worlds, in which "Admiral Dewey" laid waste to flotilla after flotilla of enemy fleets. Coney Island even had its own crazy kind of food—the hot dog, invented by Charles Feltman in 1867 to supplement his pie business.

And it had its own crazy kind of love. The Ferris Wheel had proved that momentum, properly applied, could induce romantic liaisons. At Coney Island, this became an article of faith. Drop the Dip, the Cannon Coaster, the Human Roulette Wheel—where Newtonian physics careened toward the edge of control, even the shyest of lovers found ample excuse to grab hold of each other. On the Leapfrog Railroad, two approaching trains avoided a fatal collision when one drove *over* the other. At Hell Gate, sluices carried boatloads of passengers on a harrowing ride down to a whirlpool. And of course, the most thrilling gravity ride was the roller coaster, developed by LeMarcus Adna Thompson (no relation to Frederic) in 1884 and carried to what many consider to be its apex in the Cyclone, built in 1927 by Vernon Keenan and Harry Baker.

While gravity rides worked their magic by presenting the specter of death and then whisking it away at the last possible moment, Thompson and Dundy were not averse to working real mortality into the act should the occasion arise. An elephant named Topsy provided just such an occasion when she killed a visitor who had fed her a live cigarette. It was her third offense, and her last. After she survived the effects of two poison carrots, a hanging was proposed, but the ASPCA prohibited it. And so, the War of the Currents all but forgotten, Edison's muckers were called in to do the job by electrocution. Two electrodes were applied and the switch thrown as a paying audience looked on in silent awe. In the space of ten seconds, Topsy stiffened, tottered, and fell—a latterday Jumbo felled by a Jumbo generator.

Love and death—at Luna Park, it seemed no facet of the human condition could escape the clutches of technology. Naturally then, Thompson and Dundy jumped at the chance to offer the most primal show of all: the spectacle of birth.

Martin Arthur Couney did not seem fated to sideshow work. After studying medicine in Germany, he went to Paris in the 1890s to do his postgraduate studies under Pierre Constant Budin, a pediatrician specializing in the care of prematurely born babies. At the time, little could be done for such children. As late as the 1850s, the only recourse was to keep them as warm as possible, using a combination of ovens, heated bricks, warm clothes, and hot water bottles. In the 1870s, Etienne Stéphane Tarnier added hygiene, proper feeding, and isolation to the list.

Budin's contribution was to isolate infants under glass and provide them with gas heating. For this achievement, he was appointed head of the newly organized Maternité in Paris in 1893. As the Berlin Exposition of 1896 approached, Budin used his authority to secure an exhibit there. Then he persuaded his protégé, Martin Couney, to oversee it.

Couney took to the task like an old hand. He procured his infants from Berlin's Charity Hospital, charged admission to cover expenses, and christened his display the *Kinderbrutanstalt*—the child hatchery. What might have been a somber adjunct to a medical seminar thus became a sensation. The exhibit was packed, its legend sung in music halls. Not only did Couney keep all the babies alive, he turned a profit in the process. When he took his show to the Victorian Era Exhibition at Earl's Court in London, the reception was cooler. Doctors refused to send him any babies, and he was forced to import them from Paris. The show was a hit anyway, bringing in more than thirty-six hundred spectators in a single day.

So began Couney's itinerant phase. In 1898, he turned up at the Omaha Trans-Mississippi Exposition; in 1900, at the Paris Exposition that had Henry Adams wearing down so many pencils. The year 1901 found him at the Pan-American Exposition in Buffalo, where he met Thompson and Dundy. Thompson invited him to join their fledgling enterprise down in Coney Island. Couney accepted, and it became his home for forty years.

The entire exhibit was kept meticulously clean. A dozen or so incu-

Martin Couney found no welcome for the first practical baby incubator—invented by his mentor, Pierre Constant Budin—except at Coney Island. Over the course of forty years, 6,400 out of 8,000 premature babies were saved, but many visitors refused to believe they were real. *The Brooklyn Historical Society*

bators sat in rows, their hot water pipes leading to a central boiler, their subjects safely ensconced behind a glass window. Baby boys were dressed in blue, baby girls in pink. Guides were not to venture a single joke under threat of immediate dismissal. Wet nurses were kept away from every kind of stress and made to follow strict diets (doled out by an in-house cooking staff), lest they convey any poisons to their charges.

Even after all this, the exhibit was slow to lose its stigma as a freak show. The parents often asked to remain anonymous, either from the shame of giving their children away or from the embarrassment of weaning them in such an unseemly environment as Luna Park. Couney's babies were thus a slightly lurid sight to begin with: orphans and circus children, nestled among the pachyderm shows and dance halls.

That these infants were presented without pedigree also gave visitors license to project their own desires onto them. The most frequent visitors to the exhibit were childless women, who used the opportunity to play out their own fantasies of motherhood. One such woman is said to have come every week for thirty-seven years. The more casual witnesses pushed the fantasy further and refused to believe that the infants were real at all. Operating as he did in an environment populated by some of the best hustlers in the world, Couney was hard pressed to convince them otherwise.

Indeed, for a long time, even Couney's incubation methods failed to spread beyond the confines of the nation's Electric Edens. When Dreamland opened in 1904, Couney opened another exhibit there; later still, when amusement parks opened in Chicago and Atlantic City, he expanded again. Over the course of forty years, he saved the lives of sixty-four hundred babies—a success rate of eighty percent. Yet doctors continued to rush their premature babies to him rather than undertake such procedures themselves. Not until 1937, when Cornell's New York Hospital set up its own incubators, did Budin's invention gain legitimacy outside the amusement park gates. By then, Couney, trying to keep his business afloat in an age of high overheads, was staging reunions and graduations for the survivors of his amazing incubators.

These ceremonies—and Couney's difficulties in being taken seriously—had a good deal to do with the context in which they appeared. Of course, promotions by individuals had always fared poorly in large, exhibitionlike environments. But in the case of the amusement park, there was an additional problem. For all the apparent freedom from the ordinary rules, it wasn't really true that anything went at Coney Island. After all, its machines, even its useful ones, were not supposed to *do* anything. They were supposed to make you *feel* something. Even the electrocution of Topsy by alternating current had lost the hallmarks of the inventor's contest; the fate of a technology was no longer at stake. Instead, the success of an attraction rested in its ability to involve the spectator in a more personal ritual—the first kiss atop the Ferris Wheel, the initiatory challenge of the roller coaster's first drop, the miracle of birth itself.

In effect, Coney Island, as the logical outcome of the Midway, turned the customers into actors in their own right. And that, in the end, meant an emphasis not on the inventors but on the crowds—the sprawling, carefree crowds of a nation discovering the meaning of unadulterated fun.

The technological environment that emerged from the White City, however, offered something altogether less intoxicating.

When a lean, blue-eyed Henry Ford attended the "other" Columbian Exposition at the age of thirty, he had yet to make his name in the world. As far as anyone knew, he was just another engineer from the Edison Illuminating Company in Detroit, standing awestruck before the master's exhibit at the Electricity Building. Only after the exposition had closed, in fact, did he begin work on his first gasoline-powered car.

The legacy of the Ford Motor Company suggests that the sequence is important. Ford was not primarily an inventor of cars, or of anything else for that matter. For as much as he deserved the accolades he received for his Model T, his lasting contribution was not his product but his production system. In this, oddly enough, he shared a place in history with the proprietors of Coney Island as a pioneer of technological environments. But where Thompson and Dundy mechanized play, Ford would mechanize work in a Gridlike spectacle of order and economy.

On June 4, 1896, when Ford knocked down his barn door in Detroit and drove his first Quadricycle into the light of day, the automobile industry was a textbook study in variety. Ever since Oliver Evans paraded his Orukter Amphibolos through Philadelphia's Center Square in 1805, the dream of a horseless carriage had persisted. With the invention of the internal combustion engine in Germany in the 1880s, the pace picked up considerably, and by the 1890s, manufacturers ranged in the hundreds, possibly the thousands.

Many of these efforts have left nothing behind but the outlines of a tenacious amateurism. In 1890, Achille Philion, a native of Akron, constructed a complicated steamer and promptly got stranded in the backroads of anonymity. A blacksmith named J. J. Gillinger tried his hand at a surrey car. In 1897, Earle C. Anthony built an electric car in Los Angeles at the age of seventeen. Similar efforts have left little more to posterity than the riddle of their names—Seven Little Buffaloes, Vim, Blood, Foos, Duck, and Klink.

This mass-inventor movement, so to speak, fostered anything but uniform results. In the years before the Model T, nobody could have told you exactly what an automobile was, because so many were one-of-a-kind, or nearly so. A car might have four wheels, or three, or two. It might be noisy or quiet, high-slung or low. It might even be long-slung, like the Vanell Steam Carriage, which supported two armchairs far to the aft of the rear axle. While the most common fuels were steam, gas, and electricity, the choices were by no means limited to these. The Twombly Ether Bicycle, for example, relied on arcane spiral tubing to distribute its anesthetic fuel.

Perhaps the most innovative idea for motive power came from Edward Joel Pennington. In 1895, Pennington organized a company in Racine, Wisconsin, for the purposes of touting the Kane-Pennington Hot Air Engine, which allegedly cooled itself by dissipating heat from the cylinder walls. Pennington entered his cars in races in Chicago and Great Britain, each time pulling out at the last moment because of unforeseen problems. Though his automobiles were no more tangible than his various figures on capitalization, his ideas appeared in print and were said to have made an impression on young Henry Ford.

As usual, an invention was inspiring its share of subversive antics. By the mid-1890s, however, certain names were beginning to pull ahead of the pack. In May 1892, *Scientific American* reported an automobile built by Ransom E. Olds that used both steam and gas for fuel. On September 22, 1893, Frank and Charles Duryea of Chicopee, Massachusetts— like the Wright brothers, bicycle mechanics—came out with the first practical automobile in America. On April Fools' Day, 1898, the Winton No.1 gathered the honor of being the first car to be sold in America.

Of course, claiming to be the best and proving it were two different matters, and the most persuasive way of demonstrating the superiority of any given invention was still by staging a contest. The first car race held in America took place in Chicago on Thanksgiving, 1895—a fifty-two-mile dash through a snowstorm that was won by a Duryea model. On September 7, 1896, three electrics and two Duryea wagons went at it at Narragansett Park in Cranston, Rhode Island, the first race track dedicated to automobiles. One or another of the electrics won every time, until at last the crowd began to shout what was to become an American idiom—"Get a horse!"—at the losers.

Henry Ford spent some time as a racer himself, and gained some notoriety in the process. On October 10, 1901, he went head to head with Alexander Winton, the reigning champion of the track, in Grosse Point, Michigan, and won in a dramatic upset. At first, Winton held the lead with ease; by the third lap, he was ahead by a fifth of mile. Then Ford's Spider Huff started to gain. Winton's machine began letting off an ever-larger plume of smoke, and in the seventh lap, right in front of the grandstand, Ford shot ahead. There he remained until the finish line. Hats flew into the air.

Ford stopped manning the wheel in short order, but he didn't leave racing altogether, not right away. For one thing, he put Barney Oldfield onto the path of glory by installing him in the driver's seat of his famous "999." He also briefly entertained the notion of starting up a traveling circus of roadsters with his brother-in-law, Milton Bryant, and a fellow racer named Tom Cooper.

He would not have been the first to do so. At the time, the Barnum and Bailey circus was showing off the first Duryea model (or what they claimed was the first) among its dromedaries and bearded women. Even a few years later, in 1906, cars were considered exotic enough for the

Greatest Show on Earth to acquire a miniature replica of Ransom E. Olds's two-cylinder Reo and plunk a midget behind the wheel.

But ultimately, Ford decided against the circus. He often liked to say that he had built his first ignition out of spare parts from the Edison power plant in Detroit, and the anecdote belies his preference for the organization of the White City over the thrills of the Midway show world. By 1908, the result of that preference was the Model T, an inexpensive, rugged car. By December 1909, it was an expression of precision and self-abnegation on a colossal scale—the assembly line factory.

The Highland Park factory was hailed in its time as Detroit's own Crystal Palace. Designed by Albert Kahn and built, ironically enough, atop an erstwhile racecourse, it was four stories high, and much longer than it was tall, with white exterior walls and red brickwork trim. Inside, the tile floor, brass fixtures, and dynamos were polished to perfection. Irregularly shaped balconies jutted from every floor, allowing managers to peer down onto a clockwork dance in which jobs were highly specialized and machine parts tooled to variances of one ten-thousandth of an inch. The sum effect was that of an intensely structured environment. You could not be whatever you wanted at Highland Park. You could be one thing, and that thing only.

As time went by, Ford's appetite for economy only grew stronger. In the spring of 1913, the first moving assembly line in the world went into operation in the magneto department of the Highland Park factory. That summer, he learned that production was bottlenecking in the final phase, where all parts were combined in the chassis. Timing the operations, he measured the performance of 250 assemblers and 80 part carriers, and discovered that it took twelve-and-a-half man-hours to deliver a complete chassis.

Having specialized to a degree unimaginable only a few years earlier, Ford specialized even further. "The man who places a part doesn't fasten it," he commanded. "The man who puts in a bolt does not put on the nut; the man who puts on the nut does not tighten it." When the dictum went into effect, chassis-assembly time dropped to an average of ninety-three minutes. Eventually, a single shift could put out a thousand Model T's, and a complete car rolled off the assembly line every three minutes. To let the public appreciate just how wonderful this accomplishment was, Ford had a plate-glass window fitted into the wall facing Woodward Avenue.

Ford's vision was something quite new to American culture. Except for a brief period during the lyceum movement, when public demon-strations of technology enjoyed a modicum of respect, the principles of economy and order had always been linked to an ethos of privacy. Jef-ferson had cast a cold eye on any outbreak of spectacle, and Joseph Henry had done much the same. In this, they were only following the precepts of the larger Protestant society: faced with outrageous extrava-gance, it was deemed best to batten down the hatches and ride out the storm. A window onto the precise workings of a factory, on the other hand, not to mention the sight of thousands of identical cars lined up in rows, suggested what the Renaissance clergy had once demonstrated with its rituals of public penance—that the forces of order could provide a spectacle all their own.

It was a lesson worth noting. Just as the procession of Lent ended the riotous variety of Carnival, so too did Highland Park establish a stunning uniformity, at least within the automobile industry. Only those who adopted Ford's methods could afford to stay in business, and the variety of the 1890s began to dwindle. From thousands of manufacturers pro-ducing a handful of cars, a handful of manufacturers began to produce thousands. By the late 1930s, there was no mistaking what was and was not a car.

Of course, practicality is often cited as the reason that the gas-powered car prevailed, but one could argue that mass production was capable of squeezing out sensible alternatives. By the 1920s, an able mechanic named Abner Doble had eliminated many of the vexations associated with the steam engine. His Model E, which appeared in 1923, possessed the virtues of a one-minute warm-up time, a top speed of 85 miles per hour, no boiler explosions, almost no emissions, and, perhaps most ap-pealing of all, a completely quiet ride. The car was also fairly plush, with an African ebony steering wheel and German-silver spokes. Unfor-tunately, Doble managed to build only twenty-nine examples of this steamer at a price tag of $8,000, before he was forced to sell his company in 1931.

Other innovative car manufacturers outlasted Doble, but in the end there was no competing with Ford's mass-production techniques. Nor, for that matter, was there any limiting Ford to the manufacture of cars. His vision of the technological environment, unlike the ritualistic may-hem of Luna Park, amounted to a world composed of interlocking Ford parts, and soon he was exercising this vision with great vigor. He opened an in-house school so that his immigrant workers could learn English.

He set up a foundry so he could make his own steel on the premises. Eventually, he even tried his hand at what was arguably the first supermarket chain in America.

In the 1920s, a few firms had started the practice of subsidizing small grocery stores. Du Pont, for one, built a company store in Deepwater, New Jersey; Armor had its equivalent in the Chicago stockyards. By and large, these subsidies were attempts to mute the general dissatisfaction with both factories and retail practices. Ford, however, seems to have approached the matter in a more experimental frame of mind. In October 1919, when the Bay State Fishing Company began selling fish at cut-rate prices, bragging that haddock was the "Ford of all fish," Ford took it upon himself to underwrite its transport. Perhaps he had been flattered, but after an estimated eighteen thousand pounds of fish sold that week, vanity turned to something else. There was money in the food business, and surely if he applied his mind to it, he could make the running of that business more efficient.

On December 3, 1919, Ford opened his first commissary, offering food and clothing (and eventually shoes) to his Highland Park employees at retail. Instead of the familiar fishmonger's market, however, the commissary resembled nothing so much as an assembly line for shoppers.

Arriving before their morning shift, workers (their wives were encouraged to shop during off-peak hours) beheld a single aisle about 100 feet long, with cashiers at the far end. One side of the aisle was taken up by a continuous counter, 30 inches high, with a display case running above it. Beneath the glass, samples of the wares were repeated every 15 feet or so, for easy access by the clerks, but also no doubt for the repeated suggestion that the customer buy them. The inventory, much like the inventory in his factory, was limited to a few items, each with the Ford named stamped onto the package. Everything was kept as clean as was humanly possible.

Beyond this austere scene lay Ford's totalizing system. Behind the clerks, a set of shelves led to narrow loading platforms, which in turn opened onto the warehouse itself. By 1926, entire carcasses were being brought into this warehouse to be cut and prepriced. Meanwhile, rice, peas, beans, and prunes were stored in bins three flights up and conveyed by a system of conduits and spouts to the floor below.

As might be expected, the work force was as specialized in the commissary as it was in the plant. One man cut cheese all day, another picked up reclaimed paper. When a stock clerk ordered by telephone, a conveyor belt delivered the merchandise to him. Up on the third floor, several women packaged and priced bulk goods for eight hours a day with the aid of an automatic weighing machine. For these and other repetitive services, commissary workers received as much as $7.45 a day—more than the famous Ford minimum wage.

In 1926, when Ford was running eleven commissaries, he opened three of them—the Highland Park, Fordson, and Lincoln commissaries—to the public, effectively inaugurating the first American supermarket. No one knew if efficient management accounted for the uncommonly low prices or if Ford was silently subsidizing the operations. They only knew that the stores were immensely popular. In 1927, these three locations pulled in a robust $9,322,808, for a profit of $264,761.

The experiment ended almost before it began, however. The sudden appearance of such overwhelming competition alarmed local retailers, who arranged to have the stores boycotted, and to have Ford accused of driving prices down artificially. In a time of delicate relations between management and labor, it was deemed impolitic to continue, and the stores were closed to the public for good in April 1927. The rationale for closing, given at a meeting between the warring parties by G. N. Staples, manager of Highland Park, was simple. It had all been a terrible misunderstanding. Ford had only meant to teach retailers the ins and outs of mass distribution.

And perhaps he succeeded at that. Several years later, the first officially recognized supermarkets opened—the King Kullen markets in 1930 and the Big Bear Market in 1932—and their successors evolved into exemplars of the modern technological environment.

These two parks, then, Luna and Highland, were the first significant attempts at technological environments. It would be hard to imagine two worlds more at odds. One promoted absolute play, the other absolute work. One encouraged impulse, the other demanded obeisance.

Yet they did complement each other in a way. Just as Carnival had allowed momentary relief from the rationing schedule of Lent, the pleasures of the funhouse offered workers a weekend respite before they returned to the assembly line. This arrangement may not have boded well for the fostering of new inventions (and, in fact, the Model T underwent no structural or cosmetic changes for many years), but at least it held out the possibility of a stable coexistence between chaos and order.

Then again, for a true balance to be struck, the dramatic spectacles of the factory and the amusement park had to be equally compelling, and by the 1910s, Coney Island seemed to be a first among equals. It offered revelry without end, or at least the limits of one's pocketbook. At Highland Park, people could look through a plate-glass window onto its intricate interior, or marvel at the speed with which new cars issued forth from its doors. But did the factory environment really have anything to compete with the experience of playing the fool at the arcade?

Many workers thought not. By 1913, labor unions were angrily protesting the inhospitable conditions of factory work, and intransigence was commonplace—especially at Ford's factories, where overtaxed employees had begun to complain of "Forditis." At Highland Park that year, 10 percent of the workforce failed to show up each morning, and the annual turnover rate soared to 370 percent. Impressive as it was, the assembly line was not automatically appealing to the common laborer.

Management also saw the lot of the worker as problematic, though it tended to frame the matter in its own way. Some years after the introduction of the assembly line, the worker's crucial place in the spectacle of the order was articulated by George B. Cortelyou, on the occasion of Elihu Thomson's eightieth birthday. The ordinary man, Cortelyou insisted,

> fails to see that behind the marvels of science and invention lies an exceedingly complicated and artificial system that nourishes and sustains them, nor does it occur to him that as their chief beneficiary there is an obligation resting on him to conserve them and safeguard their future; and that unless they are upheld by conscious and vigilant effort, they will vanish . . .
>
> There has been brought home to us in recent months, and still more recent days, the highly complex and artificial system of which I have spoken. When all its parts are working smoothly we are not conscious of the intricate mechanism by which it is governed, and accept its benefits as a matter of course. But when something happens to throw it out of balance—it may be one of a thousand things—causing a slowing down or stoppage of any one part, the whole machine functions poorly or not at all, and then we realize what a wonderfully constructed and inter-related affair it is, this

system of trade and commerce and finance, of exchange of goods and services, within nations and between nations.

In this description, the factory worker bears the burden of an Atlas: one wrong move and nations will fly out of kilter. Yet, regrettably, he fails to appreciate the effects his actions may have. This makes him the weak link in the chain, and in order to avert disaster, he must be brought into harmony with the system.

Here, then, was a situation without precedent in the culture of invention. Unlike the show inventor, who labored to introduce a device into the existing society, the factory owner had to fit living beings into an established technology. He had to convince his workers that their idiosyncrasies interfered with the "complex and artificial system" that joined all human affairs.

Ford, for his part, tried to meet the challenge with a system of indoctrination that came to be known as Fordism. In his most famous gesture, he began paying his employees five dollars a day. This was undoubtedly a handsome salary at the time, but it also came at a price: workers first had to pass muster with Ford's newly formed Sociological Department.

The way this organization operated was curiously reminiscent of religious novitiate rituals. Beginning in 1913, Ford operatives visited the homes of workers and scrutinized every aspect of their lives. Those who took in male boarders, spent money foolishly, or drank immoderately—to name just a few infractions—were disqualified from the higher wage, and clergymen were often sent in to corroborate the operatives' findings. Even when the operatives were genuinely helpful, their agenda had a distinctly lenten cast: they gave advice on budgeting, accounting, hygiene, and—in a fitting echo of Lent's original resource-saving purpose—instruction on how to distinguish between cuts of meat.

The religious parallels continued in the Ford English School, which instructed a largely European workforce in the language and customs of their new nation. As with the seventeenth-century penitents on the eve of Lent, workers who attended this school were disabused of their colorful native customs and made to adhere to a uniform standard. An annual commencement exercise, held in the city's largest hall, made the transition explicit:

> On the stage was represented an immigrant ship. In front of it was a huge melting pot. Down the gang plank came the members of

the class dressed in their national garbs and carrying luggage such as they carried when they came to this country. Down they poured into the Ford melting pot and disappeared. Then the teachers began to stir the contents of the pot with long ladles. Presently the pot began to boil over and out came the men dressed in their best American clothes and waving American flags.

Though Ford continued these "initiatory" practices until the early 1920s (when he declared them unproductive), they were never widely adopted by the industry at large. Other factory owners were just as anxious to bring their workers into the fold, however, and were attempting to achieve as much through a specialized application of the motion picture.

Movies had made great progress since their debut. Not long after Edison introduced the Kinetoscope at the Columbian Exposition, the French brothers Louis and Auguste Lumière succeeded in modifying the invention, so that it projected images onto a screen. They gave their first public movie screening at the Société d'Encouragement a l'Industrie Nationale on March 22, 1895, and quickly drew large crowds. Others accomplished similar feats at around the same time. Soon, rather than looking into Edison's peephole machine, people were enjoying the pleasures of the movie *theater*.

In these early days of the motion-picture industry, there was little need for plot or characterization. It was spellbinding enough to show mundane activities—a baby at his supper, a train arriving in a station, a man chopping wood. One of the most popular of the early Lumière films was a short reel that showed their workers leaving the factory.

Perhaps this fascination stemmed from vanity; people, after all, have always liked seeing themselves. At any rate, the worker turned out to be an abiding subject. In 1894, while Thomas Edison was filming his assistants in the course of their everyday activities, Charles Fremont, an engineer at Etienne-Jules Marey's lab, began using chronophotographs (multiple images printed on one photographic plate) to study the motions involved in labor. The effect of these images could be jarring to the nineteenth-century eye. One plate showed a man wielding a hammer, with the body blurred to accentuate the action of the arm in all its dynamism.

Fremont published the results of his experiments in *Le Monde Moderne* in February 1895, but nothing much came of them until a decade later, when a bricklayer named Frank Gilbreth spent half a day with Frederick Taylor and a stopwatch.

Taylor would become famous in 1911, when his *Principles of Scientific Management* described a system for determining the efficiency of factory workers. As a gang boss in an iron works, he had come to wonder what actually constituted a day's work. To find out, he began studying the motions of laborers with a stopwatch, noting the duration of each activity. When a laborer dumped the contents of a shovel, was it more advantageous to turn the arm inward, or was it better to lock the wrist? What was the minimum number of steps necessary to travel from the furnace to the coal pile? Should a bricklayer bend at the knees or the hips?

Gilbreth was excited by Taylorism, but he was also dissatisfied, so he went a step further and developed what he called the "micro-motion technique." At first, he took photographs and measured the intervals with a stopwatch, then offered the results to workers as instruction cards. Before long, he had developed an entire array of techniques (many of which actually originated with Fremont)—timed lights for distinguishing motions in a dark room, graphs that charted the motions of a typist's eyes, and actual movies, which were viewed in strip form.

Gilbreth's movies were filmed with cameras that were far more precise than the ordinary theatrical-release variety. Worried that motions made between exposures would be unavailable for study, he devised a "double cinematograph," in which two cameras were in operation at once, one moving as the other rested. By the 1940s, his efficiency movie cameras typically ran at 1,000 frames per second—some forty times faster than the standard.

With the advent of micro-motion techniques, the work of Eadweard Muybridge, with its strange attentions to women dancing naked and legless boys, was effectively trained upon the common citizen and, taking the mission of the Columbian Guard to new heights, used as a form of crowd control. The result was every bit as economy-minded as Ford's production methods. As a 1915 article on Gilbreth in *Scientific American* assessed it, "With all these methods of study and instruments of precision at his disposal, surely the industrial coach is now well equipped *to detect and eliminate the prodigal waste of effort that is going on in every line of industry.*" (Italics mine.)

There were aspects to motion studies that attained the level of drama. Gilbreth was known for the histrionics he employed whenever he paid a visit to a work site. Among bricklayers, he would sidle up to a worker and kid him about how slow he was until, inevitably, the worker challenged him to do better. Taking the trowel in hand, the industrial coach would feign ignorance for a moment, then perform the task with remarkable skill—much to the merriment of the workers who had gathered round.

Gilbreth applied much the same brio to his micro-motion demonstrations. While screening motion pictures for groups of workers, he gave brisk running commentaries meant to involve the workers on a personal level. One can imagine these sessions as a sober variant on choreography lessons, as the supplicants watched films with such austere titles as *A Study of the Time Required to Grasp Machine Screws from Various Types of Bins* and *Packing Cheddar Cheese in Cups*.

The inventor's contest lived on in the motion study as well, albeit in degenerated form. From man against nature to man against man, it had devolved into a struggle between the worker and time itself. Gilbreth made sure to highlight the waste-free feats of high-speed typists in his book *Applied Motion Study*. Miss Anna Gold, he noted, used his analytical hardware to become National Amateur Champion Typist at a 1916 Chicago heat. At 147 words per minute gross, Miss Hortense Stollinitz broke all records to walk away with the title of International Amateur Champion, even though she had to change the paper in the machine. A special machine, Gilbreth added, was available to aid those interested in learning her techniques.

Both Fordism and motion studies offered early glimpses of things to come. In the coming decades, corporate-sponsored pageants and narrative-based industrial films would rise from their ashes. At the time, however, the tradition of "supply-side" dramas was insufficiently developed, and the people were not convinced. In fact, they were more likely to develop dramas of resistance than to take up those offered by management.

In 1916, the Palace in New York exemplified the prevailing mood with a show called "12 Speed Mechanics" in which the advertised crew assembled a Ford car onstage in two minutes flat—one minute faster than Highland Park's celebrated record. If those statistics were inflated, they nevertheless served notice that some people still questioned the supremacy of the assembly line.

Gilbreth, for his part, was immortalized as a zestful, sympathetic character by his children in the book *Cheaper by the Dozen*, which had him cheerily timing his bathtub activities and marshalling midnight fire drills in his home. In real life, however, he was no more appreciated for his efforts than Ford was. As *Scientific American* felt compelled to point out, there was "a great deal of prejudice against the industrial coach or 'efficiency engineer.' " And understandably so: having one's every motion dissected down to the thousandth of an inch was not the dramatic role most workers desired.

Gilbreth was not entirely oblivious to his critics. Aware that some workers objected "to having any observer record what they are doing," he devised the formidably titled "autostereochronocyclegraph apparatus," which allowed more furtive laborers to do the job themselves, during "secret time studies." Nevertheless, the motion picture proved far more popular when it was taken up by the dissenters themselves. By the late 1910s, Buster Keaton was appearing in movie houses in the guise of a long-suffering Job beset by collapsing cars, whirling houses, and conspiratorial gadgets. Harold Lloyd thrilled crowds by hanging from a clockface far above the city streets. Soon, Charlie Chaplin expressed his opinions on mechanization more stridently in *Modern Times*, in which soulless machinery played havoc with the famous tramp.

In fact, the big surprise of celluloid was the abrupt reappearance of the zany in full-fledged form. As many historians of commedia dell'arte have noted, the comedians of the silent screen were nothing short of a paragon of the genre, foiling upperclass characters with their acrobatic prowess, using physical gags to fill in their loosely structured plots. Keaton's deadpan face even attained the character of a mask. There was one important difference, though. In their latest reincarnation, the zanies were no longer the purveyors of the latest mechanical advance. If anything, they identified the technological environment envisioned by Ford and Gilbreth, like the procession of Lent itself, as their enemy.

It may be asked why, if the commedia dell'arte players could enjoy such a renaissance, no show inventor stepped forward to commandeer the motion picture for his own purposes. What kept someone like Tesla or, say, Oliver Heaviside, from filming his achievements and projecting them before an audience? The opportunity was certainly there. Once the movie theater replaced the more intimate experience of the Kinetoscope, the familiar stage format returned, with the traditional figures of emcees and supporting acts. Edison himself, while retired from the world of spectacle, advocated movies as a valuable educational tool. One can easily imagine him releasing newsreels about his latest exploits in electric-car batteries or ore-grinding technology. Yet one looks in vain to find an important breakthrough depicted on film in the early 1900s.

Certain reasons can be offered for the omission. The predetermined nature of a demonstration on celluloid must have been worrisome from the beginning: if a machine couldn't fail, the demonstration was not much of a test. Equally problematic was the lack of sound. Actors could always draw on the dumbshow, which had arisen from various European prohibitions at fairs over the centuries, but an inventor had to explain his invention, and to sell it.

Then, too, in its early years, motion-picture technology went through constant transformations. Mutoscopes and Biographs proliferated. Revolving sets were made to follow the sunlight along specially designed tracks. And as Walter Benjamin was soon to point out, the shooting of a film created a spectacle far exceeding the film itself. So what was the point of demonstrating a plane or a radio on a movie screen, when the movie machinery itself was the main attraction?

To top it all off, movies could be sexy. Henry Adams came close to recognizing as much when he compared America's worship of the machine unfavorably to the Virgin cults of Europe. "The force of the Virgin was still felt at Lourdes," he observed in 1900, "and seemed to be as potent as X-rays; but in America neither Venus nor Virgin ever had value as force—at most as sentiment." A few years later, that would no longer be the case. Hatched from the complex of dollies and crane hoists, America's movie starlets—Lillian Gish, Jean Harlow, Greta Garbo— would exude the force of a thousand Venuses and Virgins. And what inventor could compete with visions such as these?

These explanations have the virtue of dialectical sense, but in the end, they are not strong enough. After all, the niceties of logic had never bothered show inventors before, and there was no reason why they should have this time. The use of trick photographs—such as the one in which Tesla inserted himself beneath a shower of high-voltage sparks—was proof enough that investors could be fooled with doctored visual artifacts. More to the point, in the years to come movies did eventually become a tool for promoting technological progress, as corporations learned to valorize their products through filmstrips, movies, and television shows.

In fact, there was nothing to prevent show inventors from making the motion picture their own. A film used in conjunction with a lecture could have overcome the lack of sound. (In fact, in the beginning, most movies were sandwiched between live acts.) They could have worked erotic elements into their acts, as the New York Crystal Palace and the Midway had once done for them. They might have borrowed the tech-

niques of the early filmmaker George Méliès, whose magician characters performed impossible feats through trick photography. Tesla, for
one, would surely have appreciated a tactic like that.

Only one explanation seems to suffice: show inventors didn't use movies because it never occurred to them to do so. Or rather, they didn't
use movies because they didn't know they were show inventors. Like
Great Britain, which established a worldwide empire and then all but
forgot it was there, the show inventors had changed the world without
quite knowing how. Their interdependence with theater had always
been informal; if it was easily forged, it was just as easily dissolved. As
a result, even without the many forces working against them, there was
nothing to keep their tradition intact.

The public, however, still needed proof. And while Luna Park lit up
the night and Highland Park divided the day into milliseconds, the most
important inventors of the decade were not doing much in the way of
providing it.

*Chapter Fifteen*

# KILLING THE VOLUNTEERS

At the turn of the century, few towns in America were more remote than Kitty Hawk. Set in a mile from the Atlantic coast on a barrier island, it claimed no more than a handful of houses and a nominal post office. No bridges connected it to the mainland. The only available boat for charter leaked badly. In September, when the no-nonsense Wrights, Orville and Wilbur, arrived at the railway terminal in nearby Elizabeth City and asked for directions, the first passerby they met had never heard of it.

And so on December 17, 1903, no more than five spectators stood shuddering on the dunes of Kitty Hawk, North Carolina. Not one was a journalist, a scientist, or an eminent authority. Very likely, none had ever been to a large metropolis. J. T. Daniels, W. S. Dough, and A. D. Etheridge worked at the Kill Devil lifesaving station four miles to the south. W. C. Brinkley lived in nearby Manteo. Johnny Moore, from Nag's Head, was only a boy.

A few others narrowly missed their chance to witness the experiment. The aviationist Octave Chanute would have seen it, and perhaps lent the moment some credibility, had his health not forced him to leave for more forgiving climes. Two local boys would have had a priceless story to tell their grandchildren, but they were frightened away by the sound of the motor.

Orville set a camera on a tripod, pointing it toward the spot where the machine was expected to be after takeoff. The wind speed was checked at twenty-seven miles per hour—a strong wind, to be sure, but the brothers felt secure in their calculations. Orville started up the engine, then after a few minutes, released the wire that held the machine back. Wilbur ran alongside, balancing the wings. One of the men from the lifesaving station stood ready at the camera . . .

The Wrights had chosen Kitty Hawk for its ideal wind conditions, but its remoteness made it a singularly poor location for an inventor's show. Did these two brothers from Ohio, six years into their pursuit of heavier-than-air flight, have no interest in drawing a crowd for their landmark achievement? If so, they were not alone. Many other inventors had come to believe that live shows were no longer important. Edison had abandoned all interest in performances. Bell had drifted from the public eye. Muybridge had retired from inventing altogether. The spectacles that were appearing were not entirely encouraging, either. Only eleven days before the Wrights flew, Samuel Pierpont Langley, then the director of the Smithsonian Institution, launched his own flying machine from a houseboat and crashed directly into the Potomac, bringing sixteen years of work to a heartbreaking close.

But for all this, inventors had yet to develop a viable alternative to the live show. To introduce an invention into society, it was still necessary to bring human beings—preferably a lot of them—in direct contact with the object itself. Count Rumford had articulated it well a century earlier. Unless there was something to "see and touch," ordinary citizens would "have but faint and transitory ideas of those important and highly interesting objects with which you must make them acquainted."

The Wrights, of course, had something to be seen and touched, but almost no one to do the seeing and touching. It was a mistake that cost them dearly. As their authorized biographer Fred Kelly put it, "Not only were there no receptions, brass bands, or parades in their honor, but most people paid less attention to the history-making feat than if the 'boys' had simply been on vacation and caught a big fish, or shot a bear." In fact, their first flight took place in such isolation that they were unable to convince the world of their achievement—*for five years.*

Ironically, the Wrights knew perfectly well how to bring the brass bands running. As teenagers in the 1880s, when theatrical entertainments of every kind raged, they split their time building jerryrigged printing presses and lathes, and dreaming up performances of their own. For the most precocious of these, the Great W. J. and M. Circus, they used many techniques that would have helped to popularize the airplane, if they had bothered to revive them.

The idea for the Great W. J. and M. took root when Orville was loitering in the barn of his friend Gansey Johnston one day. Johnston's father, a taxidermist, had populated the barn with a great variety of stuffed animals. As he was admiring the grizzly and the black bear, it occurred to Orville how impressive they would look in a parade. At the time, many boys had such thoughts, of course, but this was more than an idle fancy. Wilbur, who was a lover of books (among them Jules Verne novels) placed a notice in the *Richmond Evening Item*, announcing the inclusion of "thousands of strange birds from all parts of the world."

The parade, led by a procession of "iron horses," with Davy Crockett at the fore, was to wend its way to the circus, admission five cents (three cents for children under three). Taking a page from Barnum, Wilbur made good use of adjectives: the show would be "mammoth," "colossal," "stupendous." One of the *Evening Item* editors, seeing a good story in this, gave the upcoming event a prominent position in the September 10, 1883, edition, in an article titled "What Are the Boys Up To?"

Come showtime, the business section of town was lined with spectators. As promised, the two brothers led the parade atop a pair of high-wheeler bicycles, followed by the terrifying grizzly bear and a flock of stuffed birds on the platform of a buggy that had been stripped of its body. The circus itself was preempted by a jealous friend, who announced from a barn roof that no performance would take place. Still, the townspeople had enjoyed the parade, and they fondly recalled the Great W. J. and M. Circus, with its inscrutable initials, for a long time after that.

As the 1880s progressed, however, the Wrights's big-tent ambitions slowly mutated into other interests. The buggy that had supported their aviary, or one like it, soon housed a printing press, and with this makeshift machine they began printing handbills for another local circus — this one not their own — called the Great Truxell Bros. & LaRue Show. Meanwhile, their fascination with stuffed birds translated into an exploration of Etienne-Jules Marey's photographs of animals in motion. By the early 1890s, their interest in parades had given way to a passion for the bicycle, made practical in 1888 when the Scots-Irishman John

Dunlop invented the pneumatic tire. And they were already well into their careers as serious-minded bicycle mechanics when Otto Lilienthal plunged to his death on August 9, 1896.

A native of what is now Germany, Otto Lilienthal began experimenting with flight in the 1860s, and his methods reflected the hearty optimism of that era. Throughout his career, he insisted that humans had to mimic birds if they wanted to fly. He studied gulls intently, looking for answers in the minute nuances of their flight, then designed his gliders accordingly. Thus, when he jumped off cliffs, immense artificial wings sprouting from his arms and insectoid goggles obscuring his face, he effectively became a *bird-man*. Eccentric as this approach may have been, it ultimately brought results. In 1895, Otto and his brother Gustav designed the first glider that could soar above the height of takeoff, and Otto became the first human being to fly.

As might be expected for an inventor of his generation, Lilienthal also had close to ties to theater. At one point, he took it upon himself to write a play, then directed the performance himself. In his book *Birdflight as the Basis of Aviation*, he invoked the very same passage from Goethe's *Faust* that Tesla had uttered when he diagrammed his ac motor in the dirt:

> Aye, it will not be so easy
> To mate the wings of the mind with material wings.

And his conviction that balance was the key to flight derived in part from the circus.

Here he is, observing an acrobat on the high wire:

> Possibly [human flight] requires less skill than some of the tricks practised by artists on the tight rope, at least such skill would not be badly applied, and the risk which attends such experiments would not be greater, especially when starting with small wing surfaces and gradually employing larger ones.
>
> Our rope artists are sometimes not quite inexperienced in the advantages which air resistance introduces. Some years ago I witnessed a performance of a lady artist on a wire rope, during which she constantly fanned herself with a gigantic fan. Of course the object was to create an impression that the introduction of this fan made the performance more difficult; but those who have studied the utilization of air pressures could very well appreciate how the

graceful manipulation of this fan was employed by this lady, in order to constantly produce an invisible lateral support by means of the air pressure thus generated, and so to assist the maintenance of equilibrium.

All of these influences gave Lilienthal's experiments great dramatic potential. Shifting his weight high in the sky, clad in the regalia of the avian kingdom, he was a kind of "wireless" tightrope walker—a daredevil of the air.

By the same token, the circumstances of his death had the makings of a great circus legend. As his brother Gustav described it, Otto had been experimenting with flying apparatuses without incident for decades, but he had flown a motorized glider only once. The results were not encouraging. When the support for the arm broke, it threw man and machine out of balance, and only a shock absorber prevented him from being injured. Still, Otto wanted to try it again. The brothers planned to go to Stöllen to pick up a different flying machine—a glider with a carbonic acid motor that caused the wings to beat. On the day when they were to leave, however, Gustav became ill, and Otto decided to go with a servant instead.

It was a tragic mistake. Without his brother there to remind him, Otto forgot to fit the new apparatus with a shock absorber. The wind shifted abruptly, causing him to lose his balance, and he plummeted to his end. Their uncle had always predicted that their experiments would end in disaster; in retrospect his warnings seemed more like prophesy. Still, Otto's final statement betrayed no regrets. As per his own instructions, his gravestone was inscribed with the legend, "Sacrifices must be made."

Indeed, that seemed to be the general consensus: rather than deterring would-be birdmen, Lilienthal's demise only seemed to spur them into action. Percy Sinclair Pilcher (or Pilchard) of Glasgow University constructed a machine called the Bat and soon met his doom in it. Pilcher in turn inspired Samuel Pierpont Langley to install gasoline motors in his own flying machines. Even Alexander Graham Bell began investigating the possibilities of aviation, though he never manned a flying machine himself.

Among those who heeded the birdman's calling was a young Wilbur Wright. "My own active interest in aeronautical problems," he recalled, "dates back to the death of Lilienthal in 1896. The brief notice of his death which appeared in the telegraphic news at that time aroused a passive interest which had existed from my childhood."

Somewhere in those childhood memories lurked Wilbur's penchant for "mammoth" spectacles. Unfortunately, Lilienthal never brought his show influences to the fore. For all his attention to tightrope walkers, he never made the circus analogy explicit. He never advertised himself as, say, the "Blondin of the Skies." On the contrary, he invariably conducted his aeronautic adventures far from the public eye. As a result, when the Wrights turned to their own experiments, whatever Lilienthal had learned from theater was too faintly expressed to revive their own proclivities.

In the first pages of the Wrights's voluminous correspondence with Octave Chanute, a French aviationist transplanted to Chicago, Lilienthal's findings are avidly discussed. By 1901, however, they had abandoned any wild notions of imitating birds in favor of the strict tenets of engineering—flight not by airs but by aerodynamics. And in the end, it was these more prosaic efforts that led the Wrights to their boxlike biplane, and to their success on that windy December day.

The photograph is known to almost everyone in the world: Wilbur stands to the right, looking on, as Orville, lying down in their double-winged machine, is aloft for the briefest of moments. The flight lasted 12 seconds and covered a distance of 120 feet. Between the two brothers, three more flights took place that day, the longest one carrying Wilbur 859 feet in 29 seconds. The dream of controlled flight, stretching back many centuries, was fact.

The decision to forgo bird costumes was clearly the right one from a technical point of view. Nevertheless, the Wright's abandonment of theatrics was, to put it bluntly, a public-relations disaster. At the height of the brothers' career, the American people were supremely indifferent, and so they remained until a very different photograph was taken in 1908.

Like any good comedy of errors, critical mistakes took place in the very beginning. After the initial elation wore off, the Wrights began to think about what their next move would be. They had no darkroom facilities at Kitty Hawk, so they contented themselves for the moment with cabling the news to their father, Bishop Wright. Shortly after they wired him, a message came back from the operator in Norfolk, Virginia.

A local reporter wondered if he might run the story. The Wrights declined, preferring to break the news in their hometown of Dayton, Ohio. The Norfolk operator disregarded the request and informed a reporter from the *Virginian-Pilot.*

And there the troubles began. The newsman, H. P. Moore, contacted the Kitty Hawk weather bureau searching for concrete details about the flying machine. Whoever provided Moore with these details had a poor grasp of the facts. The story that ran described a three-mile flight, during which Orville ran around on the ground shouting "Eureka!" Supposedly, the plane had a six-inch propeller blade on its underside, like an inverted helicopter, and another propeller at the rear to push the body forward. The headline above the article spanned the entire front page.

Not content to leave it at that, Moore, who presumably wanted to make a name as a journalist, sent his story to twenty-one papers around the country. Of the five that bought it, only two of them ran it immediately: the *New York American* and the *Cincinnati Inquirer.* The *Washington Post* delayed publication, and the others did not bother with it at all. Though the *Virginian-Pilot* was a member of the Associated Press, the wire service did not pick it up. Wary of a hoax, they turned their minds to other events.

The Wrights's hometown served them no better. The *Dayton Journal* ignored Octave Chanute's personal appeal to cover the flight. Other Dayton papers covered it, but continued to get the facts wrong. The *Dayton Daily News,* for example, carried the headline "Dayton Boys Emulate Great Santos-Dumont." Alberto Santos-Dumont had flown a lighter-than-air gasbag, but this distinction hardly mattered in the end, since the body of the article was based on hearsay.

When the AP finally did pick up the story on December 18, it took its facts from the *Virginian-Pilot* and reported that the Wright brothers' plane had flown for three miles, starting from a hilltop and landing at a lower altitude, and had flown as high as sixty feet. The fictitious propellers were reiterated. The story ran in only a few papers, but nevertheless served to "confirm" the article in the *Virginian-Pilot.*

The misinformation could only continue from here. The Wright brothers gave their own statement to the AP on January 6, 1904; this eventually became "The Machine That Flies," in the *New York Herald* on January 17. The six-bladed and rear propellers were still among the stock references, as seen in the illustration by an artist who had never seen the Wright machine.

Reporters from Dayton and Cincinnati were treated to a performance when the Wrights moved back to Dayton, but it hardly equalled the unsubstantiated three-mile flights trumpeted by overeager reporters. On April 23, 1904, a sizable crowd gathered at Huffman Field, where the Wrights had set up a rudimentary workshop, but the wind was too strong to attempt a demonstration. The following day, the motor did not function. On the third day, the motor was still giving them trouble. The brothers made the best of it and managed to fly a distance of sixty feet, at a height of five or six feet in the air.

The Wrights invited the press to come back and witness their activities any time. But having witnessed a flight that apparently did not rate as a true flight, the journalists never returned to Huffman Field. By 1905, Frank Tunison of the *Dayton Journal* was routinely dismissing news of the plane's improvements from his desk. When his colleague Luther Beard did take an interest, it amounted to the same thing. A typical telephone conversation between Beard and Orville Wright sounded more like an exchange between a nurse and her patient than a journalistic interview.

"Done anything special lately?" asked Tunison.

"Oh, nothing much," answered Orville. "Today, one of us flew for nearly five miles."

"And where did you go?"

"Around the field."

"Oh! Just around the field. I see. Well, we'll keep in touch with you."

In the end, it took an unlikely party to make the first assays toward credulity. One day, A. I. Root of Medina, Ohio, a Sunday school teacher and beekeeper, chanced on a squib about the Wrights in an Akron paper and became convinced that something momentous had happened. He told his Sunday school class as much, and on March 1, 1904, published his own account in the intriguingly titled *Gleanings in Bee Culture*.

In September, Root made to a trip to Huffman Field, near Dayton, where the Wrights had relocated, and saw the machine for himself. Now a believer beyond all doubt, he wrote another article describing the event in his beekeeping journal on January 1, 1905, and sent a copy of it to *Scientific American*. The editors said they were interested.

But they remained uninterested for a long time yet. In 1906, they ran an article titled "The Wright Aeroplane and its Fabled Performances," expounding a theory that has since become a standard justification among the incredulous:

> If such sensational and tremendously important experiments are being conducted in a not very remote part of the country, on a subject in which almost everybody feels the most profound interest, is it possible to believe that the enterprising American reporter, who, it is well known, comes down the chimney when the door is locked in his face—even if he has to scale a fifteen-story skyscraper to do so—would not have ascertained all about them and published them a long time ago?

Only when a list of sixty reputable witnesses appeared in a letter to *Scientific American* did the editors begin to soften. The first favorable article appeared in its pages on December 15, 1906. But even then the editors had yet to see the machine for themselves.

If the newspapers seemed cavalier about the Wrights' accomplishment, the armed services were downright oblique. From the very beginning, the inventors had wanted to give their patents over to the U.S. government, but they found it difficult even to begin such a process. Disdaining the opportunity to see an airplane firsthand, army officials judged the invention to be impractical as of yet and had no interest in pursuing it. When the Wrights made another plea, the word came back, inexplicably, that the offer still stood.

Other branches of the armed services proved no more helpful. When the Wrights offered to demonstrate their flying machine for the War Department, their letters were referred to the Board of Ordnance and Fortification, which promptly relegated them to the "crank files." Finally, in October 1905, after repeated appeals from the Wrights, Captain T. C. Dickson replied that the Ordnance Board could not proceed "until a machine is produced which by *actual operation* is shown to be able to produce horizontal flight and to carry an operator." (Italics mine.) Which, of course, is exactly what the brothers were offering.

The situation seemed to improve when one Samuel Cabot, an early believer in the Wrights, related their case to a relative, Henry Cabot Lodge, at the time a senator from Massachusetts. Lodge in turn brought the matter to the attention of the War Department. Thanks to this intercession, the Ordnance Board sent another letter to the Wrights, on May 11, 1907, in which their stance appeared to soften: they were now willing to strike some sort of deal.

The brothers wrote back, offering to give a demonstration in which they would fly at least 50 kilometers, at a speed of 40 miles per hour or more, before representatives of the government. The Ordnance Board, however, had no interest in demonstrations. It wanted a formal proposal. So the Wright brothers gave them one, with the reminder that the government need not spend a penny until after it had seen the plane in action. The Ordnance Board, taking a page from the army, replied opaquely that the sum requested had to be appropriated from Congress before any other moves could be made.

And so it went. The Wright brothers took their machine to Europe, where by and large it was received favorably. H. G. Wells was sufficiently impressed to write a novel called *Tono-Bungay*, in which the hero builds a machine much like the Wright brothers' flyer. For his troubles, two American reviewers took him to task for overstepping the facts.

Meanwhile, it was still the journalists who were overstepping the facts. The brothers returned to Kitty Hawk for further flights in 1908, the tales of their feats preceding them. Before they began new tests, the irrepressible *Virginian-Pilot* published a fabricated account, describing how they had flown ten miles out over the ocean.

Ironically, it was this fantastic account that began to turn the tide. The editors at the *New York Herald* considered reprinting the story, but before doing so, they wanted Byron R. Newton, a capable journalist and devoted exposer of fraud, to verify the facts. Word of Newton's assignment leaked out, and by the time he arrived in Kitty Hawk, he had the company of four other journalists. Taken aback by the desolation of the site, the junket decided that the Wrights were operating in secret, so they arranged to make a daily trek: five miles by sailing boat across the sound, followed by a mile walk across the beach to an advantageous lookout from the beach.

Rarely had an inventor's audience expressed its interest so circuitously. Though journalists had a standing invitation from the Wrights, these newsmen preferred to brave woodticks, mosquitoes, and rain for the pleasure of observing the proceedings through field glasses. "We were aware of the presence of newspapermen in the woods," wrote Orville to Newton some time later, ". . . I am only sorry that you did not come over to see us at our camp. The display of a white flag would have disposed of the rifles and shotguns with which the machine is reported to have been guarded."

The articles that came out of this trip were the most accurate so far, and those that appeared in European papers described the experiments in a favorable light. But the pox on the Wrights' house continued to rage in America. Newton's article, for one, was mistakenly held, and in the confusion he was blamed for the error and suspended from the Herald staff. When he sent the article to another publisher, the reply came back that it did "not seem to qualify as either fact or fiction."

Meanwhile, the military was lurching toward credulity as well. Lieutenant Frank P. Lahm of the Signal Corps had been won over to the Wright machine's potential, and thanks to his lobbying, Signal Corps officials began to take a lenient view. Still, they had their reservations. It would be better, they thought, to advertise for bids on the best flying machine in the country.

In the end, this amounted to a mere formality, since no other inventor had anything that could hold up to the Ordnance Department's specifications. The Wrights' bid was accepted on February 3, 1908, and on September 3, the Wrights at long last demonstrated their invention in Fort Myer, near Washington, in the presence of Teddy Roosevelt, Jr., and a crowd of something less than a thousand.

Orville circled around the grounds, then lifted off and flew—for one minute and eleven seconds. According to the president's son, the assembly was stunned. "The crowd's gasp of astonishment was not alone at the wonder of it," he recalled, "but because it was so unexpected. I'll never forget the impression the sound from the crowd made on me. It was a sound of complete surprise."

Amazingly, doubts persisted among press and public alike until a more definitive event took place. On September 17, 1908, the Wrights were conducting another test at Fort Myer when Orville lost control of the craft and crashed, killing his passenger, Lieutenant Thomas Selfridge of the Signal Corps. The photographs taken moments after reveal a general air of pandemonium, with guards hastily calling out orders and a circle of people bending down around the fallen flyers. The death of a volunteer was a tragedy, certainly—yet it was this "proof" that put the Wrights' flying machine on the front pages of American newspapers at last.

That the Wrights had to struggle for their success was not unusual. Inventors had often been ignored, discredited, ridiculed, and usurped in the course of their careers. That much came with the territory. But for them to be disbelieved even after they had achieved success betrayed strange currents at work in American popular culture. After all, the same *Scientific American* that so willfully ignored the Wrights had delved headlong into the dubious facts of the planchette only forty years earlier.

Indeed, to find an example comparable to that of the Wrights, one must look back to the days of John Fitch and Oliver Evans.

The tradition of the show inventors was falling into decay, and as always, the potential variety of inventions suffered in kind. In this case, an entire order of invention—aviation—was delayed needlessly, much as the automobile was forestalled when Philadelphians ignored the ungainly Orukter Amphibolos.

The rise and fall of the show inventors was not entirely symmetrical, however. In the early nineteenth century, figures like Evans had presented a threat to the existing order by being too dramatic. But by the early twentieth century, inventors were forgetting the basic rules of drama—and paying the price.

This was true of the Wrights in more than just their poor choice of locations. Once they returned to civilization, they continued to display a faulty understanding of what it took to persuade crowds of their feat. Show inventors had often invited volunteers to participate in their demonstrations as a way of engaging the audience directly. Cyrus McCormick's aim had been to get his customers to straddle a reaper at the earliest opportunity. Edison had recorded the voices of bystanders on his phonograph. The use of volunteers was a highly effective technique, because in violating the division between stage and house, it allowed an invention to pass out of the realm of fantasy and into the realm of fact.

The Wrights, who had overlooked so many other lessons of the stage, overlooked this lesson as well. After they returned to Dayton, where there were plenty of people on hand to provide a crowd, they failed to solicit volunteers even in a limited capacity. No one manned the machine while it was on the ground, just to get the feel of it. No one stepped up to the wings to see their texture up close. Perhaps the Wrights didn't dare to risk audience involvement until a certain level of safety was attained. Nevertheless, Count Rumford's logic still applied: an invention was bound to be misunderstood as long as the public could not "see and touch" it. And in the case of the flying machine, the misunderstandings were destined to continue until a volunteer—Lieutenant Selfridge—paid with his life.

It may sound cynical to say that the public would demand blood before it believed, but the airplane is not the only invention to bear this point out. By the time the Wrights lifted off from the sands of Kitty Hawk, the wireless industry was two years old. Radio signals had been transmitted across the Atlantic, and many governments had already be-

After almost five years of trying to convince the public they had flown, the Wright brothers secured a series of demonstrations at Fort Myer in Virginia. During a demonstration on September 17, 1908, the plane crashed, killing passenger Lieutenant Thomas Selfridge, and suddenly heavier-than-air flight was fact. *Hugh V. Morgan/Air Force Museum*

gun to install transmitters and receivers in ships and lighthouses. Yet the pioneers of this technology also failed to engage the public directly, and as result, American citizens did not begin to think of radio as their own until it was linked to a spectacle of death.

To be sure, radio did not suffer the same stone disbelief that the airplane did. The decades had provided enough evidence—from Joseph Henry's hermetic demonstration to Mahlon Loomis's unheralded transmissions—for the public to believe that radio was imminent. What course it took as it entered society, however, was another matter.

In the first years of the new century, radio technology was designed for point-to-point transmission; rather than the familiar one-way medium of today, it was imagined as a kind of wireless telephone. Francis A. Collins was typical of early wireless enthusiasts when he described the radio community as "a vast whispering gallery" and, in a prefiguring of the late twentieth-century computer culture, as "a gigantic spider's web with innumerable threads radiating from New York more than a thousand miles over land and sea in all directions." In this view, shared by many other enthusiasts, radio was to be transmitted and received by all.

Unfortunately, the more the proponents of radio tried to achieve this democratic vision, the more it slipped from their grasp. Unlike the telephone, which moved from a plaything of the rich to a general consumer product, or the telegraph, which became accessible to anyone who wanted to send a message, point-to-point radio never passed from the realm of the specialists into the populace at large.

In the historical context of the inventor's show, this outcome is understandable enough. Quite simply, the early radio inventors failed to observe the "Rumford rule"—time and again, in their fervor, they forgot to let ordinary citizens hear the magic for themselves. As a result, the vast majority of Americans came to think of radio as a medium to be used not by them, but *by someone else*. And by the time the innovators truly needed the public's support, it was already too late.

The first to miss his chance was Nikola Tesla. In the first months of 1900, Tesla returned to New York from Colorado, riding his customary gust of enthusiasm. It had occurred to him that the electrical flames that had covered his body at the Columbian Exposition might be used as a coolant—the dim beginnings of cryogenics. Wireless transmission of power loomed ever larger in his mind. And he had developed a vision of a worldwide radio network, which in its decentralized latticework resembled nothing more than the Internet circa 1990. "[T]he entire earth," he wrote, "will be converted into a huge brain, as it were, capable of response in every one of its parts."

This was a worthy dream, of course, and no stranger than many an inventor's plan, but the press found it difficult to accept, especially in light of his newfound affinity with Martians. "Some of his sanguine conceptions," wrote the *Pittsburgh Dispatch* on February 23, 1901, "including the transmission of signals to Mars, have evoked the opinion that it would be better for Mr. Tesla to predict less and do more in the line of performance."

Sloughing off such criticisms, Tesla published an article titled "The Problem of Increasing Human Energy" in *Century* magazine. Along with the manuscript he sent a picture of himself, sitting on a chair in his Colorado Springs lab, reading quietly as a torrent of electrical discharges cascaded around him.

Perhaps Tesla was remembering the success Edison had enjoyed with his sleepless-vigil photograph in 1888. In any case, the response was just as he had hoped. Professor A. Slaby, a pioneer of German radio, declared it a unique phenomenon. The architect Stanford White read the article and was inspired to join Tesla in his plan. J. Pierpont Morgan, perhaps eager to exert more control than an unwieldy corporation allowed, had much the same reaction. The financier and the inventor met on November 26, 1900, and talked over the requirements for a worldwide radio system. Morgan agreed to finance Tesla with up to $150,000. In return, he would control his customary fifty-one percent of the operation.

It was the last great pairing of an inventor and a robber baron. For Tesla, shamanistic loner, to give so much control over to Morgan must have been unsettling. Yet he still had not submitted. What Morgan didn't know was that the photograph published in *Century* had been carefully doctored. The inventor admitted to the ruse in his diary: "Of course, the discharge was not playing when the experimenter was photographed, as might be imagined! The streamers were first impressed upon the plate in dark or feeble light, then the experimenter placed himself on the chair and an exposure to arc light was made and, finally, to bring out the features and other detail, a small flash powder was set off."

And so, with advance in hand from the unwitting Morgan, Tesla set out, ostensibly to broadcast radio around the world according to his theory of resonance. But in this, he again concealed the whole truth from his backer. Like so many before him, Tesla was planning a Lazzo of the New World, with a surprise to be revealed when Pantalone looked inside the machine.

White and Tesla settled on a site in Shoreham on the coast of Long Island. Tesla christened the site Wardenclyffe, after James D. Warden, who offered the two hundred acres of land under the auspices of the Suffolk County Land Company. The tower was to weigh 55 tons and rise 187 feet into the air. It would be built entirely out of wood, down to the pegs that held it together. Only the dome at the top would be metallic, a copper brain that transmitted wireless messages to any point on the globe.

Tesla progressed at his usual relentless pace, driving his workers to do the same, and the outlines of the tower gradually began to take shape. Then, in 1901, word came that an Italian named Guglielmo Marconi had sent a wireless message across the Atlantic without any of the expensive machinery that Tesla required. Undaunted, Tesla drove his crew even harder. He beseeched Morgan to let go of more of the advance and approached as many other investors as he could. In June 1902, he moved his offices out to Wardenclyffe, hoping to hasten the project along as fast as possible.

But as if to mock him, a series of complications cluttered his path just as his workload was reaching its peak. In the fall, he was summoned to jury duty. When he forgot to show, the newspapers derided him as being un-American. No sooner was he released from serving (because of his opposition to the death penalty) than old creditors surfaced, demanding payment. Desperately trying to keep distractions to a minimum, he turned reporters away, allowing only crew members onto the grounds. When Edison had done this, the press had grown all the more excited and speculated wildly. But Tesla had failed to produce a tangible invention for the crowds for some years now, and it seemed likely that he would fail to do so this time as well. At Wardenclyffe, journalists began to denigrate the project with headlines that disparaged "Nikola Tesla—His Work & Unfulfilled Promises."

After the last of the $150,000 was gone, Tesla reluctantly asked Morgan for more money. Months passed with no reply. Finally, on July 3, 1903, the inventor decided to reveal his true reasons for building Wardenclyffe Tower. He wanted, he confessed, to transmit electrical power itself.

Morgan, a businessman to the end, was hardly able to muster any interest in a project designed to provide free energy to his customers, whether it was feasible or not. "I should not feel disposed at present," he wrote back, "to make any further advances."

In defiance, Tesla unleashed a dazzling stream of electrical charges into the Long Island sky that night. But from then on, his electric Tower of Babel was doomed. He tried to scrape money together from other sources. In July, he began laying off workers. His friends began to avoid him, including his old mentor, George Westinghouse. On June 26, 1906, Stanford White was murdered on the roof of Madison Square Garden, for an alleged adulterous act, leaving the unfinished tower as his final legacy.

It was a poignant sight. The dome that was to be covered in copper remained a wooden skeleton. Inside the office were glass-blowing machines, lathes, x-ray devices, Tesla coils, a radio-controlled boat, thousand of bulbs and tubes, electrical transformers and generators, and miles of cable—all lying unused. One witness recalled seeing scraps of documents blowing down the street.

Whether Tesla transmitted power over any significant distance is still unknown. Perhaps these documents would have told us. As it was, they blew backward into the nineteenth century, and with them went Tesla's career. He continued to utter gripping predictions for himself, and continued to attract devoted followers, but potential backers thought long and hard before they put any money on him. As to any radio sets he may have imagined, the public never saw a single one.

Guglielmo Marconi was already well into his career by the time Tesla laid the foundations for Wardenclyffe Tower, but he benefited from its machinery nonetheless. At the very least, he availed himself of Tesla's Patent no. 645,576, issued in March 1900, for his famous transatlantic demonstration, and probably he used many more.

When it came to personality, however, Marconi borrowed very little from his predecessor, sharing more with the get-it-done Wright brothers. Like Orville and Wilbur, Marconi weaned himself of an early aptitude for performance (in his case, the receding talent was musical) and devoted himself instead to a life of prodigiously hard work. Like the aviators, he chose an exceedingly remote location to put on his most exciting show, and like them, he sought his backing primarily from the armed services. The Faust-inspired figures of the nineteenth century, it seems, were destined to give way to a more practically minded breed of men.

One thing that did distinguish Marconi from the Wrights—and from all the other show inventors, for that matter—was his upper-class background. His father, Giuseppe Marconi, was a highly successful businessman. His mother, Annie Jameson, belonged to the Irish distillery dynasty. Guglielmo himself was born in the Marescalchi Palace in Bologna. It was on the third floor of this heavily shuttered palace that, as a young man, he first rang a bell without the use of wires.

When Marconi came of age, his privileged position gave him entrée into circles generally denied the common citizen. He arrived in England in 1896, a thin-lipped, clean-shaven Italian (he sometimes shaved twice a day), with a letter of introduction to Sir William Preece, late of his battles with Oliver Heaviside and presently the chief engineer of the

British post office. Preece had already been making advances in wireless telegraphy, and the two men immediately fell to work together.

Marconi soon discovered the benefits of a standing in the scientific community. In November 1896, Preece enlisted no less a personage than Lord Kelvin to send a "Marconigram" from Needles, England, to the Isle of Wight. Kelvin in turn was able to pull strings for Marconi and get him appointed as assistant marine attaché to the Italian embassy in London—a sinecure. On July 20, 1897, the Wireless Telegraph and Signal Company was capitalized at 100,000 pounds.

In this early stage, Marconi put on a public face, or at least allowed the public to notice what he was doing. At the Needles station, locals wondered at the strange masts rising up beside the Needles Hotel. They puzzled at a wire that ran to a window, casting off sparks in the wind. As the surf broke below, men moved about in silhouette, talking in the ether.

Meanwhile, Marconi was also evincing a knack for business. Soon, lighthouses along the coast of England were being fitted with his wireless sets. In May 1898, the Lloyds Corporation installed Marconi's invention in its own lighthouse stations. In July, Marconi was able to send wireless reports of a yacht race off the Irish coast. Three decades after the Loomis Aerial Telegraphy Company perished, wireless technology was finally being put to commercial use.

But despite the interest of both businessmen and the public, Marconi believed from the beginning that radio's best hope lay with the military. From September 2, 1896, on, observers from the British army and navy were on hand to scrutinize his progress. Early in his experiments, when he asked about initial applications for radio, he explained, "The first may be for military purposes, in the place of a field telegraph system." On another occasion, he said, "I believe one of the greatest uses to which these instruments will be put, will be signaling in wartime."

After making successful transmissions from England to France on March 27, 1899, Marconi was ready to expand his horizons and sailed for New York, where he gave several demonstrations to the public. But America was not destined to remember them. Marconi's appearance was completely overshadowed by the surprise arrival of Admiral Dewey— the uncontested hero of the Spanish-American War.

Americans might still have witnessed Marconi in action had fate not intervened. In July 1900, as his wireless was beginning to be used in

the first ship-to-ship and ship-to-port communications, he began construction on a transmitter a hundred times more powerful than his previous models, in Poldhu, Cornwall, for the purpose of transmitting
messages across the Atlantic. The Poldhu station resembled a Tesla
creation, with a ring of twenty wooden masts, each 200 feet high,
arranged in a semicircle about 200 feet in diameter and joined by 400
wires to form a conical aerial. Unfortunately, a cyclone demolished it
in August 1901. Marconi had erected a similar station in Cape Cod,
but it too blew down, so he moved his New World site to Cabot Tower
in St. John's, Newfoundland, a site every bit as inaccessible as Kitty
Hawk.

In December 1901, a heavy snow lay on the ground, and the surf
crashed against the cliff some 300 feet below. Marconi flew a test kite
into the air, hoping to pick up a signal. Then he sent up a test balloon
measuring 14 feet in diameter and containing 1,000 cubic feet of hydrogen gas. When the balloon broke, the tether flew out to sea. He went
back to kites.

At the time, there was no way to measure the wavelength of the
transmission; without the benefit of a tuning dial, Marconi could only
guess the frequency of the Poldhu transmitter. On December 12, after
a long wait, he guessed correctly. A series of clicks sounded in his ear-
phones—a series of S's, rendered in Morse code, were coming out of
the receiver. Soon the kite, let out higher into the sky, was receiving
continuous messages.

Though this feat received critical acclaim, the American public remained skeptical. For years, in fact, many doubted whether Marconi
had actually received a message at all. Of course, the fact that the transmission took place far from view did little to heighten the general credulity. Nor did it help matters much that Marconi's American "rite of
passage" proved to be no demonstration of his invention at all, but an
expression of the financial community's satisfaction.

The celebration was held at the Waldorf-Astoria on January 3, 1902,
in the Astor Gallery. On a table at the back wall sat a black tablet framed
in smilax, with Marconi's name emblazoned in studded lights. On the
east and west walls, additional electrical lights spelled out *Poldhu* and
*St. John's*, and a silken cable connected these two "destinations," with
the letter *s* appearing regularly along it. (Not even a wireless there!) The
guest table boasted many more lights, American beauty roses, and a half-
tone picture of Marconi transmitting a wireless message across the

ocean. There were three hundred diners, and countless spectators in the galleries.

The gala event began with a procession of waiters bearing ices on miniature telegraph poles, steamships, and sailing vessels. The poles themselves were made of solid ice. The guests predicted the demise of the telegraph when they saw these poles and cried, "Frozen out!" Charles Steinmetz—Elihu Thomson's inestimable partner at General Electric—called the crowd to attention, and letters from Edison and other inventors were read. Then Marconi stood up and spoke of the rapid application of the wireless aboard ships. Rousing applause followed.

In the hands of a blood-and-thunder showman, this dinner would have taken a very different form. One can only imagine what kind of radio show, say, Isaac Singer might have put on. No doubt the public would have had to contend with suave company agents, seductive financing plans, and, above all, persuasive technical demonstrations. But rather than a real inventor's show, the Waldorf reception offered only the *trimmings* of one: ice sculptures, American beauty roses, and white linen. To the citizens in the gallery, radio itself must have seemed as abstract and unattainable as ever.

Of course, Marconi had never planned to make wireless a consumer product to begin with, but his success galvanized many who did. Indeed, after his transatlantic feat, there appeared a breed of enthusiasts who devoted themselves to the vision of democratic radio with the zeal of religious converts.

In 1902, an avowed follower of Tesla named Lee de Forest equipped his Wireless Auto No.1 with a transmitter and careened around New York, showing off a spark gap before stopping at the stock exchange to send closing prices to a mysterious receiver nearby. That same year, Reginald Aubrey Fessenden, a former mucker in Edison's lab, joined forces with Ernst F. W. Alexanderson of GE to devise a high-frequency alternator, which along with John Ambrose Fleming's vacuum tube of 1904, made voice transmissions possible. On Christmas Eve 1906, Fessenden sent out a broadcast of a woman singing, a violin solo, and an address—officially, the first wireless telephony broadcast.

De Forest made another leap forward in 1907 when he patented an improved version of the vacuum tube called the Audion tube and opened his own broadcasting studio in the Parker Building in New York. An indefatigable believer, he dreamed of "attuning a new Aeolian harp" that could capture the melodies of musicians in a distant auditorium. On January 10, 1910, he realized this dream when he broadcast the voice of Enrico Caruso live from the stage of the Metropolitan Opera Company.

Meanwhile, Hugo Gernsback, a science-fiction writer, inventor, and yet another devotee of Tesla, opened a shop on Fulton Street in New York that doubled as a "junk collector's heaven." Those who braved its interior beheld a hodgepodge of aerials and crystal detectors, all of which could be ordered from the Electro-Importing Company.

By and large, these early radio promoters saw radio much as Tesla did, as a democratic tool designed for two-way communications. Yet who could make sense of what they were doing? Was there really a mysterious recipient at the other end of de Forest's Wireless Auto transmitter? And who could possibly listen to Fessenden's Christmas tidings, or wade through Gernsback's arcane inventory, except for the wireless amateurs—the hackers of the time?

Admittedly, for a time, it seemed as if the amateurs were becoming dramatic figures in their own right. An operator named Jack Binns even managed to become a brief sensation in 1909, when he relayed the news that his ship, the *Republic*, had collided with the *Florida*—thus saving the lives of all those on board both ships. But Binns never thought to give the public a clear demonstration of point-to-point wireless transmission. Nor, for that matter, did any of the other amateurs. Unlike Bell, whose two-way communications device ostensibly set the pattern for radio, they did not invite any volunteers to speak into a transmitter before a thrilled crowd, or fascinate any audience by making strange voices jump from speaker to speaker.

On the contrary, rather than promoting the wider adoption of radio, the amateurs tended to revel in their rarefied status as information brokers. Bragging about receiving reports "long before the country has heard the news from the papers," they came to think of themselves as belonging to an exclusive brotherhood, or what they described as a "superior class." "The eagerness and frankness in distributing the results of our findings," remembered one amateur, "undoubtedly molded the form of fellowship which is such a striking quality of the amateurs." "We were undoubtedly romantic about ourselves," recalled another, "possessors of strange new secrets that enabled us to send and receive messages without wires." This was not spreading the gospel. It was a way of closing ranks.

That radio continued to be associated with the military only made it more esoteric—and ultimately, more likely to provoke suspicion. As Marconi developed a clientele made up of various branches of the armed services, the public began to think of the technology in slightly paranoid terms. The wireless operator was imagined at times as a hypothetical "electrical expert who slips in somehow and steals the secrets of the enemy's tunes." When a Frederick Collins developed a commercial wireless telephone service between Portland, Maine, and nearby Casco Bay, the *New York Times* wrote that "the inventor says he has solved the problem of selectivity thus making the wireless telephone *even more secret* than the present wire telephone systems." (Italics mine.)

This secret, such as it was, was finally revealed to the public on April 14, 1912, at 10:25 P.M., when Marconi operators at Cape Race received word that the *Titanic* oceanliner was sinking. Besides saving the lives of about seven hundred passengers who otherwise would have perished, the wireless reports turned the catastrophe into a blow-by-blow account. Through it, the world learned that the orchestra continued to play to the end, that some passengers acted like cowards and some heroes, that still others stood smoking on deck as the ship went down. Most important, radio brought news of the survivors. Relatives of the passengers clamored outside Marconi's wireless stations, begging for news.

With the *Titanic* disaster, radio and drama met at last. Marconi understood the implications immediately and allegedly went so far as to delay confirmation of some of the survivors, in order to prolong the drama as long as possible. One of Marconi's operators turned the situation to his advantage as well. Soon it was said, erroneously, that one young man had been the sole operator at the wireless set at Wanamaker's department store throughout the disaster. This was the young Russian-Jewish immigrant David Sarnoff. Later, as president of RCA, Sarnoff beamed: "The *Titanic* disaster brought radio to the front. And also me."

So it was. The spectacle of death made radio a reality in the minds of the public, just as a crash had done for the Wright flyer. When the lives of loved ones were at stake, wireless suddenly didn't seem so arcane anymore.

The technological drama of the *Titanic* disaster also proved far more effective than Gilbreth's motion studies as a tool for furthering the public order. Over the years, the navy had grown increasingly annoyed with wireless amateurs, who took up air space and often played practical jokes on their own operators. In 1909, it published a report disparaging the fact that "seemingly semi-intelligent and wholly irresponsible operators at any time through carelessness or stupidity may render hopeless the case of a shipwreck." The news of the *Titanic* itself, many claimed, had been slowed by the ceaseless chattering of amateurs on the airwaves.

This was not entirely true, as heroic amateurs like Jack Binns had demonstrated. Even so, immediately after the disaster, a movement began that sought to curtail the amateur's freedom. Marconi himself, seeing a monopoly in the making, advocated "control of amateur experimenters." With the *Titanic* fresh on the minds of its constituency, Congress followed suit and passed a law that imposed professional standards on operators and their equipment. The public, still largely unaware of what was at stake, put up no resistance to the law at all.

Ostensibly, the Radio Act of 1912 was designed to prevent the woefully poor response to the *Titanic* from occurring again, but it also awarded undamped airwaves to complete stations, restricting amateurs to the short-wave bandwidths of 200 meters or less. Those found guilty of malicious interference would be fined up to $500. And while private stations were allowed to use wavelengths above 1,600 and below 600 meters, the entire spectrum between 600 and 1,600 meters was given over to the government. Naval operators were required to transmit commercial messages in zones where there were no commercial stations, and to meet these new standards, they had a standing order to develop better radio technology.

The heyday of the wireless amateurs was over almost before it had begun, and long before the idea of radio as a two-way consumer product had a chance to spread to the general public. The defeat was perhaps best symbolized by the condition of the "living brain" Tesla had imagined for the world. In 1915, Wardenclyffe Tower was in ruins. Much of the equipment had been stolen. The stairs leading up to the dome had rotted away. In the office, drawers were thrown open, windows smashed, the rooms ransacked. Eventually, Tesla was forced to sign over the contents of the building to the Waldorf-Astoria in lieu of rent. On the Fourth of July, 1917, Wardenclyffe Tower was dynamited, and the remains were sold for scrap.

Scrap was what was needed. By this time, radio was not the only technology being given over to the armed forces. The Dayton-Wright Company was building more planes for the government than for anyone else. Corporations and factories of every variety were being put upon to fill massive orders. Machine parts, steel, clothing—anything that could possibly be mass-produced was needed for the ordeal ahead.

The spectacle of death and the technological environment were about to come together.

## Chapter Sixteen

# TEMPORARY LOSS
# OF "MEMORAY"

T he scenes are familiar. Tanks rolling over devastated landscapes. Soldiers in gas masks peering up from foxholes. Biplanes wheeling overhead. Firebombs setting cities ablaze at night. As if to make a ghastly play on the phrase "theater of war," World War I turned vast stretches of Europe into a mechanical spectacle of mass destruction.

Of course, world war, which brought on widespread death and suffering, was a spectacle of a very different order from the small-time stagings of itinerant tricksters. Put on by entire nations, it called for a multitude of volunteers to appear on its stage, and for tremendous suspension of disbelief. As a technological environment, world war also required an immense deployment of goods—not only food and supplies, but unprecedented amounts of machinery as well. In fact, it has often been noted that the conflict resembled a factory system.

This is an apt analogy, since for the first time the U.S. government, as much as any other, became concerned with war as a problem of efficiency. The government's scope, however, exceeded that of American corporations and factory owners by many magnitudes. Far more commanding than any CEO, the government acted as a central "headquarters" for all of the manufacturers of the nation, making it, in effect, a metafactory. Between the urgency of the moment and the rule of law, it also became appropriative in a way that previous economizing forces could not. The entire intellectual capital of the nation was presumed to be at the service of the state, and inventors, as much as soldiers and munitions workers, were expected to mesh with the "exceedingly complicated and artificial system that nourishes and sustains them."

The effect of these emergency measures was to limit the freedom of inventors to a degree that American manufacturers had never imagined. As the war dragged on and scarcity pressed the government to dire extremes, many inventors were intimidated and harassed into silence. Others had their inventions seized practically by fiat. While the world was at war, domestic disorder could not be tolerated.

It goes without saying that, in such an atmosphere, the ability of inventors to put on shows became increasingly strained as well. Only the most powerful figures in technology could afford to make flamboyant gestures, and even then, the customary absurdities of the inventor's spectacle were bound to conflict with the inexorable momentum of wartime production. Zany extravaganzas simply did not fit into the scheme of things.

Ironically, it took Henry Ford, the factory king himself, to prove just how far wrong an innovative mind could go in such times. Setting himself dead against the war, he organized a spectacle that seemed expressly designed to go nowhere at all. And it got there in no time flat.


It all began innocently enough. One day in June 1915, while speaking to a reporter from the *Detroit Free Press*, Ford offhandedly proclaimed his willingness to do almost anything to promote peace in Europe. The reporter took this vague statement and turned it into a headline that read, "Henry Ford To Push World-Wide Campaign For Universal Peace."

Almost immediately, solicitors descended on the Model T manufacturer, promoting every sort of peace plan imaginable. Among them was a Hungarian Jew named Madame Rosika Schwimmer, suffragette, peace activist, and ardent self-promoter. She came to Highland Park on November 17, 1915, toting a black handbag stuffed, she said, with notes of conversations she had had with a number of European leaders. With Ford's help, she was convinced that they could make great progress in ending the war.

Ford took a liking to Schwimmer, and on November 22, held a meeting to toss around ideas on how to further her plan. He seemed distracted during this meeting, but became alert when someone mentioned the possibility of staging an activity aboard a ship. Although some objections were also raised, Ford ignored them. Here was another chance to create a grand-scale spectacle, not a factory this time, but a "Peace Ship." (Unfortunately, notes were never taken during Ford's business meetings, so the originator of the Peace Ship can't be identified with any certainty.)

The very next day, Ford met with President Wilson, his pitch already formed: he invited Wilson and his family to join him on a voyage to Europe aboard the Peace Ship, which was leaving "next Saturday week." No use wasting any time! When Wilson declined, Ford returned home, called the president "a small man," and forged ahead. By November 24, he had his slogan: "We'll get the boys in the trenches home by Christmas"—a line, incidentally, that was revived without irony during the Vietnam War.

A natural when talking to two or three reporters, Ford was often lost in the presence of a roomful of them. Nevertheless, he chose to give a press conference. The results were rich in pathos. "Repeated questions," wrote the *Detroit Free Press*, "disclosed not the slightest evidence that Mr. Ford has a definite plan as to what he is going to do when he gets to Europe." Meanwhile, Madame Schwimmer booked a suite at the Biltmore Hotel, ran up $1,000 a day in cable bills, and ordered a "peace wardrobe" of fur coats and evening gowns, all bankrolled by Ford. Clara Ford, Henry's wife, regarded Schwimmer with disgust and refused to go on the trip, explaining delicately to her husband that the European coasts were ringed with mines.

The weather was cold and harsh at the Hoboken pier on December 14. The faithful *Detroit Free Press* reporter noted with dismay that "Nobody knew where to go, nobody was in charge of anything, nobody knew anything." Fifteen thousand people showed up to see off fifty paying passengers, eight of whom arrived at the dock unaware that the ship had been chartered for such an unusual purpose. A social director hired by Schwimmer arrived in beret, smock, and yellow spats to rally the crowd. Edison showed up and pretended to be deaf when Ford pleaded with him to come along. Then Clara cried, Ford threw roses to her, and the band played "I Didn't Raise My Boy to Be a Soldier." An unannounced Mr. Zero leaped into the arctic waters for a peace swim. As the Peace Ship pulled away from shore, someone on board discovered a gift: two squirrels in a cage and a supply of raisins bearing the legend, "To Go with the Nuts."

On the open sea, one thing soon became clear: With so much time on their hands, the passengers had nothing to do but argue about their nonexistent plans. Schwimmer immediately began firing off memoranda to her thirty-one administrative staff members, and continued to do so throughout the voyage. The forty-four journalists brought along at Ford's expense watched the contretemps unfold with great satisfaction and plied Ford for quotes.

When the travelers arrived in Oslo, Norway, on December 18, the mood was considerably less jovial than it had been in Hoboken. The temperature was twelve degrees below zero. Worse, during the journey, a wave had curled over the deck and engulfed some of the passengers, making them quite ill. Among the sick were the bespatted social direc-tor, who died of pneumonia within days, and Ford, who went to his hotel and collapsed.

By December 22, Ford had improved enough to let the press into his room. As the reporters scribbled, he regaled them with his plans for a tractor that was certain to save Europe once the war was over. The reporters smiled and recorded his every word.

That night at four in the morning, a member of the team appeared in Ford's room, woke him, and presented him with his steamer trunk, already packed. A liner was leaving in a few hours, he was told. Too weak to protest, Ford sighed. "Guess I better go home" he said, "to Mother." Schwimmer, who was up late drafting yet another of her em-phatic manifestoes, managed to learn of her sponsor's plans and ran down to the hotel lobby. She was met by a flying wedge of Ford em-ployees concealing their leader as they raced outside to an idling taxi. In the confusion, the word *kidnapping* pierced the air.

Thanks to Ford's good relations with the journalists, the press treated the Peace Ship affair in a remarkably favorable light. Ford never voiced regrets over the venture, but it was clear that his inchoate notions about military conflicts left a good deal to be desired. In wartime, more com-prehensive and sober methods had to be used. In fact, by the time Ford returned to American shores, those methods were already in place.


With the Radio Act of 1912, the government had become more involved with radio than ever before, and the following year, when the newly elected President Wilson appointed Josephus Daniels to the post of sec-retary of the navy, it became still more involved. A teetotaling newspaper editor from Raleigh, North Carolina, Daniels favored low-brimmed hats and bow ties, and distinguished himself in his new post by banning wine from the officers' mess and extolling the virtues of "beautiful Christian women." He was anything but a sailor, but he knew what was good for the navy. At every opportunity, he petitioned for control of the airwaves. And when lobbying before Congress or appealing to cabinet members fell short of his goals, he found a potent ally in AT&T.

A decade earlier, AT&T had squelched the dispute between George Campbell and Oliver Heaviside on one hand, and Michael Pupin on the other, and so gained uncontested control over the long-distance telephone lines. Since then, it had built on this technique to gain a foothold in the burgeoning radio industry. As new patents emerged, it was quick to gain control over them—and to downplay the importance of the inventors responsible for bringing them into being. The corporation advanced, and Campbell and Heaviside began to have company on the sidelines.

One of the first to join them was Lee de Forest. In 1907, this button-eyed, cigar-smoking American had invented the Audion tube, which improved on John Ambrose Fleming's vacuum tube by allowing wireless voice transmissions to cover great distances. De Forest also held the distinction of transmitting voice messages from the Eiffel Tower, of driving his Wireless Auto through the streets of New York, and of sleeping in his own radio tower at the St. Louis World's Fair of 1904—none of which made him a likely candidate to understand the ways of a large corporation.

Short on cash in 1912, de Forest decided to sell his patents for the Audion tube and began negotiating with AT&T. The initial offer of $100,000 was attractive. But by July 1913, he had heard nothing further, and when an anonymous client offered $50,000, he accepted. Only later did he learn that this unnamed client and AT&T were one and the same.

George Squier received much the same treatment, despite his precautions to the contrary. A fragile-looking man who invariably posed for photographs in full military regalia, Squier was the sort of soldier who felt compelled to act on his imagination. At West Point, and later as an officer in the Signal Corps, he became notorious for his mechanical aptitude, using various telegraph technologies to ring bells, activate machinery, detonate canons, and explode mines. In the Spanish-American War, he devised the Squier Synchrograph, which tracked and timed projectiles by electrical means. Soon his interests began to broaden into other fields. When the Wrights conducted their demonstrations at Fort Myer, he had the honor of being among the first passengers in an air-

plane, flying in their machine only a day or two before Lieutenant Selfridge was killed.

Squier's main contributions, however, were to the radio industry. His
entry into the field was unconventional enough. By driving a spike into
the base of a tree and another high in the trunk, he was able to create
an extemporaneous radio for soldiers in combat. He dubbed this tree
radio the "floroscope" and received a patent for the use of "vegetable
organisms" as radio antennae on February 7, 1905.

Squier's interest in radio soon led him to experiment with the transmission of signals at high frequencies over telephone lines, a technology
that came to be known as "wire-wireless." The idea was that if two
conversations could travel the telephone lines simultaneously—one as
a radio signal, and the other as an ordinary wire transmission—it would
allow secret communications during wartime. This technology had tremendous implications, since it linked radio and telephony together for
the first time.

In 1910, Congress gave Squier $30,000 to develop wire-wireless tech-
nology for the Signal Corps, with the particular aim of sending radio
frequencies along phone lines while the phone was in regular use. The
feat was accomplished on September 18, 1910, on seven miles of underground cable between 1710 Pennsylvania Avenue and the Bureau of
Standards. The results were presented to the American Institute of Electrical Engineers on June 28, 1911, in Chicago, and Squier received four
patents for wire-wireless technology soon afterward. Then he surprised
everyone by dedicating them to the public.

The importance of wire-wireless was understood by industry insiders
in its time. "A new art has been born to us," wrote John Stone Stone
in 1912. "The infant art of high-frequency multiplex telephony and
telegraphy is the latest addition to our brood of young electrical arts. It
is certainly a most promising youngster and should, after the manner of
its kind, call lustily for its share of attention and sustenance."

But encouraged as he was, Stone also took time to lament Squier's
decision. "Major Squier has dedicated to the public his patents relating
to this new art—an act, though laudable in the spirit it displays, is nevertheless unfortunate, as it is more likely to retard the progress of the
new art than to advance it."

Stone's opinion is curious in light of the many compliments paid to
Wilhelm Roentgen and Michael Faraday for refusing to patent their
inventions. After all, nothing prevented any inventor who felt so inclined

from jumping on wire-wireless, as others had jumped on the x-ray and the dynamo before them. The only logical inference is that AT&T saw an opportunity in wire-wireless to expand into the radio business, and that Stone was speaking on their behalf.

As it turned out, a monopoly was unnecessary. When AT&T began using wire-wireless for its own purposes, Squier brought a lawsuit against the company, insisting that some of its profits should go to the public. The court decided against him, and AT&T emerged as the de facto owner of his invention.

Thus, by the time Josephus Daniels became secretary of the navy, AT&T controlled three inventions, which, when used together, allowed the human voice to be transmitted virtually around the planet. Daniels recognized as much and, hoping to further the glory of the navy through radio, enlisted the help of AT&T in setting up a demonstration of long-distance radio communication. The phone company, which by this time was receiving generous government contracts, had no reason to object.

It was a global-scale show, suitable for a global-sized navy. The campaign began at the Pan-American Exposition of 1915, when Alexander Graham Bell and Thomas Watson were summoned from their busy schedules as freelancers to re-enact their first telephone conversation—this time, across a continent. When Bell uttered the famous phrase, *Watson, come here, I want you,* from his perch in San Francisco, Watson was able to hear it clearly three thousand miles away in New York. Then the two threw aside the scripts that AT&T had prepared for them and, for twenty-three minutes, extemporized much as they had almost forty years earlier. The Ziegfeld Follies went one further and produced a song—"Hello, Frisco"—to commemorate the event; it became the Broadway hit of the season.

AT&T gave Bell and Watson the recognition they deserved in a brochure titled *The Story of a Great Achievement: Telephone Communication From Coast to Coast.* But any mention of famous inventors disappeared from the proceedings after that. In September 1915, the voice of AT&T president Theodore Vail traveled by telephone lines from New York to a naval station in Arlington, Virginia, where it was relayed by a wireless transmitter (built by AT&T) to Pearl Harbor, Hawaii—some 4,600 miles away. On October 22, the team produced a similar feat, transmitting a human voice across the Atlantic for the first time. The press wrote up both events in favorable terms. A reporter from the *New York Times* noted that the September transmission traveled further than the distance between New York and the North Pole.

For all intents and purposes, these were the first technological spectacles produced by the government itself. Beyond the obvious contributions of Bell and Watson, it was clear who deserved credit for their success. Oliver Heaviside, while pontificating on sea serpents, had solved the problem of telephoning from New York to Arlington. Lee de Forest, between stints in his radio car, had made possible the transmission of Vail's voice to Hawaii. And George Squier, author of the talking tree, had developed the all-important technology for linking these telephone and radio transmissions together. Yet AT&T and the navy made no mention of any of these inventors in connection with these demonstrations.

None of them were happy about the omission. Heaviside was still routinely firing off truculent letters to the scientific community for denying his critical role in the development of the distortionless circuit. An enraged de Forest published a brochure that was identical to AT&T's, down to the typeface and paper stock, except that it gave prominent place to his own contributions to transcontinental telephony. And Squier, of course, had filed a lawsuit for the express purpose of preventing AT&T from hoarding wire-wireless technology for itself.

For all that, Daniels went on to speak by wireless from Washington to a ship off the coast of Virginia in May 1916 and, with AT&T officials gathered around his desk, delivered what seemed to be an irrefutable defense. The demonstrations, he said, offered "indisputable proof that whether American businessmen are acting as individuals or as corporations, their hearts respond readily and unreservedly to the call of their country." Apparently a mechanical feat performed by the navy belonged to the navy, and nothing more could be said about it.

The radio demonstrations put on by the navy and AT&T were a benchmark in the annals of technology. Buying out inventors was one thing, making a spectacle of their spoils (by stationing a famous inventor at an exposition, no less) was another. For the first time, an economizing force had stolen the thunder of inventors outright.

Yet fatuous as it was, Daniels's "indisputable proof" was really only half wrong. The inventors of peacetime technology may have coveted their stardom as staunchly as ever, but the inventors of wartime devices experienced no such conflicts. In fact, when it came to supplying the government with military technology, some Americans were altogether *too* anxious to help. On May 6, 1915, an advertisement in the *American Machinist*, for a projectile manufactured by the Cleveland Automatic Machine Company, captured the patriotic fervor at its most zealous:

> The material is high in tensile strength and VERY SPECIAL and has a tendency to fracture into small pieces upon the explosion of the shell. The timing of the fuse for this shell is similar to the shrapnel shell, but it differs in that two explosive acids are used to explode the shell, in the large cavity. The combination of these two acids causes a terrific explosion, having more power than anything of its kind yet used. Fragments become coated with the acids in exploding and wounds caused by them mean death in terrible agony within four hours if not attended to immediately.

Secretary of Commerce Redfield denounced Cleveland Automatic for dreaming up such an atrocity—to no avail. When copies were laid on every desk at the Reichstag, it provoked an uproar. The American ambassador to Berlin tried to finesse the matter, politely explaining that the advertisement was a hoax designed to provoke anti-American sentiment. Provoke it did, but the announcement was real. The *American Machinist* finally came forward with a confusing statement about an error in the composition room.

Clearly, when inventors held the power to surprise everyone with new and ungodly weapons, it behooved Washington to be the first to know what was on their minds. And so, even as the *American Machinist* gaffe was being smoothed over, Daniels set up an organization designed to find out. Officially known as the Naval Consulting Board, the Inventors Board was organized in May 1915 and included Leo Baekeland, Peter Cooper Hewitt, Lee de Forest, Hudson Maxim, and Elmer Sperry on its roster—with Thomas Edison as their chairman.

The Inventors Board did have some effect during World War I. Edison, for one, saw several of his recommendations taken up. On his advice, the navy gave radios and various other listening devices to American merchant ships. It was also Edison who suggested that merchant ships travel in convoys by night, and that they keep to shallow waters and British ports by day—tactics that may have minimized the damage inflicted by German U-boats.

Most of Edison's recommendations went nowhere, though, and as time went by he became increasingly frustrated. "The Naval officer resents any interference by civilians," he concluded. "Those fellows are a close corporation." Perhaps Edison failed to fit in because, at seventy years of age, he revived some of his old zaniness and demonstrated a high kick for Daniels that smashed a chandelier globe to pieces. But in the end, less demonstrative members of the board felt just as neglected as Edison did. Most likely, the navy never intended to heed the advice of these inventors and simply wanted to keep apprised of their whereabouts.

Much the same could be said for the many unknown inventors who sent their suggestions by post. Shortly after the board was made public, Daniels was swamped with mail. By November 13, 1915, *Scientific American* could report that the office was glutted. A similar deluge visited upon the War Department gives some idea of the volume. As opposed to the usual two hundred letters a year, the War Department was receiving two hundred letters a week, "with a range and variety of subjects corresponding to the numerical product."

Few if any of the letters delivered to the Inventors Board received a reply of any kind, much less found their way into application. Like the Inventors Board itself, their purpose seems to have been largely decorative. Then again, Daniels may have rested easier knowing that the nation's intellectual captial was being funneled to him and not to the *American Machinist*.

For those who dreamed up military inventions, or inventions with potential military applications, the prewar years offered very few options. Daniels seemed to be cultivating the role of a latterday Thomas Jefferson: even as he called for the unswerving support of his countrymen, he seemed intent on defeating them. Meanwhile, the alternative—to proceed along commercial lines—meant flirting with political mayhem. With the specter of mechanized war at hand, getting an invention before the right audience called for an unusual combination of intelligence, luck, and stamina.

One inventor blessed with this combination—or cursed with it—was a young man from Massachusetts named Robert Goddard. Like so many others, Goddard submitted a proposal to the government (he proposed a rudimentary form of sonar to the navy in May 1917), and like so many others, he received no reply. But Goddard was a man possessed, and in the end he managed not only to put on an inventor's show before an audience of decorated warriors but to give it a touch of the old magic as well. The only thing he failed to factor into the equation was the harassment he would get from the government along the way.


Robert Goddard was fated to look eternally old, as if he had been born in a suit and packed off to school a bald and serious boy. In fact, quite the opposite was true: a sense of wonder seized him early and stayed with him for the rest of his life. At sixteen, he read H. G. Wells's *War of the Worlds* while laid up with kidney trouble; for the next year, he could think of nothing else. On October 19, 1899, he climbed a cherry tree and imagined a machine that could take him to Mars. Thereafter, he often wrote in his diary under this tree, and referred to October 19 as Anniversary Day.

Goddard's enthusiasm soon translated into a wide variety of interests. At nineteen, he wrote to Edward F. Bigelow, editor of *St. Nicholas Magazine*, about the possibility of steering a flying machine by tilting one wing. In a nod to his literary mentor, he wrote a short story called "The High Speed Bet" in which speeds of 1,200 miles per hour could be obtained on the earth's surface. Before he was twenty, he had tried his hand at wireless technology, laughing gas, a toy firefly (with phosphorescent oil in a glass abdomen), a reusable pen wiper, a necktie press, an attachment to remove leaves from rakes, and a kinetic advertising sign powered by electromagnets.

But throughout it all, Goddard's first love was space technology. In December 1901, he could be found studying the problem from a technical standpoint. "The interesting problem of space navigation seems to be much neglected," he wrote, with no apparent sense of irony. "Occasionally, however we may hear of a plan suggested. The method generally advanced is causing the recoil of a gun placed in a vertical position with the muzzle directed downwards, to raise itself with a car containing the operator."

If that sounds like Verne revisited, it's because Goddard had read the French author and was consciously preparing to update his initial proposal. Indeed, Goddard was soon surpassing anything Verne had imagined. In 1905, he pondered the length of time a space voyage would take, which led him to contemplate the potential of cryogenics. Not long after, he was entertaining the notion that the electrical waves surrounding the earth—Hertzian waves—could be used to eject a vehicle into outer space. At a time when few people believed that the Wrights had really flown, he was ready to leave the earth's atmosphere altogether!

Goddard got his first drubbings soon enough. When he submitted an article titled "On the Possibility of Navigating Interplanetary Space" to *Scientific American* and *Popular Astronomy*, both publications rejected it. *Popular Astronomy* stated flatly that space flight was an impossibility. Undaunted, he postulated a multistage rocket in 1909.

In March 1913, Goddard became so ill that the doctors gave him two weeks to live. To say he recovered is an understatement. He applied for his first rocket patent on October 1, 1913. A second rocket patent, filed May 15, 1914, mentioned liquid fuel as a propellant. Far from behaving like a sickly man, he wrote Franklin D. Roosevelt, acting secretary of the navy, about his ideas for wireless control of torpedoes. (Unlike his successor, Roosevelt actually wrote back, though ultimately nothing came of it.)

In the years 1915 and 1916, almost every entry in Goddard's diaries is taken up by his rocket experiments. So immersed was the inventor that he lived out his expeditions by night. One dream had him "going to moon, and interested, going and coming, on where to land respectively on moon and earth . . . Was cold, and not enough oxygen density to breathe—got into chamber for a while. Saw and took photos of earth with small Kodak while there—two for stereoscopes—and glimpsed earth once during return—South America? Not enough oxygen when I opened my helmet to see if so."

Though few people were willing to countenance the idea of space travel, least of all the government, it was in Washington that Goddard eventually found a willing ear. Writing to Charles Walcott, secretary of the Smithsonian, in December 1916, he described the benefits of his rockets, which used liquid propellants and exceeded the highest altitudes of sounding balloons. For the moment, he kept the idea of space travel to himself and spoke only of military and meteorological applications. In January 1918, Walcott prevailed upon none other than George Squier—now promoted to major general—to give Goddard ten thousand dollars from the coffers of the Signal Corps' aviation division. Squier, who had flown in the Wright airplane and invented wire-wireless technology, saw something of himself in Goddard and agreed to finance his technology for military applications.

But support from the government came with its own kind of baggage, which was as ominous in its way as anything the Cleveland Machine Company could dream up. A few years earlier, Goddard had met the president of a sprinkler company named G. I. Rockwood, and the two had talked briefly about forming a partnership. When Goddard insisted on calling the product the Goddard rocket and retaining the rights to future patents, the negotiations became strained. The more reluctant Goddard became, the more Rockwood wanted a part of the business. Finally, Rockwood broke rank and began telling his friends that "All he has is a nozzle attached to an ordinary rocket."

In the spring of 1918, the imbroglio took a nastier turn. Rockwood went to Washington and contacted one Colonel E. M. Shinkle of the gun division of the Ordnance Department, asking for a letter saying, in effect, that the department wanted him to produce a rocket based on Goddard's design. To get the necessary information, Rockwood proposed to compromise a Mr. Haigis, then a foreman for Goddard. How Rockwood justified this treachery is unknown. In any event, Shinkle went to the chief signal officer of the army and, apparently without mentioning Rockwood, obtained permission to visit Goddard's lab in Worcester, Massachusetts, to see the designs for himself.

Goddard managed to be an elusive quarry. When Shinkle failed to provide any credentials, he refused to speak with him, then called the Smithsonian and told them not to give out information about his experiments to anyone. Shinkle responded by enlisting an intelligence officer, a Mr. Hammond, to pay a visit to Goddard as well.

C. G. Abbot, a Smithsonian liaison, provides a sense of the mood at Goddard's shop in a letter written to Walcott on March 19, 1918:

> People are very curious about the work, and indications are that spies are active. Drunken men ring the bell, etc., etc., but disappear quickly when the watchman brings his repeating Winchester shotgun. The building is of thick stone with but one door. I recommend to wire all windows and the door so as to alarm Mr. Haigis, who rooms nearby, if an attack should be made. They will do this at once. I also cautioned them not to talk even remotely about the work outside.

This letter suggests that Goddard had yet to suspect Haigis of any betrayal, though Rockwood apparently made some headway with him, as a letter from Walcott to Squier on May 31, 1918, alludes to the "Rockwood-Haigis-Shinkle intervention." Nevertheless, Shinkle eventually became so frustrated that he threatened the inventor's father, Nahum Goddard, by telephone: "You can tell your son that if he doesn't come to see me immediately [at the Bancroft Hotel]," he bullied, "I'll close up his laboratory, and he can put *that* in his pipe and smoke it!"

Nahum, sturdy soul, informed his caller that "Dr. Goddard doesn't smoke a pipe" and hung up.

By this time, the normally unflappable Goddard feared for his safety. On the advice of Walcott, he left for Washington, boarding the train one stop beyond Worcester, feeling as if he were being followed. A subsequent report revealed that his suspicions were well founded: Shinkle had searched the train at Worcester.

In Washington, Squier reassured Goddard that his invention would remain his own and offered further financial support from the Signal Corps. Abbot, for his part, secured Mount Wilson Solar Observatory in Pasadena, California—a kind of inventor's safehouse—for Goddard to continue his experiments. Goddard returned to Worcester, where he deliberately mistitled his writings on space travel "Special Formulae for Silvering Mirrors," attached a note that read "To be opened only by an optimist," and had them locked away in a safe. Then he embarked for Pasadena.

The brief respite from surveillance served Goddard well, not least because he made the acquaintance of an assistant named Clarence Hickman. A graduate of Clark University, Hickman doubled as a clarinet player, an archer, and, most important, a stage magician, whose stated interest in physics was as research for his magical tricks.

This interest proved beneficial when Hickman was given the task of making a practical multiple-charge machine gun rocket. Noting that in Goddard's prototype each charge left a gummy residue, and that there was too much pressure on the breech block, he decided to feed the charges from a magazine into the nozzle end by force of a gas piston. His subsequent experiments caused him to lose part of three fingers and a thumb, but it also led to a fully demonstrable rocket.

Goddard was more than pleased. When he returned east in November 1918 to deliver his results, he made sure to bring his assistant along—and, in fact, made him master of ceremonies for a demonstration at the Aberdeen Proving Grounds.

To an audience that included members of Army Ordnance, Aircraft Armaments, Trench Warfare, the Bureau of Standards, and the navy's Bureau of Ordnance, Hickman distributed program notes describing what they would see. Three rocket launchers, each five and a half feet long, would fire rockets of different weights, including one that weighed fifty pounds. For the moment, they would be set off manually, though an electrical mechanism was in the works. Also on the schedule of events was a rocket fired from trench mortar and the demonstration of stabilizing spin. And last but not least, a multiple-stage rocket would be fired, gaining velocity as it traveled.

For one of the demonstrations, Hickman set up a rack launch between two music stands placed two feet apart, and fired a rocket into distant sandbags. The rocket penetrated the third layer of the sandbags, but left the music stands upright, with the launcher intact. For the other items on the bill, the stage magician remembered holding "the launchers in my hands, under my arms, in slender supports. Every rocket went further than the Army's trench mortar. They seemed pretty impressed."

Of course, this demonstration had been carefully tailored to fit its audience. Goddard let slip no mention of his plan to send these rockets into outer space. Instead, he allowed the officers to see what was for all intents and purposes the prototype of the bazooka. It was a prudent move. For his reward, the army's aircraft armament section promised a special appropriation, and it undoubtedly would have honored the pledge had Germany not surrendered four days later.

The tradition of the show inventor still lived, but only just barely. For Goddard to demonstrate the forerunner of the modern rocket, he had the help of an eccentric major general and an able stage magician. Others were not so lucky.


Of all the inventions to come out of World War I, none was as ambitious, or so apocryphal, as the death ray. The typical death ray is described as an electrical current that causes combustion or an explosion at a distance—the wireless transmission of power gone awry. A man named Harry Grindell-Mathews supposedly invented one, as did the ever accommodating Nikola Tesla. Yet the facts surrounding death-ray machines were inevitably exaggerated by the press, dismissed by governments, and ridiculed by scientists. Inevitably, such conditions cast these machines in a political light; in what was to become an abiding twentieth-century tradition, it became possible to think of inventions as being suppressed. Viewed this way, the unpublished papers left behind by Paul Mallmann, if difficult to substantiate, offer a glimpse into a conspiracy culture at its inception.

In 1914, Mallmann was an American metallurgist and geologist living in England. He had tried without success to interest the British government in an explosive of his called Mallmannite. Then one day, he chanced upon a phenomenon so peculiar that he hesitated to reveal it to anyone. He described his reluctance to pursue the subject in a letter, dated October 29, 1917, to the British Secretary of the Board of Inventions and Research—the British equivalent of the Inventors Board in the United States:

> Leaving the conference room, while talking in the corridor I briefly described to Commander Brady the results I had obtained with my specially designed Searchlight in June 1914.
>
> Commander Brady immediately asked me *why* I had not placed this before the Admiralty long ago, and I answered that since the results obtained were so weird I had refrained from doing so, because not wishing to be laughed at, and not desiring that what I said would be taken as the imagination of a scientifically highly trained but overwrought brain, I had tried to reason it out but though I could do again what I had done in 1914, I was up against a series of phenomena I could not explain.

What exactly was this machine that had produced such weird results? Mallmann initially described it as a searchlight. "[M]y apparatus," he wrote, "has the semblance of a huge searchlight—provided with two reflectors and a rejector apparatus, a series of wire cases [or 'cages'] and a high frequency generating outfit in which light rays and heat rays of light were separated and charged."

In a letter to U.S. Secretary of State Robert Hastings, dated September 6, 1917, he was more specific. During experiments conducted in May and June of 1914, he directed the beam from an ordinary searchlight onto a toy balloon thirty yards away. Nothing happened. Then he concentrated the rays onto another balloon of the same size but sixty yards distant, and fastened to a glass rod by a thin thread. The balloon burst into flames. Next, he trained his death rays on a bundle of hay positioned in front of a reflecting board ninety yards away. The bundle of hay caught fire when the rays were reflected back off the board.

From what remains of Mallmann's papers, it seems he sent an "electric" light through a series of hollow lenses filled with various chemical compounds. When other conditions were met, he claimed to be able to send a stream of hydrogen "encased" in this electric light to a focal point, whereupon the end of the beam flattened out and produced a burst of flames.

After discovering that he could ignite objects from a considerable distance, Mallmann dismantled his apparatus with the intent to return to America, or as he invariably put it, "my country, the United States of America." But he did not go back to the States. Instead, he stayed on at his 88 Leadenhall Street address in London and met with a Commander Brady in late 1917. Then he spent about two months making eight drawings, two sketches, and specifications for a plant that could manufacture death-ray machines capable of igniting a target two miles away. He gave these papers, completed December 17 and 19, 1917, to a Flight Commander Brock on January 16, 1918.

A letter from Brock, posted from Air Board Service, Strand, W.C.2., came back in February 1918, indicating that the proposal was too expensive: "If you could reduce your demands very considerably, say to get a beam projected 1,000-ft., this would be quite enough to prove whether the idea is of value." Encouraged, Mallmann wrote to a Lieutenant Carmichael on February 25. A company called Schall & Company, he reported, would probably loan "5 High Frequency Outfits" to the Admiralty, with an option to buy after three months.

Around this time, Mallmann met with his liaisons, Brock and Carmichael. He explained the math behind his death ray, and the two officers confirmed it. When the inventor asked them how much it might be worth to them, they estimated—a little gratuitously perhaps—a figure of five million pounds sterling and asked that it be designed to work in bombers.

Then the tale, like Goddard's, went sour. Carmichael died of pneumonia in Italy on March 19, 1918. Brock fell on April 19, "supervising his Smoke Screen"—a detail that suggests that he might have been an inventor in his own right. When Mallmann asked what had become of the papers he had submitted to Brock, nobody seemed to know. Recalling that a black canvas roll containing his papers had disappeared around March or April at "the Cecil," he worried that his ideas might have fallen into the wrong hands and began to pursue the matter relentlessly. Or, as he wrote in his own synopsis, *"Then the fun begins."*

The first signs of trouble came when Scotland Yard refused to accept Mallmann's U.S. passport, his British registration papers, his invitations by the embassy, and even what he called "complimentary" letters from the Admiralty. Soon afterward, Mallmann concluded that Scotland Yard—along with the intelligence departments of the Admiralty, the War Office, the "new branch," and the Ministry of the Air—was making clandestine entries into his apartment. Nevertheless, he continued his efforts to retrieve his papers.

In the midst of these troubles, Mallmann found an ally in a man named Colonel Kirby—the potential equivalent of Goddard's General Squier. But Kirby did not put Mallmann at ease. Instead, he sent word through a Captain McCormick that the two of them had done "all they knew" to frustrate Mallmann's arrest by the Secret Service. "Capt. McCormick also informed me at this interview," wrote Mallmann, "that priority certiciates [sic] would be granted to me to assemble and manufacture the apparatus, but in spite of these and in spite of special permits I would be arrested by the Admiralty as soon as I would demonstrate the efficacy of my Death Ray apparatus at His Majesty's Royal Air Force workshops on Kirtling Street, but that Colonel Kirby would arrange for my release."

On July 16, 1918, Mallmann received a phone call from a Major John Jones, asking to meet the following day at the Carlyle Club in London. Mallmann arrived at the appointed time to behold a man in the uniform of a wing commander, who said he was familiar with Mallmann's work and offered Brock's name.

Having become more circumspect after the apparent breakins at his apartment, Mallmann asked if his name was really Jones.

"It isn't Jones," the man replied. "But for the purposes of the interview it is sufficient."

"Jones" then asked if he could come to Mallmann's den at Duke Street, an address known only to a few people. Mallmann was alarmed at this man's familiarity with his personal affairs and declined the offer. Undaunted, Jones wondered aloud if Mallmann "had not anticipated trouble with my winker and whether or not my fluids X and Z deteriorated under action of the light passing through the lenses, particularly when the inner reflector was in operation."

Stunned by this display of knowledge, Mallmann allowed his contact to come to his lab. Once there, Jones pressed for more information, then offered a revelation. It was Mallmann's machine, he said, that "he had used when from a bombing plane he attacked the Moselle Valley with disastrous results." (Whether *disastrous* meant a military success or failure is unclear.)

Now it was Mallmann's turn to pump the major. But Jones would not be softened, replying that his orders were to receive information, nothing more.

Eventually, Mallmann lost patience with this mysterious and recalcitrant man. If the government wanted more information, he said, it should wait for a demonstration. Such was every inventor's inborn desire, of course, but Jones did not see it that way and "left very annoyed."

The mood lightened on July 22, 1918, when Mallmann was allowed to begin his project anew under Colonel Kirby's authority. He began at once on a set of new drawings and sketches. Then, on September 10, he received another phone call, requesting that he meet Major John Jones again, this time at the Savoy Hotel, on the following day, at four in the afternoon. The caller also indicated that he knew of the meeting between Jones and Mallmann at the Carlyle on July 17.

When Mallmann arrived, Jones wasn't there. In his place, a naval officer appeared, informing him that Jones was dead and that he should get out of the country—fast. Mallmann, in the fashion of an entitled American, answered, "I intend to stay as long as I please."

Mallmann did stay, but he never achieved closure. Like a character in a Greek myth, he was consigned to search for his lost papers eternally and to find only vapors. In the end, he concluded that the British government was building his machine without his consent. On November 18, 1918, he wrote to an E. Polack, Esq. "You know from your own sources," he railed, "that my principles, my lenses, my Rays and the application of my discovery and my invention is being used today. . . . I know from unimpeachable and different sources, that my Invention is being used, both in Defences and in Attack." Even the British Parliament, he noted, was puzzled by the death ray's disappearance from governmental discourse.

Soon after this letter, Mallmann's notes become scattered and redundant. There are endless appeals to obscure government offices, complex suppositions as to what happened, the careful, plodding recriminations of a man defeated. Perhaps the most haunting detail in this one-man deposition is a fragment left behind as an afterthought. Typed on the back of one of his letters, on an otherwise white page, are the words, "temporary loss of memoray." Lost in a maze of half-truths and innuendo, Mallmann was not only disappearing from history. He was disappearing from himself.

Situated at an armchair's remove, it is almost impossible to know what to make of Mallmann's troubled tale. If it is true, then what became of the death ray? If it is false, in what way is it false? Because no death ray existed? Because it existed but did not work? Because Mallmann was imagining conspiracies that weren't there? Mallmann apparently never attempted to publish his papers. Why then did he spend so much time detailing his woes, to the point of losing his "memoray"?

In the face of so many unanswerable questions, the easiest course would be to dismiss Mallmann as delusional, yet the treatment of Robert Goddard at the hands of intelligence agents forestalls hasty judgment. In fact, the difference between the two men's accounts illustrates quite neatly how important the inventor's show really was. The credibility Goddard gained in putting on a demonstration at Aberdeen Proving Grounds allowed him to go on and develop the nation's first multistage liquid-fuel rockets. In a very real sense, a live show allowed his achievements to enter objective reality. And it allowed *him* to enter objective reality.

Mallmann, on the other hand, remained in a wholly subjective universe. The results were not salubrious. As long as his death ray went undemonstrated, he could only become what Anthony West had once described as "a person impenetrably concealed within his own special frame of private references, resentments, obsessions, and compulsions, and altogether set apart from the generality of mankind." He could only become the Invisible Man.

As has often been noted, the First World War exacted a loss of innocence, of a basic animal trust. This loss was experienced in many ways — through shellshock, through grief, through lingering nightmares of mustard gas and firebombs. For inventors, it meant a passage from Ford's improbably sunny outlook into an uncertain darkness, inside which awaited a monolithic force.

This force was recognized in its time. Harry Houdini, for one, made it the subject of his first movie. Filmed in 1918, at the height of America's involvement in the war, *Master Mystery* centers on the overlord of International Patents Inc., who suppresses any inventions that threaten his interests and hoards models of them in the basement of his castle. Houdini, hero from an earlier age, is charged with the mission of getting to these inventions and freeing them for all mankind. Along the way, he eludes barbed wire, acid streams, and freight elevators; conquers a steel robot named the Automaton; bursts free from a box thrown into the sea; and escapes from an electric chair—his own perhaps, inherited from the War of the Currents.

As the war came to a close, Houdini's cinematic opus described the situation accurately enough. The real-life overlords had begun the process of appropriating the inventions of others. In the case of AT&T and Josephus Daniels, they had gone further and demonstrated their ability to stage spectacles of their own. To ensure their hold over the world's inventions, all that was needed was to turn those spectacles into a vibrant tradition—and it would surely take a Houdini to stop them.

## Chapter Seventeen

# THE CORPORATE SHOW

**W**ar," said General James G. Harbord, "is a permanent factor in human life and a very noble one." The statement had a special resonance coming from the man who became president of RCA in 1923. After the armistice was signed, American corporations were quick to make their achievements during the war as permanent as possible. Having grown strong and efficient filling government contracts, they grew stronger and more efficient again. And having learned to fleece inventors of their intellectual property, they continued to appropriate whatever technologies they could, turning a blind eye to the rightful owners as they went. In the process, they gained almost complete control over the introduction of new inventions to the public.

The complete transference of power from inventor to corporation was not yet complete, however. Where wartime had called for unusual measures, peace brought with it a different sort of market, and to reach it, the corporations had to remake the spectacle of death into a spectacle of life. Of course, they could always invoke the memory of the war when they staged a publicity stunt—and so they did. But in the end, they had to go further than Josephus Daniels had in his long-distance radio transmissions; they had to create an ongoing corporate show.

There had been preliminary assays in this direction. Manufacturers had already made their first inconclusive bids at a "lenten" style of showmanship with Ford's employee spectacles and Gilbreth's unpopular typing contests. Elsewhere, department store owners had been perfecting their own kind of technological shows, in the form of lavish window displays and extravagant floor designs. Even so, efforts by retailers were inevitably local, and only as good as the proprietor's individual imagination. Mass production, meanwhile, had created a mass market, and there was as of yet no form of promotion capable of matching this vast new buying public.

Creating an entirely new tradition of showmanship was not an easy challenge for corporations to meet. Not only did they need to project a widespread sense of celebration that had no counterpart inside their factories and offices, but they needed to do so without calling on the inventors, who were likely to start making claims for themselves. How, then, was the gap to be bridged?

To say that the corporate show evolved from the advertising techniques of the department stores would be accurate on one level. On a deeper level, though, it arose from the wreckage of the inventor's show itself. After all, inventors had been divested of more than just their patents in the preceding decades. They had also been separated from the public and divorced from their one-time liaisons: the actors. And it was these two stray elements—the audience and the players—that ultimately supplied the crucial missing pieces in the burgeoning corporate-sponsored drama.

The seeds first took root, appropriately enough, in the soil of paranoia. In 1919, America was in the grips of its first Red Scare, and with public sentiment against foreigners running high, Guglielmo Marconi was denied permission to continue broadcasting in the United States. Alarmed, the corporate community immediately moved to keep the Italian inventor's intellectual capital in the country. Owen Young, then vice president of General Electric, and Edward J. Nally, the vice president of American Marconi, took the first step, pooling the radio patents owned by their companies and organizing RCA—the Radio Corporation of America. Then, David Sarnoff made his move.

Sarnoff had been busy since his moment as the "sole" wireless operator on duty during the *Titanic* disaster. His Jewish background kept him from receiving a commission in the navy, so he stayed on at the Marconi Company and got married to Lizette Hirmant, a Frenchwoman with whom he shared no common language. Promoted to commercial manager, he began amassing all the other important radio patents in the country. Before long, he had turned RCA into a virtual monopoly, controlling the patents that had been ceded to the navy during the war and boasting a stockholder list that included United Fruit, General Electric, Westinghouse, and AT&T.

But it was what Sarnoff did with all this power that mattered. Though the amateur wireless operators had been effectively curbed with the Radio Act, the medium still belonged to a specialized audience, who spoke almost exclusively among themselves. Sarnoff's gamble was that if he put on exciting radio programs, as the Westinghouse company had recently tried, people would buy RCA's "radiola" sets and become engrossed in dramas that came into their homes.

The Dempsey-Carpentier fight was an ideal proving ground for this idea. It was scheduled to take place on July 2, 1921, near the Lackawanna railroad yards in Jersey City, New Jersey, in a hexagonal stadium called Boyle's Thirty Acres. Visitors from all over the country had booked rooms in New York hotels to see the French war hero, Georges Carpentier, go up against hulking Jack Dempsey for the heavyweight championship. The promoter, Tex Rickard, announced that he was enlarging the stadium expressly for the occasion.

Seeing a chance to capitalize on ready-made fervor, Sarnoff played his hand. The navy, he knew, was still feeling proprietary about its patents, so he gave his show a perfunctory link to the military by turning the event into a benefit for the Fund for a Devastated France. Who could argue with that? Within three months, RCA had erected a transmitter at the Lackawanna yards.

When the fight began, at three P.M., to the blow-by-blow commentaries of *Wireless Age* editor and boxing enthusiast Major Andrew White, the nation jumped. More than 300,000 people heard the match on the radio that day—easily the largest audience ever at that time. Roughly 100,000 gathered around the loudspeaker outside the *New York Times* building in Times Square. Many others listened through wires strung hastily together. Callers reported hearing the match in Schenectady, on the Long Island Sound, in Pennsylvania.

Sarnoff's gamble paid off handsomely. Immediately after the fight, RCA's Radio Music Boxes began to sell. An estimated 60,000 households had a radio in 1922. The next year the number jumped to 400,000. General Electric and Westinghouse began offering their own lines of radio sets; so did others. Soon, there were stations in such far-flung places as Iowa, Illinois, West Virginia, and Arkansas. As programming blossomed, radio owners gathered around the set to listen to "things to tell the housewife about cooking meat," lectures, poetry readings, or most often, music. Radio enthusiast "Doctor" Goldsmith proclaimed the new technology "CONSOLER OF THE LONELY/BOND OF THE SCATTERED FAMILY."

Even the advent of movies had not marked such a radical departure. After the Kinetoscope faded away, the motion-picture industry developed along relatively conventional lines, with a stage, a house, a box office—with everything, in fact, that a theater had, except for live actors. But it was a very different thing for listeners to take a spectacle into their homes. With radio, the drama of the machine became as far-reaching as it was intimate—a nationwide domestic affair. And like the amusement park, radio was an ongoing event, which the public could tap into at any time.

The only real problem was funding. Though it was becoming painfully obvious that the sale of radio sets couldn't cover the costs of broadcasting, the idea of commercial radio was considered odious, even by those who stood to benefit from it. The old bugaboo of Thomas Jefferson's day had never been completely banished. Herbert Hoover, while secretary of commerce, decried the notion of "advertising clatter." Sarnoff was of the same opinion. Hoping to solve the problem by other means, he recommended that the major radio-set manufacturers—RCA, General Electric, and Westinghouse—shunt two percent of their sales on radio sets into a single broadcasting company. Others imagined offers by a Carnegie or a Rockefeller to underwrite the business. But the costs kept rising and no such act of largesse seemed imminent.

AT&T's radio station—WEAF—was in an especially difficult position. According to RCA's terms of incorporation, AT&T did not enjoy the luxury of selling radio sets and therefore was making no profit in radio at all. The company did control the means of transmission, however. At the time, radio signals were of the highest quality when sent by telephone lines from a central location to local points, whence the signal would continue through the air to home receivers. This was the wire-wireless system that George Squier had invented and subsequently given to the world. But only AT&T had the financial clout to construct the actual lines, and so the business was theirs by default. Thus, with its WEAF station on Walker Street in New York, the telephone company set its sights on having the best radio station in the business.

Not wanting to be accused of "direct" advertising, AT&T came up with the idea of a toll station, which, like its telephone lines, could be rented regardless of the nature of the communications. WEAF would create none of its own programming. Instead, it would lease air time to anyone who wanted to pay for it. In effect, the telephone company was putting out the call for the first infomercial.

The response was slow in coming. Finally, on August 28, 1922, from 5 to 5:30 P.M., the Queensboro Corporation went on the WEAF airwaves to promote the sale of its new Nathaniel Hawthorne apartments in Jackson Heights, Queens. To keep the commercial appeal from being too blatant, the announcer provided a short account of Nathaniel Hawthorne and his accomplishments. Within a few weeks, toll broadcasts followed from Tidewater Oil and American Express. WEAF moved from its address on Walker Street to a more sumptuous building on Broadway, and the idea began to gather steam.

With the toll station, advertising gained its first foothold in the modern technological drama—and so, for that matter, did the mountebank, none the worse for wear as he arrived at the radio microphone. Much like his predecessor on the trestle stages of Venice, the radio pitchman appeared amid a jumbled dramatic presentation, using masterful flights of rhetoric to cajole his audience into purchasing the latest goods. He was the purveyor of the commercial drama, scourge of the eighteenth-century clergy—only now his voice was being piped directly into the private spaces that the church had once so assiduously protected.

When the mountebank could infiltrate the private home, the American story was being turned inside out. Nevertheless, these radio pitchmen operated under greater limitations than the mountebanks ever had. For one thing, they were not masters of the show. In fact, they were simply hired actors, with no influence on the products they touted, and only a marginal say in the writing of their pitch. As they worked their wiles on the listener, the real controls lay in the boardrooms, where production schedules were determined.

For the moment, the radio pitchmen could not be direct about their intentions, either. While the mountebanks of old had devised various payment schemes—from *saltimbanchis* flipping off the stage to money-back guarantees ("For the poor, Gratis")—radio announcers could only insinuate their message and hope that the listener would catch on. But that would change soon enough. Surrogates the radio pitchmen would remain, but before long they would be blatantly hawking every product imaginable over the air waves.

Direct advertising came about in part because corporations like RCA were able to exert influence over the government, but it also came about because they discovered an alternative to Gilbreth's punishing micro-motion studies: the gift of song.

Workers may not have cared to have their every move analyzed, but they quite enjoyed participating in company-sponsored spectacles as actors and singers in their own right, especially when those spectacles paid homage to the war effort. And as these spectacles came to be performed on radio, they left no part of life untouched. The worker was the listener, the listener was the worker, and in the end no one could remember what was really so wrong with direct advertising in the first place.

The roots of employer-sponsored music run fairly deep. During the Centennial Exposition of 1876, department-store owner John Wanamaker had been inspired to install an organ in the rotunda of his Philadelphia store. Wanamaker employees soon developed the habit of opening the store with a round of their favorite hymns and tunes. Out of this practice a store chorus was formed.

Few people bothered to imitate this practice at first. It took World War I, with its attending low morale, for workers to seek uplift through melody on a large scale. But by the 1920s, department-store groups were booming. The Wanamaker stores, for their part, boasted the John Wanamaker Cadet Choir of four-hundred voices: a chorus made up of "cash girls, wrappers, pneumatic-tube girls, and sales people"; the J. W. C. I. Military Band; a girls' band; a bugle corps; a bagpipe band; and a band made up of "40 colored employees."

Other department stores were nearly as prolific. Strawbridge & Clothier had a choral society and an operatic society, which gave a theatrical performance of *Pirates of Penzance* in 1923 for the Japanese Relief Fund. In Boston, Filene's store had a twenty-four-piece orchestra, an "animal presentation of musical comedy," a military band, and a dance orchestra. The list goes on and on: Woodward & Lathrop, Marshall Field, L. Bamberger & Company, Kaufmann's, the Joseph Horne Company, Abraham & Straus, F. C. Nash, L. S. Ayres, Hutzler Brothers, the Herbst store, the Meyers store, and the Rhodes brothers' stores all had musical outfits of one kind or another.

These groups were not designed merely for the worker's enjoyment.

Music in the workplace was seen as a tonic to fatigue and an inspiration to loyalty. Much like Gilbreth's forboding autostereochronocycleograph, the work song was meant to increase productivity. The difference was that it actually did. The beneficent effects extended to the customers as well, as music dramatized the department-store experience and made them more productive shoppers. Behind the plate-glass windows, it seemed, a world of goods vibrated with bonhomie.

Many department-store musical groups performed as Wanamaker's employees had—in the store, before and after hours, as a way of uplifting morale. Clark again marks the origins of the "singing employee" craze in his description of events at the R. H. Macy department store:

> Ever since the war, this store has been fairly active as to community singing, under various leaders. This writer has had a pleasant personal experience as a leader of the singing at store rallies held there during recent years. These have been chiefly in connection with special sales drives. For these occasions the employees report a few minutes earlier than usual and assemble underneath the mezzanine skirting the main floor. The equipment for the sing consists of a small orchestra and an amplifying system. After fifteen minutes of lively singing there is always a talk by one of the store executives, and then a stanza of "America." Afterwards, one can sense throughout the store an atmosphere of energizing animation as the doors are opened to the customers.

Department-store groups gradually diversified their activities, giving formal concerts, holding dinners, presenting awards. Wanamaker's even set up schools in which workers could be readied for musical service. Macy's was probably best known not for its before-hours renditions of "America," but for its annual musical show called the *Red Star Revue*, in which the "damsels of the store" took part in a theatrical presentation by and for Macy's employees. Though the public was not invited to these stage shows, the publicity department saw to it that photographs were taken of the proceedings for the Sunday supplements of New York papers.

The listening public *was* soon privy to these soothing tones, however. Sometime in December 1922, Macy's paid for programming on AT&T's WEAF station—the brand-new toll station—with a show featuring Santa Claus and "other seasonal characters then stalking the halls of the giant store at Herald Square." This program in itself was not terribly auspicious, except that it married the domestic spectacle of radio to the economic spectacle of the department store. From the home to the store and back again, the brand name was bouncing through the ionosphere.

This connection soon became commonplace. The chorus from Shepard's store of Boston sang regularly on WNAC in the 1920s. Its counterpart at the Scruggs, Vandervoort, Barney store in St. Louis delivered Christmas carols on KMOX. When the Joseph Horne Company Chorus (of the eponymous Pittsburgh department store) sang for wounded soldiers at the U.S. veteran's hospital in Aspinwall (Panama), it was heard over the airwaves of WCAE and Westinghouse's famous KDKA. The A. Harris & Company store of Dallas went so far as to send out postcards to favored customers before radio concerts that featured its choral club and orchestra. Such advertising might not have been "direct," but it was perilously close to it.

Meanwhile, factory workers were learning to warble over the airwaves as well. The idea of providing entertainment outlets for factory workers had been dormant ever since Samuel Colt set up Charter Oak Hall in the mid-nineteenth century. But as with department-store music, the idea was taken up with greater vigor as the specter of war approached. In 1915, Thomas Edison installed phonographs in factories to relieve fatigue. Around the same time, a cigarette factory employed three musicians to play from a platform while three hundred women rolled cigarettes by hand. At Westinghouse, music to labor by was born when workers testing radio parts discovered that prolonged exposure to melodic strains lightened their load. After the war, General Electric continued to use the pianos and phonographs left over from their morale-building days to broadcast music once or twice a week throughout the Schenectady shops.

Like their department-store cousins, factory workers did not confine themselves to listening. As early as 1910, the International Harvester Company, Cyrus McCormick's progeny, had started a chorus that performed at the Ziegfeld Theater. By the late 1920s, this practice was virtually ubiquitous. In 1929, United States Steel could count no fewer than twelve bands, eleven orchestras, nine glee clubs, and four choruses.

It was common for factory groups to perform on the radio, but it was probably Remington Typewriter that made the final jump into direct advertising. In 1926, the Electric Light Commission built a band shell in Ilion, New York, in a park dedicated—naturally—to the veterans of the World War. The Remington company built a studio in its cafeteria, and for the next two years, the Remington Typewriter Company Band was broadcast once a week on WGY. Letters expressing listener approval came from as far as Canada, England, and South America.

At the end of the decade, the conductor of the Remington band, Edwin Daniels, freely admitted to using the dreaded direct-advertising technique. "The broadcasting," said Daniels, "is, of course, connected with the advertising department of this company and Mr. A. C. Reiley, the advertising manager, is greatly interested in our band's efforts."

As both audience and actor, factory and department-store workers came to identify radio as a self-contained world of technological entertainments. And this world was growing by leaps and bounds. By 1925, there were 563 stations. On September 9, 1926, the National Broadcasting Company was incorporated (merging RCA, General Electric, and Westinghouse radio concerns together) and inaugurated its Red and Blue networks. The Columbia Broadcasting System, formed by Columbia Records, came the following year. The networks, which broadcast from affiliated stations across the country, were too strong a lure for advertisers to resist. When NBC president Merlin Aylesworth appeared before a Senate committee in 1930, he defined direct advertising as "stating prices."

Once workers had paved the way, the pitchmen had plenty of room in which to operate. Testifying before the Federal Communications Commission in 1935, an implausibly named Dr. Cramp espoused the view that "impressionable young people do not, as a rule, read 'patent medicine' advertisements in newspapers or magazines. These same people can hardly avoid listening to the 'patent medicine' ballyhoo that comes into their homes over the radio."

Cramp complained specifically about a number of products, including Alka-Seltzer, Peruna (a tonic for stimulating digestion, containing 18 percent alcohol), Crazy Crystals, Willard Tablets, and Ex-Lax, "the delicious chocolate laxative that will not form a habit." At the time, six out of nine of the top spenders in radio advertising were medico-cosmetic companies. Procter & Gamble, Colgate-Palmolive-Peet, Bayer's Aspirin, California Syrup of Figs, Fletcher's Castorina, ZBT Baby Powder, Dr. Lyon's Tooth Powder, Anacin, Bisodol, Kolynos, Lady Esther Company, and Pepsodent—all plied their trade in the ether.

Even those who proffered goods unrelated to pharmaceuticals found themselves behaving like latter-day medicine men. In 1925, Alfred P. Sloan of General Motors had introduced the annual model car, which was sold as new whether it really was or not. With this, the corporations absconded with yet another element from the inventor's show; planned variety reappeared as planned obsolescence. By the 1930s, even Ford, the champion of the all-purpose automobile, capitulated and was advertising his own yearly models through the Ford Victory Hour radio program.

The age-old tradition of the mountebank show had returned with greater vigor than ever, but it was no longer an unregulated spectacle. It was a front for private interests—a front, in fact, for the corporate procession of Lent. For the first time, the economizing forces of society were *manufacturing* Carnival, even as they organized their production schedules for maximum thriftiness. Moreover, commercial radio was a continuous parade—and had to be, in order to safeguard the continuing growth of the corporations themselves. Everybody remembered the war, everybody played a part, and the conflict between technological disorder and control found its most stable form in American history.

But the corporate show was stable only because one figure was left out of it. While the eloquent oratories of the patent-medicine man pulsed through the air, the actual inventors of the wares he promoted were laboring at the far end of the production chain, stripped of their names and concealed from the public view.

On May 20, 1924, the *New York Times* ran a headline on the front page that read "Pictures by Wire Sent With Success For The First Time." The full-page article inside described the culmination of a project by AT&T, in which a picture was sent from Cleveland to New York, then developed only forty-four minutes after it had been taken. Most important, however, was the fact that this achievement was overtly celebrated for having no tangible inventor behind it.

> The demonstration was anonymous, as far as the names of the engineers and other employees of the telephone company were concerned. It was said that so many engineers and scientists had cooperated in developing the new process that it would be unfair to mention a few names only and difficult to apportion the credit among those who played a part . . . It was not a case of one man coming forward with a great discovery that cut the Gordian knot.

This announcement served formal notice that theatrics from inventors would not be indulged in peacetime any more than they had been during the war. Babies weaned in sideshows, men illuminated by fire, these were actions fraught with risk, and risk was a thing of the past.

It is interesting in this respect to speculate what might have happened if Joseph Henry had publicized his radio experiments in the 1840s. Would such an action have hastened the development of radio? And would Samuel Colt have subsequently used radio at Charter Oak Hall, setting a precedent that preempted the stage-oriented triumphs of the golden age?

The question is moot of course, but it remains useful for pointing out the effect of the developments in the home, the store, and the workplace in the 1920s. By selling radio, and then selling the factory and the department store, the corporations had categorically stolen the show. Against such a formidable juggernaut, the show inventor, who at this point had to make do with the pejorative label of "outside" inventor, could do nothing but make increasingly futile gestures.

General Squier, for one, watched WEAF ply its infomercials on the strength of the wire-wireless technology that he had invented, and he knew that one battle had been lost. But he had yet to surrender. Seeking to create a niche for himself, he learned how to send radio signals through electrical power lines, and in 1922, with this technology in hand, he organized Wired Radio, Inc., as a subsidiary of the North American Company, a Cleveland-based utility concern. In part, he saw Wired Radio as an answer to increasingly crowded airwaves. More important, by offering programming on request—essentially, a dial-a-tune service—he hoped to compete with the wireless sets being put out by RCA.

North American began conducting experiments in Ampere, New Jersey, and got far enough by 1930 to conduct a test run. That year, the Cleveland Electric Illuminating Company piped a choice of dance music or news (on three channels) from its substation into households in the old Lakeland area of Cleveland, and into a new domain for industrial music: restaurants and hotel dining rooms. The cost, $1.50 a month.

In 1933, Squier was still sufficiently optimistic to pen a tract titled *Telling the World*. Dedicated to the "Telephone Girls" of World War I, the book pretended to a history of the telephone in which Squier's own inventions formed the culminating act. In the appendix, the major general waxed utopian, proposing "new words for the radio art."

> Radovia—A road, street or way where radio is exhibited.
> Radiocracy—A radio operated community.
> Radiopolitan—Pertaining to a radio city.
> Radiodonna—A grand opera singer who broadcasts.

Such grandiose visions were not to be, however. The first blow came when noise on the power lines made the Cleveland venture impractical and forced him to lease telephone lines from his old nemesis, AT&T. The rest came posthumously. Squier's company would outlive him (he died of pneumonia on March 24, 1934), and the music piped over his Monophone—which would come to be known as Muzak—would go on to replace the many Remington Typewriter Company Bands of the nation.

These developments were fraught with irony. Though Squier was the one to combine *music* with *Kodak* to form the famous portmanteau, he remained a strong advocate of public involvement in technology. He dedicated his original patents to the public, supported Robert Goddard's space technology, and dared to imagine a "radiopolitan" world in which ordinary citizens participated. Social control was simply not his style. In fact, it was not Squier, but his successor at Muzak, Inc., Waddill Catchings, who first engineered canned music to increase the worker's output and soothe the shopper's soul. And it was Catchings, too, who rendered Squier's lifelong battle against AT&T in vain in 1939, when he broadcast Muzak on WEAF, the very station that had used wire-wireless to bring commercial radio into being.

There would be no "radio operated communities," no "radovias" where the wireless art was celebrated. There would however, be a Radio City, and it would belong to David Sarnoff when he ascended to the presidency of RCA. And as the inventor of FM radio, Major Edwin Howard Armstrong, discovered soon enough, the zany gestures of inventors had no place in Sarnoff's world.

One of radio's great geniuses, Armstrong had much in common with Squier. Like the major general, he had a passing interest in aviation and an overriding passion for radio. Armstrong had also served in the Signal Corps during the war, a fact that technically made Squier his boss. Whether the two ever met remains an unexplored question, but if they did, they certainly would have recognized each other as kindred inventors battling against the tides.

Before the war, the bald, quietly intense Armstrong had distinguished himself by inventing the feedback, or regenerative, circuit, which made radio signals many times more powerful than they had been. During his tour of duty, he had topped that feat with the superheterodyne, the precise tuning technology that exists in some form in every radio and television today.

Much to Sarnoff's dismay, Armstrong had licensed these patents to Westinghouse, a fact that forced RCA to pay out large amounts of money for their use. Consequently, when Armstrong invented superregeneration, which promised to make radio signals even more powerful, Sarnoff negotiated directly with him to secure the patent. Armstrong would receive $200,000 and 60,000 shares of RCA stock—an enormously generous offer. Delirious with joy, Armstrong took a longpostponed tour of Europe, watching his stocks rise. On his return, his euphoria continued unabated, spurring him to a feat that would have done his *saltimbanchi* forebears proud.

In the early part of May 1923, a photographer accompanied Armstrong to the roof of RCA's twenty-three-story Aeolian Hall on Fortysecond Street. Leaving the photographer behind, Armstrong then climbed one of the twin 115-foot towers that projected from the roof. Each of these towers had a 36-foot-long crossarm, with wires connecting them. As the photographer shot away, Armstrong swung from the crossarm by his legs, then climbed up to the iron ball at its peak and performed a handstand. Proud of his gymnastic flourish, he sent the photos to Sarnoff.

In the very same year, the actor Harold Lloyd attained posterity by hanging from a clockface in the movie *Safety Last*. But hanging from a radio tower was apparently a different matter. "If you have made up your mind that this mundane universe of ours," wrote Sarnoff to Armstrong, "is not a suitable place for you to be spending your time in, I don't want to quarrel with your decision, but keep away from the Aeolian Hall Towers or any other property of Radio Corporation. . . . I don't want you to take this letter as a joke because I am perfectly serious about it."

Officially barred from a building that existed in large part because of his inventions, Armstrong disregarded Sarnoff's warnings and, on May 15, climbed the tower again. He balanced high over Manhattan, his hat pulled down low, defiantly surveying the scene spread out before him. Model Ts and Cadillacs coursed the avenues below. The lights twinkled in a dense matrix of human endeavor. The photographer snapped away.

Show inventors had beheld many aerial views in the past century and a half—Fulton his panorama, Otis his elevated Manhattan, Muybridge his outlook onto Yosemite Valley, the Wrights the open stretches of North Carolina. This was to be the last of them, or at least the last to

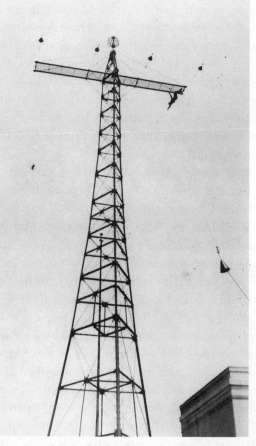

In 1923, inventor Edwin Howard Armstrong decided on the spur of the moment to climb the radio tower atop RCA's Aeolian Hall and engage in some acrobatics four hundred feet in the air while a photographer documented the stunt. *Columbia University Libraries*

have a triumphant tone. Thirty-one years later, on the losing end of a protracted battle against Sarnoff over his own FM radio technology, Armstrong put on an overcoat, a scarf, and pair of gloves, removed the air conditioner from his thirteenth-floor apartment in New York City, and jumped—the first famous American inventor to commit suicide since John Fitch poisoned himself in 1798. (Sarnoff's first reaction upon hearing the news was to say: "I did not kill Armstrong.")

Everything about the 1920s portended the end for show inventors. Yet in the mysterious calculus of drama, until the corporate show was truly complete, the demonstration of an important invention by a ramshackle character was still possible. Indeed, even as the AT&T engineers flatly predicted that television "would never happen" (in the same *Times* article that described the company's success in sending photographs by wire), such a figure was preparing its unveiling.

The name John Logie Baird is not likely to elicit nods of recognition from the average Californian or midwesterner. Anyone inquiring about him at the Museum of Television and Radio in New York is apt to receive a blank stare. Yet Baird's story is so central to American technological culture that it cannot properly be left out. Not only has the invention he pioneered come to influence almost every aspect of life in the United States, but as one who earned the nickname "Personality Joe" for a reason, he was also the last best hope that show inventors might leave their imprint on American society. After all, whoever controlled television would control the most important show of all.

John Logie Baird was born 1888 and raised in Helensburgh, Scotland, near Glasgow. As a child, he showed an interest in photography, aviation, and the usual show inventor's scripts; even after he had grown up, he was able to recite Goethe's *Faust* and much of *Macbeth* and *Hamlet*.

After graduating from the Royal Technical College in Glasgow, Baird suffered a spate of Dickensian engineering jobs, to which he forever attributed his poor health. But it was only when he became assistant mains engineer at the Clyde Valley Company that his true character began to surface. In 1919, he tried to make diamonds by electrifying carbon, and ended up replaying a Tesla scene in miniature. "There was a dull thud from the pot, a cloud of smoke," he once reminisced, "and then the main current-breaker tripped and the whole power supply went off. Thereafter I was regarded as a dangerous character."

Indeed, Baird continued to provide thought-provoking sights after that. One day, his landlady stumbled upon the inventor—a lean young man with wire-rimmed glasses and a stylish shock of hair on his brow—sitting in his chair, a wad of toilet paper wrapped around his feet. A man whose feet were forever cold, he had developed the habit of wrapping them in newspaper before donning socks and shoes. Toilet paper, he thought, might make for a more marketable material.

Baird was quite serious about this remedy. Eventually he went to Hinckley, Leicestershire—bustling hub of gentlemen's hosiery—ordered six unbleached, half-hose samples and sprinkled them with borax. Satisfied with the result, he took an office at 196 Vincent Street in Glasgow and advertised in the *People's Friend*: "The Baird Undersock—medicated, soft, absorbent, worn under the ordinary sock, keeps the feet warm in winter and cool in summer. Ninepence per pair, post free."

When Baird received exactly one order, he redoubled his efforts. He put an ad in the *Glasgow Herald*, asking for "travellers," meaning traveling salesmen. He put sandwich boards on women and proudly announced the "First sandwich women in Glasgow." When Scottish retailers were still slow to sell the Baird Undersock, he took a page from Barnum and had his friends besiege their stores. With this, the Baird Undersock went through a phase as a local fad. The managers at Clyde Valley did not like seeing one of their workers profiting so much on a personal project, but before they could fire him, Baird quit.

Footloose and, for the first time, in a position to expand his horizons, Baird came in contact with a childhood friend, Godfrey Harris, who urged him to go to Trinidad. Harris's tales of tropical climes sounded like opportunity knocking, so the sock man promptly closed his company with a profit of sixteen hundred pounds and left for the New World.

It seems that Baird planned to spend his stay in Trinidad as a wholesaler. It also seems to have been a misguided adventure from the start. After three weeks, he managed to sell five pounds of safety pins, but that was about the size of it. The inevitable fever hit him, and in the throes of it, he decided to set up a jam factory.

Baird commenced operations with two locals, known to history only as Ram Roop and Tony. As soon as they started to boil the jam, thousands upon thousands of insects descended on the pot, astounded by their good luck. Soon, the team was overrun with cockroaches, spiders, and insects that defied categorization.

When Baird came down with another fever and no interest in his jam developed whatsoever, he returned to England, his head hung low. Taking a small shop at 166 Lupus Street in London, he offered his mango chutney and guava jelly to a nation very much accustomed to the finest jams in the world. In the end, he sold the lot for fifteen pounds, to a butcher who used it to stuff sausages.

Downtrodden and miserable, Baird took a room in a Bloomsbury boardinghouse. His life there was a far cry from that of a Glaswegian engineer. A constant stream of transients tried to interest him in patent medicines. An offer to trade in iron buckets resulted in something close to a shakedown. The only moderately successful venture from this period was Baird's Speedy Cleaner, which was not necessarily a very good brand of soap, but as Baird pointed out, it didn't cost much either.

Fortunately, at this point, another childhood friend reappeared to offer thoughtful advice. Guy Robertson, known to his friends as "Mephy" (which, in the time-honored link between inventors and Faust, was short for "Mephistopheles"), convinced Baird to get out of Bloomsbury and retreat to Hastings. Sick as ever, Baird sold his soap company for two hundred pounds. The two of them moved into a flat on Queen's Avenue, or Queen's Arcade, opposite the Leighton Brothers photographers and above an artificial-flower shop. Apparently, the architecture left them highly exposed to the public, because they soon aroused interest among the locals by walking around the flat sockless, eating nothing but buns with tea.

No socks and no jam—and no immediate change in fortunes, either. Baird's first project at Hastings was a glass razor, an idea that came to a swift end when he cut his face badly. Next he tried pneumatic shoes and "walked a hundred yards in a succession of drunken and uncontrollable lurches, followed by a few delighted urchins" before one of the balloon inserts in his shoes burst.

But in the end Hastings looked kindly on Baird. One day, rummaging around for a new project, he recalled some experiments he had conducted before the war, when he still considered himself an engineer. He decided to resume where he had left off, this time availing himself of the recent advances in vacuum-tube technology.

Inventors had been trying their hands at television for many years. Tesla, of course, had entertained the idea of television as a thought-transference machine, but most inventors confined themselves to the more attainable goals offered by the Nipkow disk. Devised in 1880 by a German named Paul Nipkow, this disk was little more than a circle with holes arranged in a spiral pattern. When it was spun, however, any light passing through it was dissected and carried by a selenium cell to a sister disk, which reversed the process and reproduced the particulars of the original light.

Max Dieckmann of Germany and Boris Rosing of St. Petersburg were among the early inventors who used the Nipkow disk in an attempt to "see by wireless." By the 1920s, a Russian named Vladimir Zworykin and Charles Jenkins of Ohio were also making progress. And so, for that matter, were the AT&T engineers, despite their having predicted that television would never happen. In fact, in 1924, just after the company had successfully sent photographs over telephone lines, Dr. Herbert E.

Ives, an engineer at AT&T, was asked to draw up plans for television research. On January 23, 1925, Ives submitted his proposal and received funding. (As per corporate protocol, Ives never won the recognition he deserved. Neither did his staff: Frank Gray, John R. Hofele, Robert C. Mathes, and Ralph V. L. Hartley.)

The last great inventor's contest was fated to have many contestants, even a few who had the might of a corporation behind them. Still, no one went about it the way Baird did. Improvising as best he could in his Hastings flat, he used, among other things, a tea chest, a "bull's-eye" lens from a local cycle shop, sealing wax, glue, surplus army wire, knitting needles, a hat box, a serrated biscuit tin, an ordinary lamp, and an electric fan. With this Rube Goldberg assemblage, the resourceful inventor defied all expectations and, probably in 1922, sent the silhouette of a Maltese across a distance of two feet.

Baird received a little money for this achievement, but not enough to get very far, so on June 27, 1923, he advertised in the personals of the *Times of London:* "Seeing by Wireless—Inventor of apparatus wishes to hear from someone who will assist (not financially) in making working models. Write Box . . . The Times, E.C.4."

Apparently, the ad created the desired effect, because on April 3, 1924, an article by F. H. Robinson appeared in *Kinematograph Weekly.* One of the earliest printed references to a working television, "The Radio Kinema" described an experiment in which Robinson saw "the letter 'H,' and the fingers of my own hand reproduced . . . across the width of the laboratory."

Unlike AT&T's negative predictions for television, made a month and a half later to the *New York Times,* Baird avidly seconded the belief voiced in Robinson's article "that no technical difficulties stand in the way of the transmission of moving images by wireless." Responding to this pledge of success, the fledgling radio company BBC expressed interest. More important, a man named Will Day bought a third interest for two hundred pounds. Baird used the money to buy an assortment of lamps.

Television work could be as perilous as the glass-razor business at times. As shoppers strolled along Queen's Arcade one day, they saw a flash of light emanate from Baird's flat, followed by a noisy fall. A crowd gathered, speculating about what had happened to this interloper in their midst. Someone finally gained entry into the flat and found Baird unconscious, felled by a surge of 2,000 volts.

When an article came out detailing this "Serious Explosion in Hastings Laboratory," Baird's landlord, Mr. Twigg, decided that the inventor was a liability and told him to pack his bags. Baird ignored the order. Soon afterward, Twigg saw him working in his lab in plain view and waved his arms as if to say, "What are you doing here?" When Baird turned his back to Twigg, the crowd—seemingly everpresent in the Baird literature—erupted in peals of laughter. In plunging his hands into his pockets, Baird had ripped the back seam of his pants.

The spirit of commedia dell'arte was alive and well in the Hastings flat, but the landlord prevailed and Baird was compelled to return to London, this time to 22 Frith Street, where Will Day had offered him a lab. Again he met with reservations. Somewhere around 1925, he tried to solicit the interest of the Marconi corporation, only to be told they had no interest whatsoever. When he was invited to see an editor at a London paper, one newspaperman saw him arrive at the office and cried out, "Watch him; he may have a razor on him!"

Meanwhile, Baird's competition in the United States had gone a different route and was receiving better treatment as a result. Charles Jenkins in particular was being lauded for transmitting silhouettes at the navy radio station NOF to an audience made up of government officials and his assistant, D. McFarlan Moore. But Baird's star began to rise again when Gordon Selfridge offered him twenty pounds a week to give three shows a day in his London department store.

Spanning three weeks in April 1925, the Selfridge demonstrations drew long queues of spectators, most of whom were shoppers, though the occasional scientist dropped in to sate his curiosity. One woman balked, asking Baird's assurance that the machinery wouldn't damage the racks of clothing nearby. The rest simply looked into the funnel and, by way of a crude wireless transmitter, saw the outlines of objects that stood a few yards away.

After the Selfridge demonstrations, Baird's former classmate Jack Buchanan, now a musical star of the West End and Broadway, threw a party for him at Romano's restaurant. Tired and ill once again, Baird nevertheless had cause to be optimistic. His performances had prompted a cousin to forward him five hundred pounds, and this money would allow him to take his most important step.

On October 25, 1925, Baird used his new "flying-spot" mechanism—a modification in the way the light passed through the Nipkow disk—to televise what most experts agree was the first image with a full range of half-tones. Fittingly for a show inventor, he chose the leering face of "Stukey Bill," a ventriloquist's dummy, to be television's first star. Unable to contain his excitement, he immediately buttonholed a young office boy, William Taynton, who worked in the building. Moments, later, Taynton became the first living face seen on a television screen.

Television was out from the shadows.

On January 27, 1926, Baird unveiled his half-tone television for more than forty members of the Royal Institution, where Humphry Davy had gassed his socialite audiences so long ago. In full evening dress, a pride of eminent scientists and their wives climbed three flights of narrow stone stairs, then stood in a cramped, drafty passage while groups of six were led into two tiny attic rooms. Here, a picture made up of thirty lines, seven inches high by three inches wide, traveled through a wall to a receiver on the other side.

Of course, no bona fide inventor's show was complete without the age-old dynamic of disorder giving way to order. In Baird's demonstration, this took place when one hirsute gentleman peered a little too close to the fascinating device and found his long white beard being sucked into it. Fortunately, he was rescued in time. A few minutes later, he approached the camera again and had the pleasure of seeing his face—and most of his whiskers—on a television screen.

The Royal Institution demonstration, like so many live shows, had a pronounced and charismatic effect. Afterward, the press responded enthusiastically, publishing accounts of "Magic in a Garret" and the "Young Scotsman's Magic Eye." As always when a demonstration was involved, some accused Baird of hiding a boy in the box, harking back to the automaton chess players of yore. But the reality of television could no longer be denied with any conviction.

The next chapter in Baird's career offers a particularly revealing example of how the inventor's show could lead to an outpouring of diverse inventions. According to the television historian Albert Abramson, Baird's system had a fatal weakness. While he was inarguably the first to demonstrate the flying spot technology, others were developing their own flying spot independently of him. Thus, although Baird could have patented his version, the chances of defending his claims in court were slight. (Some scholars have also suggested that Baird's television of 1926 contained a secret device at its heart, though Baird himself did not support this claim.)

Having exposed his invention to the public, then, Baird risked exposing the workings of his flying spot. His response, Abramson says, was to take a page from John Keely, the old-time master of misdirection, and whip up "a profusion of equipment made for publicity purposes only," making sure that certain models were "often re-built or relabeled so as not to reveal the real apparatus."

What exactly were these publicity-generating machines? Soon after his landmark 1926 demonstration, Baird transmitted images that had been filmed in darkness. (For this contribution to infrared television, he used a light bulb covered with a thin coat of ebonite. Sir Oliver Lodge, present in the next Royal Institution entourage, liked it, but complained of the heat.) In 1926, he invented an early prototype of fiber optics and received British Patent no. 285,738. That same year, he obtained the first television license, with the call letters 2TV. On January 26, 1927, he filed for a patent on a magnetic recording system capable of recording a single frame or of playing back a recording at high speed—the ancestor of videotape, complete with recording and playback heads. For someone trying to distract the public from an indefensible invention, Baird was making quite a few contributions to the television industry that are commonly believed to have appeared much later.

Of course, it is true that Baird valued the publicity that such advances could bring. For him, television was a live medium in every sense: he appeared in person and presented instantaneous imagery to crowds. In his hands, television was immediate and alive. And on one occasion, he seemed to want to bring it to life in the literal sense.

On April 7, 1927, AT&T demonstrated its version of television with the slogan "Television At Last!" The American transmission took place, as usual, using the wire-wireless system invented by George Squier. The visage of Secretary of Commerce Herbert Hoover originated in Washington, D.C., and traveled two hundred miles by wire to a two-foot screen in New York. An amateur vaudeville act followed, transmitted by radio from Whippany, New Jersey, to New York. Much was made of the thousand engineers it took to effect the demonstration.

Baird, not one to be caught short, became more public in his efforts than ever. He promptly sent an image from London to Glasgow, a distance of 483 miles. On February 9, 1928, his company made a crude transatlantic transmission from London to America. On his return aboard the *Berengaria*, Baird's assistant, Ben Clapp, received a picture of Miss Dora Selvy, fiancée of the ship's radio operator. A photograph arriving in the middle of the Atlantic caused considerable stir among the passengers.

But it was on the following day, back in London, that Baird worked up his most unlikely experiment of all. On February 10, 1928, he contrived to procure a human eye from a London surgeon. "As soon as I was given the eye," Baird recalled,

> I hurried in a taxicab to the laboratory. Within a few minutes I had the eye in the machine. Then I turned on the current and the waves carrying television were broadcast from the aerial. The essential image passed through the eye within a half an hour after the operation. On the following day the sensitiveness of the eye's visual nerve was gone. The optic was dead. . . . Nothing was gained from the experiment. It was gruesome and a waste of time.

With that idea out of his system, Baird turned to publishing. "The World's First Television Journal" was *Television*, a monthly magazine put out by the Television Society, of which Baird was a member. The debut issue, in March 1928, revealed these cover slugs:

> All About Television, the Invisible Ray, etc. etc.
> Also an exclusive Constructor article/How to make a Simple
>    "TELEVISOR"/fully described in this issue.
> How to Make a Selenium Cell/and other interesting features.

Here was an appeal that harked back to the do-it-yourself days of the previous century. Rather than selling premade sets, Baird's approach was to turn his customers into active participants. One is hard-pressed to see how secretive he could have been if he was teaching the public to build its own sets!

In any event, AT&T was catching up fast. The telephone company achieved daylight television—using sunlight rather than artificial light—on May 10, 1928. AT&T engineer Ives expected to reveal this advance to the public in three or four weeks. When, on the other side of the Atlantic, Baird demonstrated the daylight television on June 18, the major British newspapers did not cover the event, leaving three reporters from his own magazine to publish the results. In July, he surpassed himself and transmitted *color* television in a closed circuit in his lab. "We found that strawberries came out particularly well," he remarked with typical good humor, "and they were popular with the staff." But again, it was *Television* that reported the event, in two articles written by J. C. Wilson.

A career peak came on July 28, 1929, when Baird televised a per-

In 1922, John Logie Baird built the world's first working television from, among other things, a hat box, a tea-biscuit tin, knitting needles, and army surplus wire. He went on to improve his television and to give demonstrations of it at department stores and theaters. *Science & Society Picture Library*

formance from the Coliseum, in London's Charing Cross theater district, to those who had bought his sets. The bill illustrates Baird's abiding interest in showmanship. Three shows daily (at 2:15, 5:15, and 8:15 P.M.) featured M. Santiago; A Fete at the Royal Hunting Box; The Bird of Paradise, A Poem of Artistry, Color and Movement; Allison Troupe of Nine Acrobatic Wonders; Chris Charlton, Europe's Illusionist; Beryl Beresford, The Cheerful and Tearful Comedienne; and two editions of British Movietone News.

After the Charing Cross performance, Baird never again did as well. When the BBC television station 2LO went on the air on September 30, 1929, public acceptance of television grew even more. Baird himself was never associated with the station, however. A rift developed between him and John Reith, founder of the BBC and a friend of Baird's from childhood. The discord only grew worse as time wore on, and eventually Baird was forced to operate an independent station out of a building at 133 Long Acres, where the admiralty at Whitehall complained of interference on their radio frequencies.

Cut adrift, Baird demonstrated his television in Parisian theaters and saw the French press deride it as "The Bombastic Phantom." Back in

England, he aired one of the first teleplays, a vignette called *Box and Cox*. In 1932, he broadcast the Epsom Derby live to the Metropole Cinema fourteen miles away. A packed house watched the immense, nine-by-six-foot screen as the race commenced, and Baird recalled that "when Optimist the winner was seen flashing past the post, the demonstration ended with thunderous applause." Horses, theaters, ovations—the age-old obsessions of the show inventors seemed to live again for a moment.

But the moment quickly vanished. In 1929, while AT&T and Baird were battling for the television prize, David Sarnoff had quietly hired Vladimir Zworykin, recently emigrated from St. Petersburg, to develop an all-electronic television system. By 1933, Zworykin was able to report success. In the subsequent years, a brilliant and unobtrusive inventor from Utah, Philo T. Farnsworth, laid claim to the same achievement, but the end result was the same. The early contestants were blindsided, and RCA, having cornered the market on the electronic versions of both Zworykin and Farnsworth, emerged as the preeminent power in American television.

With Baird's defeat, the reign of the show inventors was effectively over. There would continue to be colorful shows, important inventors, and high-profile performers, but very few indeed who succeeded in combining all three of these attributes into one career. The ranks were scattered, the world was forgetting, a tradition was dying away.

Baird continued to work on television for the rest of his life. During the Second World War, he experimented with electronic and 3-D television, and transmitted a secret television system from the towers of the London Crystal Palace. After the war, he spoke optimistically of the use of television in theaters, and openly discussed the possibility of using television to explore mysteries of spiritualism. At times, an assistant might stumble into a room and find "Personality Joe" deep in a yogic trance. But as interesting as he continued to be, the last best hope for the show inventors had drifted to the sidelines. The BBC tacitly acknowledged as much by failing to utter his name over its air waves until an announcer read his obituary in 1946.

AT&T was also excluded from broadcasting television, but it was not destined to be excluded from its transmission. Having built an empire from the all-important wire, it developed a new telephone line capable of transmitting superhigh frequencies. The improved picture definition that this line provided emboldened radio stations around the country to begin building television stations, and the idea of a national network suddenly seemed viable.

And so on April 20, 1939, David Sarnoff stood in a light wind outside the RCA Exhibits Building at the New York World's Fair. It had been a cold spring, and the few trees that dotted the grounds had yet to put forth buds. A camera dollied up to the makeshift lectern, capturing Sarnoff's beneficent face and beaming it to a row of receivers inside the hall.

"Today," Sarnoff said, "we are on the eve of a new industry, based on imagination, on scientific research and accomplishment." With that, he introduced television, not for the first time but for the last.

Two years later, the first commercial television stations in the United States received their licenses. In the years to come, they would provide everything the show inventors had in the way of crass fascinations and more, causing the FCC chairman Newton Minow to deride the "procession of game shows, violence, audience participation shows, formula comedies about totally unbelievable families, blood and thunder, mayhem, sadism, violence, murder, western badmen, private eyes, gangsters, more violence and cartoons . . . and commercials, many screaming cajoling and offending." This time, however, the screamers, cajolers, and offenders were not authentic personalities saddled with strange, irrepressible dreams, but large, efficient organizations with names like General Electric and General Motors.

Two hundred years after Benjamin Franklin concealed the facts about his famous experiment, the show inventors were right back where they started—on the margins of society—even as their legacy played on and on in every American home.

*Epilogue*

# THE LAZZO OF
# THE NEW WORLD

Histoy is often summed up in a single phrase: *things change.* Why do political parties go out of favor or customs disappear? Because things change. Why do cultures die out or grow strong? Because things change. Having reached the end of my tale, I am tempted to join in and employ this phrase myself. But somehow, it is not enough for me to say that the show inventors simply rose, flourished, and faded away. To do so, I think, would be to miss the lessons that their story has to offer.

If nothing else, the show inventors had a tremendous capacity for taking what fate threw their way and making it everyone's business. This relentless airing of their psyches in public must have been taxing at times, but it also evinced a depth of morality that one strains to detect in today's celebrities. Some of the show inventors were cruel, and most were self-centered, but none of them placed themselves above ridicule. They understood themselves to be part of a narrative large enough to contain pathos, hilarity, evil, disaster, and heartache, all of which they freely bestowed on the world. In this, they were comic, in the fullest sense of the word. Their actions always presupposed a coherence beyond themselves. They believed in a happy ending.

On one level, this boundless optimism paid off. Their dreams of rockets and automobiles and movies slowly came to fruition, and as they did, the nation prospered. One cannot walk three feet in a populated area of the United States today without seeing their handiwork and without concluding that, at least in some way, the happy ending did come.

Yet on another level, their story is anything but happy, because it was one that didn't have to end. There were many moments when the show inventors could have reversed their decline. Tesla might not have become his own worst enemy. Squier might have retained the rights to his wire-wireless patents. Baird might have explored electronic television earlier. If none of these things happened, it was simply because so few inventors realized the crucial role that drama played in their careers. They had risen along with American theater, enjoying a parallel boom, yet the connection was never consciously made. Ironically, it took a noninventor, David Sarnoff, to see that drama was not just an exciting thing, it was the *only* thing.

Many causes can be cited for the show inventor's continued absence from the public discourse: the onset of the depression, the nontheatrical nature of miniaturized technology, the incremental achievements of R & D labs. But it was certainly commercial television (and subsequent additions to the corporate show, such as the theme park and the stadium-sized sponsored event) that took over the task of providing the public with a framework for understanding new technologies.

The corporate takeover of the inventor's show has had a stunning effect on the world of technology. Until the rise of the modern corporation, inventors existed in a dualistic universe. They might have enjoyed lesser or greater power, but in either case the territories were clear: the inventor approached from the kingdom of disorder, his opponent from the kingdom of order, and their meeting called for a spectacle that placed the disruptive machine within an understandable framework, which in turn eased its transition into society.

Once commercial television arrived, this dynamic was doomed. After all, the television ad, as a pitch inserted among various dramatic performances, is in many respects identical to the mountebank's banter. It uses the same elements of disorder—sexual come-ons, implausible scenarios, visions of unbridled fun—in order to sell the latest product. It has the same grating but seductive effect. Yet the result is markedly different, because instead of threatening the status quo, as did the appeals of a John Fitch or an Amos Eaton, the corporate pitch actually supports it. There is no disorder to be muted, only disorder to be simulated, behind which stability prevails.

Indeed, in the past half century, corporate stability has come to dictate the introduction of major inventions so regularly as to suggest a dogma. The computer was revived from the depths of the nineteenth century to unburden engineers of the complex calculations needed to improve long-distance power and telephone lines. The transistor was born of the desire to renovate AT&T's cumbersome switching systems. Today, new computer hardware arrives on the market with such regularity as to suggest a highly sophisticated rationing schedule. Everywhere the lesson is the same. The invention that benefits the large corporation, for one reason or another, is an invention that will find its way into the stores. The invention that does not, will not.

So the show goes on, with its very real conservative agenda and its outward message of disarray. In its dazzle and glare, America has come to exist in an atmosphere of permanent Carnival even as it abides by the rules of a totalizing system of Lent. Our disbelief is suspended at all times, even as the bottom line rules. We have become the most hedonist of Stoics.

Meanwhile, the inventor—the real voice of disarray—has been marginalized to a degree that is truly amazing. To find a comparable situation, you would have to imagine a world in which no one knew the names of the latest pop musicians. But so it is. How many people know who invented the microwave oven, or patented the first genetically engineered mouse? This is not the place to explore the lives of the great inventors of the Cold War era; it would take another book to do their stories justice. Suffice it to say that twentieth-century geniuses of the machine have generally become famous to the degree that they have failed. Like Master Carnival dealt the fatal blow by Lady Lent, they have been able to offer little more than their "credits not yet acquired" and "property not yet bought," in the form of inventions that have never seen the light of day.

And more and more, even this last gesture has been denied them. As time goes by, the names of inventors have traced a line of diminishing renown. The trend that began with Goddard, Mallmann, and Armstrong follows a long arc, at the end of which stand the late-night avatars of the infomercial and Jack Marchand, wandering the streets of New York with his briefcase full of visions.

As a columnist writing about patents, I have had occasion to interview many inventors. They come in all shapes and sizes, and all sorts of temperaments, but they all have considerably lower expectations than, say, Hiram Maxim, who announced the arrival of a "totally different breed." Sometimes, they are genuinely unstable, their outlook darkened by fears of conspiracy. Whether such conspiracies are true is beside the point. Many inventors today remain in a more or less permanent state of disorder, not because they are maladapted from birth, but because they are marooned in the rehearsal phase. Without access to an audience, they remain unable to enact the rite of passage that might lead both themselves and the public to a new kind of coherence. Not surprisingly, some of their inventions have taken on mythical dimensions. Does the 100-mile carburetor exist? Is there such a thing as zero-point energy? If you don't know what those terms mean, there is reason for it: the public and the inventor have been parted.

An unhappy ending indeed—unless perhaps it is not the end. Recently, an unexpected opening has appeared, first with cable television and more lately with the explosion of on-line technology. In the past few years, the Internet has achieved a sprawl of activity very much like that of the post–Civil War era, when Jules Verne could imagine Americans voting to tilt the world on its axis. After a long moratorium, anarchy has suddenly regained its voice.

The very nature of the Internet bodes well for a new paradigm. Unlike radio or television, it does not suffer from scarcity, but is open to endless contributions by people of all backgrounds and viewpoints. And as long as this is so, the age-old justification of rationing—stretching all the way back to the church of Renaissance Italy—cannot be convincingly invoked.

Cyberspace has already done exceedingly well by code writers and software companies, but does it presage a more general show inventor's revival, with an authentic audience and a true sense of risk? Perhaps. What remains to be seen is whether it will become a full-fledged dramatic medium. The signs are encouraging, since on-line technology, like theater, has the capability of being a two-way, real-time medium. In fact, in some ways it is happening as I write. Dubious merchants have become a staple of the Web, coming on like hustlers at a latterday St. Mark's Square, and here and there, the Internet is proving itself capable of producing the genuine sensation of an event. Virtual reality, as it becomes commercially available, seems especially promising as a dramatic vehicle, and perhaps it provides the most prescient image of what tomorrow holds in store. . . .

It could happen almost anywhere. You could be strolling along at a convention center, or mall, or outdoor fair. As you pass a nondescript booth, a salesperson gets your attention and implores you to try something new. Put on this headset, you are told, and a three-dimensional fantasy world will open out before you—and behind you, and beside

Tomorrow's technological dramas are taking shape in inventions such as Sim-Graphics's Mario In Real Time (MIRT) System, which, as seen here, transfers the expressions of the human face to a cartoon character on a screen. *Courtesy of SimGraphics Engineering Corp. & Nintendo America*

you. You'll find yourself in the center of a completely artificial experience. Do you dare try it out?

With some difficulty, you put on the headset. Instantly you begin to behave as if you're somewhere else altogether. You flap your arms as if to fly, pucker up to an unseen paramour—bystanders can't help but laugh at your delusionary gestures.

Is what you see faintly ridiculous? Probably. Is it transfixing? No doubt about it. A sleeked-down version of a peepshow machine has transported you into another universe, and by dint of an ancient trick, you're suddenly playing the fool. Comic and breathtaking, cruel and seductive, the Lazzo of the New World simply cannot be kept down.

# Notes

## Chapter One: Rumors of Lightning

11    *"[Master] Carnival must die"*: Winifred Smith, pp. 37–38.

13    *"These Mountebankes at one end"*: Rudlin, p. 25.

13    *An early French illustration*: Ibid., pp. 25–27.

15    *The zany was even popular*: In one English version of Goethe's masterpiece, the role of the Player is translated as "Merry Andrew."

17    *Soon he was making marionettes*: Maurice Sand writes: "There existed in the nineteenth century of Bologna a type which, like all the rest, entered the realm of marionettes . . . Usually he was the father of Columbine, and allied with the Doctor. He is the Bolognese Cassandre or Pantaloon." Sand, p. 237.

17    *two other men immediately reported*: These men were Giovan Giuseppe Veratti and a doctor named Bianchi.

18    *In 1723, a commedia dell'arte troupe*: Howard Taubman asserts this scenario on page 30 of *The Making of American Theatre*. That he calls the actors "professional players" strongly suggests that this was a commedia dell'arte troupe, which was defined by its professional status and its tendency to perform outdoors.

18    *Even so, protests continued*: For a more detailed account of this conflict, see "Difficult Territory: Philadelphia," by William Dunlap, reprinted in Nagler, pp. 513–15.

18    *the Philadelphia clergyman William Smith*: Smith was also Benjamin Franklin's avowed nemesis, at least in part because he went out of his way to try to discredit Franklin's electrical experiments.

18    *"Quacks abound like locusts in Egypt"*: McNamara, p. 6.

18    *"Be it therefore enacted by the Governor"*: Ibid., p. 8.

19    *the occasional dirty joke*: As in: "It is hard for an empty sack to stand up straight," or "A hundred Thieves cannot strip one naked man; especially if his Skin's off." Paul Leicester Ford, pp. 393–404.

19    *"upon Wax"*: Bowen, p. 53.

19      *"Chagrin'd a little"*: Ibid, p. 56.
19      *"electrical Jack, before a Fire"*: Ibid.
20      *"a Dangerous Man"*: Seavey, p. 159.
20      *"a Shower of Sand"*: Cohen, *Franklin's Experiments*, p. 406.
20      *"An Experiment"*: Ibid.
21      *"To determine the question"*: Ibid., p. 23.
22      *Kant, who called Franklin*: Flatow, pp. 4–5.
22      *"more universal"*: Ibid.
23      *Scholars still debate*: Carl Van Doren, perhaps as even-handed a biographer
        of Franklin as there has been, admits that "Every simple explanation of
        the kite mystery leaves it still confounded. . . . Whether Franklin is sup-
        posed to have flown the most famous of all kites in June, or later, or
        never, little is known about him during this mysterious time." Van Doren,
        pp. 167–68.
24      *After all, a man climbing*: In fact, Christ Church was conducting a lottery
        to raise the money needed to complete its steeple while Franklin was con-
        sidering it as a site. No doubt Franklin's appearance in the midst of such
        a campaign would have cast him in an unflattering promotional light.
26      *"Immense sums"*: Garrett, p. 133.
26      *"You know the just esteem"*: Meier, p. 23.
27      *"abundance of projectors"*: Hindle, p. 287.

## Chapter Two: A Passion for Privacy

28      *Jefferson described*: Dumbauld, p. 38.
30      *"Whereas, frequenting play-houses"*: Tyler, p. xii.
30      *"No cure, no pay"*: McNamara, p. 9.
31      *"I could not suppress"*: Hawke, p. 79.
31      *"It would be too much"*: Boyd, p. 241.
32      *"Nobody will believe"*: Hoopes, p. 26.
32      *The playwright Royall Tyler*: Tyler, p. 52. A closer study of this play begins
        to turn up interesting results. Not only is its title reminiscent of the *Con-
        trasto between Master Carnival and Lady Lent*, but the name *Jonathan* is
        the rough English equivalent of *Giovanni*, the origin of the word *zanni*.
33      *"the compass of the private family"*: Hawke, p. 88.
33      *"I can conceive"*: Meier, p. 29.
33      *the third in U.S. history*: The first patent went to Samuel Hopkins on
        July 31, 1790, for a new method of making pot and pearl ash.
33      *"I thought this was sufficient"*: Bathe, pp. 68–69.
34      *"to many new uses"*: Ibid., p. 69.
34      *Orukter Amphibolos*: William Lutz, who worked with Evans during this
        period, remembered years later that the Orukter Amphibolos was not the
        first steam dredge built by Evans, merely the first he brought before the
        public. Bathe, p. 110.
35      *"ridiculous project"*: Ibid., p. 66.
35      *"If the bringing together"*: Meier, p. 29.
36      *"I have labored hard"*: Mirsky, p. 133.
37      *"there is no branch of the work"*: Ibid., p. 197.
37      *"One of my primary objects"*: Merritt Roe Smith, p. 47.

37     *"by taking the first pieces"*: Ibid.

38     *"Whitney must have staged"*: Ibid., p. 48.

38     *being embarrassed*: Jefferson often saw the world through the filter of this
       particular emotion: "to embarrass society with monopolies for every utensil
       existing," he wrote, ". . . would be more injurious to them than had the
       supposed inventors never existed." Meier, p. 30.

39     *"give a pleasing and innocent direction"*: William Howard Adams, p. xxxviii.

39     *"You see that I am an enthusiast"*: From the half-title page of William
       Howard Adams's *The Eye of Thomas Jefferson*. No citation is given, except
       that Jefferson wrote this in a letter to James Madison on September 20,
       1785.

40     *"a circular picture"*: Philip, p. 89.

41     *"[p]atrons . . . become so absorbed"*: Ibid., p. 90.

41     *"Everybody goes or is going"*: Dickinson, *Robert Fulton*, p. 96.

41     *True to patrician form*: Fulton biographer Cynthia Owen Philip speculates
       on Livingston's absence: "Perhaps he thought it beneath his dignity as the
       U.S. minister plenipotentiary to be connected with a commercial venture.
       More probably he was overcome by fear the experiment would fail and
       preferred to hide his association with it." Philip, p. 148.

43     *"The young ladies were delighted"*: Ibid., p. 196.

43     *and Jefferson himself*: One of Benjamin West's students, Mather Brown,
       painted what is believed to be the first portrait of Jefferson, and went on to
       become the favorite portrait artist of John and Abigail Adams.

43     *"elegant in spotless ruffles"*: Hawke, p. 79.

44     *"I number a few"*: Reigart, p. 174.

45     *interchangeable parts at such an early date*: Interchangeability of machine
       parts, however crude, was not achieved until the 1850s.

46     *"take one third"*: Philip, p. 215.

46     *"I was desirous not only"*: Jones, p. 10.

## Chapter Three: Cross Currents

48     *"A well arranged House of Industry"*: Bradley, p. 155.

49     *"oils, wax, resinous bodies"*: Rolt, p. 120.

49     *"Thoughts upon Patents"*: For more of what Watt wrote on the subject, see
       Robinson and Musson, pp. 213–28.

50     *"I have not the least doubt"*: *Proceedings of the American Philosophical
       Society* 3, no. 27 (25–30 May, 1842), p. 105.

51     *"Nothing exists but thoughts"*: Stansfield, pp. 164–65.

51     *"Not in the ideal dreams"*: Davy, p. 97.

52     *"[W]e do not look"*: Knight, p. 42.

52     *"The sensation created by"*: Carrier., p. 66.

52     *"those eyes were made"*: Ibid., p. 63.

53     *"the globules flew"*: Johnson, p. 547.

54     *"Hence Genius draws"*: Knight, p. 51.

54     *Michael Faraday came to represent*: Both Davy and Faraday thought of
       themselves not as inventors but as "natural philosophers," but they pro-
       duced inventions nevertheless.

55    *"Every part illustrative"*: L. Pearce Williams, p. 325.

55    *"A lecturer falls deeply"*: Ibid., p. 327.

55    *"We all know how Faraday"*: Remarks from a meeting of the Institution of Electrical Engineers of London on May 16, 1889, cited in Dunlap, p. 31.

57    *"My principal patrons"*: McAllister, p. 184.

57    *"I give most of the experiments"*: Ibid.

58    *"[S]tudents shall be exercised"*: Ibid., p. 491.

58    *"apply the sciences"*: "Association of Adults for Mutual Education." *American Journal of Education* 1, no. 10 (October 1826), p. 595.

59    *"apparatus for illustrating the sciences"*: Ibid., p. 595.

59    *"It may be questioned"*: Ibid.

60    *"To embody, as far as possible"*: Bigelow, Jacob. "Art. III.—Elements of Technology, taken chiefly from a Course of Lectures delivered at Cambridge, on the Application of Sciences to the Useful Arts." *American Journal of Education* 4, no. 4 (July-August 1829), p. 318.

60    *Fanny Kemble introduced:* Kemble had been a passenger on the maiden voyage of the Liverpool & Manchester Railway and later confessed to having fallen in love with its inventor, George Stephenson.

61    *"Gentlemen will be particular"*: Trollope, p. 133.

61    *"grand colossal figure of Minos"*: Ibid., p. xxxi.

61    *"unearthly sounds, horrid groans"*: Ibid., p. xxxiii.

61    *"While the timid and ignorant"*: Ibid.

62    *"His young Norval"*: Reingold, p. xxi.

63    *"believed that there was a way"*: Ibid.

63    *"after a long and anxious mental struggle"*: Ibid., p. xxii.

63    *"though a pretty good felow"*: Coulson, p. 18.

63    *"It . . . caused me"*: Shelton, p. 29.

64    *"When classes resumed"*: Coulson, p. 63.

65    *he saw himself as the keeper of the Faraday flame:* Faraday invited Henry to lecture at the Royal Institution in later years. Henry, characteristically, turned down the offer and remained in the house.

66    *Henry didn't even want the Smithsonian:* Henry's successor, Spencer Fullerton Baird, was responsible for making museums part of the Smithsonian agenda.

66    *"contribute essentially to the increase"*: Hellman, p. 36.

66    *the Lazzaroni:* This word has no apparent etymological connection to the word *lazzo. Lazzaroni* derives from the Italian word for "wolf." The root meaning of *lazzo* is of uncertain origin but probably derives from a word meaning "sticks."

67    *"foolish speculations on Atomic theory"*: Daniels, p. 170.

67    *"The public"*: Ibid., p. 171.

## Chapter Four: The Amazing Talking Nation

70    *"first-rate disgusting"*: Frances Trollope, in her *Domestic Manners of the Americans*, gives a list of such colloquialisms in Appendix A, p. 428.

70    *"the time will come"*: Hawke, p. 62.

70    *"Whether it would be expedient"*: Cameron, p. 114.

71 *On June 1, 1831:* Cooper himself did not join this subsequent contest, but augmented his immortality some years later by inventing the gelatin dessert.

72 *"I have not the slightest doubt":* Trollope, p. 349.

72 *At least one investor:* Mack, p. 101.

72 *"it is time that":* Taubman, p. 72.

72 *This promoter had no credentials:* The methods of the early promoters are described in greater detail in McKennon, p. 25.

76 *"Scientific Amusement—Nitrous Oxide Gas":* Quoted from Rohan, pp. 36-37. For more of the endlessly colorful exploits of Samuel Colt, see Rohan's outstanding biography, *Yankee Arms Maker.*

79 *"We never beheld such an anxiety":* Ibid., p. 14.

81 *where reaper-inventor Cyrus McCormick was living:* Apparently, the two inventors did not meet at this point.

82 *asked for a thousand of his six-shooters:* Ellsworth Grant believes that Colt was making five-shooters at this time, and that the Colt six-shooter did not arrive until the 1870s. Extant drawings seem to contradict this view, however.

82 *he became the hero:* Twain, pp. 14-15. Twain wrote *Connecticut Yankee,* between jokes a kind of compendium of American technology, while trying to market an invention called the Paige typesetting machine. The venture was one of the biggest financial disasters of his life.

83 *"the honest but poor printer":* Hutton, p. 48.

84 *"Original, Aboriginal":* Ibid., p. 165.

85 *"inventors in large numbers":* Barnum, p 84.

85 *Perhaps his most outrageous foray:* The prospects for black inventors in the nineteenth century were dim, and became doubly so when they tried to give presentations. Elijah McCoy, inventor of many forms of lubricants, often arrived at business meetings only to be turned away because of his color. Such obstacles prevented blacks from becoming show inventors at all, and they were not overcome to any degree until after the tradition of show inventors had fallen into decline. The most comprehensive history of black inventors in America that I have found is *Created Equal,* by James Michael Brodie.

85 *what Colt had discovered about fireworks that went wrong:* Robert-Houdin, the famous French magician and manufacturer of automata, also learned this rule of thumb when he made his too-perfect devices hiss: "Admiration increased in a ratio to the intensity of the noise." Harris, p. 89.

86 *"late Mr. Barnum":* Ibid. p. 280.

86 *"a wilderness of wonderful":* Barnum, pp. 102-3.

86 *"The curiosity exhibitor":* Ibid., p. 374.

87 *"It is almost a sublime sight":* Kasson, p. 141.

87 *"Double-headed snake":* Hellman, p. 69.

87 *to look like a Turk:* The general predilection for dressing automata as "Turks" can be seen as a fetishizing of the Other, but it can also be understood as an acknowledgment of their origins: eighteenth-century Europeans traced the source of automata to ancient Egypt.

88 *"words might be spoken":* Bruce, p. 5.

88 *"anything and everything":* Saxon, p. 150.

89    *"The Professor was none too clean"*: Altick, p. 354.

89    *Thackeray, writing in* Punch: Thackeray, like Henry, sympathized with the toiling preacher, if in less lofty terms: "A parson might set up the Compound Machine in his pulpit, and a clerk or curate work it from the reading-desk, whilst his Reverence was smoking his pipe in the vestry; or an under-secretary might set the bellows going with a speech of LORD JOHN'S whilst his Lordship was taking his usual glass of brandy-and-water at BELLAMY'S." Altick, p. 355.

## Chapter Five: Like a Gentleman

91    *"with a sight of the sketch"*: Alberts, p. 359.

92    *"If I cannot live"*: Flexner, p. 24.

92    *"If this be so"*: Mabee, p. 149.

93    *the rotunda of the Capitol building*: The architecture of the rotunda itself was based on a design submitted by patent chief Dr. William Thornton.

93    *"Painting has been"*: Morse, p. 31.

94    *"My first instrument"*: Ibid., p. 38.

94    *"printed five hundred"*: Ibid., p. 79.

95    *"THE TELEGRAPH"*: Ibid., p. 75.

96    *"Extraordinaire! Très admirable!"*: Mabee, p. 218-19.

96    *"Professor Morse"*: Ibid., p. 274.

97    *"Nothing could have been"*: Ibid., p. 276.

99    *to make ceremonial speeches*: In his last public appearance, on January 17, 1872, Morse unveiled a statue of Franklin in Printing House Square, New York City, in the company of Horace Greeley.

99    *"EXTRAORDINARY PHENOMENON"*: Scientific American 1, no. 1 (28 August 1845), p. 1.

100   *the Northern Central Railroad*: The main line of the Northern Central ran between Baltimore and Sunbury, the branch line between Rockdale and Canton.

100   *Whether the two Barnums*: Social contact between Zenus and Phineas resists confirmation. Zenus, as mentioned, was for a time president of the Northern Central Railroad, though the dates of his tenure are obscure. In 1853, the Railroad Circus and Crystal Amphitheater, owned by Gilbert R. Spalding, became the first rolling show to travel entirely by rail, making it tempting to link the circus on rails to the good graces of Zenus. But Spalding's circus ran mostly on New York Central, not Northern Central, tracks. While the show did go south for one leg of this tour, the connection with Zenus's railroad would have been short-lived at best, since Spalding quit the rail idea in 1854.

100   *Field's personal notes*: Field's papers are available in the Brooke Russell Astor Reading Room for Rare Books and Manuscripts at the main branch of the New York Public Library.

101   *"The Cable Carnival"*: Quoted in Judson, p. 115.

101   *"The crowd upon Broadway"*: Ibid., pp. 115–16.

102   *"while thus employed"*: Morse, p. 130.

103   *thus creating the first daguerrotype*: Also spelled "daguerreotype."

103 *François Arago endorsed it in 1839*: This was the same Arago who developed Arago's wheel, which Faraday studied in developing the dynamo.

104 *In the end, Mathew Brady*: Mathew Brady also capitalized on Barnum's renown by setting up a portrait studio across the street from the American Museum.

104 *"[I had] tasted"*: The Charles Currier Beale papers.

105 *"as the pupil and friend"*: Mabee, p. 233.

106 *to refer to the daguerrotype subject*: Taft, p. 43.

106 *"the golden key"*: Fauvel-Gouraud, p. 473.

106 *"One of M. Gouraud's lectures"*: Ibid., p. 542, quoted from *New World*, 17 February 1844.

107 *these crowds*: So said the press: "We believe the size of the class of Gouraud's is unprecedented in the history of lecturing in this country." *New York Herald Tribune*, 15 February 1844.

107 *"especially"*: Taft, p. 52.

107 *"from daguerrotypes"*: Davies, p. 48.

107 *"of all the advantages"*: From E. Littell, editor. *Littell's Living Age* 9, no. 110 (June 1846), p. 552.

108 *"The Magnetic Daguerrotype"*: Trachtenberg, pp. 70–71.

108 *a town on the banks*: *Daguerreian Journal*, vol. 3 (1852) p. 20.

109 *"MORSE'S INVIGORATING ELIXIR"*: *New York Times*, 13 October 1853.

## Chapter Six: Thundering Caravans

111 *"You brothel-bred shithead"*: Rudlin, p. 145.

112 *got mention for*: *Lexington Union*, 14 September 1833.

113 *"In view of"*: Hutchinson, p. 327.

115 *"Tremendous showbills"*: *Brattleboro Messenger*, 29 August 1834.

115 *five menagerie men*: The five principals of the Zoological Institute were James Raymond, Hiram Waring, Caleb Angevine, Lewis Titus, and William Howe, Jr.

115 *"to more generally diffuse"*: Thayer, p 39.

116 *"We put our foot down flat"*: McKennon, p. 20.

116 *Massie announced a visit*: Letter from William Massie to Robert McCormick, April 21, 1837, Cyrus McCormick Collection, State Historical Society of Wisconsin.

116 *shown in their advertising records*: Thayer (vol 2), p. 198. Thayer's *Annals*, drawn from primary materials, is an invaluable compendium of information on circuses and menageries. See also "Wisconsin, Incubator of the American Circus," by Ayries Davies, reprinted from the *Wisconsin Magazine of History* 25, no. 3 (March 1942), pp. 283–96, by the State Historical Society of Wisconsin.

117 *"I warrant them superior"*: McCormick, p. 46.

118 *"McCormick warrants"*: Hutchinson, p. 349.

120 *"showing the connection"*: Ibid., opp. p. 358.

120 *This practice*: McCormick applied this idea to himself as much as to his machines. Once, after he had achieved renown, he was scheduled to go to Philadelphia to have his portrait rendered. When he realized that he

wouldn't be able to make it on time, he simply sent a letter to the painter asking him to start work anyway. "[M]y hair is a very dark brown," he wrote, "—eyes dark, though not black, complexion fresh and health good, 5 ft. 11½ inc. high, weighing 200 lbs. I prefer my portrait taken with more of a front face." Ibid., p. 455.

121   *three rolling shows joined together*: The shows that merged were Barnum's Greatest Show on Earth, Howe's Great London Circus, and Sanger's Royal British Menagerie.

121   *"Centralization of All"*: Harris, p. 253.

121   *"Prince and lord"*: Rudlin, p. 141.

122   *"a cross between"*: McCormick, p. 55.

122   *"a brilliant chronicle"*: Hutchinson, p. 329.

123   *"industrial products"*: Luckhurst, p. 93.

123   *"To wed mechanical skill"*: Ibid., p. 94.

124   *"a sea of heads"*: Tallis, p. 22.

124   *"The philosopher and the savage"*: Ibid., p. 207.

125   *"the general idea"*: Ingram, p. 32.

126   *"very showy"*: Hawke, p. 262.

126   *"extra gew-gaw show"*: Ibid., p. 260.

127   *"Ornament as a characteristic"*: "The International Exhibition of 1876," *Scientific American Supplement* 1 (17 June 1876), p. 386, reprinted from "Machine Tools at the Philadelphia Exhibition," *Engineering* 21 (26 May 1876), pp. 427–28.

## Chapter Seven: The Star System

131   *"The star is the light"*: Nagler, p. 550.

132   *"I would have it move"*: Brandon, p. 45.

134   *"Howe and all his associates"*: *New York Times*, 14 April 1854.

134   *"CAUTION."*: Ibid.

135   *"[T]he plan promised"*: Barnum, p. 284.

136   *to be someone else for a day*: One hand continued to wash the other. Even as Singer was dramatizing his sewing machine as an essential prop of the home, Tony Pastor, the father of vaudeville, was giving away sewing machines as promotions for his tasteful family shows, which he put on in luxurious theaters.

136   *"steamboat on wheels"*: *New York Family Herald*, 5 December 1859.

136   *"The Herald of Civilization"*: Brandon, p. 140.

## Chapter Eight: A Big Bang

141   *"Instantly there was a terrifying"*: Verne, *From the Earth to the Moon*, p. 175.

142   *"Some of them"*: Jules-Verne, p. 104.

143   *the report from Lee*: *Scientific American*, 25 January 1868.

143   *"Hesitations, doubts"*: Verne, *Earth to Moon*, p. 20.

143   *"An artilleryman is like"*: Ibid., p. 53.

144   *"Well, then"*: Ibid., p. 126.

| 144 | *This was not so different:* Scientific American, 11 September 1869. |

144    *This was not so different:* Scientific American, 11 September 1869.
145    *"After reading Edgar Allan Poe":* Costello, frontispiece.
146    *"crates of champagne, food":* Jules-Verne, p. 58.
147    *"An unknown writer had":* Costello, p. 73.
147    *"This fictional journey":* Verne, *Journey to the Centre of the Earth*, p. 232.
147    *Thinking more like an inventor:* Some electrical engines had been proposed for submarines at the time, but it is not likely that he knew about them.
148    *an American named George Francis Train:* In his travels, Train had met Dumas, and it is likely that Dumas related his exploits to Verne.
149    *"It had the same weight":* Jules-Verne, p. 93.
149    *In fact, the essentially theatrical:* Some have gone even further, seizing on the fruitless nature of the Eagle landing to declare the entire project a hoax—in other words, the work of mountebanks!
150    *"producing a dazzling star":* Scientific American, 20 June 1868, pp. 385–86.
150    *"The entire phalanx":* Ibid.
151    *"in every stationers' in England and America":* Scientific American, 29 July 1868, p. 70.
153    *In France, the matter:* Scientific American, 26 August 1868, p. 130.
153    *"having subsided from the discharge":* Scientific American, 16 September 1868, p. 182.
154    *"He narrowly escaped being put":* Ibid.
154    *"More ghastly was the sight":* Fant, pp. 61–62.
154    *"dictatorial powers":* Ibid., p. 66.
154    *"someone apparently dead":* Ibid., p. 67.
155    *"When youth has lost its faith":* Evlanoff, p. 59.
155    *". . . my love is with":* Ibid., p. 62.
156    *Ironically, the Nobel family:* The only surviving manuscript is kept at the Nobel Foundation in Stockholm.
157    *"the mountainous slopes":* New York Times, 5 May 1866.
159    *"kites covered with fine light gauze":* Dunlap, p. 27. Dunlap erroneously cites the *Washington Chronicle*, 1 November 1872.
159    *"electrical vibrations or waves":* Ibid.
160    *"a new and Improved Mode":* U.S. Patent no. 129,971.
160    *"I also dispense with":* Ibid.
160    *"the fragments careering":* Scientific American, 6 June 1868.
161    *"I once drove an engine":* MacDougall, p. 71.
161    *Bullets flew:* Scientific American, 3 December 1898, p. 354.
161    *"divine element is shown":* MacDougall, p. 71.
161    *"a new substance;":* Scientific American, 1 September 1877, p. 137.
162    *his "inter-etheric liberator" used vacuum tubes:* These were not vacuum tubes in the modern sense but tubes with the air exhausted.
162    *Clarence B. Moore:* Moore was a friend of the scientific-management pioneer Frederick Taylor.
162    *"a vibrator magnet":* Josephson, p. 127.

## Chapter Nine: How the Golden Age Was Made

164    *"He called it 'etheric force' "*: Josephson, p. 129.

167    *"How much I have improved"*: Bruce, p. 29.

167    *"somewhat prematurely into a man"*: Ibid., p. 34.

167    *Play of Douglas*: There is some debate about the authorship of this play. It is signed by Alexander Bell, suggesting that it was perhaps Grandfather Bell who wrote it. Yet according to Bell's biographer, it is written in the inventor's hand. Supporting this view is the fact that it doesn't bear the writerly style of the older Bell. What's more, one page is filled with an attempt at an alphabet much like Melville Bell's Visible Speech, which Alexander Graham Bell was working on at the time.

167    *"Pat: Ach!"*: Box 2, Alexander Bell family papers, Library of Congress.

168    *Wheatstone had invented "an enchanted lyre"*: Wheatstone also invented the Wheatstone telegraph. He did not invent the Wheatstone bridge, though; this machine bore his name because he was the one to popularize it.

169    *"the extreme poverty"*: Bruce, p. 47.

170    *He also began to avail himself*: Bell was admired at the Williams shop for using a fork instead of a knife for putting food into his mouth. He knew about all kinds of forks, it seems.

171    *Bell then confessed that*: Some accounts have Bell saying, "Watson—come here—I want to see you." Perhaps Bell said "to see," but the crude telephone line failed to pick it up.

171    *"black eyes that could look"*: Bruce, p. 219, from Providence Star, "Salem Witchcraft."

172    *"When these our ceremonies"*: Ingram, p. 763.

173    *"The International Exhibition"*: Ibid., p. 766.

173    *"When the machine"*: Joseph Wilson, p. 32.

174    *"We may say"*: Hyman, p. 198.

174    *"I have my hopes"*: Moore, pp. 215–16.

175    *Alethes and Iris*: This play is recounted in greater depth in Hyman, p. 207.

175    *"This invention produces"*: Ingram, p. 720.

176    *"By our method"*: Jones, pp. 151–52.

177    *"the women of America"*: Ingram, p. 85.

178    *"Women can also apply"*: Macdonald, p. 12, quoting from *Scientific American*, 1861.

178    *a huge leap*: The number of patents issued to men increased during the same period, but not by as much.

178    *Gillespie went at it*: Macdonald, p. 77.

179    *"no better than if men had made them"*: Ibid., p. 77-78.

179    *"mottoes worked in worsted on cardboard"*: Ibid., p. 101.

180    *"I turned to the audience"*: Bruce, p. 197.

182    *"astonished him more than all else"*: *Scientific American*, 8 July 1876, p. 17.

182    *"As I placed my mouth"*: Bruce, p. 217.

183    *"The effect was"*: *Scientific American*, 24 February 1877, p. 120.

183    *"to gain his private ends"*: Josephson, p. 135.

183    *"Who will be the next"*: Bruce, p. 217.

183    *"We await"*: *Scientific American*, 3 March 1877, p. 133.

184    *"the sound produced"*: Scientific American, 2 June 1877, p. 342.
184    *"It is a most bewildering sensation"*: Scientific American, 9 June 1877, p. 351.
185    *"But for Henry"*: Coulson, p. 315.

## Chapter Ten: Escape from Menlo Park

186    *"I paid my money"*: Tyler, pp. 57–58.
186    *"[p]lays and most other"*: Edison, p. 44.
187    *"a new business"*: Scientific American, 10 January 1880, p. 16.
187    *"a minor invention"*: Josephson, pp. 133–34.
188    *"the Moody Sankey meetings"*: Moulton, p. 85.
189    *"As yet it is not"*: Josephson, p. 144.
189    *"the machine must talk"*: Ibid., p. 163.
191    *". . . now is the winter"*: Allen Koenigsberg. "The Wizard of Menlo Park and the Amazing Food Machine," *Antique Phonograph Magazine* 10, no. 2 (1992), p. 10.
191    *"burlesque or parody"*: Josephson, p. 173.
191    *"A Food Creator"*: Koenigsberg, p. 4.
192    *"Lavoisier dismissed it"*: Ibid., p. 5.
192    *"I am receiving letters"*: Ibid. p. 9.
193    *"to indicate the heat"*: Scientific American, 22 June 1878, p. 385.
193    *"I think I can"*: Josephson, p. 178.
194    *"I can produce"*: Ibid., p. 185.
197    *"For I am the Wizard"*: Ibid., p. 216.
198    *"For a minute or more"*: Ibid., p. 220
199    *"sick headaches, neuralgia"*: Ibid., p. 243.
199    *"mental kaleidoscope"*: Edison, p. 3.
199    *"in the depth of space"*: Ibid., p. 35.
200    *"because I protest"*: Engelbrecht, p. 86.
201    *"I said, 'If it' "*: Maxim, p. 146.
201    *"I am a totally"*: Ibid., p. 163.
202    *a medical inhaler*: This inhaler caused Maxim to suffer the censure of his friends, who thought patent nostrums lowly but machine guns noble.
202    *"seeing by telegraph"*: Scientific American, 5 June 1880, p. 355.
202    *through the medium of sunlight*: The early 1880s were good years for the sun. In 1882, The *Soleil-Journal*, a solar-powered printing press run by Abel Pilfre and Augustin Mouchot, put out 500 copies per hour.
202    *"would prove far more"*: Bruce, p. 338.
204    *"Having shown the tendency"*: Bell, p. 48.
204    *"When a word was spoken"*: Cheney, p. 11.
204    *"The sun's rays"*: Tesla, My Inventions, pp. 42–43.
205    *"The glow retreats"*: As translated in Cheney, p. 22.
206    *"running around at night"*: Cheney, p. 31.
207    *"have nothing to do"*: Josephson, p. 318.

## Chapter Eleven: Anatomical Museums

209    *Some set up dental parlors:* In 1916, there were an estimated five thousand unlicensed dentists practicing in New York.

210    *"Fireworks with Dramatic Accessories":* Albert Hopkins notes in *Magic* that a typical show was staged at Manhattan Beach in 1879 by James Paine.

210    *set the fireworks bursting:* The scenery for this display was hinged in irregular places, so as to "fall apart" haphazardly when the rockets were released. Yet it was also constructed in uniform dimensions, allowing troupes to present "new" dramas with the same sets when the current show grew too familiar.

210    *This "elevator stage":* Mackaye created many impressive stage devices. "Cloud creators," or "nebulators," were pieces of cloth suspended to cast cloud shadows onto the stage. His fog producer consisted of a trough filled with lime, which was lowered into water out of the audience's view. Perforated pipes sufficed to make rain. For terminology alone, we can thank Mackaye for his "luxauleator," a method of obscuring the area between the audience and actors. When the actors went to the extreme upstage for changeovers, it shone lights at so many angles as to leave no inch of the stage untouched.

      Mackaye also planned a stage for the Spectatorium at the Columbian Exposition, which was to have several cars riding on parallel semicircular tracks. The cars telescoped into one another to save space. They also opened up at variable speeds, so that they could be swung out to a single line on the stage and arrive at the same time, or as desired. Imagining the spectacle of Columbus discovering America or the like, Mackaye arranged for water to flow over these tracks and devised "wave makers"—in effect, paddles attached to the stage that disturbed the water.

211    *One night, Edison:* The following year, the "Edison Darky," a black performer, appeared at the Philadelphia Electrical Exposition standing on copper squares and wearing a headpiece with a lamp that was joined by wires to copper disks on his heels. When he moved his feet, the lamp lit up.

214    *Reviews of his work:* One rival put a Muybridge reject in his window to indicate shoddy workmanship. Muybridge responded in a newspaper with a moral tale from Aesop.

215    *discovered that Flora was pregnant:* According to the *Sacramento Union,* the child was born on April 29, 1874.

215    *shot him dead:* The shooting was reported in the *San Francisco Examiner,* October 19, 1874.

216    *Muybridge was acquitted:* The *Alta California* reported his acquittal on February 7, 1875.

216    *"The horse trotted by":* MacDonnell, p. 24.

217    *"a period limited only by":* Muybridge, *The Human Figure in Motion,* p. ix.

218    *Marey then modified the Astronomical Revolver to resemble a rifle:* An often reproduced picture, which depicts Marey aiming this primitive movie camera at an unseen subject, fails to give a good idea of its appearance. It looked exactly like a rifle.

219    *"I saw":* Rabinbach, p. 115.

219   *Freud responded:* Freud's articulation of the psychic apparatus can be found in *Interpretation of Dreams,* pp. 574–77.

219   *Or did the Astronomical Revolver:* Another possible link between Freud and Marey can be teased from the December 30, 1893, issue of *Scientific American,* which ran an article titled "Photochronography in the Medical Sciences." The article describes a motion-study system based on Marey's, built by A. Londe between 1890 and 1893, specifically for Professor Charcot at his Salpetriere clinic in Paris. Freud, of course, considered Charcot a major influence, and came to Paris in the early 1880s to learn from him. That Charcot could have mentioned Janssen's Astronomical Revolver to Freud is supported by Londe's comment that Charcot "always encouraged our research in the so interesting field of medical photography."

220   *With initial funding:* The University of Pennsylvania was entertaining other unusual notions at the time. In 1883, just before Muybridge began his studies, Mr. Henry Siebert donated $60,000 to the institution on the condition that it be used solely to study spiritualism. The university complied, accumulating books on the occult and conducting tests, up to and including seances. In May 1887, the results gave no indication that spiritualism was anything but a mass of deceptions, and the inquiry was discontinued.

222   *"The baneful effects":* Dercum, p. 176.

222   *From the resulting photographs:* The source for Harvard's early posture-photo programs is Harley P. Holden, curator of Harvard's archives. It is also known that Muybridge had the attention of several medical professors besides Dercum, any one of whom could have communicated with colleagues at other universities. These medical men included Dr. Joseph Leidy, a professor of anatomy in the Medical School, and Dr. Harrison Allen, a professor of comparative anatomy in the Auxiliary School of Medicine. (Allen provided the text for the original publication of *Animal Locomotion.*) The best-known champion of the posture-photo movement was William H. Sheldon, who established himself at the University of Pennsylvania in 1951 and made this pseudo-science a cause célèbre.

　　　See Ron Rosenbaum, "The Great Ivy League Nude Posture Photo Scandal," *New York Times Magazine,* 15 January 1995, p. 31. Also see Sheldon.

223   *Animal Locomotion:* This book included 781 plates in eleven volumes. Justifying the retail cost of $600 was the fact that it cost more than $30,000 to produce.

223   *"personalities, that are":* D. H. Lawrence, "When I Went to the Circus," *The Complete Poems,* pp. 445–46.

## Chapter Twelve: The Birth of the Grid

228   *his father:* A year's worth of research on the Gourauds has revealed, among other things, that François was in Niagara around the time of George's birth, and that in 1844 he had children, whereas in 1839 he did not. Another compelling proof of patrimony is a registered parcel receipt in George's pension records, delivered to Col. G. E. Gouraud and signed by "H. V. Carriere," or "H. U. Carriere," for "G. Fauvel-Gouraud." This is the only reference to George Gouraud's hyphenated name in his pension

records. Fauvel-Gouraud was an exceedingly rare name in the Northeast in the nineteenth century; I have not found any other instance of it being used.

229    *"Gouraud is a man"*: Letter from Francis B. Keene to General Davis, August 24, 1909, from the pension records of Col. George E. Gouraud, National Archives.

229    *"Lebaudy"*: Ibid.

231    *"Not since the appearance"*: Cheney, p. 39.

233    *"Newly empowered"*: Kennelly went on to discover the ionosphere at the same time as Oliver Heaviside.

234    *"alternating current will kill"*: James F. Penrose, "Inventing Electrocution," *American Heritage of Invention and Technology* 9, no. 4 (spring 1994), p. 38.

235    *"already had a record"*: Ibid., p. 40.

235    *"like overdone beef"*: Ibid., p. 42.

236    *"I have not failed"*: Josephson, p. 348.

237    *"You tell me"*: Cheney, p. 46.

237    *"I can only invent"*: Josephson, p. 360.

237    *a new entity called General Electric*: Edison owned shares in General Electric at first, but soon sold them.

238    *In the same lecture*: For a more detailed description of the carbon-button lamp, see Cheney, pp. 55–59.

238    *"The ideal way of lighting"*: Martin, p. 189.

239    *Except for his long-windedness*: Some of Tesla's lectures ran as long as eighty pages in print.

239    *"a magician of"*: Cheney, p. 59.

239    *"take through his body"*: *New York Times*, 18 December 1888.

239    *"I thought that"*: Cheney, pp. 64-65.

240    *"Tesla awoke"*: Tesla, *My Inventions*, p. 80.

240    *"When we look"*: Martin, p. 294.

240    *Vision, he said, was the key to all understanding*: Compare the pitch of the mountebank Taborin's straight man in the seventeenth century with Tesla's lecture two hundred years later. This is Taborin: "Sight is one of the first organs of the body, and the most delicate part of it, being of an incredible and admirable construction, in which the Author of the Universe has enclosed all that is rarest and most excellent in this world." And this is Tesla: "Of all organs, the eye is most wonderful. It is the most precious, the most indispensable of our perceptive or directive organs, it is the great gateway through which all knowledge enters the mind."

240    *"in order to enable"*: Ibid., p. 318.

240    *"Were the potentials"*: Ibid., p. 319.

241    *"female savage"*: King, p. 52.

242    *The delegates of*: These concerns gained some credence in 1901, when President McKinley was assassinated by an anarchist in the Temple of Music at the Pan-American Exposition in Buffalo.

242    *6 out of the 100,000 visitors*: Hilton estimates an opening-day attendance of 75,000; Muccigrosso puts the number between 100,000 and 150,000.

242    *"incidents of vital human gaiety"*: Muccigrosso, p. 86.

242    *"opportunity for isolating"*: Ibid., p. 154.

243    *"The rabble let"*: Scientific American, 11 November 1893, p. 307.
244    *pervasive loveliness*: Scientific American, 21 October 1893, p. 259.
245    *"These Zoetropic devices"*: Josephson, p. 392.
247    *"Mr. Tesla has been seen"*: Cheney, p. 73.
247    *"And if I give up"*: Ibid., p. 48
248    *Tesla tore up both contracts*: The Westinghouse annual report of 1897 indicates that Tesla received a lump sum of $216,000.

## Chapter Thirteen: Century's End

251    *"except, perhaps"*: Tesla, My Inventions, p. 17.
251    *"Whatever may be the cause"*: Cheney, p. 87.
252    *"Tesla took a picture"*: Ibid., p. 101.
253    *"I had hardly finished"*: Anderson, p. 30.
253    *The x-ray burst upon*: Roentgen announced his discovery on December 28. Carnival traditionally commenced on December 26. The public reaction, in Europe anyway, may have drawn strength from this parallel.
253    *"the rays were used"*: Nitske, p. 121.
253    *"Speculations, mostly"*: As translated in Anderson, p. 96.
255    *"I had no refuge"*: Wells, The Invisible Man, p. 105.
255    *"the story does not deal"*: West, p. 234.
255    *"No, not those Röntgen"*: Wells, The Invisible Man, p. 92.
256    *The public did not know*: According to Cheney, "The inventor did not disclose more than the fundamental idea in his basic patent No. 613,809—a means he had learned to use to protect his discoveries." Cheney, p. 124. This is a curious defense if true, since complete patent claims would have protected his discoveries better than almost anything else.
256    *"attack and destroy"*: Cheney, p. 125.
256    *"Judging from the comments"*: Scientific American, 26 November 1898, p. 338.
257    *"immense objects appear"*: Tesla, Colorado Springs Notes, pp. 127–28
259    *"into that tenuous realm"*: Lewis, p. 31.
259    *"it is popularly"*: Nahin, p. 270.
259    *In December 1899, American Telephone and Telegraph*: As a measure of the loaded line's importance, American Telephone and Telegraph had been organized on March 3, 1885, specifically to handle long-distance telephony, and the board of directors had shifted the assets of American Bell Telephone over to it, making AT&T the parent company.
260    *"bob and dick also at some future time"*: Nahin, p. 81.
261    *"The daily newspapers"*: Ibid., p. 105.
262    *his reward for aligning with a pariah like Heaviside*: Heaviside remained defiant until his death in the 1920s, refusing even to accept an award in lieu of recognition for his invention of the loaded line.
263    *But lately the structure seemed to be tinkering with him*: W. Bernard Carlson has noted that Thomson imagined the organization of GE to be much like a machine with interdependent parts. Other historians such as John Law have described this organization as a set of "actor networks." In the context of the show inventors, however, GE's dramatic elements in the 1890s were too faint to qualify as live theater. Given the compartmentalized nature of

the organization, perhaps the closest analogy would be to the production of a studio-based motion-picture.

263   *"We certainly cannot"*: Carlson, p. 323.

263   *"[M]y opportunities to work"*: Ibid., p. 331.

264   *"[I]t has grown upon me"*: Ibid., p. 335.

## Chapter Fourteen: A New Universe

269   *"In these seven years"*: Henry Adams, pp. 381–82.

269   *"thousands of pages"*: Ibid., p. 390.

275   *By then, Couney*: For a more complete description of Couney and his incubators, see Gary R. Brown, "The Coney Island Baby Laboratory," *American Heritage of Invention and Technology* 10, no. 2 (fall 1994), pp. 24–31.

276   *manufacturers ranged in the hundreds*: Automobiles proliferated partly because of the bicycle, which came into prominence a few years earlier, and partly because of the increase in paved roads. Car companies were also relatively simple to finance, with parts suppliers selling on credit. As repairs were generally do-it-yourself propositions, the line between owner and builder was blurry at best.

277   *On September 22, 1893*: In the same year, the Duryea brothers contributed the Davidson-Duryea Semi-Armored Car. Any guard manning this vehicle had the right to look grim. It was equipped with a Colt automatic gun and an armored shield, but other than that it was open to the air.

277   *the first Duryea model*: In 1896, Barnum and Bailey's Greatest Show on Earth hailed "The Famous Duryea Motor-Wagon or Motorcycle. The Identical Carriage That Won the Great Race in Chicago Last November. To Been Every Day in the New Street Parade."

278   *"The man who places a part"*: Lacey, p. 109.

279   *Unfortunately, Doble managed*: For a firsthand account of an excursion in a Doble, see Ralph Stein, *The American Automobile*.

281   *Several years later*: I have drawn my information on Ford's commissaries from a much neglected industry paper by Stanley C. Hollander and Gary A. Marple entitled "Henry Ford: Inventor of the Supermarket?"

282   *"fails to see that"*: "Elihu Thomson Eightieth Birthday Celebration," pp. 48–49.

283   *"On the stage was represented"*: Zunz, p. 312.

285   *By the 1940s*: Barnes, *Motion and Time Study*, p. 335.

285   *"With all these methods of study"*: *Scientific American*, 6 November 1915, p. 403.

286   *A Study of the Time*: These titles come from a list of films that were available from the Industrial Engineering Film Library at the University of Iowa, circa 1940.

287   *"a great deal of"*: Ibid., p. 402.

287   *And understandably so*: Gilbreth's case was also complicated by conflicts within his own ranks. When a dispute arose over who had originated time studies, Taylor's followers cut the interloper from their midst. Gilbreth blithely continued to promote Taylorism anyway, and to lecture in "Fred-

erick W. Taylor Hall," an impressive-sounding locale that was actually a room in his sister's music school in Providence.

287     "to having any observer record": Gilbreth and Gilbreth, p. 70.

287     As many historians of commedia dell'arte: Rudlin, p. 7.

287     Keaton's deadpan face even attained the character of a mask: The demands of the mask explain why, contrary to many interpretations, Keaton never smiled for the camera.

288     the shooting of a film created a spectacle: Benjamin, p. 232.

288     "The force of the Virgin": Adams, p. 383.

## Chapter Fifteen: Killing the Volunteers

291     "Not only were there no receptions": Kelly, p. 68.

292     "thousands of strange birds": Ibid, p. 7.

292     One of the Evening Item editors: Ibid., p. 8.

293     Throughout his career: Lilienthal, p. 129.

293     "Possibly [human flight] requires": Ibid., p. 111.

294     "My own active interest": McFarland, p. 103.

296     H. P. Moore, contacted the Kitty Hawk: In another account, Moore showed up when the type had already been set and asked if anyone knew about the story.

297     "Done anything special lately?": Kelly, p 85.

298     "If such sensational": Ibid., p. 87, quoted from Scientific American, 13 January 1906.

298     "until a machine is produced": Ibid., p. 94.

299     "We were aware of the presence": Ibid., pp. 137–38.

300     "not seem to qualify as either fact or fiction": Ibid., p. 138.

300     "The crowd's gasp of astonishment": Ibid., p. 139.

301     And in the case: On the surface, the effects of the Selfridge disaster would seem to be contradicted by calamities such as the Hindenburg crash and the Challenger explosion, both of which led to a decline in the technologies involved. The difference can be explained by the fact that these later catastrophes occurred within an existing dramatic framework (the Hindenburg crash was both filmed and broadcast on radio; the Challenger exploded on television), which meant that their failures interrupted a well-established suspension of disbelief. The Selfridge disaster, on the other hand, took place without the benefit of a sufficiently developed dramatic structure, and so was received according to an entirely different set of expectations.

303     "a vast whispering gallery": Susan Douglas, pp. 199–200.

303     "[T]he entire earth": Tesla, Fantastic Inventions, p. 232, from Electrical World and Engineer, 5 March 1904.

303     "Some of his sanguine conceptions": Cheney, p. 155.

304     "Of course, the discharge": Ibid., p. 154.

305     "Nikola Tesla—His Work & Unfulfilled Promises": Electrical Age, February 1903.

306     Guglielmo Marconi was already: Cheney, p. 176.

306     sought his backing primarily from the armed services: Many other inventors, Tesla and Edison among them, had connections with the armed services,

but these were generally detours in the course of their careers. For their part, Tesla and Edison both walked away from their dealings with the military feeling dissatisfied.

307   *"The first may be for military purposes"*: Dunlap, p. 65.

307   *"I believe one"*: Ibid.

307   *and sailed for New York, where he gave several demonstrations to the public*: Neither Marconi nor Tesla provided the American public with its first good look at radio. This came at the Electrical Exposition of 1898, held in New York, when W. J. Clarke, general manager of the United States Electrical Supply Company, exhibited a wireless transmitter and a storage battery, transmitting the letters *nynyny*—Morse code for "New York City." The apparatus also rang a bell on the other side of the hall, some three hundred feet distant, without the use of wires. Unfortunately, Clarke managed to overshadow his own demonstration with another one, in which a facsimile of the battleship *Maine* was blown from a nautical tank four times daily by remote control—hardly an example of radio as a two-way communications device. See *Scientific American*, 28 May 1898, p. 340.

310   *Hugo Gernsback, a science-fiction writer*: An article titled "Nikola Tesla: The Man," reprinted in Tesla's own *My Inventions*, finds Gernsback praising Tesla's longevity and his diet. He also arranged to have Tesla's death mask made.

310   *"junk collector's heaven"*: George Douglas, p. 39.

310   *"long before the country"*: The quoted material in this paragraph is drawn from Susan Douglas, pp. 203–4.

311   *"electrical expert who"*: Dunlap, p. 120.

311   *"the inventor says he has solved"*: Leonard Reich, p. 156.

311   *With the* Titanic *disaster*: Lewis, p. 106.

311   *"The* Titanic *disaster brought radio to the front"*: Ibid., p. 105.

312   *"seemingly semi-intelligent"*: Susan Douglas, p. 210.


## Chapter Sixteen: Temporary Loss of "Memoray"

316   *"Repeated questions"*: Lacey, p. 139.

316   *"Nobody knew where to go"*: Ibid., p. 141.

316   *"To Go with the Nuts"*: Ibid., p. 142.

317   *"Guess I better go home"*: Ibid., p. 144.

319   *"A new art has been born"*: John Stone Stone, "The Practical Aspects of the Propagation of High-Frequency Electrical Waves Along Wires." *Journal of Franklin Institute* (October 1912), p. 353.

319   *"Major Squier has dedicated"*: Ibid., p. 354.

320   *AT&T emerged as the de facto owner of his invention*: Congress later split the difference by requiring that some of the royalties go to the National Academy of Sciences.

321   *"indisputable proof that"*: Lewis, p. 109.

322   *"The material is high in tensile strength"*: Engelbrecht, p. 182.

323   *"The Naval officer resents"*: Josephson, *Edison*, p. 454.

323   *"with a range and variety"*: *Scientific American*, 13 November 1915.

324   *"The interesting problem of space navigation"*: Goddard, p. 57.

324   *which led him to contemplate the potential of cryogenics*: Late one night,

Goddard wrote: "If there were some substance like formaline, which would permeate every tissue, and kill all bacterial life except the spores, and besides, the body were placed in a sealed glass containing nitrogen, and, perhaps, the temperature remained constant, and a little above freezing, there seems to be no reason why the body might not remain in this passive condition indefinitely, since decay is absolutely arrested from the moment passivity is assumed, although the same amount of moisture is present, as when the body is active . . ." Lehman, p. 47.

325    "going to moon, and interested": Goddard, p. 163.
326    "All he has is a nozzle": Lehman, p. 90.
326    "People are very curious": Goddard, p. 218.
326    the "Rockwood-Haigis-Shinkle intervention": Goddard, p. 232.
326    "You can tell your son": Lehman, p. 90.
328    "the launchers in my hands": Lehman, p. 97.
329    "Leaving the conference room": Mallmann's papers, from which this passage and the quotations in the succeeding pages of the chapter are drawn, can be found in the Rare Books and Manuscripts Department of the New York Public Library.
329    "the results obtained were so weird": The word weird is handwritten in an otherwise typed letter.

## Chapter Seventeen: The Corporate Show

335    "War": Lewis, p. 176.
337    a stockholder list that included United Fruit: United Fruit had been manufacturing wireless technology for its Central American plantations.
338    "CONSOLER OF THE LONELY": Lewis, p. 150.
338    shunt two percent of their sales: George Douglas, pp. 81-82.
340    It took World War I: Kenneth S. Clark, writing on the increase of music performed in department stores, observed that "many of the . . . activities are a definite outgrowth of the semi-public department store music of wartime." Kenneth Clark, p. 69.
341    "Ever since the war": Ibid., p. 71.
341    "other seasonal characters": George Douglas, p. 87.
342    The A. Harris & Company store: Kenneth Clark, p. 81.
343    "The broadcasting," said Daniels: Ibid., p. 101.
343    "impressionable young people": Brindze, p. 93.
344    "The demonstration was anonymous": New York Times, May 20, 1924, p. 9.
345    "Radovia—A road": Squier, p. 163.
347    "If you have made up your mind": Lewis, p. 167.
349    Anyone inquiring about him at the Museum of Television and Radio . . . is apt to receive a blank stare: This is what happened to me when I inquired about Baird at the bookstore there.
349    "There was a dull thud": Moseley, pp. 45–46.
350    "The Baird Undersock": Ibid., p. 47.
350    "First sandwich women in Glasgow": Ibid.
351    "walked a hundred yards": Ibid., p. 61.
352    As per corporate protocol: Abramson, p. 77.

352     *"Seeing by Wireless"*: Moseley, p. 64.

352     *"the letter 'H,' "*: F. H. Robinson, "The Radio Kinema," *Kinematograph Weekly*, April 3, 1924. Today, a plaque is screwed to the Hastings building: "Television. First demonstrated by John Logie Baird from experiments started here in 1924." The plaque was unveiled on November 7, 1929.

352     *"that no technical difficulties"*: Ibid.

352     *"Serious Explosion in Hastings Laboratory"*: Moseley, p. 69.

353     *"Watch him; he may have a razor on him!"*: Ibid., p. 72.

354     *On January 27, 1926*: Abramson dates the event the 26th, but most other sources have settled on the 27th.

355     *"a profusion of equipment"*: Abramson, p. 84.

356     *"As soon as I"*: Ritchie, p. 25.

356     *Rather than selling*: The prices of the Baird televisions were exorbitant at first, but they soon came down. In 1928, the Televisor Model "C" fetched a price of 150 pounds. Three years later, a Baird Televisor ran for a mere 18 pounds. The Baird "Junior" Kit could be bought one piece at a time— with only twelve parts in total.

356     *"We found that strawberries"*: Baird, p. 81.

357     *Three shows daily*: Ibid., p. 105.

358     *"when Optimist the winner"*: Ibid, p. 117.

359     *"Today," Sarnoff said*: Sarnoff, p. 3.

359     *"procession of game shows"*: Marcus and Segal, p. 328.

# Bibliography and Related Reading

Abramson, Albert. *The History of Television, 1880 to 1941.* Jefferson, N.C.: McFarland & Co., 1987.

Adams, Henry. *The Education of Henry Adams: An Autobiography.* Boston: Houghton Mifflin Co., 1918.

Adams, William Howard, ed. *The Eye of Thomas Jefferson.* Washington: National Gallery of Art, 1976.

Alberts, Robert C. *Benjamin West: A Biography.* Boston, Houghton Mifflin Co., 1978.

Aldridge, Alfred Owen. *Franklin and His French Contemporaries.* New York: New York University Press, 1957.

Allott, Kenneth. *Jules Verne.* London: Cresset Press, n.d.

Altick, Richard D. *The Shows of London.* Cambridge: Harvard University Press, Belknap Press, 1978.

Anderson, Leland I., ed. *Nikola Tesla: Lecture Before the New York Academy of Sciences, The Streams of Lenard and Roentgen and Novel Apparatus for Their Production, April 6, 1897.* Breckenridge, Colo.: Twenty First Century Books, 1994.

Arthur, Tom, and Peter Waddell. *The Secret Life of John Logie Baird.* London: Century Hutchinson, 1986.

Augur, Helen. *The Book of Fairs.* New York: Harcourt, Brace and Co., 1939.

Austrian, Geoffrey D. *Hermann Hollerith: Forgotten Giant of Information Processing.* New York: Columbia University Press, 1982.

Babbage, Charles. *Passages from the Life of a Philosopher.* 1864. Reprint, New York: Augustus M. Kelley, 1969.

Baird, John Logie. *Sermons, Soaps and Television.* London: Royal Television Society, 1990.

Barnes, Ralph M. *Motion and Time Study.* New York: John Wiley & Sons, 1949.

Barnes, Ralph M. *Motion and Time Study Applications.* New York: John Wiley & Sons, 1942.

Barrett, Ada Louise. *George Stephenson: Father of Railways.* New York: Paebar Co., 1948.

385

Bates, Richard O. *The Gentleman from Ohio: An Introduction to Garfield.* Durham, N.C.: Moore Publishing Co., 1973.

Bathe, Greville, and Dorothy Bathe. *Oliver Evans: A Chronicle of Early American Engineering.* Philadelphia: Historical Society of Philadelphia, 1935.

Beach, Mark. "Was There a Scientific Lazzaroni?" In *Nineteenth-Century American Science: A Reappraisal,* edited by George Daniels. Evanston, Ill.: Northwestern University Press, 1972.

Beale, Charles Currier. Papers. Box 14. Rare Manuscripts Division, New York Public Library.

Bell, Alexander Graham. Family Papers. Box 2, Room 101. The Library of Congress.

Benjamin, Walter. *Illuminations: Essays and Reflections.* Translated by Harry Zohn. New York: Harcourt Brace Jovanovich, 1968.

Bleich, Dr. Alan Rudolph. *The Story of X-Rays: From Röntgen to Isotopes.* New York: Dover Publications, 1960.

Bode, Carl. *The American Lyceum: Town Meeting of the Mind.* New York: Oxford University Press, 1956.

Bowen, Catherine Drinker. *The Most Dangerous Man in America.* Boston: Little, Brown and Co., 1974.

Boyd, Thomas. *Poor John Fitch: Inventor of the Steamboat.* New York: G. P. Putnam's Sons, 1935.

Bradley, Duane. *Count Rumford.* Princeton: D. Van Nostrand Co., 1967.

Brandon, Ruth. *A Capitalist Romance: Singer and the Sewing Machine.* Philadelphia: J. B. Lippincott Co., 1977.

——. *The Life and Many Deaths of Harry Houdini.* New York: Random House, 1993.

Brindze, Ruth. *Not to Be Broadcast: The Truth about the Radio.* New York: Navguard Press, 1937. Reprint, New York: Da Capo Press, 1974.

Brodie, James Michael. *Created Equal: The Lives and Ideas of Black American Innovators.* New York: William Morrow and Co., 1993.

Brown, Dee. *Hear That Lonesome Whistle Blow.* New York: Simon and Schuster, Touchstone, 1977.

Brown, Sanborn C. *Count Rumford: Physicist Extraordinary.* Garden City, N.Y.: Doubleday, 1962.

Brown, William H. *The History of the First Locomotives in America.* New York: D. Appleton and Co., 1874.

Browne, Waldo R. *Barnum's Own Story: The Autobiography of P. T. Barnum.* New York: Dover Publications, 1961.

Bruce, Robert V. *Bell: Alexander Graham Bell and the Conquest of Solitude.* Ithaca, N.Y.: Cornell University Press, 1973.

Burke, James. *Connections.* London: Macmillan, 1978.

Buxton, H. W. *Memoir of the Life and Labours of the Late Charles Babbage Esq. F.R.S.* Cambridge: MIT Press, 1988.

Cameron, Kenneth Walter, ed. *The Massachusetts Lyceum during the Renaissance: Materials for the Study of the Oral Tradition in American Letters: Emerson, Thoreau, Hawthorne and Other New-England Lecturers.* Hartford: Transcendental Books, 1969.

Campbell, George Ashley. *The Collected Papers of George Ashley Campbell: Re-*

*search Engineer of the American Telephone and Telegraph Company.* New York: American Telephone and Telegraph Co., 1937.

Carlson, W. Bernard. *Invention as a Social Process: Elihu Thomson and the Rise of General Electric, 1870–1900.* Cambridge: Cambridge University Press, 1991.

Carrier, Elba O. *Humphry Davy and Chemical Discovery.* London: Chatto & Windus, 1967.

Casson, Herbert N. *Cyrus Hall McCormick: His Life and Work.* Chicago: A. C. McClurg & Co., 1909.

Chanute, Octave. *Progress in Flying Machines.* New York: American Engineer and Railroad Journal, 1894.

Cheney, Margaret. *Tesla: Man Out of Time.* New York: Dell, 1981.

Cheyney, Edward Potts. *History of the University of Pennsylvania: 1740–1940.* Philadelphia: University of Pennsylvania Press, 1940.

Clark, Kenneth S. *Music in Industry: A Presentation of Facts Brought Forth by a Survey, Made by the National Bureau for the Advancement of Music, on Musical Activities among Industrial and Commercial Workers.* New York: National Bureau for the Advancement of Music, 1929.

Clark, Paul. "Major General George Owen Squier." Master's thesis, Case Western University, 1974.

Clymer, Floyd. *Treasury of Early American Automobiles: 1877–1925.* New York: McGraw-Hill, 1950.

Cohen, I. Bernard. *Benjamin Franklin: Scientist and Statesman.* New York: Charles Scribner's Sons, 1975.

——— *Benjamin Franklin's Science.* Cambridge: Harvard University Press, 1990.

———. *Franklin's Experiments.* Cambridge: Harvard University Press, 1941.

Costello, Peter. *Jules Verne: Inventor of Science Fiction.* London: Hodder & Stoughton, 1978.

Coulson, Thomas. *Joseph Henry: His Life and Work.* Princeton: Princeton University Press, 1950.

Crary, Jonathan. *Techniques of the Observer: On Vision and Modernity in the Nineteenth Century.* Cambridge: MIT Press, 1994.

Crowther, J. G. *Men of Science: Humphry Davy, Michael Faraday, James Prescott Joule, William Thomson, James Clerk Maxwell.* New York: W.W. Norton & Co., 1936.

Daniels, George. *Science in American Society.* New York: Alfred A. Knopf, 1971.

Davies, John D. *Phrenology Fad and Science: A 19th-Century American Crusade.* New Haven: Yale University Press, 1955.

Davy, John. *Memoirs of the Life of Sir Humphry Davy.* London: Longman, Reese, Orme, Brown, Green & Longman, 1836.

De Pambour, Chev. F. M. G. *A Practical Treatise on Locomotive Engines on Railways.* Philadelphia: E. L. Carey & A. Hart, 1836.

Dercum, Francis X. *Rest, Suggestion and Other Therapeutic Measures in Nervous and Mental Diseases.* Philadelphia: P. Blakiston's Son & Co., 1917.

———. "A Study of Some Normal and Abnormal Movements Photographed by Muybridge." In *Animal Locomotion: The Muybridge Work at the University of Pennsylvania.—The Method and the Result.* Philadelphia: J. B. Lippincott Co., 1888. Reprint, New York: Arno Press, 1973.

Dickerson, Edward N. *Joseph Henry and the Magnetic Telegraph: An Address De-*

*livered at Princeton College (June 16, 1885)*, New York: Charles Scribner's Sons, 1885.

Dickinson, H. W. *James Watt: Craftsman and Engineer*. New York: Augustus M. Kelley, 1967.

Dickinson, H. W. *Robert Fulton: Engineer and Artist, His Life and Works*. London: John Lane, 1913.

Dickinson, H. W. *A Short History of the Steam Engine*. New York: Augustus M. Kelley, 1965.

Douglas, George H. *The Early Days of Radio Broadcasting*. Jefferson, N.C.: McFarland & Co., 1987.

Douglas, Susan J. *Inventing American Broadcasting: 1899–1922*. Baltimore: Johns Hopkins University Press, 1987.

Draper, John William. *Life of Franklin*. Washington: Library of Congress, 1977.

Dumbauld, Edward. *The Constitution of the United States*. Norman, Okla.: University of Oklahoma Press, 1964.

Du Moncel, Theodore A. L. *The Telephone, the Microphone and the Phonograph*. New York: Harper & Brothers, 1879. Reprint, New York: Arno, 1974.

Dunlap, Jr., Orrin E. *Marconi: The Man and His Wireless*. New York: Macmillan, 1937.

Eckley, Wilton. *The American Circus*. Boston: Twayne Publishers, 1984.

Edison, Thomas Alva. *The Diary and Sundry Observations of Thomas Alva Edison*. Edited by Dagobert D. Runes. New York: Greenwood Press, 1968.

"Elihu Thomson Eightieth Birthday Celebration at the Massachusetts Institute of Technology," Cambridge: Technology Press, March 29, 1933.

Engelbrecht, H. C., and F. C. Hanighen. *Merchants of Death: A Study of the International Armament Industry*. New York: Dodd, Mead and Co., 1934.

Evlanoff, Michael, and Marjorie Fluor. *Alfred Nobel: The Loneliest Millionaire*. N.p.: Ward Ritchie Press, 1969.

Fagen, M. D., ed. *A History of Engineering and Science in the Bell System: The Early Years, 1875–1925*. N.p.: Bell Telephone Laboratories, 1975.

Faith, Nicholas. *The World the Railways Made*. New York: Carroll & Graf, 1991.

Fant, Kenne. *Alfred Nobel: A Biography*. Translated by Marianne Ruuth. New York: Arcade, 1993.

Fauvel-Gouraud, François. *Phreno-Mnemotechny, or the Art of Memory, The Series of Lectures Explanatory of the Principles of the System, Delivered in New York and Philadelphia in the Beginning of 1844*. New York: Wiley and Putnam, 1845.

Fäy, Bernard. *Bernard Fäy's Franklin, Apostle of Modern Times*. Boston: Little, Brown and Co., 1929.

Fife, Gordon, and John Law, eds. *Picturing Power: Visual Depiction and Social Relations*. London: Routledge, 1988.

Flatow, Ira. *They All Laughed . . . From Light Bulbs to Lasers: The Fascinating Stories behind the Great Inventions That Have Changed Our Lives*. New York: HarperCollins, 1992.

Flexner, James Thomas. *Nineteenth-Century American Painting*. New York: Putnam's Sons, 1970.

Ford, Edward. *David Rittenhouse: Astronomer-Patriot, 1732–1796*. Philadelphia: University of Pennsylvania Press, 1946.

Ford, Paul Leicester. *The Many-Sided Franklin.* 1898. Reprint, Freeport, N.Y.: Books for Libraries Press, 1972.

Freud, Sigmund. *The Interpretation of Dreams.* Edited and translated by James Strachey. New York: Avon Books, 1965.

——. "The Origin and Development of Pyschoanalysis." *American Journal of Pyschology,* vol. 21 (April 1910). Reprint, N.p.: Gateway Editions, 1965.

Fucini, Joseph J., and Suzy Fucini. *Entrepreneurs: The Men and Women behind Famous Brand Names and How They Made It.* Boston: G. K. Hall & Co., 1985.

Fuller, R. Buckminster. *Ideas and Integrities: A Spontaneous Autobiographical Disclosure.* Englewood Cliffs, N.J.: Prentice-Hall, 1963.

Gale, T. *Electricity, or Ethereal Fire, considered.* Troy, N.Y.: Moffitt & Lyon, 1802.

Garrett, Wendell D. *Thomas Jefferson Redivivus.* Barre, Mass.: Barre Publishing Co., 1971.

Gilbreth, Frank B., and L. M. Gilbreth. *Applied Motion Study: A Collection of Papers on the Efficient Method of Industrial Preparedness.* New York: Macmillan, 1917.

Gilbreth, Jr., Frank B., and Ernestine Gilbreth Carey. *Cheaper by the Dozen.* New York: Thomas Y. Crowell Co., 1948.

Goddard, Esther C., ed. *The Papers of Robert H. Goddard, Including the Reports to the Smithsonian Institution and the Daniel and Florence Guggenheim Foundation.* Vol. 1: 1898–1924. New York: McGraw-Hill, 1970.

Gordon, Mel. *Lazzi: The Comic Routines of the Commedia dell'Arte.* New York: Performing Arts Journal Publications, 1983.

Grant, Ellsworth. *The Colt Legacy: The Colt Armory in Hartford, 1855–1980.* Providence: Mowbray Co., 1982.

Gray, Elisha. "Experimental Researches in Electro-Harmonic Telegraphy and Telephony: 1867–1878," New York: Russell Brothers, Printers, 1878. Reprinted in *The Telephone: An Historical Anthology,* edited by George Shiers. New York: Arno Press, 1977.

Greene, Abel, and Joe Laurie, Jr. *Show Biz: From Vaude to Video.* New York: Henry Holt and Co., 1951.

Greenwood, Isaac J. *The Circus Its Origin and Growth prior to 1835.* New York: Dunlap Society, 1898.

Haas, Robert Bartlett. *Muybridge: Man in Motion.* Berkeley: University of California Press, 1976.

Hammond, J. R., ed. *H. G. Wells: Interviews and Recollections.* Totowa, N.J.: Barnes and Noble Books, 1980.

Handwerker, Murray. *Nathan's Famous Hot Dog Cookbook.* New York: Grosset and Dunlap, 1968.

Hansen, Harry. *North of Manhattan: Persons and Places of Old Westchester.* New York: Hastings House, 1950.

Harris, Neil. *Humbug: The Art of P. T. Barnum.* Boston: Little, Brown and Co., 1973.

Hawke, David Freeman. *Nuts and Bolts of the Past: A History of American Technology, 1776–1860.* New York: Harper & Row, 1988.

Hellman, Geoffrey T. *The Smithsonian: Octopus on the Mall.* Philadelphia: J. B. Lippincott Co., 1967.

Hilton, Suzanne. *Here Today and Gone Tomorrow: The Story of World's Fairs and Exhibitions.* Philadelphia: Westminster Press, 1978.

Hindle, Brooke. *David Rittenhouse.* Princeton: Princeton University Press, 1964.

Hollander, Stanley C., and Gary A. Marple. "Henry Ford: Inventor of the Supermarket?" Marketing and Transportation Paper no. 9, Bureau of Business and Economic Research, College of Business and Public Service, East Lansing: Michigan State University, 1960.

Homer, William Innes. *Thomas Eakins: His Life and Art.* New York: Abbeville Press, 1992.

Hoopes, Penrose Robinson. "Connecticut's Contribution to the Development of the Steamboat." In *The Tercentenary Commission of the State of Connecticut, Committee on Historical Publications* 53, New Haven: Yale University Press, 1936.

Hopkins, Albert A., ed. *Magic: Stage Illusions, Special Effects and Trick Photography.* New York: Munn & Co., 1898. Reprint, New York: Dover Publications, 1976.

Hubbell, Douglas Kent. "The *Scientific American* and Its Supplement as Sources of Information About Theatre Technology." Ph.D. diss., Indiana University, 1978.

Hughes, Debra K. *Artifacts of Invention: Patent Models at the Hagley Museum and Library.* York, Penn.: York Graphic Services, 1993.

Hutchinson, William T. *Cyrus Hall McCormick: Seed-Time, 1809–1856.* New York: Century Co., 1930.

Hutton, Laurence. *Curiosities of the American Stage.* New York: Harper & Bros., 1891.

Hyman, Anthony. *Charles Babbage: Pioneer of the Computer.* Princeton: Princeton University Press, 1982.

Iles, George. *Leading American Inventors.* New York: Henry Holt and Co., 1912.

Industrial Recreation Association. *Music in Industry: A Manual on Music for Work and for Recreation in Business & Industry.* Chicago: Industrial Recreation Association, 1944.

Ingram, J. S. *The Centennial Exposition.* Philadelphia: Hubbard Bros., 1876.

James, Marquis. *Andrew Jackson: Portrait of a President.* New York: Bobbs-Merrill Co., 1937.

Jehl, Francis. *Menlo Park Reminiscences.* Vol. 1. New York: Dover Publications, 1990.

Johnson, Paul. *The Birth of the Modern: World Society, 1815–1830.* New York: HarperCollins Publishers, 1991.

Jones, Alexander. *Historical Sketch of the Electrical Telegraph: Including Its Rise and Progress in the United States.* 1852.

Jones, Stacy V. *The Patent Office.* New York: Praeger Publishers, 1971.

Josephson, Matthew. *Edison: A Biography.* New York: John Wiley & Sons, 1959.

———. *The Robber Barons: The Great American Capitalists, 1861–1901.* Orlando, Fla.: Harcourt Brace & Co., 1962.

Judson, Isabella Field, ed. *Cyrus Field: His Life and Work, 1819–1892.* New York: Harper & Bros., 1896.

Jules-Verne, Jean. *Jules Verne: A Biography.* Translated and adapted from the French by Robert Greaves. London: Macdonald and Jane's, 1976.

Kasson, John F. *Civilizing the Machine: Technology and Republican Values in America, 1776–1900*. New York: Grossman, 1976.

Kelly, Fred C. *The Wright Brothers*. New York: Bantam Books, 1983.

Kenner, Hugh. *Bucky: A Guided Tour of Buckminster Fuller*. New York: William Morrow & Co., 1973.

King, Erika G. *Crowd Theory as a Psychology of the Leader and the Led*. Lewiston, N.Y.: Edwin Mellen Press, 1990.

Knight, David. *Humphry Davy: Science and Power*. Oxford: Blackwell Publishers, 1992.

Lacey, Robert. *Ford: The Men and the Machines*. Boston: Little, Brown and Co., 1986.

Lanza, Joseph. *Elevator Music: A Surreal History of Muzak, Easy-Listening and Other Moodsong*. New York: St. Martin's Press, 1994.

Larsen, Egon. *An American in Europe: The Life of Benjamin Thompson, Count Rumford*. New York: Philosophical Library, 1953.

Larsen, Egon. *Ideas and Invention*. London: Spring Books, 1960.

Law, John. *Organizing Modernity*. Oxford: Blackwell Publishers, 1994.

Lawrence, D. H. *The Complete Poems*. Edited by Vivian De Sola Pinto and Warren Roberts. New York: Penguin, 1971.

Leach, William. *The Land of Desire: Merchants, Power, and the Rise of a New American Culture*. New York: Vintage, 1994.

Lehman, Milton. *This High Man: The Life of Robert H. Goddard*. New York: Farrar, Strauss and Co., 1963.

Lewis, Tom. *Empire of the Air: The Men Who Made Radio*. New York: Harper-Perennial, 1991.

Lilienthal, Otto. *Birdflight as the Basis of Aviation: A Contribution Towards a System of Aviation: Compiled from the Results of Numerous Experiments made by O. and G. Lilienthal*. London: Langman, Greens & Co., 1911.

Lipman, Jean. *Rufus Porter: Yankee Pioneer*. New York: Clarkson N. Potter, 1968.

Luckhurst, Kenneth W. *The Story of Exhibitions*. London: Studio Publications, 1951.

Mabee, Carlton. *The American Leonardo: A Life of Samuel F. B. Morse*. New York: Alfred A. Knopf, 1943.

Macdonald, Anne L. *Feminine Ingenuity: Women and Invention in America*. New York: Ballantine Books, 1992.

MacDonnell, Kevin. *Eadweard Muybridge: The Man Who Invented the Moving Picture*. Boston: Little, Brown and Co., 1972.

MacDougall, Curtis D. *Hoaxes*. New York: Dover Publications, 1968.

Mack, Edward C. *Peter Cooper: Citizen of New York*. New York: Duell, Sloan and Pearce, 1949.

Mallmann, Paul. Papers. Box 1. Manuscripts Division, New York Public Library.

Marcus, Alan I., and Howard P. Segal. *Technology in America: A Brief History*. Orlando, Fla.: Harcourt Brace Jovanovich, 1989.

Marey, J.-E. *Le Vol des Oiseaux*. Paris: G. Masson, 1890.

Martin, Marianne W. *Futurist Art and Theory: 1909–1915*. Oxford: Clarendon Press, 1968.

Martin, Thomas Commerford. *The Inventions, Researches and Writings of Nikola Tesla*. New York: Barnes & Noble, 1992.

Maxim, Sir Hiram S. *My Life*. London: Methuen & Co., 1915.

McAllister, Ethel M. *Amos Eaton: Scientist and Educator*. Philadelphia: University of Pennsylvania Press, 1941.

McCormick, Cyrus. *The Century of the Reaper*. Boston: Houghton Mifflin Co., 1931.

McCullough, David. *The Great Bridge: The Epic Story of the Building of the Brooklyn Bridge*. New York: Avon Books, 1972.

McCullough, Edo. *World's Fair Midways*. New York: Arno Press, 1976.

McFarland, Marvin W., ed. *The Papers of Wilbur and Orville Wright, Including the Chanute-Wright Letters and Other Papers of Octave Chanute*. Vol. 1: 1899–1905. New York: McGraw-Hill, 1953.

McKennon, Joe. *A Pictorial History of the American Carnival*. Vol. 1. Sarasota: Carnival Publishers of Sarasota, 1971.

McNamara, Brooks. *Step Right Up*. Garden City, N.Y.: Doubleday & Co., 1976.

Mead, David. *Yankee Eloquence in the Middle West: The Ohio Lyceum, 1850–1870*. East Lansing: Michigan State College Press, 1951.

Meador, Roy. *Franklin—Revolutionary Scientist*. Ann Arbor: Ann Arbor Science Publishers, 1975.

Meier, Hugo A. "Thomas Jefferson and a Democratic Technology." In *Technology in America: A History of Individuals and Ideas*. Edited by Carroll W. Pursell, Jr. Cambridge: MIT Press, 1990.

Millard, Andre. *Edison and the Business of Innovation*. Baltimore: Johns Hopkins University Press, 1990.

Miller, John T. *Applied Character Analysis*. Boston: Gorham Press, 1922.

Miller, Walter James. *The Annotated Jules Verne: From the Earth to the Moon*. New York: Thomas Y. Crowell, Publishers, 1978.

Mirsky, Jeannette, and Allan Nevins. *The World of Eli Whitney*. New York: Macmillian Co., 1952.

Moore, Doris Langley. *Ada, Countess of Lovelace: Byron's Legitimate Daughter*. London: John Murray, 1977.

Morse, Edward Lind, ed. *Samuel F. B. Morse: His Letters and Journals*. Vol. 2. Boston: Houghton Mifflin Co., 1914.

Moseley, Sydney. *John Baird: The Romance and Tragedy of the Pioneer of Television*. London: Odhams Press, 1952.

Moulton, H. J. *Houdini's History of Magic in Boston, 1792–1915*. Glenwood, Ill.: Meyerbooks, 1983.

Muccigrosso, Robert. *Celebrating the New World: Chicago's Columbian Exposition of 1893, The American Ways Series*. Chicago: Ivan R. Dee, 1993.

Mund, Vernon A. *Open Markets: An Essential of Free Enterprise*. New York: Harper and Bros., 1948.

Muybridge, Eadweard. *Animals in Motion*. Edited by Lewis S. Brown. New York: Dover Publications, 1957.

———. *The Human Figure in Motion*. New York: Dover Publications, 1955.

Nagler, A. M., ed. *A Sourcebook in Theatrical History*. New York: Dover Publications, 1959.

Nahin, Paul J. *Oliver Heaviside: Sage in Solitude—The Life, Work, and Times of an Electrical Genius in the Victorian Age*. New York: Institute of Electrical and Electronics Engineers Press, 1987.

Neely, Wayne Caldwell. *The Agricultural Fair.* New York: Columbia University Press, 1935.

Neering, Rosemary. *Continental Dash: The Russian-American Telegraph.* Ganges, British Columbia: Horsdal & Schubart, 1989.

Nelson, Daniel. *Frederick W. Taylor and the Rise of Scientific Management.* Madison, Wisc.: University of Wisconsin Press, 1980.

Newhall, Beaumont. *The Daguerreotype in America.* New York: Duell, Sloan and Pearce, 1961.

Nitske, W. Robert. *The Life of Wilhelm Conrad Röntgen: Discoverer of the X Ray.* Tucson: University of Arizona Press, 1971.

Norman, Bruce. *The Inventing of America.* New York: Taplinger Publishing Co., 1976.

Nyce, James M., and Paul Kahn. *From Memex to Hypertext: Vannevar Bush and the Mind's Machine.* San Diego, Calif.: Academic Press, 1991.

Pacey, Arnold. *The Maze of Ingenuity: Ideas and Idealism in the Development of Technology.* Cambridge: MIT Press, 1992.

Philip, Cynthia Owen. *Robert Fulton: A Biography.* New York: Franklin Watts, 1985.

Phillips, Ulrich Bonnell. *Life and Labor in the Old South.* Boston: Little, Brown and Co., 1929.

Presbrey, Frank. *The History and Development of Advertising.* Garden City, N.Y.: Doubleday, Doran & Co., 1929.

Prout, Henry G. *A Life of George Westinghouse.* New York: American Society of Mechanical Engineers, 1921.

Pupin, Michael. *From Immigrant to Inventor.* New York: Charles Scribner's Sons, 1923.

——. *Romance of the Machine.* New York: Charles Scribner's Sons, 1930.

Rabinbach, Anson. *The Human Motor: Energy, Fatigue and the Origins of Modernity.* Berkeley: University of California Press, 1990.

Rae, John B. *The American Automobile: A Brief History.* Chicago: University of Chicago Press, 1965.

Reich, Leonard S. *The Making of American Industrial Research: Science and Business at GE and Bell, 1876–1926.* Cambridge: Cambridge University Press, 1985.

Reich, Wilhelm. *Listen, Little Man!* Translated by Theodore P. Wolfe. New York: Noonday Press, 1948.

Reigart, J. Franklin. *The Life of Robert Fulton.* Philadelphia: C. G. Henderson & Co., 1856.

Reingold, Nathan, ed. *The Papers of Joseph Henry.* Vol. 1. Washington: Smithsonian Institution Press, 1972.

Rice, Elmer. *The Living Theatre.* New York: Harper & Bros., 1959.

Richter, Stefan. *The Art of the Daguerreotype.* London: Viking Penguin, 1989.

Ridge, Martin, and Ray Allen Billington, eds. *America's Frontier Story: A Documentary History of Westward Expansion.* New York: Holt, Rinehart and Winston, 1969.

Ritchie, Michael. *Please Stand By: A Prehistory of Television.* Woodstock, N.Y.: Overlook Press, 1994.

Robinson, Eric, and A. E. Musson. *James Watt and the Steam Revolution, A Documentary History.* New York: Augustus M. Kelley, 1969.

Rohan, Jack. *Yankee Arms Maker: The Incredible Career of Samuel Colt*. New York: Harper & Bros., 1935.

Rolt, L. T. C. *James Watt*. New York: Arco Publishing Co., 1962.

Rudlin, John. *Commedia dell'Arte: An Actor's Handbook*. London: Routledge, 1994.

Runes, Dagobert D., ed. *The Diary and Sundry Observations of Thomas Alva Edison*. New York: Greenwood Press, 1968.

Sand, Maurice. *The History of the Harlequinade*. New York: B. Blom, 1968.

Sante, Luc. *Low Life: Lures and Snares of Old New York*. New York: Vintage, 1991.

Sarnoff, David. "The Birth of an Industry." *RCA Review: A Quarterly Journal of Radio Progress* 4, no. 1 (July 1939), pp. 3–5.

Saxon, A. H. *P. T. Barnum: The Legend and the Man*. New York: Columbia University Press, 1989.

Schieldrop, Edgar B. *Conquest of Space and Time: The Railway*. London: Hutchinson & Co., 1956.

Schubert, Paul. *The Electric Word: The Rise of Radio*. New York: Macmillan, 1928.

Seavey, Ormond. *Becoming Benjamin Franklin: The Autobiography and the Life*. University Park: Pennsylvania State University Press, 1988.

Sheldon, W. H. *The Varieties of Human Physique: An Introduction to Constitutional Psychology*. New York: Harper & Bros., 1940.

Shelton, Harry. *The Invention of Television*. Sugar Land, Tex.: Bell Towne Publishing, 1988.

Shenton, James, ed. *Free Enterprise Forever!* Scientific American *in the 19th Century*. New York: Images Graphiques, 1977.

Shurkin, Joel. *Engines of the Mind: A History of the Computer*. New York: W.W. Norton & Co., 1984.

Siegel, Mark. *Hugo Gernsback: Father of Modern Science Fiction*, Popular Writers of Today, vol. 45. San Bernadino, Calif.: Borgo Press, 1988.

Smiles, Samuel. *The Life of George Stephenson, Railway Engineer*. Boston: Ticknor and Fields, 1859.

Smith, Merritt Roe. "Eli Whitney and the American System of Manufacturing." In *Technology in America: A History of Individuals and Ideas*. Edited by Carroll W. Pursell, Jr. Cambridge: MIT Press, 1990.

Smith, Winifred. *The Commedia dell'Arte*. New York, 1912.

Smithsonian Institution. *Smithsonian Miscellaneous Collections* 21, Washington: Smithsonian Institution, 1881.

Snow, Richard. *Coney Island: A Postcard Journey to the City of Fire*. New York: Brightwaters Press, 1984.

Squier, G. O. "The Monophone." *Journal of the Maryland Academy of Sciences* 1, no. 1 (January 1930).

Squier, Major George Owen. *Telling the World*. Baltimore: Williams & Wilkins Co., 1933.

Stage, Sarah. *Female Complaints: Lydia Pinkham and the Business of Women's Medicine*. New York: W.W. Norton & Co., 1979.

Stanley, Autumn. *Mother and Daughters of Invention: Notes for a Revised History of Technology*. Metuchen, N.J.: Scarecrow Press, 1993.

Stansfield, Dorothy A. *Thomas Beddoes M.D., 1760–1808: Chemist, Physician, Democrat*. Dordrecht, South Africa: D. Reidel Publishing Co., 1984.

Stein, Ralph. *The American Automobile*. New York: Random House, n.d.

Stourzh, Gerald. *Benjamin Franklin and American Foreign Policy*. Chicago: University of Chicago Press, 1954.

Strauss, Linda Marlene. *Automata: A study in the interface of science, technology, and popular culture, 1730–1885*. San Diego: University of California Press, 1987.

Sutton, Sir Graham. *Mastery of the Air: An Account of the Science of Mechanical Flight*. New York: Basic Books, 1965.

Taft, Robert. *Photography and the American Scene: A Social History, 1839–1889*. New York: Dover Publications, 1938.

Tallis, John. *Tallis's History and Description of the Crystal Palace*. London: John Tallis and Co., n.d.

Taubman, Howard. *The Making of American Theatre*. New York: Coward McCann, 1965.

Taylor, Frederick Winslow. "Scientific Management: Comprising Shop Management, The Principles of Scientific Management," Testimony Before the Special House Committee. Westport, Conn.: Greenwood Press, 1947.

Tesla, Nikola. *Colorado Springs Notes: 1899–1900*. Belgrade: Nolit, Terazije, 27, 1978.

———. *The Fantastic Inventions of Nikola Tesla*. (Additional material by David Hatcher Childress.) Stelle, Ill.: Adventures Unlimited Press, 1993.

———. *My Inventions*. Zagreb: Školska Knjiga, 1984.

Thayer, Stuart. *Annals of the American Circus*. Vol. 2, 1830–1847. Seattle: Peanut Butter Publishing, 1986.

Thompson, Robert Luther. *Wiring a Continent: The History of the Telegraph Industry, 1832–1866*. Princeton: Princeton University Press, 1947.

Thompson, Slason. *A Short History of the American Railways, Covering Ten Decades*. New York: D. Appleton and Co., 1925.

*The Thousand and One Nights, or Arabian Nights Entertainments*. Boston: Lee and Shepard, 1865.

Throgmorton, Todd H. *Roller Coasters: An Illustrated Guide to the Rides in the United States and Canada, with a History*. Jefferson, N.C.: McFarland & Co., 1993.

Tisdall, Caroline, and Angelo Bozzolla. *Futurism*. New York: Oxford University Press, 1978.

Trachtenberg, Alan. "American Response to the Daguerrotype, 1839–1851." In *The Daguerrotype*. Edited by John Wood. Iowa City: University of Iowa, 1989.

Trollope, Frances. *Domestic Manners of the Americans*. Edited by Donald Smalley. New York: Vintage Books, 1960.

Twain, Mark. *A Connecticut Yankee in King Arthur's Court*. New York: Harper & Row, 1963.

Tyler, Royall. *The Contrast: A Comedy in five acts*. New York: Publications of the Dunlap Society No. 1, 1887.

Van Doren, Carl. *Benjamin Franklin*. London: Putnam, 1939.

Verne, Jules. *From the Earth to the Moon*. Translated by Lowell Blair. New York: Bantam Books, 1993.

———. *Journey to the Centre of the Earth*. Translated by William Butcher. Oxford: Oxford University Press, 1992.

———. *'Round the World in Eighty Days*. N.p.: Didier, 1949.

Ward, John William. *Andrew Jackson: Symbol for an Age*. London: Oxford University Press, 1955.

Weiner, Norbert. *Invention: The Care and Feeding of Ideas*. Cambridge: MIT Press, 1993.

Welch, Walter L. *Charles Batchelor: Edison's Chief Partner*. Croton-on-Hudson, N.Y.: North River Press (Syracuse University), 1972.

Wells, H. G. *Experiment in Autobiography: Discoveries and Conclusions of a Very Ordinary Brain (Since 1866)*. New York: Macmillan, 1934.

——. *The Invisible Man* and *War of the Worlds*. New York: Washington Square Press, 1962.

Werner, M. R. *Barnum*. New York: Harcourt, Brace and Co., 1923.

West, Anthony. *H. G. Wells: Aspects of a Life*. New York: Random House, 1984.

Williams, A. N. "What Hath God Wrought!" A Newcomen Address (May 24, 1844), Princeton University Press, 1944.

Williams, L. Pearce. *Michael Faraday: A Biography*. New York: Da Capo Press, 1965.

Wilson, Grove. *Great Men of Science: Their Lives and Discoveries*. New York: New Home Library, 1942.

Wilson, Joseph M. *The Masterpieces of the Centennial International Exhibition*. Vol. 3. Philadelphia: Gebbie & Barrie, 1876. Reprint, New York: Garland Publishing, 1977.

Yeomans, Edward. *Men, Steam and the Driven Wheel*. Rutland, Vt.: House of Tuttle, 1939.

Young, J. Lewis. *Edison and his Phonograph*. London [?]: Edison United Phonograph Co., 1890 [?] .

Zunz, Oliver. *The Changing Face of Inequality*. Chicago: University of Chicago Press, 1982.

# Index